Voters Under Pressure

COMPARATIVE POLITICS

Comparative Politics is a series for researchers, teachers, and students of political science that deals with contemporary government and politics. Global in scope, books in the series are characterized by a stress on comparative analysis and strong methodological rigour. The series is published in association with the European Consortium for Political Research. For more information visit
www.ecprnet.eu

The series is edited by Nicole Bolleyer, Chair of Comparative Political Science, Geschwister Scholl Institut, LMU Munich, and Jonathan Slapin, Professor and Chair of Political Institutions and European Politics, University of Zurich.

OTHER TITLES IN THIS SERIES

Minority Governments in Comparative Perspective
Edited by Bonnie N. Field and Shane Martin

The Government Party
Political Dominance in Democracy
R. Kenneth Carty

The New Kremlinology
Understanding Regime Personalization in Russia
Alexander Baturo and Johan A. Elkink

Reimagining the Judiciary
Women's Representation on High Courts Worldwide
Maria C. Escobar-Lemmon, Valerie J. Hoekstra, Alice J. Kang, and Miki Caul Kittilson

Coalition Governance in Western Europe
Edited by Torbjörn Bergman, Hanna Back, and Johan Hellström

Beyond Turnout
How Compulsory Voting Shapes Citizens and Political Parties
Shane P. Singh

Voters Under Pressure

Group-Based Cross-Pressure and Electoral Volatility

RUTH DASSONNEVILLE

Great Clarendon Street, Oxford, OX2 6DP,
United Kingdom

Oxford University Press is a department of the University of Oxford.
It furthers the University's objective of excellence in research, scholarship,
and education by publishing worldwide. Oxford is a registered trade mark of
Oxford University Press in the UK and in certain other countries

© Ruth Dassonneville 2023

The moral rights of the author have been asserted

Impression: 1

All rights reserved. No part of this publication may be reproduced, stored in
a retrieval system, or transmitted, in any form or by any means, without the
prior permission in writing of Oxford University Press, or as expressly permitted
by law, by licence or under terms agreed with the appropriate reprographics
rights organization. Enquiries concerning reproduction outside the scope of the
above should be sent to the Rights Department, Oxford University Press, at the
address above

You must not circulate this work in any other form
and you must impose this same condition on any acquirer

Published in the United States of America by Oxford University Press
198 Madison Avenue, New York, NY 10016, United States of America

British Library Cataloguing in Publication Data

Data available

Library of Congress Control Number: 2022943686

ISBN 978–0–19–289413–7

DOI: 10.1093/oso/9780192894137.001.0001

Printed and bound by
CPI Group (UK) Ltd, Croydon, CR0 4YY

Links to third party websites are provided by Oxford in good faith and
for information only. Oxford disclaims any responsibility for the materials
contained in any third party website referenced in this work.

Voor papa

Acknowledgements

This book is the result of a long process, which began when I started my PhD at the University of Leuven. As a doctoral student, I spent several years trying to better understand the causes and consequences of the surge in electoral volatility and gained much insights in the micro- and macro-correlates of volatility. However, I was not able to pinpoint what it was exactly about the decision process of voters that made their electoral choices so fickle. Several years later, I decided to turn back to this very question, determined to shed light on the ways in which voters' decision-making process renders vote choices stable or volatile. This book summarizes my thinking on the question and makes the argument that cross-pressures, which result from the connections between different determinants of the vote choice, are key to understanding volatility.

Over the past few years, I have been able to spend much time thinking about volatility and how it connects to cross-pressure because of the excellent research conditions that are provided by the Canada Research Chairs program. At the Université de Montréal, I also benefit greatly from the fact that I teach courses on elections. Interactions with students have greatly shaped and enriched my thinking about elections and voting behaviour. This especially holds for the students whose research I have had the opportunity to supervise. Thanks to Semih Çakır, Maxime Coulombe, Klara Dentler, Fernando Feitosa, Nadjim Fréchet, Marta Gallina, Fanny Geoffrion, Alexandra Jabbour, Juliette Leblanc, Baowen Liang, Jeanne Marlier, Philippe Mongrain, Valentin Pautonnier, Semra Sevi, Dieter Stiers, Matthew Taylor, Florence Vallée-Dubois, and Virginie Vandewalle for the research discussions over the years and for (sometimes unsolicited) advise on the look of the graphs in the manuscript. Several students also contributed directly to the project by providing excellent research assistance. I particularly thank Fernando Feitosa, Nadjim Fréchet, and Baowen Liang for their help with the data. Alexandra Jabbour helped with the visualization of the theoretical argument. Baowen Liang provided invaluable help at the production stage.

Even though big chunks of this book were written in lockdown or while teleworking, I owe a big thank you to my colleagues at the Université de Montréal. Throughout the years, they have not only supported me with feedback on my research and helped me to navigate the institution, but they have also been incredibly kind and fun to hang out with at lunchtime *Chez Valère*, in a bar for after-work drinks, or during winter-time quarantine walks. I am especially grateful to Vincent Arel-Bundock for advice on best practices for typesetting a book-length manuscript and to Jean-François Godbout for sharing his experience about the book publishing process.

The over-time analyses of citizens' voting decisions and volatility are only possible because many countries collect high-quality election data and make those data publicly available. They provide the infrastructure for election scholars to study voting behaviour and to do so comparatively and longitudinally. I am particularly grateful to Henrik Oscarsson and to Rune Stubager for guidance in accessing and working with election survey data from Sweden and Denmark. I also thank Ian McAllister for pointing out that earlier surveys from the 1960s could be used to extend the time series that the Australian National Election Study provides.

Rüdiger Schmitt-Beck provided valuable feedback on the book proposal early on, and Susan Scarrow was key in talking me into putting together a proposal and elaborating my research on volatility in a book-length manuscript.

I presented parts of this book manuscript at the 2020 Meeting of the American Political Science Association and the 2021 Meeting of the Midwest Political Science Association. I benefited greatly from the advice of Jae-Jae Spoon, Arndt Leininger, and Eric Guntermann at these occasions. I also presented the project in seminars at Western University, at Nuffield College, and at the University of Siena and received fantastic suggestions from Geoffrey Evans, Roosmarijn de Geus, Mattia Guidi, Pierangelo Isernia, Jae-Hee Jung, Matt Lebo, Laura Stephenson, Mattieu Turgeon, and Luca Verzichelli, among others.

Jean-François Daoust, Patrick Fournier, Jane Green, Liesbet Hooghe, Herbert Kitschelt, and Philip Rehm participated in an online book workshop. They provided detailed comments and precious feedback on a draft of the manuscript. The comments I received during that workshop were of tremendous help and have led me to make substantial changes to the argument and its framing, as well as to the empirical analyses that are presented. I also want to thank Philip Rehm for sharing the syntax for decomposing the explained variance and am grateful to Patrick Fournier for suggesting a more punchy title for the book.

I revised and finalized the manuscript as a Jean Monnet Fellow at the European University Institute's Robert Schuman Centre. The fellowship provided me with the best possible conditions to focus on the book. It provided me with time to focus on research while simultaneously being intellectually challenged in discussions with the many members and visitors at the Robert Schuman Centre and the European University Institute (EUI). My research and the book manuscript has been enriched by the discussions I had at the EUI with Daniele Caramani, Elias Dinas, Simon Hix, and Hanspeter Kriesi. I thank Liesbet Hooghe and Gary Marks in particular for encouraging me to apply for a Jean Monnet Fellowship and for discussions about the book and follow-up work on the topic of cross-pressure.

André Blais, Michael Lewis-Beck, and Ian McAllister—three of my dearest collaborators—read the full manuscript and provided extremely detailed feedback on it. Their comments have helped me to refine the argument and clarify the demonstration. I am extremely grateful, not only for their time and engagement with this research but also for their mentorship over the years. I count myself lucky and privileged to be able to collaborate with these giants in the field and am inspired by the examples they set.

I also thank the anonymous reviewers who provided comments on the book proposal and am especially grateful to Dominic Byatt for guiding me through all the stages of publishing with Oxford University Press.

Finally, I thank my family for their encouragement and support. I dedicate this book to my dad, with whom I shared an interest in politics. I miss him every day.

Contents

List of figures   xi
List of tables   xiii

1. Introduction   1

PART I. VOTER VOLATILITY, LONG-TERM DETERMINANTS, AND SHORT-TERM DETERMINANTS OF THE VOTE

2. How change has been explained   21
3. How socio-demographic factors have fared over time   32
4. Have party attachments weakened?   51
5. Increasingly short term?   75

PART II. A NEW FRAMEWORK FOR EXPLAINING CHANGE: GROUP-BASED CROSS-PRESSURES AND VOTER VOLATILITY

6. Sources of instability: Cross-pressures and unconstrained vote choices   99
7. Cross-pressured voters   119
8. Increasingly cross-pressured   141
9. The impact of cross-pressures: Less constraint   161
10. Cross-pressures, late deciding, and volatility   177
11. Conclusion   199

Bibliography   214

PART III. SUPPLEMENTARY MATERIALS

Appendix A.	Data sets used for the analyses	233
Appendix B.	Percentage of campaign deciders by election	244
Appendix C.	Socio-demographic variables	248
Appendix D.	Change in the role of socio-demographics	257
Appendix E.	Partisanship in Germany: West versus East	262
Appendix F.	Partisanship over time	263
Appendix G.	Wording of partisan strength measures	266
Appendix H.	Strength of partisanship, stacked area graphs	269
Appendix I.	Long-term and short-term factors, illustration	272
Appendix J.	Economic voting over time, alternative analytical approaches	273
Appendix K.	Measurement and wording of short-term variables	281
Appendix L.	Change in the role of economic and leader evaluations	296
Appendix M.	Full variation method	300
Appendix N.	European Election Study voter survey analyses	314
Appendix O.	Age, period, and cohort effects	319
Appendix P.	Party system fragmentation over time	323
Appendix Q.	Group-based cross-pressure and strength of partisan attachments	326
Appendix R.	Broader indicator of cross-pressure	329
Appendix S.	Measures of sophistication and frustration	336

Bibliography Supplementary Materials   341
Index   342

List of figures

1.1. Net volatility over time	4
1.2. Percentage of self-reported switchers, election survey data (1)	7
1.3. Percentage of self-reported switchers, election survey data (2)	8
2.1. Representation of the theoretical funnel of causality	22
2.2. Connection between long-term factors, short-term factors, and the vote choice (1)	28
2.3. Connection between long-term factors, short-term factors, and the vote choice (2)	29
3.1. The impact of socio-demographic variables over time (1)	45
3.2. The impact of socio-demographic variables over time (2)	46
3.3. The over-time explanatory power of socio-demographic variables in the United States, excluding race	48
4.1. Partisans over time (1)	59
4.2. Partisans over time (2)	60
4.3. Strong partisans over time (1)	63
4.4. Strong partisans over time (2)	64
4.5. Average marginal effect of partisanship on volatility	66
4.6. The likelihood of switching among partisans and non-partisans (1)	68
4.7. The likelihood of switching among partisans and non-partisans (2)	70
5.1. Violin plot of sociotropic retrospective evaluations of the economy by partisan group, ANES 2016	82
5.2. Effect of sociotropic retrospective evaluations of the economy by partisan group, ANES 2016	84
5.3. The effect of economic evaluations on the vote over time (1)	88
5.4. The effect of economic evaluations on the vote over time (2)	89
5.5. The added explanatory power of leader evaluations over time (1)	92
5.6. The added explanatory power of leader evaluations over time (2)	93
6.1. A strongly constrained voting decision	101
6.2. An unconstrained voting decision	102
7.1. Distribution of group-based CP score measure by country (1)	129
7.2. Distribution of group-based CP score measure by country (2)	130
7.3. Mean cross-pressure score for group- and non-group-deciders	134

7.4.	Cross-pressures and the most preferred party	138
7.5.	Cross-pressures and differences between parties	139
8.1.	Change in CP scores in Australia and Canada	143
8.2.	Change in CP scores in Denmark and Germany	143
8.3.	Change in CP scores in Great Britain and the Netherlands	144
8.4.	Change in CP scores in Sweden and the United States	144
10.1.	Marginal effect of cross-pressure on likelihood to decide late	180
10.2.	Marginal effect of cross-pressure on likelihood to switch parties	185
D.1.	Bivariate association between time and pseudo-R^2 statistic of a socio-demographic-only model	258
E.1.	Partisans over time, East and West Germany	262
H.1.	Strength of partisanship over time (1)	270
H.2.	Strength of partisanship over time (2)	271
J.1.	The added explanatory power of economic evaluations over time (1)	274
J.2.	The added explanatory power of economic evaluations over time (2)	275
J.3.	The effect of economic evaluations on voting for the prime minister's party over time (1)	277
J.4.	The effect of economic evaluations on voting for the prime minister's party over time (2)	278
J.5.	The effect of economic evaluations over time, effects of worsening and improving conditions (1)	279
J.6.	The effect of economic evaluations over time, effects of worsening and improving conditions (2)	280
M.1.	Change in full variation CP scores in Australia and Canada	302
M.2.	Change in full variation CP scores in Denmark and Germany	303
M.3.	Change in full variation CP scores in Great Britain and the Netherlands	304
M.4.	Change in full variation CP scores in Sweden	305
P.1.	Effective number of electoral parties by decade	324

List of tables

1.1.	Net volatility by decade and country	5
1.2.	Percentage of campaign deciders by decade and country	9
1.3.	Election surveys included in the analyses	14
4.1.	Wording and coverage of the party identification measures	57
4.2.	The percentage of switchers among partisans and non-partisans in British panel studies	72
4.3.	The percentage of switchers among partisans and non-partisans in Swedish panel studies	73
5.1.	Economic evaluations and support for the incumbent, ANES 2016	83
6.1.	The connection between the number of cleavages and the likelihood of being cross-pressured	110
6.2.	Trade union density by decade	115
6.3.	Trends in church attendance	116
7.1.	Explaining vote choice in the US 2008 presidential election, socio-demographic determinants	127
7.2.	Examples of respondents' socio-demographic profile and their CP score	128
7.3.	Selected vote-choice motivations	132
8.1.	Explaining CP score, change over time	152
8.2.	Explaining CP score, age, period, and generation effects	153
8.3.	Explaining CP score, change over time and the effective number of parties	157
8.4.	Trend in party ambivalence, EES data	159
9.1.	Cross-pressures and partisanship (1)	164
9.2.	Cross-pressures and partisanship (2)	165
9.3.	Levels of partisanship among the least and most cross-pressured	166
9.4.	Explaining short-term cross-pressure	171
9.5.	Explaining short-term cross-pressure, within-election effects	172
9.6.	Group-based and issue-based cross-pressure, EES data	175
10.1.	The association between group-based cross-pressure and campaign deciding, accounting for linear time trend	182
10.2.	The association between group-based cross-pressure and campaign deciding, within-election effects	183

10.3.	The association between group-based cross-pressure and volatility, accounting for linear time trend	187
10.4.	The association between group-based cross-pressure and volatility, within-election effects	188
10.5.	The association between group-based cross-pressure and volatility, control for partisanship (1)	191
10.6.	The association between group-based cross-pressure and volatility, control for partisanship (2)	192
10.7.	Explaining party switching in UK panel studies	193
10.8.	Explaining party switching in Australia, Germany, the Netherlands, and the United States, alternative explanations	197
B.1.	Percentage of campaign deciders by election, Australia	244
B.2.	Percentage of campaign deciders by election, Canada	244
B.3.	Percentage of campaign deciders by election, Denmark	245
B.4.	Percentage of campaign deciders by election, Germany	245
B.5.	Percentage of campaign deciders by election, Great Britain	246
B.6.	Percentage of campaign deciders by election, The Netherlands	246
B.7.	Percentage of campaign deciders by election, Sweden	247
B.8.	Percentage of campaign deciders by election, United States	247
D.1.	Association between election year and McFadden pseudo-R^2 statistics of a socio-demographic vote-choice model	259
D.2.	Association between election year and McFadden pseudo-R^2 statistic of a socio-demographic vote-choice model (old cleavages only)	260
D.3.	Association between election year and McFadden pseudo-R^2 statistic of a socio-demographic vote-choice model (new cleavages only)	261
F.1.	Association between election year and the share of partisans	264
F.2.	Association between election year and the share of strong partisans	265
I.1.	Economic evaluations and support for the incumbent, ANES 2016	272
L.1.	Association between election year and coefficient of economic evaluations	297
L.2.	Association between election year and decomposed McFadden pseudo-R^2 statistic of leader evaluations	298
M.1.	Explaining full variation CP score, change over time	306
M.2.	Association between group-based cross-pressure and campaign deciding	307
M.3.	Association between group-based cross-pressure and campaign deciding, accounting for linear time trend	308
M.4.	Association between group-based cross-pressure and campaign deciding, within-election effects	309
M.5.	Association between group-based cross-pressure and volatility	310

M.6.	Association between group-based cross-pressure and volatility, accounting for linear time trend	311
M.7.	Association between group-based cross-pressure and volatility, within-election effects	312
N.1.	Cross-pressure and the most preferred party	317
N.2.	Cross-pressure and differences between parties	318
O.1.	Explaining CP score, age, period, and cohort effects	320
O.2.	Explaining CP score, old and young generations	322
P.1.	Effective number of parties by decade and country	325
Q.1.	Cross-pressure and partisan strength (1)	327
Q.2.	Cross-pressure and partisan strength (2)	328
R.1.	Association between overall cross-pressure and campaign deciding	330
R.2.	Association between overall cross-pressure and campaign deciding, accounting for linear time trend	331
R.3.	Association between overall cross-pressure and campaign deciding, within-election effects	332
R.4.	Association between overall cross-pressure and volatility	333
R.5.	Association between overall cross-pressure and volatility, accounting for linear time trend	334
R.6.	Association between overall cross-pressure and volatility, within-election effects	335

1
Introduction

> [C]itizens today no longer react as a group and are no longer bound by structures, but decide in an individual and volatile way about the fate of politicians whose job is more and more limited to gaining votes. Politicians no longer have time to think and plan in the long term, but instead must respond immediately to everything, and those rapid responses can determine their political survival.
>
> Jean-Luc Dehaene,
> former Prime Minister of Belgium (2012)

During a 2012 interview, former Belgian Prime Minister Jean-Luc Dehaene reflected upon his long career in politics. Thinking about the changes that he had witnessed while active in politics, Dehaene concluded that politics had fundamentally transformed. The main source of change, according to Dehaene, was to be found in voters' behaviour. More specifically, Dehaene's analysis holds that, in contrast to what was the case in the twentieth century, current-day voters are no longer taking decisions as a group and are no longer guided by social structure when choosing whom to elect as their representatives. Instead, voters are taking voting decisions individually and independently. And in making such individual choices, voters appear whimsical.

While contemplating the changes that he was witnessing, Dehaene appeared to worry most about the consequences of short-termism for politics and governing. His diagnosis, that politicians no longer have time to govern and plan in the long term, echoes the concerns of many political scientists. As a general observation, '[w]hether politicians are willing to invest in the long run at short-run expense should (…) depend on how vulnerable they think their policy initiatives are to the predations of future governments' (Jacobs, 2016: 440). When volatility is up and parties and governments are very uncertain about their electoral future, that should thus impact the policy choices they make. Mair (2007), for example, observed a growing tension between responsible decision making on the one hand and short-term responsiveness to public opinion on the other (see also Goetz, 2014). Observers and students of politics thus seem to agree that a growth in volatility is a phenomenon with important

Voters Under Pressure. Ruth Dassonneville, Oxford University Press. © Ruth Dassonneville (2023).
DOI: 10.1093/oso/9780192894137.003.0001

policy consequences. Unstable voting behaviour limits the extent to which governments can plan in the long term. And such 'short-termism' is a cause for concern because it limits the effectiveness—and therefore the legitimacy—of representative democracy (Mair, 2013).

Dehaene decidedly pointed to voters as the main source of change. According to the former prime minister, it is citizens who have become more volatile, and their whimsical decisions are putting a strain on the system. On this point, the scholarly literature is divided. While some work that seeks to explain changes in electoral politics takes a voter perspective (Dalton, 2013; Franklin, Mackie, and Valen, 1992; Stubager et al., 2021), others have drawn attention to the role of parties in bringing about change (De Vries and Hobolt, 2020; Evans and Tilley, 2012; Evans and De Graaf, 2013). My goal is not to determine which factor is most important or what came first. In the end, electoral change most likely results from an interaction between citizen-driven change and parties' reactions to social change. Instead, I take a close look at the individual level and I theorize about the ways in which individual-level change has contributed to more instability.

While acknowledging that parties are important actors in this process, this book thus takes a voter perspective to explain change. I examine over-time changes in voters' electoral choices and investigate how these changes are linked to a growth in instability. The core argument that is made in this book is that it is *group-based cross-pressures* that lead to instability in voters' choices. More specifically, I theorize and empirically show that when citizens' socio-demographic characteristics and their membership of social groups do not consistently push them to support one party, but instead lead them to feel cross-pressured between parties, their voting decision process lacks constraint; that is, voters who are group-based cross-pressured are less likely to feel an attachment to a party and have less guidance when assessing the state of the economy, taking positions on issues, or evaluating leaders too. The different factors that influence voters' choices, as a result, do not add up to strengthening a preference for one specific party but instead lead a voter to consider different parties. While all elements within the metaphorical funnel of causality (Campbell et al., 1960) are still relevant to explaining the vote of a cross-pressured voter, instead of all elements within the funnel being closely connected and inter-related, for a cross-pressured voter the different determinants are separate elements that are at best loosely connected with each other and that push a voter to prefer different parties, ultimately leading to volatile voting behaviour.

In this book, I show that group-based cross-pressures, through their impact on the extent to which citizens' voting decision process is structured, are an important source of instability. This is evident from the fact that cross-pressured voters are more ambivalent between parties, make their voting decision later, and are more likely to switch parties from one election to the next. In essence, the argument that is laid out and tested in this book is the intuition of former Prime Minister Dehaene that voters have grown whimsical because their choices 'are no longer bound by social groups and structures'. This lack of an anchoring, which I capture by means of the concept of cross-pressures, is a key variable to explain the instability in citizens' political behaviour and in electoral outcomes.

1.1 Signals of change

The observation that elections and voting behaviour are seemingly in flux, and increasingly unstable, is not new at all. Since at least the 1970s, political scientists have drawn attention to patterns of change in electoral behaviour (Crewe and Denver, 1985; Pedersen, 1979; Dalton, 1984; Franklin, Mackie, and Valen, 1992). While there was initially debate about the importance and the strength of the change, by now few would dispute the claim that election outcomes in many democracies have grown more volatile and more uncertain over time. Several indicators in fact show a picture that leaves no doubt that election outcomes are in flux and that voting behaviour is growing more volatile.

A first and often-used indicator of change is Pedersen's index of net volatility. The index is based on a comparison of election results between consecutive elections, and uses the summed wins and losses of parties between elections to obtain an estimate of size of voter flows between elections (Pedersen, 1979). The over-time trend in this indicator of net volatility, which can theoretically take values between 0 and 100, gives a good sense of the extent to which elections have grown more unstable over time.[1] Using data on this index[2] for elections in sixteen established democracies since 1945, Figure 1.1 plots the level of net volatility in elections in these sixteen countries by election year. The graph takes the form of a scatter plot, but to ease the assessment of the

---

[1] It should be noted that there are different approaches to dealing with party system changes when comparing electoral results, and such coding decisions strongly affect outcomes (Casal Bertoa, Deegan Krause, and Haughton, 2017). However, when consistently applying the same methods to categorizing parties and comparing results, the Pedersen index is a very powerful tool for comparing aggregate level volatility between countries and—importantly for my purposes—over time.

[2] For the European countries, I use the data from Chiaramonte and Emanuele (2017), who have proposed ways to distinguishing between party- and electorate-induced instability. The focus here is on 'total volatility', the most general application of Pedersen's formula.

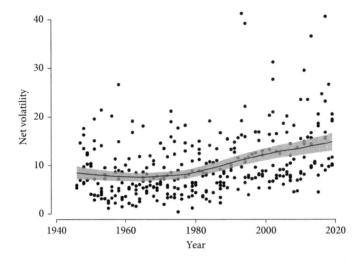

Figure 1.1 Net volatility over time

Note: Dots are observations of net volatility in elections in Australia, Austria, Belgium, Canada, Denmark, Finland, France, Germany, Ireland, Italy, Luxembourg, the Netherlands, Norway, Sweden, Switzerland, and the United Kingdom. Data on European countries come from Chiaramonte and Emanuele (2017), data for Australia and Canada are the author's calculations. A local polynomial smoother line and 95 per cent confidence intervals are included.

over-time trend I also include a local polynomial smoother line and 95 per cent confidence intervals on top.

Looking at the trend line first, we see a pattern of stability in electoral outcomes until around 1980, after which net volatility starts to increase in a fairly continuous way. The surge in volatility, once it occurs, is rather sharp. While rates of net volatility were, on average, around 8.5 until 1980, they have risen to almost 15 by 2020. In the set of established democracies included in Figure 1.1, net volatility has increased by 75 per cent in about two decades of time.

Beyond this average trend line, Figure 1.1 shows substantial variation in levels of net volatility. Even before 1980, there were high volatile elections in some countries, and also after 1980 there are still elections that show a moderate level of net volatility. However, it is striking that there are many more high volatile elections post 1980, and definitely post 1990. At the same time, extremely low levels of net volatility (with a value below 5) are no longer observed in recent time periods.

In fact, virtually all countries have witnessed an increase in net levels of volatility. This is evident from Table 1.1, which lists net volatility levels by country for elections in the 1950s, the 1970s, the 1990s, and the 2010s. With the exception of Luxembourg, net volatility levels in the 2010s are systematically higher than they were in the 1950s. In many countries, levels of net volatility

Table 1.1 Net volatility by decade and country

Country	1950s	1970s	1990s	2010s
Australia	4.08	5.93	8.00	9.43
Austria	4.22	2.58	9.74	16.95
Belgium	7.50	5.15	11.23	15.07
Canada	9.93	6.27	24.40	15.07
Denmark	5.51	15.56	10.70	17.00
Finland	3.95	7.95	12.47	11.00
France	22.15	13.63	18.08	32.15
Germany	15.05	4.98	8.28	16.80
Ireland	10.97	5.60	10.63	27.18
Italy	9.70	6.87	22.42	31.68
Luxembourg	11.12	13.20	7.18	9.70
The Netherlands	5.85	12.77	19.55	20.90
Norway	3.38	15.28	16.63	11.73
Sweden	4.78	6.35	13.77	10.32
Switzerland	2.57	6.43	7.75	8.15
United Kingdom	4.38	8.34	8.85	12.86

Note: Data on volatility per election in European countries retrieved from Chiaramonte and Emanuele (2017); entries for Australia and Canada are the author's calculations.

have more than doubled, and in some cases the average level of volatility in the 2010s is more than three- or four-fold what it was for elections in the 1950s.

Clearly, when considering electoral outcomes, there is strong evidence of a trend towards more instability in elections. The shifts in parties' vote shares from one election to another have grown larger over time, with a strong uptick from around the 1980s onward.

The over-time trend in levels of net volatility indicates that election outcomes are increasingly volatile from one election to the next. Such shifts in election results, however, can in part be driven by changes at the party system level. Survey data, however, offer suggestive evidence of change at the individual level as well. In particular, using longitudinal election survey data from eight established democracies, I find ample evidence of increased volatility among voters—with larger shares of respondents reporting that they switched parties between elections now than was the case a few decades ago.

Specifically, election surveys provide indications of the amount of party switching between elections. While panel studies are ideally suited to studying such change, cross-sectional election surveys allow approximating the importance of voter flows by means of a 'recall-question'. Such a question asks survey respondents to think back to the previous election and indicate what party they voted for then. By comparing respondents' reported votes in the current election with their recalled vote choice in the previous election, we obtain an estimate of the percentage of voters having switched parties from one election to another and gain insights into the number of switchers over time.

This approach is not perfect and likely leads to an underestimation of the true amount of switching—both because of memory problems on the part of respondents and because of the presence of a consistency bias (Dassonneville and Hooghe, 2017*b*). What I am most interested in, however, is not the precise level of switching per se but rather the trend in volatility. And a reliance on recall data allows trends to be traced since the 1950s and 1960s in some countries.

Figures 1.2 and 1.3 show trends in the share of election survey respondents who report having voted for a different party in the previous election than in the current one in eight established democracies.[3] These are the eight countries that are analysed in more depth in this book. In fact, each of these eight countries has a long tradition of election survey research, allowing for a longitudinal comparative analysis of individual-level party switching.

By and large, these individual-level trends show a picture that is consistent with the aggregate-level evidence of change; that is, the survey evidence as well shows an increase in electoral volatility over time. There is, however, important variation between the countries. The United States follows a different pattern to the other countries. After a surge in the earlier time period, the United States is marked by a decline in the share of party switchers in the most recent elections. This pattern contrasts with that of the other countries, which—when disregarding a few outlier elections—tend to show substantially higher shares of switchers in recent elections than was the case for elections in the 1970s and 1980s. In some cases, such as in Great Britain or in Australia, this increase is the result of a fairly gradual process. In both countries, levels of volatility increased in the first few elections observed, to remain at a higher level in more recent elections. In Sweden and also in Germany, the level of party switching has more strongly increased, with a continued increase to higher levels of level volatility in the more recent time period. Finally,

---

[3] Note that those who abstain are excluded from the analyses, implying that the focus is solely on respondents who report to have voted in two subsequent elections. Given that there is no consistent information on what party abstainers would have voted for, they cannot be clearly categorized either as volatile voters (perhaps they would have voted for the same party but could not participate for other reasons) or as stable voters. There is also work which shows that the determinants of party switching and switching to/from abstention differ somewhat (Dassonneville, Blais, and Dejaeghere, 2015). Finally, the exclusion of abstainers in the empirical analyses is motivated by the fact that my theory specifically relates to hesitating between and switching parties.

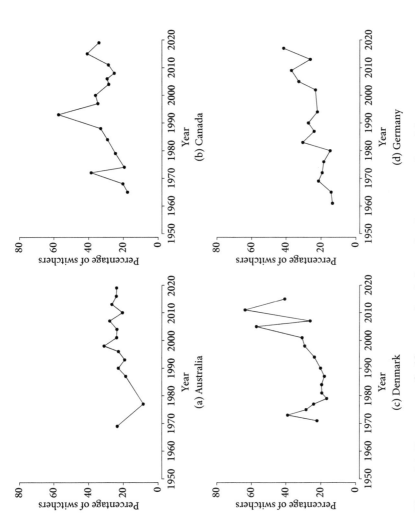

Figure 1.2 Percentage of self-reported switchers, election survey data (1)

Note: Percentage of recalled party switchers in election surveys. For details on the surveys, see Appendix A.

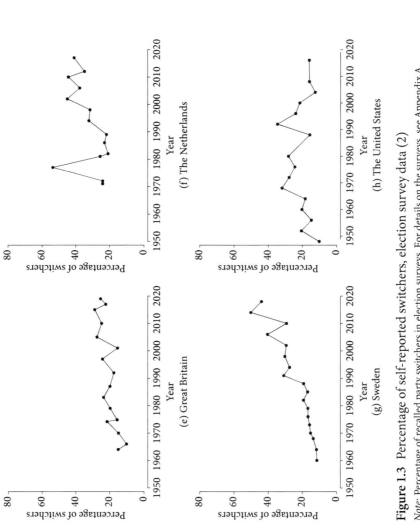

Figure 1.3 Percentage of self-reported switchers, election survey data (2)

Note: Percentage of recalled party switchers in election surveys. For details on the surveys, see Appendix A.

Table 1.2 Percentage of campaign deciders by decade and country

Country	1940s	1950s	1960s	1970s	1980s	1990s	2000s	2010s
Australia	–	–	–	–	–	36.8	30.1	33.3
Canada	–	–	48.1	44.0	43.1	54.6	47.0	43.2
Denmark	–	–	–	24.6	24.0	25.8	35.8	47.3
Germany	–	–	8.6	8.0	12.5	11.8	27.0	33.0
Great Britain	–	–	11.5	20.2	21.4	25.2	28.3	34.4
The Netherlands	–	–	–	21.6	25.0	41.3	45.4	60.0
Sweden	–	–	20.6	45.7	19.7	30.7	35.1	36.6
United States	12.6	10.6	15.5	18.8	18.9	21.2	18.8	18.3

Note: Detailed information on the percentage of campaign deciders in each election and information on the elections included in the estimations can be found in Appendix B.

Canada, Denmark, and the Netherlands show a more erratic pattern. While the trend of volatility is clearly increasing in these countries, what is most striking in these settings is the regular occurrence of extreme levels of party switching. Canada, Denmark, and the Netherlands have all had multiple elections for which more than one in four survey respondents indicated having changed parties. Without a doubt, shifts of this size imply a lot of instability in politics and a substantial amount of uncertainty for political parties and elected politicians.

Growing numbers of citizens thus admit to have switched parties from one election to the next. These trends are suggestive of an important decline of loyalty in electorates—especially in Western Europe. However, voters do not only appear to switch parties more, but they also seem to hesitate more about the choice that they are making. This is evident from survey questions that ask respondents to report when—approximately—they decided to vote for the party they cast a vote for.

Table 1.2 shows the percentage of respondents that indicates they made their voting decision during the campaign.[4] In five of the eight countries, the percentage of self-reported campaign deciders has strongly increased.[5] This increase is particularly strong in Denmark, where the percentage of campaign deciders increased from less than 25 per cent in the 1970s and 1980s to, on average, 47 per cent for elections in the 2010s. In the Netherlands, the surge

---

[4] Answer options to such questions differ somewhat between countries and within countries over time. For the purposes of comparison, all respondents indicating to have decided what party to vote for during the campaign, after leader debates, in the last weeks before the election, in the last days before the election, or on election day, are considered 'campaign deciders'.

[5] See Appendix B for the percentages by election.

in campaign deciding is even more pronounced, as the percentage of self-reported campaign deciders has increased from just over 20 per cent during elections in the 1970s to 60 per cent in the 2010s. In Germany, the rise in the share of late deciders is more recent but is very strong as well. At the start of the time series, around 9 per cent of the German respondents indicated that they decided during the campaign. This number has strongly increased. On average, about one in three Germans decided during the campaign for elections in the 2010s and around 40 per cent of Germans reported that they had decided during the campaign in the 2017 German election. In Sweden, the increase is less pronounced but still substantial. In the 1960s, around 20 per cent of voters made their voting decision during the campaign, while this number had increased to almost 37 per cent by the 2010s. In contrast to those five countries, the percentage of campaign deciders has remained more stable in Australia, Canada, and the United States. In the former two countries, the level of campaign deciding is consistently at a high level, but the time series is particularly short for Australia. In Canada, the estimates suggest that the percentage of respondents who decided during the campaign is consistently more than 40 per cent. This differs from the United States, where the percentage of campaign deciders hovers around 20 per cent of survey respondents since the 1970s.

Aggregate-level data of net volatility and individual-level data that capture the share of respondents who indicate that they have switched parties from one election to the next both show evidence of a surge in volatility in many established democracies. In addition, there are indications that voters hesitate more and decide later what party to vote for, at least in European democracies. While these trends are not universal, in many countries, election outcomes are now more volatile than they were before 1980. A substantially larger share of the electorate admits to switching parties between elections and hesitates longer about their vote choice.

Why are election outcomes now more volatile, and why are more voters now changing parties from one election to the next and hesitating more between options than was the case a few decades ago? The argument that I make in this book is that the surge in volatility is driven by a change in the way in which voters choose parties. In particular, the theoretical argument that I present and test in this book holds that more voters now are cross-pressured between parties, based on their socio-demographic characteristics. These group-based cross-pressures, in turn, result in a vote-choice decision process that lacks an anchor, resulting in choices that are more fickle.

1.2 Long-term determinants, short-term determinants of the vote, and cross-pressured voters

As indicated earlier, political scientists have drawn attention to patterns of electoral change for multiple decades already. In doing so, they have pointed to different sources of the change. A number of scholars have highlighted changes in party systems, with the arrival of new parties with a left-libertarian agenda spurring change in election outcomes (Kitschelt, 1988). In a more general way, Budge (1982: 161) has drawn the connection between the number of issues that are discussed in campaigns and volatility, stating that 'systems which consistently bring larger numbers of issues to prominence will experience greater shifts than others'. Such aggregate-level work was complemented by survey analyses, which showed evidence of an erosion of the links between citizens and parties (Dalton and Wattenberg, 2002) and a weakening of the role of social cleavages on the vote (Franklin, Mackie, and Valen, 1992). While some scholars drew attention to the early indications of change in electoral behaviour, others quickly nuanced and stressed patterns of continuity underneath. Peter Mair, for example, writing in the early 1990s, stressed that examples of electoral change remained exceptional and argued that 'the impression of persistence often remains much more striking than does that of discontinuity' (Mair, 1993: 123). To substantiate this argument, Bartolini and Mair (1990) analysed the role of ideological party blocks. Observing that most volatility was still confined within left- and right-wing blocks of parties (Bartolini and Mair, 1990), they argued that cleavages still stabilized electoral behaviour and that change was largely 'mythical' (Mair, 1993). Electoral change seems to have really kicked in after the publication of Bartolini and Mair's (1990) work, however. And even Mair (2008) later on came to conclude that by the 1990s, '[v]irtually every west European polity had become more unstable' (Mair, 2008: 237–238).

One question that has motivated much work on this topic is whether the changes in electoral behaviour are—in part—driven by a transformation in *how* voters choose parties. This has led scholars of elections to rethink what influences voters' choices. In particular, much previous work on the causes for the rise in volatility and the growing unpredictability of voters' choices explains these changes as a result of a shift in importance from long-term—stabilizing—determinants to short-term factors of the vote choice.

The distinction between long- and short-term vote-choice determinants was first made by Campbell et al. (1960), who described the vote-choice process as a 'funnel of causality'. In short, within the funnel, one finds 'long-term' stable determinants of the vote choice, such as an individual's socio-demographic characteristics, but also short-term factors. The latter—which include leaders, economic conditions, and issues—not only influence the vote closer to election day but also are more unstable (see also Lewis-Beck et al., 2008). A commonly invoked interpretation of the changes in electoral behaviour is that they result from a decline in the importance of long-term determinants (i.e. socio-demographic factors but also party attachments). This alleged decline of long-term factors, furthermore, is argued to be 'counterbalanced' by an increasing importance of short-term factors (Dalton, 1996; Costa Lobo, 2006; Walczak, van der Brug, and de Vries, 2012). For a voter who is not influenced by their socio-demographic characteristics and who has not developed an attachment with a party, all that is left to influence their choice are short-term factors. Given the instability of such factors, with leaders changing at each election, economic conditions varying over time, and the salience of different issues varying over time as well, the party choice of such a voter would indeed be very volatile.

The evidence for the idea that long-term determinants have become less important over time and that their decline has been partially compensated by an increased importance of short-term variables does not appear to be conclusive, however. First, some attention has been given to the decline of long-term factors for explaining voters' choices. Work along these lines claims that the era of 'frozen cleavages' (Lipset and Rokkan, 1967) is over and that factors such as social class and religion now structure people's vote choices less than they did some decades ago. While there is some evidence to support this view (Best, 2011; Franklin, Mackie, and Valen, 1992), others claim that cleavages have simply taken a different form or affect the vote differently (Oesch and Rennwald, 2018; van der Waal, Achterberg, and Houtman, 2007). Still others draw attention to the emergence of new cleavages that are also long-term factors of the vote. For example, scholars have discussed the emergence of an 'ideological gender gap' in voting (Inglehart and Norris, 2003), while Stubager (2010) has described the appearance of an education cleavage in voters' behaviour. Second, the evidence for the idea that short-term determinants of the vote choice are gaining in importance is altogether weak. While the possibility of a 'personalisation of politics' has received much attention in the literature, there is little systematic evidence of a growing impact of candidate or leader evaluations on voters' choices (Holmberg and Oscarsson, 2011; Karvonen, 2010). Furthermore, a longitudinal analysis of voting behaviour in seven European democracies shows that the weight of the economy on the vote is stable (Dassonneville and Lewis-Beck, 2019), casting further doubt on the premise that short-term factors are gaining weight.

In Chapters 3, 4, and 5, I provide a more systematic review of previous work that has tested the argument of a shift in importance from long- to short-term determinants. I also analyse the available election survey data to test what evidence there is of an over-time shift from long- to short-term determinants of the vote. Combined, these three chapters show that even though the idea of a shift from long-term to short-term determinants guiding voters' choices is an intuitively compelling theoretical framework, the empirical evidence that supports the theory is altogether weak.

It is the lack of strong empirical evidence for the idea of a shift in weight from long- to short-term factors that motivates me to examine in more depth what it is about the way in which voters choose parties that makes their choices stable or unstable. And the core argument that I make is that an important source of electoral instability can be found in the extent to which citizens are cross-pressured between parties, based on their membership of social groups. The presence of a feeling of group-based cross-pressure has consequences for the role of long- and short-term determinants in voters' decision processes. But the implication is *not* that long-term factors matter less and short-term factors matter more for citizens' electoral choices. My theory instead assumes that both long- and short-term factors are still affecting the choices that cross-pressured voters make but that the connections between different determinants are weak when a voter is cross-pressured, leading to a vote-choice process that I label as unconstrained instead of one in which all factors—from the mouth of the funnel onwards—push a voter towards one specific party.

The lack of constraint in the vote-choice process of a cross-pressured voter should be visible in two ways. First, long-term factors, while still present and relevant, should be linked in a less stable and structural way with a preference for a particular party. Second, the correlation between socio-demographic (i.e. long-term) characteristics and short-term factors, such as citizens' evaluations of leaders, the state of the economy, or their issue positions, should be weaker for the cross-pressured as well. The reason is that in the absence of a group-based attachment to one specific party and the guidance such an attachment provides, short-term factors are not interpreted in line with long-standing predispositions. These mechanisms result in vote choices that are still influenced by both long-term factors and short-term factors but that are substantially less 'anchored' by a single and all-encompassing long-term, group-based identity.

Given that cross-pressured voters are no longer 'bound by structures', as Prime Minister Dehaene claimed, their choices are more volatile.

1.3 Empirics

The patterns of change in electoral behaviour and the trend of increasing levels of volatility have been observed and described most extensively for established democracies (Dalton, 2013; Dalton and Flanagan, 2017; Franklin, Mackie, and Valen, 1992). In line with earlier work, my goal is therefore to better understand and explain electoral change in advanced democracies. To be sure, the connection between group-based cross-pressures and instability in voters' choices is an association that likely applies broadly and that therefore should be observed across countries and institutional settings. From a practical point of view, however, my empirical focus is exclusively on a limited number of established democracies.

The bulk of the book makes use of existing and publicly available election surveys[6] from countries that have a long history of conducting election research. These surveys are conducted using high-quality standards, rely on probability samples, and provide data on a representative section of the electorate. The full data set includes information on 133 elections in 8 established democracies, as summarized in Table 1.3. For more details on these election studies, see Appendix A. For most countries, the first election studies were

Table 1.3 Election surveys included in the analyses

Country	Time period	Number of elections
Australia	1966–2019	16
Canada	1965–2019	18
Denmark	1971–2015	17
Germany	1961–2017	16
Great Britain	1964–2019	15
The Netherlands	1971–2017	14
Sweden	1956–2018	19
United States	1948–2016	18

[6] The exception are the early studies from Australia. While the Australian Election Studies time series started in 1987, three earlier public opinion surveys allow the correlates of voting behaviour to be examined from the mid-1960s onward. I thank Ian McAllister for pointing me to these early opinion surveys.

conducted in the 1960s or 1970s, which results in a wealth of data for tracing over-time change in voters' electoral behaviour.

The selection of countries, furthermore, offers significant variation. The sample includes five European and three non-European democracies, a presidential system[7] as well as parliamentary systems, and ample variation in terms of electoral rules and party systems.

While there are important differences in the survey questions between countries and within countries over time, the core of the questionnaires is fairly standard. In addition, measures that differ only slightly between surveys are harmonized to allow for cross-sectional and longitudinal comparisons.

In some chapters, the analyses of these longitudinal and country-specific datasets are complemented with analyses that draw on the data from the European Election Studies (EES) project, with a focus on the data from the five European countries listed in Table 1.3. The advantage of these data is that the project asked the exact same questions in respondents in different European countries. Furthermore, the EES data provide information on respondents' self-reported propensity to vote (PTV) for different parties—which are particularly useful indicators for capturing citizens' feelings of cross-pressure between parties.

All the datasets that are used in this book are high-quality surveys that provide information on a representative sample of the electorate. The scope of the data, which include measures of voters' preferences, attitudes, and their political behaviour during several decades in each of the eight countries, make these data ideally suited to investigate patterns of change and provide an answer to the central research puzzle of the book. For some of the analyses, I also present results that draw on election panel data, which is especially important given the focus on voters' likelihood to change parties between elections. Overall, the combination of longitudinal cross-sectional data and a select number of more short-term panel studies provides unique insights in the dynamics of electoral behaviour and its correlates. That said, it should be kept in mind that the data are purely observational, meaning that I can only offer correlational evidence of the connection between cross-pressure and voter volatility.

---

[7] While the American National Election Studies provide data for midterm elections as well as presidential elections, to enhance the comparability of the results within the United States over time, I only make use of the data for presidential elections.

1.4 Plan for the book

The questions why some voters switch parties and others do not and why more voters switch parties in recent elections have already been given much attention by the scholarly literature. Yet, a key determinant of instability has been overlooked by most previous work: group-based cross-pressures. This book argues that citizens who are cross-pressured between parties, based on their socio-demographic characteristics, lack the guidance of strong social anchors and are pulled towards different parties. The lack of constraint in their voting-decision process leads to a choice that is ultimately more unstable. As a corollary of this core argument, this book makes the claim that the surge in electoral volatility in recent elections finds its origins in an increase in the number of cross-pressured voters in the electorate.

The book is divided in two parts. The first part of the book serves to provide more context, to connect the book's argument to the literature on change in electoral behaviour, and to strengthen the case for the introduction of a new theory to explain electoral volatility. The core argument—that group-based cross-pressures are key to explaining voter volatility—is presented and empirically tested in the second half of the book.

Before focusing on the idea that group-based cross-pressures are key to explaining this change and serve as an important determinant of volatility, I thus take the time to review the available evidence for existing theories of change. In Chapter 2, I first provide some context by reviewing how previous work has interpreted changes in voters' electoral behaviour. I particularly focus on the argument that the surge in volatility results from a shift in importance from long- to short-term determinants. Having presented recurrent theoretical arguments about the sources of change and their premises, I then turn to empirically assessing their validity. More specifically, I evaluate to what extent the effect of socio-demographic characteristics (Chapter 3) and partisan attachments (Chapter 4) have weakened over time and what the evidence is for the idea that short-term factors have gained importance in recent decades (Chapter 5). The evidence that is presented in these three empirical chapters strengthens the need to complement existing theories with an alternative explanation for the volatility in voters' electoral behaviour, setting the stage for the second part of the book.

I start the second part of the book by developing the theoretical argument in more depth. In Chapter 6, I expand on the intuition that group-based cross-pressures are key to explaining volatility. I elaborate on the ways in which group-based cross-pressures affect the role of both long- and short-term factors in voters' decisions. I also explain in more detail why group-based cross-pressures should have effects that trickle down in the funnel of causality and lead to voting-decision processes that can be characterized as unconstrained.

In Chapter 7, I then introduce the empirical measure of cross-pressure that is used in the subsequent chapters. I make the case, on theoretical grounds, that the measure captures to what extent individuals are bound by structure. In addition, I present a number of tests to validate that the measure indeed captures the theoretical concept of group-based cross-pressure.

The following chapters test the main expectations that follow from the argument that cross-pressures are key to understanding instability in voters' electoral choices. In Chapter 8, I use longitudinal cross-sectional election survey data from eight established democracies to evaluate whether levels of group-based cross-pressure have increased over time. In Chapter 9, I turn to testing the expectation that the effects of feeling cross-pressured based on one's socio-demographic characteristics trickle down in the funnel of causality. More specifically, I study the association between cross-pressure and party attachments and examine whether group-based cross-pressures correlate with more short-term determinants of the vote *also* providing less guidance in voters' decision-making process.

Finally, in Chapter 10, I assess whether higher levels of group-based cross-pressure are associated with volatility. I examine the association between an indicator of cross-pressure and different indicators that capture the instability of voters' electoral behaviour. This includes a measure of volatility but also the timing of survey respondents' voting decision. To overcome the limitations of cross-sectional data, this chapter also presents analyses of the connection between cross-pressure and voter volatility that rely on panel data. The evidence that is presented in this chapter shows evidence of a strong association between cross-pressure and voter volatility. This association, furthermore, is robust to accounting for alternative explanations of volatility.

In the concluding chapter of the book, I summarize the main findings and discuss the broader implications of the results. The observation that the increase in levels of cross-pressure appears to drive the surge in electoral volatility also motivates a discussion about what the future might bring in terms of voters' electoral behaviour and the stability of their choices. Finally, the concluding chapter points to some avenues for future research to deepen our understanding of the way in which group-based cross-pressures shape voting decisions.

PART I
VOTER VOLATILITY, LONG-TERM DETERMINANTS, AND SHORT-TERM DETERMINANTS OF THE VOTE

2
How change has been explained

Changes in electoral behaviour, and the surge in electoral volatility in particular, have spurred a stream of research studying the underlying causes of this change. In this book, I focus more specifically on an explanation that looks at voters' decision process and that seeks to establish whether changes in the way in which voters choose parties are key to explaining volatility. The puzzle that I seek to solve is why voters used to make choices that they tended to stick with over the course of an election campaign or from one election to the next, while voters now change their party preference much more.

A large number of studies have already sought to identify the changes in voters' decision-making processes that are associated with more volatile behaviour. This work has pointed to changes in the role of specific sets of vote-choice determinants, such as individuals' socio-demographic characteristics, partisanship, or more short-term determinants of the vote choice, including the economy, leaders, or issues.

In this short chapter, I review the main sources for change that earlier work has pointed to. I then turn to highlighting the limitations of these accounts and indicate why I think these explanations fall short of explaining the increase in electoral volatility that can be observed across established democracies. I more systematically review the evidence for these explanations in Chapters 3–5.

2.1 The funnel of causality

To summarize the different ways in which scholars have argued that voters' decision-making processes have changed to provoke more unstable electoral behaviour, it is useful to keep in mind the position of different determinants of the vote choice within the metaphorical funnel of causality. This way of thinking about the voting decision process was introduced by the authors of *The American Voter* (Campbell et al., 1960). Figure 2.1 shows a simplified version of the funnel of causality with a focus on three sets of factors; long-term socio-demographic factors, partisanship, and short-term determinants of the vote choice.

22 HOW CHANGE HAS BEEN EXPLAINED

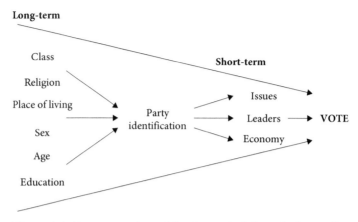

Figure 2.1 Representation of the theoretical funnel of causality

In line with how Campbell et al. (1960; see also, Lewis-Beck et al., 2008) conceived of the funnel of causality, Figure 2.1 clarifies that different factors within the funnel of causality are connected. For example, long-term sociodemographic factors shape whether citizens develop an attachment with a party and what party they identify with (Green, Palmquist, and Schickler, 2004). This party attachment subsequently influences how voters evaluate more short-term factors, including how they position themselves on specific issues and where they perceive parties' positions on these issues, their evaluation of party leaders or candidates, and their assessment of the state of the economy. To be sure, the representation of the funnel of causality in Figure 2.1 is a simplification as long-term factors, as well as party identification, not only have indirect effects on voters choices (e.g. via party identification and/or short-term factors) but can also influence the vote in a more direct way. For the sake of simplicity, Figure 2.1 also does not include values. The main point that is illustrated with this figure, however, is the idea that vote-choice determinants within a funnel of causality are interconnected and that more short-term factors are in part shaped by the long-term determinants of voters' electoral choices.

Within the funnel of causality, different determinants of the vote choice are organized according to a time dimension. Moving from the mouth to the tip of the funnel, the focus is on factors that are increasingly 'short-term', impacting voters' choices shortly before election day. This time dimension in the funnel is particularly important for an analysis of the sources of a trend towards more instability. Long-term factors have been described as 'enduring, stable, lasting' and short-term factors as 'fickle, unstable, at the moment' (Lewis-Beck and

Stegmaier, 2016: 168). An individual's socio-demographic characteristics are mostly stable over time, and partisanship as well is thought of as an enduring attachment with a party. In contrast, the saliency of issues for politics fluctuates from one election to the next and even over the course of an election campaign. Leaders and candidates change as well, and the state of the economy too is variable. Given this difference in stability, the role of long- and short-term factors in voters' decision-making processes is a natural place to look for the sources of their increasingly volatile behaviour (Dassonneville, 2016).

In the literature on the topic, three broad sets of arguments have been made to connect the increasingly volatile behaviour of voters to changes in their decision-making processes. These arguments each focus on one of the three sets of factors that are depicted in the funnel in Figure 2.1; socio-demographic variables, partisanship, and short-term factors. Section 2.2 discusses each of these arguments in turn.

2.2 Three explanations of change

A first explanation focuses on the role of individuals' socio-demographic characteristics and makes the argument that the effect of such variables has weakened over time. This work points to the erosion of cleavages in society and a weakening impact of individuals' positions on these cleavages on their vote choices. Current-day voters are contrasted with those voting in a period and in party systems that Lipset and Rokkan (1967) described as 'frozen', and particular attention is given to the weakening role of class and religion in voters' choices (Best, 2011; Goldberg, 2020; Oskarson, 2005; van der Brug, 2010; Walczak, van der Brug, and de Vries, 2012). This work offers quite some nuance in terms of the sources of change. It has been pointed out that it is important to make a distinction between a decline due to changing group compositions and a weakening of effects within cleavage groups (Best, 2011) and that it is important to separate the effects on voters' choices from effects on their likelihood to turn out to vote (Goldberg, 2020). Making abstraction of those important differences, however, the key claim of work along these lines is that there is a 'decline in the ability of social cleavages to structure individual voter choice' (Franklin, Mackie, and Valen, 1992: 385).

Admittedly, scholars studying over-time changes in the effects and impact of socio-demographic characteristics on voters' choices highlight that new cleavages might appear and take over the role that class or religion used to play in advanced democracies (Ford and Jennings, 2020). Even so, the thrust of the argument is that social cleavages contribute less to explaining voters' choices nowadays than was the case a few decades ago. Dalton (2020: 134) characterizes the change as follows:

> [S]ocial modernization weakened class alignments. Similarly, secularization is decreasing the influence of religion on voting behavior. To a lesser degree, other social traits—such as race or generation—have held steady or even gained in importance because of their relationship to new cultural issues. But the overall impact of social cleavages today is weaker than in the mid-twentieth century.

In summary, a first explanation to account for the over-time increase in electoral volatility focuses on the role of citizens' socio-demographic characteristics. The impact of these long-term factors, which are electorally relevant because they capture citizens' positions on the main societal and political cleavages, is argued to have eroded over time. Given the stable nature of individuals' social characteristics, a weakened role of such stable factors in voters' decision-making processes could logically imply that voters change their party preferences more often.

A second explanation turns the attention to the central role of party identifications within the funnel of causality. Party identification, which is conceived of as a psychological attachment to a party (Huddy, Bankert, and Davies, 2018) not only reflects one's socio-demographic characteristics (Green and Palmquist, 1990) but also shapes perceptions of more short-term political objects (Bartels, 2002; Bisgaard, 2019) and stabilizes voters' choices. Whether party identifications continue to play such a crucial role within voters' decision-making processes, however, is being questioned. In particular, scholars who have identified a trend of declining levels of partisanship point out that this dealignment serves as a breeding ground for more volatile electoral behaviour (Dalton, McAllister, and Wattenberg, 2002; Dalton, 2020; Fieldhouse et al., 2020). The argument of work along these lines is that the number of people that hold a party identification, or the strength of individuals' attachments, is in decline. This implies that the share of the electorate that is guided by such party attachments when voting is decreasing, resulting in more party switching overall.

A third account that connects the surge in electoral volatility to changes in the ways in which citizens decide what party to vote for gives particular attention to the role of short-term determinants of the vote. The starting point of work along these lines is that the importance of long-term factors—such as individuals' socio-demographic characteristics—is in decline and that party attachments are eroding. This observation is then connected to the role of short-term factors, and it is argued that the vacuum that is left by a weakening of the roles of socio-demographics and partisanship in voters' decision-making processes is being filled by the increased importance of short-term factors. As argued by Dalton (2020: 151), 'the eroding influence of long-term sources of partisanship suggests that factors further along the funnel of causality will play a larger role in voter choice.' Furthermore, the increased (relative) weight of short-term factors within the funnel of causality is thought of as a catalyst of electoral volatility. Arguably, as electorates rely more on specific issue positions, on leaders and candidates, and on their evaluation of the state of the economy when voting than on strong party attachments or their socio-demographic characteristics, their choices grow more volatile (Kayser and Wlezien, 2011).

2.3 The limitations of explanations of change

Each of the three explanations presented in section 2.2 contributes to our understanding of the sources of strong and consistent increase in electoral volatility across established democracies. None of the accounts by themselves, however, offer an entirely satisfying answer to the question of how change in voters' decision-making processes has spurred electoral volatility. In what follows, I summarize the main ways in which these theories of change should be qualified.

The argument that the rise in volatility is driven by a declining role for socio-demographic factors can be challenged on a number of grounds. First, a number of studies point out that factors related to individuals' class, social status, or religion continue to guide voting behaviour—though perhaps in different ways. The work of Oesch and Rennwald (2018), for example, draws attention to the fact that social structure still strongly shapes voting behaviour, but in different ways. More specifically, the radical right has joined the left and the centre-right to compete for specific classes of voters. Radical right-wing parties compete with the left in particular for the support of working-class voters and with center-right parties for the votes of small business owners. Along the same lines, a restructuring of the effects of religion on voters' electoral choices is being discussed too. Christian-Democratic parties are losing electoral support (Duncan, 2015), but scholarly work also points to the emergence of a new 'coalition of the religious' (Putnam and Campbell, 2010) that is drawn to radical right-wing parties (Marcinkiewicz and Dassonneville, 2022).

For the rural–urban cleavage, recent work argues that the divide has gained in importance over time in both the United States (Gimpel et al., 2020; Lyons and Utych, forthcoming) and in Europe (Huijsmans et al., 2021; Maxwell, 2020).

Second, most work that has studied the declining impact of socio-structural characteristics on voters' choices has focused on the role of class or religion (Best, 2011; Jansen, de Graaf, and Need, 2012; Nieuwbeerta, de Graaf, and Ultee, 2000). However, others are pointing out that new social divides are emerging and that differences based on individuals' gender (Norris and Inglehart, 2001), their age (Erk, 2017), or educational background (Gethin, Martínez-Toledano, and Piketty, 2022; Stubager, 2009, 2013) have the potential to develop into political cleavages (Ford and Jennings, 2020).

These are important nuances to accounts that posit that the impact of long-term socio-demographic factors on voters' choices has declined substantially. The ways in which socio-demographic factors correlate with the vote have definitely changed, and there is also change in terms of the precise factors that shape electoral behaviour. But to argue that citizens' choices are no longer or hardly affected by socio-demographic factors seems premature. Thus, despite changes in the connections between individuals' social characteristics and their electoral choices, links between these characteristics and voting behaviour are still present, and new links are being observed. Given the nature of socio-demographic characteristics, which are all fairly stable traits of individuals, the expectation would therefore be that long-term socio-demographic factors continue to have a stabilizing impact on electoral behaviour. The empirical reality, however, is one of increasing levels of electoral volatility in many established democracies.

The second way in which the scholarly literature has linked changes in the funnel of causality to a rise in electoral volatility puts the spotlight on the role of partisanship. As a long-term psychological attachment to a political party, partisanship arguably serves to stabilize voters' electoral choices (Campbell et al., 1960). Empirical research confirms this expectation, with work finding that partisanship is by far the strongest individual-level predictor of volatility (Dejaeghere and Dassonneville, 2017). As a result, the observation of a trend towards dealignment in established democracies (Dalton and Wattenberg, 2002)—implying that a shrinking share of the electorate is still partisan—would logically be associated with a surge in electoral volatility. This theoretical framework for explaining the rise in electoral volatility, however, deserves closer scrutiny as well.

First, while a number of scholars have provided evidence of a drop in the share of partisans in electorates across established democracies (Crewe,

Sarlvik, and Alt, 1977; Dalton and Wattenberg, 2002; Dassonneville, Hooghe, and Vanhoutte, 2012; Garzia, Ferreira da Silva, and De Angelis, 2022) or of a decline in the strength of party attachments (Fieldhouse et al., 2020), others have argued that this decline was restricted to a particular time period or is limited overall (Bartels, 2000; Green, Palmquist, and Schickler, 2004). There are even indications that the trend of dealignment has been reversed again more recently (Arzheimer, 2017). A recent weakening or reversal of the trend in dealignment is at odds with the observations in Chapter 1 that volatility is increasing at an increasing rate with particularly high levels of volatility in recent elections.

The third argument that has been made in previous work studying the impact of changes in voters' decision-making processes on volatility stands out for theorizing explicitly about the connections between different vote-choice determinants within the funnel of causality. More specifically, the rationale behind this account is that the weakening impact of long-term factors has resulted in more room for short-term determinants to guide voters' choices. This work thus conceives of long- and short-term determinants as communicating vessels, with a diminishing impact of long-term factors being compensated by an increased role for short-term factors. Focusing on generational differences in what determines voters' choices, van der Brug (2010: 603) states that 'since the long-term determinants of the vote are less important for [younger generations], it seems plausible that their vote will be more and more decided by short-term considerations, such as issues, evaluations of government performance and candidate evaluations'. In a more general sense, Dalton (2020) argues that '[a]s the long-term determinants of party choice have decreased in influence, there has been a counterbalancing growth in the importance of short-term attitudes....'.

If short-term factors have gained in electoral importance and have a larger impact on voters' choices now than was the case a few decades ago, that would indeed be consistent with a trend towards increasingly volatile vote choices. After all, choices that are driven by the issues of the day, or motivated by an appreciation for a party's current leader, are more unstable than choices that are shaped by one's stable social characteristics or a strong attachment to a party.

This theory of change, however, is not entirely compelling either. The idea that short-term factors counterbalance the decline of long-term determinants of the vote choice can be criticized on empirical and theoretical grounds. At an empirical level, the few studies that have explicitly studied over-time changes in the impact of short-term factors have failed to find strong support for the idea that the effect of short-term determinants has grown over time. Spending an entire edited volume looking for indications of a surge in the effects of short-term factors such as the economy, leaders, or issues, Thomassen (2005: 263) concludes there is not the 'slightest evidence' of such a pattern. Other studies that have analysed trends in the impact of specific short-term factors on the vote have similarly failed to show support for the expectation that the effect of economic conditions (Dassonneville and Lewis-Beck, 2019) or leaders (Karvonen, 2010) on the vote has grown over time.

Oscarsson and Oskarson (2019: 275) characterize the fact that despite a decline in the effects of long-term factors, there is no strong evidence of a surge in the impact of short-term determinants of the vote as a 'conundrum in electoral research'. I would argue, however, that the expectation that short-term factors will counterbalance a decline of long-term determinants of the vote choice is more nuanced and complex than this theoretical account suggests.

To understand why, take another look at the representation of the funnel of causality in Figure 2.1. Within the funnel, the scheme shows that long- and short-term factors are connected. Long-term determinants, such as an individual's social class or their religion, influence their party attachment, and citizens' identifications with parties structure how they view and evaluate political objects. In the absence of a connection between long- and short-term factors, a reduction of the effects of long-term factors on the vote choice implies that the stabilizing role of these factors weakens, giving more room for short-term factors to influence the vote. Given their short-term nature, these determinants do not anchor voters' choices but can lead voters to support another party or candidate from time to time. Figure 2.2 illustrates a scenario where long- and short-term factors are unrelated. Under such conditions, an erosion of the impact of long-term factors implies that only the more fickle short-term factors still influence voters' choices—which would result in more volatility.

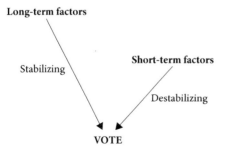

Figure 2.2 Connection between long-term factors, short-term factors, and the vote choice (1)

Campbell et al. (1960) have already pointed out that long- and short-term factors are not unrelated, however, and that the more long-term determinants of the vote shape citizens' short-term political attitudes and preferences. A voluminous literature has offered empirical evidence of such a connection (see, e.g. Anduiza, Gallego, and Muñoz, 2013; Bartels, 2002; Bisgaard, 2019). We know, for example, that during election campaigns, citizens 'learn the issue positions of the candidates or parties and (...) adopt the position of their preferred party or candidate as their own' (Lenz, 2009: 934). There is also considerable evidence which shows that citizens' perceptions of objective facts—like the state of the economy—are shaped by elite cues (Bisgaard and Slothuus, 2018) and moderated by party identities (Bailey, 2019). In this way, the long-term determinants of the vote—such as citizens' attachments to a specific party—can be thought to structure and stabilize their more short-term preferences and attitudes.

Figure 2.3 illustrates the connections between the three factors, including the stabilizing and structuring effect that long-term factors have on short-term factors. Following such a model of the vote-choice process, a voter who developed an attachment with party X is more likely to evaluate the party's accomplishments positively regardless of their actual performance, to like the leader or candidates of party X regardless of their leadership traits and characteristics, and generally to agree with party X on specific issues. In a rather stable fashion, therefore, this voter's performance evaluations, assessments of leaders and candidates, or their positions on specific issues will push them further to vote for party X—in this way, stabilizing their vote choice.

Importantly, if voters' decision-making processes resemble a scheme such as the one depicted in Figure 2.3, the role of short-term factors in the voting decision will differ depending on the presence and impact of long-term stabilizing factors. More specifically, for voters that are strongly influenced by

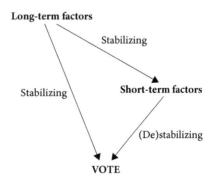

Figure 2.3 Connection between long-term factors, short-term factors, and the vote choice (2)

long-term factors and that have developed an attachment with a specific party, their short-term determinants will largely line up with their partisan predispositions. If anything, the role of short-term factors under such conditions will be to further confirm one's preferences and stabilize the vote.

In the absence of long-term predispositions towards a specific party, in contrast, citizens' short-term attitudes are not anchored and change from one election to the next. It is only in the absence of an influence of long-term factors that short-term factors are really unstable and ultimately can render voters' choices more volatile as well.

It is on this intuition, which takes as a starting point the idea that different determinants of the vote choice are inter-connected, that I build to develop a framework for understanding the effects of changes in voters' decision-making processes for electoral volatility. Before presenting that theory, which highlights the role of group-based cross-pressures as a source of instability, in Chapter 3–5 I more systematically review what evidence there is for each of the three main existing theories of change that I presented in this chapter.

2.4 Summary and implications

The observation that electoral behaviour is in flux in many established democracies, with a surge in levels of electoral volatility in particular, has spurred a discussion on the sources of the growing instability in voters' choices. This debate has focused on the role of different types of vote-choice determinants, with particular attention given to the roles of long- and short-term determinants of the vote. The assumption that much of this work makes is that long-term factors—such as individuals' socio-demographic characteristics or their partisanship—always have a stabilizing effect on voters' decisions. Short-term determinants, such as individuals' positions on specific issues, their assessment of the candidates and leaders of parties, or their evaluation of the state of the economy, are thought of as factors that consistently destabilize the choices that voters make.

In this chapter, I have argued that such a perspective overlooks the strong connections between long- and short-term determinants of the vote choice. And because of these strong connections, citizens' short-term views can either line up with a pre-existing partisan predisposition and contribute to more stability or be a source of instability if such predispositions are missing. Along the same lines, the connections between different long-term determinants also matter in determining whether long-term factors will anchor and stabilize voters' choices or not. In summary, both factors that are categorized as long-term determinants and variables that are conceived of as short-term factors can either stabilize or destabilize voters' choices.

This conceptual discussion serves as a motivation to develop an alternative theory to explain changes in voters' electoral choices and how those changes have led to a surge in electoral volatility. But there are also empirical grounds for pursuing the search for good explanations of what is causing the growing instability in electoral behaviour. That point is clarified in Chapters 3–5, which serve to systematically assess how socio-demographic variables, partisanship, and short-term determinants of the vote have fared over time in the eight established democracies that are analysed in this book.

3
How socio-demographic factors have fared over time

Of all possible determinants of voters' choices, socio-demographic factors have probably received most scrutiny in terms of the over-time trend in their effect and importance for explaining voters' choices. The motivation for most of this work is the observation that party systems are no longer 'frozen' (Lipset and Rokkan, 1967) and that this is likely a consequence of the weakening effects of cleavages. Given that party systems in many countries were traditionally structured around conflicts between owners and workers, state and church, land and industry, and centre and periphery (Lipset and Rokkan, 1967), most attention has been given to the structural decline of factors that determine what side an individual is on with respect to each of these conflicts: their social class, their religious denomination or religiosity, and their place of living.

More recently, students of elections have also begun to give more attention to the role of socio-demographic factors that were not traditionally linked to the cleavages that structured political competition. There is a growing attention being given to the role of gender in explaining voters' electoral choices, to the role of age in structuring citizens' party preferences, and to the likely appearance of an educational cleavage. To evaluate to what extent the impact of long-term factors on voters' electoral choices has declined, it is important to assess both the effects of 'old' variables—which are linked to historical cleavages—and the effects of the socio-demographic variables that have seemingly gained political relevance: gender, age, and education.

The central thesis of this book, detailed in Chapter 6—is that the 'constraining' role of socio-demographic factors on citizens' vote choices is weakening over time because voters are increasingly cross-pressured. My focus is thus on how different socio-demographic determinants of the vote choice interact, push a voter in one direction, or instead lead a voter to feel cross-pressured between parties. In focusing on the extent to which socio-demographic characteristics push voters towards the same or different parties, my work differs from previous work which has assumed that the increase in volatility results from an over-time weakening of the impact of long-term socio-demographic

Voters Under Pressure. Ruth Dassonneville, Oxford University Press. © Ruth Dassonneville (2023).
DOI: 10.1093/oso/9780192894137.003.0003

factors on the vote. My argument thus implies that the increase in electoral volatility can occur even if voters' electoral choices are still influenced by their socio-demographic characteristics.

Before elaborating on my argument, however, it is important to verify whether there is indeed a need for an alternative explanation of the changes in voters' behaviour. Therefore, this chapter zooms in on the impact of individuals' socio-demographic characteristics on their vote choices. After reviewing the main findings of earlier work that has studied the effects of socio-demographic variables on the vote, the chapter empirically assesses the explanatory power of both 'old' and 'new' socio-demographic factors in vote-choice models. The inclusion of indicators that capture both the old and newer social cleavages is important because it is theoretically possible that even if the political role of class, religion, or place of living has declined over-time, other long-term factors have gained in importance.

3.1 'Old' cleavages: Class, religion, and place of living

A number of socio-demographic characteristics have long been known to correlate with voters' choices. These variables, which I refer to as indicators of 'old' cleavages, reflect citizens' positions on the main political cleavages that Lipset and Rokkan (1967) identified, that is, a cleavage capturing the opposition between the working class and the bourgeoisie, a church–state cleavage, a centre–periphery cleavage, and an urban–rural cleavage.

A first variable is citizens' social class—which serves as an indicator of whether they are on the owner or on the worker side of the cleavage that resulted from the Industrial Revolution. In most established democracies, there was traditionally a strong association between citizens' social class and their vote. More specifically, the lower social classes were more likely to support left-wing parties than members of higher social classes (Alford, 1962). Labour parties in particular mobilized the working classes, leading to a fairly strong connection between social class and voting for the left. The connection between social class and the vote for left-wing parties, however, has weakened over time. This decline is particularly stark in the British context, as shown by Evans and Tilley (2011). They note that in the 1960s, the working class was fifty percentage points more likely to vote for Labour than the upper service class. In the early 2000s, the size of this gap had already more than halved—to less than twenty percentage points (Evans and Tilley, 2011: 148–149).

Observations of a weakening link between social class and the vote have given rise to a whole sub-field in electoral behaviour evaluating the extent to which the impact of social class on the vote has either weakened or been transformed. The central question in this literature is whether 'social classes are dying' (Clark and Lipset, 1991). Key to answering this question is finding out whether social classes are losing their political relevance. The conclusions of studies that have examined this question are nuanced. On the one hand, they show clear evidence that as a consequence of the weakening of class stratification over time, politics has become less organized by class (Clark and Lipset, 1991; Clark, Lipset, and Rempel, 1993). As a result, the impact of class on voters' choices is declining over time (Nieuwbeerta and Ultee, 1999; Nieuwbeerta, de Graaf, and Ultee, 2000). In part, this is a consequence of the fact that the size of certain social groups—such as blue-collar workers—is shrinking over time and in part it is the result of social class membership losing political relevance (Best, 2011; Brooks, Nieuwbeerta, and Manza, 2006). Focusing on the sources of the decline of social-democratic parties across Europe, for example, Benedetto, Hix, and Mastrorocco (2020) find that the losses of these parties are a consequence of both the declining presence of industrial workers in the electorate and their declining propensity to vote for social democratic parties. In addition, changes in parties' behaviour have been argued to further contribute to the decline of the role of class in electoral politics. By blurring their positions on the class cleavage, and by moving towards the ideological centre, left-wing parties have made it harder for voters to vote based on class identity (Evans and Tilley, 2012; Jansen, Evans, and de Graaf, 2013).

In contrast to these accounts, others have stressed a continued relevance of the class cleavage for the vote. For example, van der Waal, Achterberg, and Houtman (2007) argue that, even if other issues have gained political relevance over time, this does not mean that the absolute impact of class on the vote has declined. More recently, it has also been shown that the effects of class on the vote are being expressed differently now than was the case a few decades ago. Having lost the support of their working-class base, parties on the left now also appeal to members of the middle class (Gingrich and Häusermann, 2015). Furthermore, radical-right parties in particular seem to be competing with both left- and right-wing parties for part of their traditional class base (Oesch and Rennwald, 2018), weakening the link between social class and a vote for the traditional left. The view that the role of class has changed rather than declined is also the conclusion of Enyedi (2008: 291). Based on a review of the literature, he states: '[v]arious aspects of social position continue to be channelled into political attitudes and votes, but the links between parties and social groups have transformed'.

Turning to the religious cleavage, both its presence and how religion is expressed politically, varies considerably between countries. Focusing on countries where Catholics or Protestants are the dominant denominational group, religion tends to be associated with higher support for parties to the right of the ideological spectrum (Knutsen, 2004a). Traditionally, conservative parties or religious parties (e.g. Christian-Democratic or Catholic parties) hence appealed to religious voters, while left-wing parties fared less well among this group. A rich literature has reported on an over-time decline of the religious cleavage (Best, 2011; Franklin, Mackie, and Valen, 1992; Jansen, de Graaf, and Need, 2012), and in line with what holds for class, this work has referred to both group size effects and effects due to the political relevance of religion for voters. The group size effects in this case relate to the process of secularization, a trend that is visible in most Western democracies (Evans and Northmore-Ball, 2017; Inglehart, 2021). In addition, it has been investigated whether adherence to a certain religion or the attendance of religious service are losing their political relevance among the group that still is religious. On that front, the picture is not as clear. Knutsen (2004a), for example, who studied the link between religion and the vote in eight West-European countries, found evidence of 'stability in the correlations between religious denomination and party choice in most countries' (Knutsen, 2004a: 121). Studying the religious cleavage in the British context, Tilley (2015) also does not find much evidence of a decline. He attributes this finding to the fact that religion is 'simply a marker of parents' and grandparents' party affiliation from an era when religion did matter' (Tilley, 2015: 923). Other work does hint at a weakening of the effects of religion on the vote, though the trends vary a great deal between countries (Goldberg, 2020; Jansen, de Graaf, and Need, 2012).

As holds for the role of class, there are indications that despite the decline, religion still serves as an important predictor of the vote. Church attendance is still a powerful predictor of support for Christian-Democratic parties (Duncan, 2015; Marcinkiewicz and Dassonneville, 2022). Studying the connection between religion and conservative support in the United States, Germany, and Great Britain, Raymond (2011: 132) concludes that 'religious voters today continue to support parties of the right much as they did in the 1960s'. However, he also notes that this effect of religion on the vote appears to have become more indirect and mediated by more short-term political attitudes (Raymond, 2011). Furthermore, van der Brug, Hobolt and de Vreese (2009) show hints of an uptick in the importance of religion in recent times.

Others stress that the role of religion on the vote is transforming rather than declining. Putnam and Campbell (2010: 376) in particular note that while differences between religious denominations are becoming less politically relevant, a 'coalition of the religious' is emerging. A similar pattern has been observed in Canada, with Wilkins-Laflamme (2016) noting that even though the role of religious denomination in Canada is in decline, religiosity increasingly shapes voters' choices. Finally, the rise of radical right-wing parties across Europe has led to a renewed scholarly attention for the association between religion and the vote. By stressing the Christian roots of European societies, and by opposing that heritage to the values of Muslim newcomers, radical right-wing parties appeal, with some success, to the dominant religious groups (Arzheimer and Carter, 2009; Immerzeel, Jaspers, and Lubbers, 2013; Marcinkiewicz and Dassonneville, 2022), suggesting that religion might be gaining political relevance again.

Finally, citizens' place of living is traditionally thought of as an important factor influencing their vote. Two of the four cleavages that Lipset and Rokkan (1967) identified relate to where one lives. First, the centre–periphery cleavage is reflective of a conflict between the centre and populations of a different ethnic background or linguistic minorities living in the provinces. This cleavage is mostly visible from the fact that people living in different regions within a same country vote for different parties and from minorities voting for ethnic parties (Knutsen, 2013; Oskarson, 2005). While the presence and strength of this territorial cleavage varies substantially between countries, the observation that party systems and vote choices are 'nationalising' suggests a weakening of this cleavage over time (Caramani, 2004). Second, the rural–urban cleavage also relates to where citizens are living. The cleavage originated in a conflict between landowners and a new city-based elite that accumulated wealth following the Industrial Revolution (Lipset and Rokkan, 1967). In the polls, this cleavage takes the form of a contrast between rural and urban populations, with the former being more likely to support conservative and religious parties than the latter (Knutsen, 2013). In the comparative literature, the rural–urban cleavage has been given considerably less scrutiny than the class and religious cleavages. In part, this is probably because the rural–urban cleavage is rather weak comparatively, with the exception, perhaps, of the Nordic countries (Oskarson, 2005). The few longitudinal analyses that have examined the impact of the rural–urban cleavage over time, however, suggest that its importance might be in decline (Knutsen, 2004b, 2013; Oskarson, 2005). In contrast to such an account, a number of recent studies have drawn attention to the continued—and perhaps increased—importance of rural–urban divides in shaping citizens' political identities (Cramer, 2016) and attitudes (Maxwell, 2020).

The insights of Lipset and Rokkan (1967) have received most attention and have been empirically scrutinized most thoroughly in Western Europe. It is the party systems in these countries that were traditionally characterized as 'frozen', and it is also in Western Europe that scholars have observed and studied the emergence of cracks in the stable and cleavage-based political landscape (Best, 2011; Franklin, Mackie, and Valen, 1992; Knutsen, 2004*b*; Nieuwbeerta and Ultee, 1999).[1] Hence, of the eight countries that are covered in this book, there are three countries for which expectations are less clear. Politics and voting behaviour in Australia, Canada, and the United States have never been structured by social characteristics to the same extent as what holds for countries in Western Europe. Studying the role of social structure on the vote in Australia and Canada, for example, Irvine and Gold (1980: 213) concluded that '[i]n neither case is the society systematically and deeply fractured politically, as might be observed of Holland or Austria'. Of the three countries, the impact of the old cleavages is perhaps strongest in Australia—which has been described as strongly resembling the Great Britain in terms of the presence and importance of a class cleavage (Hayes, 1995).

3.2 'New' cleavages: Gender, age, and education

While discussions on the weakening impact of the 'old' cleavages continue, scholars have also started to draw attention to 'new' cleavages, such as gender, age, education, or ethnicity—to name just a few. These new cleavages are not connected to the structural cleavages that Lipset and Rokkan (1967) have described, but it has been argued that major societal transformations across established democracies are 'creating the conditions' for the emergence of a number of new cleavages (Ford and Jennings, 2020: 300). Given the longitudinal perspective that is taken in this book, I focus on three 'new' cleavages for which election studies in the eight countries analysed in this book consistently include measures that can be used to operationalize these cleavages: gender, age, and education.

Starting with the effect of gender on the vote, it is obvious that the political impact of gender is different to that of class, religion, or place of living. Even if women might have different ideological and party preferences than men,

---

[1] But see Goldberg (2020) for a comparative analyses of the weakening of cleavages that includes the United States.

gender does not structure vote choices in the same way as old cleavages (used to) do. This crucial difference was highlighted in the work of Inglehart and Norris (2003: 75):

> Gender differences in party preferences were never as marked as the classic electoral cleavages of class, region, and religion; there were no mass 'women's parties' like those associated with trade unions, regions, and churches.

Gender differs from the 'old' cleavages in two main ways. First, gender differences in party preferences are generally smaller than those based on class, religion, or place of living. Second, in contrast to factors such as class or religion, gender is hardly mobilized by political parties that claim to represent or defend the interests of either men or women.

The fundamental differences between gender and the old, cleavage-based variables might imply that gender does not fit standard definitions of a political cleavage (Bartolini and Mair, 1990; Deegan-Krause and Enyedi, 2010), but this does not mean that gender is of little political relevance. Studies regularly report on gender differences in the vote choice, and work on the topic has shown evidence of an over-time reversal of ideological gender differences. Inglehart and Norris (2003) show that while women were traditionally more conservative and right-leaning than men, starting from around the 1980s this gender gap first shrank and then eventually began to reverse; that is, since around the 1980s in the United States and from around the 1990s in Europe, women are on average more liberal, more left-leaning, and have a higher likelihood of voting for left-wing parties than men (Inglehart and Norris, 2000, 2003). The electoral rise of radical right-wing parties also appears to be gendered, as work shows that women are significantly and substantially less likely to vote for the radical right (Harteveld and Ivarsflaten, 2018; Oshri et al., forthcoming).

Subsequent studies have confirmed the reversal of the ideological gender gap, while also giving insights in to the reasons for the remarkable reversal of men's and women's ideological positions and party preferences. In particular, it has been argued that women's turn to the left is linked to a number of important changes in women's role and position in both society and family life (Abendschön and Steinmetz, 2014). Research on the topic shows, for example, that as women participate more in the labour market and often experience pay disparities, as they become higher educated, and as they become more secularized, they shift to the left (Abendschön and Steinmetz, 2014; Giger, 2009; Inglehart and Norris, 2000; Iversen and Rosenbluth, 2006).

While the reversal of the ideological gender gap is a remarkable development, it is important to stress that gender differences in party preferences are still fairly modest. Across thirty-six Organisation for Economic Co-operation and Development (OECD) countries, the estimated difference between men's and women's left–right self-placement on a 1–10 scale is about 0.2 points only (Dassonneville, 2021). This is partly due to the fact that the over-time change in women's ideological positions has been a very slow process that is driven by generational replacement (Harsgor, 2018; Shorrocks, 2018). What is more, given that among most recent generations (Generations X and Y), women are not more left-leaning than the generation of women before them, there is little reason to expect the gender gap to increase much more in the foreseeable future (Dassonneville, 2021).

A number of recent elections have drawn scholars' attention to the role of age in voters' choices. Studying the determinants of the vote choice in Great Britain, Sloam and Henn (2017: 110) argue that '[i]n 2017, age replaced class as the key predictor of party choice'. Just one year earlier, during the Brexit referendum, age had already been an important predictor of citizens' preferences—along with education (Hobolt, 2016). Such observations contrast with the work of Goerres (2008), who found altogether small effects of age on the choices of British and German voters. Similarly, Wagner and Kritziger (2012: 285) report 'surprisingly small' age group differences in the context of the 2009 Austrian election.

The increased salience of age in voters' choices therefore seems a very recent phenomenon. Studying the question of whether we are witnessing the emergence of an age cleavage in more depth, O'Grady (2021) finds that ideological differences between the young and the old are in fact fairly stable over time. His analysis of ideological preferences in European countries since the 1980s suggests that the young have always been more left-leaning than older voters—in particular, on social issues and immigration. However, O'Grady (2021: 38) also acknowledges that an increased salience and party-level polarization on those issues might have 'allowed the young and old to better express their long-standing and distinctive non-economic preferences in their votes'.

Finally, I consider the impact of education on voters' choices. According to Ford and Jennings (2020), education has real potential for developing into a true cleavage that structures the vote. Its emergence is linked to an important societal change; the strong and rapid expansion of higher education across established democracies. In addition, Ford and Jennings (2020) contend that education also reflects shared values and identities. There are indeed strong indications that the low and the higher educated have opposing views on the liberal/authoritarian dimension (Langsæther and Stubager, 2019; Stubager, 2013), which might be reflective of the fact that the former are losers and the latter are winners of globalization (Kriesi, 2010). In addition, Stubager (2009) has shown that the lower educated in particular develop a group consciousness, while Kuppens et al. (2018) find evidence of education-based in-group bias among the higher educated. Such work points to the presence of education-based identities, which is a key ingredient for the development of a strong political cleavage.

In terms of the vote choice, the new educational cleavage is visible most clearly in the likelihood to voting for parties that take a clear stance on the liberal/authoritarian or the new politics dimension. More specifically, higher educated voters are more likely to vote for green parties (Schumacher, 2014) but also for radical left-wing parties (Rooduijn et al., 2017). The lower educated turn to the other end of the spectrum and are more likely to support radical right-wing parties (Rooduijn et al., 2017; van der Brug and Fennema, 2009). A number of recent 'earthquake elections' in particular have been characterized by stark educational differences in the vote. The higher educated were much more likely than the lower educated to vote remain in the Brexit referendum (Hobolt, 2016) or to support Macron in the 2017 French presidential elections (Evans and Ivaldi, 2018), giving further credence to the idea that education might be developing into a real cleavage.

3.3 Old and new: The explanatory power of socio-demographic variables over time

Even though research on the topic is quite nuanced, it is fair to say that the literature generally shows that the electoral impact of class, religion, and place of living has changed over time. Of the variables that have received attention more recently, age and definitely education seem to be increasingly important for explaining voters' choices. There is a crucial difference, however, between factors such as class and religion, on the one hand, and age and education, on the other. The former variables are linked to cleavages that structure societies and that gain visibility through civil society organizations, trade unions, or churches that defend the interests of a certain side of the cleavage. Partly through the links with these organizations, there is also an obvious link to certain parties (Enyedi, 2008). It is clear that labour parties are there to represent the interests of the working class, while religious voters know that candidates of Christian-Democratic parties share their values. In contrast, age and education might well be correlated with citizens' vote choices, but there are no civil society organizations equivalent to trade unions or churches that bring together, mobilize, and defend the interests of, for example, the lower educated or the young. Finally, with the exception of a few minor parties in some countries,[2] there are no parties that clearly state they are defending the interests of groups at one side of the gender, age, or education cleavages.

Given this difference between the two sets of variables, the impact of gender, age, or education might be smaller than that of the old cleavage variables class, religion, and place of living. In terms of the expected patterns of change over time, the review of the literature leads to the expectation that the impact of old cleavage variables has declined over time,[3] while the effects of the new cleavage variables is expected to have strengthened over time. To shed light on the over-time relative importance of old and new cleavage variables I proceed with an analysis of the over-time trend in the explanatory power of socio-demographic variables on the vote in each of the eight established democracies that are considered in this book.

3.3.1 Empirical strategy

To examine the role of socio-demographic factors over time, I turn to an analysis of the election survey data from each of the eight established democracies that are the focus of this book. I estimate a series of election-specific vote-choice models in each country, with the reported vote choice as the dependent variable and socio-demographic variables class, religion, place of living, gender, age, and education as the independent variables.

In the United States, where racial identities are known to strongly structure voters' behaviour (Sides, Tesler, and Vavreck, 2019; Stokes-Brown, 2006), I additionally include race as an indicator of an important social cleavage. Given the long history of a connection between race and the vote in the United States, I group this variable with the 'old' cleavage variables.

To account for the fact that cleavages might be expressed differently over time, with, for example membership of the working class increasing the

---

[2] Exceptions include the 50PLUS Pensioners' Party in the Netherlands (Otjes and Krouwel, 2018) and the Women's Equality Party (WEP) in the UK (Evans and Kenny, 2019). 50PLUS has gained seats in the Dutch Parliament but has not gained more than 4 per cent of the vote. The WEP has not succeeded in gaining representation in the British Parliament.

[3] Previous work, in particular studies that focus on transformations in the effects of these variables rather than their decline, is more nuanced. Still, the prevailing narrative is that the effect of these variables—especially class and religion—has declined.

likelihood of voting for labour parties in the 1970s but increasing the chances of voting for radical right-wing parties more recently (Oesch and Rennwald, 2018), I do not specify what parties should receive the support of certain social groups. Instead, I estimate models that include all parties that receive the support of at least 2 per cent of the respondents in a survey.[4] Abstainers are excluded from the analyses, and the same holds for those indicating they voted for an 'other' party than the options provided to them in the election survey. For the United States, the models are logistic regression models that distinguish between a vote for the Democratic and the Republican party. For all other countries, I estimate multinomial logistic regression models. This approach is well suited to estimate a vote-choice model when citizens have multiple options to choose from (Whitten and Palmer, 1996).[5]

The focus of my analyses is not on the precise coefficients of the independent variables but on the explanatory power of the models. Different pseudo-R^2 statistics could be used to approximate the explanatory power of the socio-demographic models of the vote choice.[6] I report the results for the McFadden R^2 statistic.

In order to assess whether and to what extent the new cleavage variables have compensated for a potential decline of old cleavages, I also need information on how much different sets of variables contribute to explaining variation in the vote choice. To do so, I decompose the pseudo-R^2 statistic to obtain an estimate of the marginal contribution of 'old' and 'new' cleavage variables, respectively (Huettner and Sunder, 2012). To decompose the pseudo-R^2 statistic, I calculate the Shapley values by comparing the pseudo-R^2 of models that include all socio-demographic predictors, only the variables that I categorize as old cleavage variables, only the variables that are categorized as indicators of new cleavages, and a null model (for a similar approach, see Kitschelt and Rehm, 2018).[7] The decomposition of the pseudo-R^2 value for the 'old' and 'new' variables gives three different pseudo-R^2 statistics for each election; one that captures the marginal contribution of measures of class, religion, and place of living (and also race in the United States); one that indicates the part of the variation that is explained by indicators of gender, age, and education; and the overall pseudo-R^2 statistic, which provides an indication of the part

---

[4] From a practical point of view, doing so ensures that there are a sufficient number of observations in each cell to allow for estimating the models.

[5] In addition, previous work has shown that the simpler multinomial logit models in practice are often preferable over multinomial probit estimations (Dow and Endersby, 2004).

[6] It should be acknowledged that the use of pseudo-R^2 estimates and the value of different types of pseudo-R^2 are debated. For a discussion on this topic, see Hagle and Mitchell (1992).

[7] I am grateful to Philipp Rehm for recommending this empirical approach.

of the variation in vote choices that is explained by all socio-demographic determinants combined.

An important point of discussion in previous work on the role of cleavages and their over-time impact relates to the measurement and the operationalization of cleavage variables. For social class, for example, scholars have relied on self-identified membership of a certain social class, indicators based on citizens' job occupations such as the Goldthorpe–Erikson scheme, or income (Evans, 2010; Evans and Northmore-Ball, 2017). Similarly, the impact of religion has been assessed with regards to different denominational groups, attendance of religious services, and religiosity (Duncan, 2015; Knutsen, 2004a). To decide which indicators to include in the vote-choice models, I prioritized continuity, meaning that I make use of indicators that were included and measured in a consistent way in as many election studies in a particular country as possible. Given that the focus is on variation within countries over time, the independent variables vary somewhat between countries—depending on their availability in a country's election surveys. In general, this implies that the 'old' variables that are included capture self-identification with a social class (the alternative to this measure is usually income), religious denomination, urbanization, race (in the United States only) and an indicator of region if there is a politically salient regional difference in a country. More specifically, for Canada, a variable is included to distinguish respondents in Québec and the rest of Canada; in Germany, a dummy variable is distinguished to distinguish Länder in the East and in the West since unification; and in the United States, a variable is included to distinguish between North and South. To capture the importance of new cleavages, all models include indicators of gender, age, and education. Education is generally captured by means of a respondent's highest level of education. When such a measure is not included, the age of leaving school is used as an alternative.

In some countries, not all old cleavages are surveyed consistently over time. In particular, religion—either denomination or attendance—is not consistently included in election surveys in Denmark and Sweden, which likely reflects the absence of a denominational cleavage in these contexts.[8] In these two countries, the old cleavages that are included in the models are therefore limited to class and urbanization. In other countries, the rural–urban cleavage is not consistently measured and is therefore excluded from the

---

[8] For example, in Swedish surveys that do measure religious denomination, it is apparent that the number of individuals who indicate they are religious is very low and that among that group there is not much variation in denominations. I am grateful to Henrik Oscarsson for clarifying this point.

estimation. Details on the variables that are included in the models and their operationalization can be found in Appendix C.

3.3.2 Results

Figures 3.1 and 3.2 summarize the results of the analyses. Each panel shows, for a specific country, the share of the explanatory power that is explained by variables capturing old cleavages (long dashed line), the pseudo-R^2 statistic that can be attributed to the variables capturing new cleavages (short dashed line), and the R^2 of a fully specified socio-demographic model (solid line). These statistics are calculated for each election separately, and values for different elections are connected by means of a line to gauge over-time trends in the explanatory power of socio-demographic variables. This visual presentation allows us to evaluate (1) what the relative importance of old and new cleavage variables is; (2) whether the impact of the old socio-demographic variables on the vote has decreased over time; and (3) whether an increased explanatory power of new variables—gender, age, and education—compensates for the decline of old variables.

A number of conclusions can be drawn from the results in Figures 3.1 and 3.2. Before discussing the results in more detail, it should be pointed out that the graphs show a lot of between-country heterogeneity. There are important differences between countries in terms of the over-time trends and in terms of the extent to which socio-demographic variables—both old and new— explain voters' party choices. Clearly, the picture is not one of a generalized change in the effect of long-term factors on voters' choices across established democracies.

A first observation that can be made based on the graphs in Figures 3.1 and 3.2 is that the explanatory power of the old cleavage variables (long dashed line) is generally larger than that of the new cleavage variables (short dashed line). The difference between the two is often quite substantial. See, in particular, the difference in the estimated pseudo-R^2 value for old and new cleavage variables in Australia, Canada, the Netherlands, and also the United States—where race is grouped with the old cleavage indicators. Even if this is the predominant pattern, there are also two countries where the explanatory power of the old cleavage variables is not (consistently) larger than that of indicators capturing the role of new cleavages; Denmark and Sweden. In fact, the combined explanatory power of the old cleavage variables is comparatively small in these countries. In that regard, it should be recalled that these are the

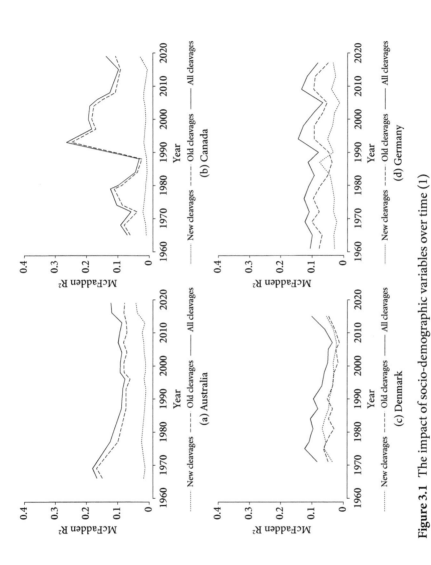

Figure 3.1 The impact of socio-demographic variables over time (1)

Note: Estimates from election specific-vote choice models. For details on the variables included, see Appendix C.

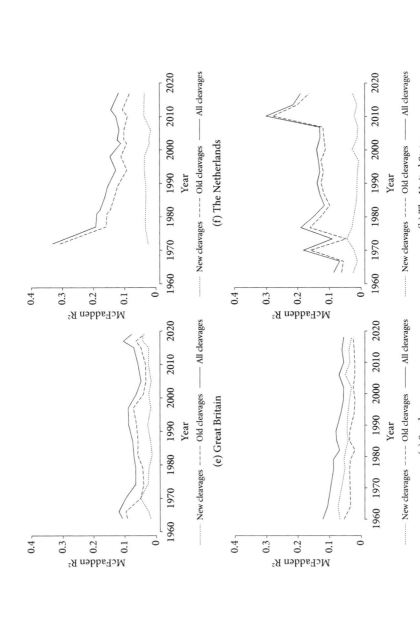

Figure 3.2 The impact of socio-demographic variables over time (2)

Note: Estimates from election specific-vote choice models. For details on the variables included, see Appendix C.

two countries for which the survey data only allow systematically including indicators of social class and place of living, but not religion. Even so, gender, age, and education (i.e., indicators of new cleavage) explain a comparatively important share of the variance in voters' choices in Denmark and Sweden. Finally, Germany appears to be an intermediate case. While the indicators that capture the effects of the old cleavages generally explain a larger share of the pseudo-R^2 in this country, the difference between the estimates for old and new cleavages remains limited and is even reversed for the 1987 election.

Focusing on patterns of change over time, I examine the role of the old cleavage variables first. The long dashed line in the graphs in Figures 3.1 and 3.2 indicates the explanatory power of a model that only includes indicators of class, religion, place of living, and race (in the United States only). Examining the country-specific patterns, it is obvious that the evidence of a declining impact of the old cleavages is strongest in the Netherlands. Examining the choices of Dutch voters, the McFadden R^2 statistic of an old cleavages model drops from 0.31 in 1972 to a mere 0.08 in 2017. In Australia as well, the trend is one of a clear decline in the explanatory power of old cleavages. In all other countries, the trend is less clear. In Canada and Germany, the absence of a decline can partly be explained by the fact that a regional cleavage gained political salience at some point in time. In Canada, the spike in the explanatory power of an old cleavages model corresponds to the 1993 election that marked the breakthrough of the Bloc Québecois and Reform—two parties that appealed to specific regions and mobilized regional grievances (Bélanger, 2004). Since the 1993 election, however, the explanatory power of old cleavages has been declining in Canada. In Germany, the surge in the explanatory power of old cleavages coincides with unification and reflects the need to account for differences between East and West in election surveys after unification. Unlike what holds for Canada, however, in Germany, the more recent period does not show evidence of a strong decline in the explanatory power of old cleavages. For Great Britain, old cleavages explain a somewhat smaller part of the vote in elections in the 2010s than in the earliest elections that are included. The difference, however, is very small, with a McFadden R^2 value of around 0.09 for the 1964 and 1966 election, dropping to an average R^2 value of 0.04 for elections since 2000. In Denmark and Sweden, not only are old cleavages not particularly important, but there is also no clear trend in the explanatory power of old cleavages variables. Finally, in the United States, the role of old cleavage indicators has seemingly increased—and quite strongly so—over time. This pattern, however, is almost entirely driven by the role of race, which peaked in the 2008 election and has remained an important predictor of voters' choices since. When excluding race from the analyses, the impact of old cleavage variables appears to be rather stable in the United States. This can be seen in Figure 3.3, which replicates panel (h) in Figure 3.2 while excluding race from the estimations.

Turning to change in the explanatory power of new cleavages, the short dashed lines in the graphs in Figures 3.1 and 3.2 show the estimated pseudo-R^2 statistic of a model that only includes indicators capturing the impact of new social cleavages on the vote choice. This thus corresponds to the combined explanatory power of gender, age, and education in a model of the vote choice. Gauging over-time trends in the impact of these new cleavages, the graphs in Figures 3.1 and 3.1 suggest a great deal of stability. Within countries, the estimated pseudo-R^2 statistic that corresponds to the contribution of the new cleavage variables varies little from one election to another. Furthermore, if there is variation, this seems to be mostly related to specific elections rather than indicative of an over-time trend. This is an important null result as it suggests that the decline of the old cleavages—where it occurred—has not been compensated by a growing impact of new socio-demographic cleavages.

Finally, if we consider the combined explanatory power of all socio-demographic variables (represented by the solid lines in the graphs),

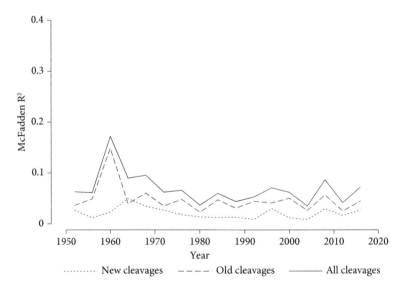

Figure 3.3 The over-time explanatory power of socio-demographic variables in the United States, excluding race

Note: Estimates from election-specific vote choice models. For details on the variables included, see Appendix C

Figures 3.1 and 3.2 do not point to an overall decline of the explanatory power of long-term socio-demographic determinants on voters' choices. In several countries, the explanatory power of a socio-demographic-only model for recent elections is either higher or very similar to what it was at the start of the time series. This holds for Canada and the United States, but in Denmark, Germany, and Great Britain, the evidence for the idea that socio-demographic variables are less predictive of the vote than they were at the start of the time series also appears to be very thin. There is more evidence of a decline in Sweden and also in Australia. The Netherlands is the only country where there has been a strong and fairly systematic decline in the combined impact of socio-demographic variables. But even there, it is useful to point out that the pseudo-R^2 statistic has been fairly stable since the early 1990s. This pattern contrasts with the trends in volatility and campaign deciding in the Netherlands, as depicted in Figure 1.3 and Table 1.2, which suggested that choices of Dutch voters have become more unstable and uncertain in the recent period as well.

To complement this visual assessment of change over time, Appendix D presents the estimates of more formal tests of the association between time and the explanatory power of socio-demographic characteristics for the vote choice. These tests confirm that the Netherlands is the only setting where there is a significant and substantively important decline in the pseudo-R^2 statistic of socio-demographic vote-choice models.

3.4 Summary and implications

The observation that electoral behaviour is increasingly volatile and that party systems are increasingly fragmented has led many scholars to study the possibility that the electoral effect of long-term factors is in decline. Much attention has been given to the role of socio-demographic characteristics, with a particular focus on variables that are connected to the cleavages that Lipset and Rokkan (1967) identified.

A declining impact of long-term socio-demographic variables on the vote would indeed be consistent with more instability in voters' choices. However, a rich literature on the impact of socio-demographic characteristics on the vote choice casts some doubt on the validity of this explanation for the changes in electoral behaviour. In particular, it has been argued that 'old cleavages' continue to shape voters' choices—though perhaps in different ways, for example, with radical right-wing parties increasingly gaining the support of the working class (Oesch and Rennwald, 2018). It has also been claimed that even though the impact of class or religion might be decreasing, new cleavages are emerging across established democracies (Ford and Jennings, 2020).

This chapter took stock of ongoing debates on the topic, while paying particular attention to the role of indicators that capture the effects of old cleavages as well as socio-demographic variables that capture more newly emerging cleavages. Given that both the old and the new cleavage indicators reflect citizens' socio-demographic characteristics, earlier work assumes that if they strongly influence citizens' behaviour, they will have a stabilizing effect on the choices that voters make.

The empirical analyses that decompose the pseudo-R^2 statistic to identify the contributions of indicators of old cleavages, new cleavages, and both shed light on the extent to which different sets of variables have explained voters' choices over time. The results suggest that variables that are related to the cleavages that Lipset and Rokkan (1967) identified are generally and still fairly predictive of voters' choices. In several countries, the explanatory power of the old cleavage indicators has either remained stable or increased somewhat. In fact, there are only three countries where there is clear evidence of a decline of the impact of variables capturing the role of religion, class, and place of living on voters' choices (i.e. Australia, the Netherlands, and Sweden). Furthermore, the analyses also suggest that the explanatory power of the new cleavages—gender, education, and age—is rather stable over time. This result suggests that these variables are not compensating for the (somewhat) decreased explanatory power of class, religion, and place of living.

The results that are presented in this chapter offer some evidence of change. In most countries that are characterized by a change in the explanatory power of socio-demographic factors, the trend is downwards. However, the results also highlight that for explaining the increase in volatility, the decline of the explanatory power of cleavage variables is not the full story. There is no evidence of a strong across-the-board decline of the impact of the old cleavages on the vote. With the exception of the Netherlands, and perhaps Australia, the decline is either very weak or not present at all. In several countries, furthermore, for the most recent elections, which Chapter 1 showed were the most volatile, the combined explanatory power of socio-demographic variables is not particularly low.

4
Have party attachments weakened?

Following a Michigan-perspective, the variable that is situated closest to the socio-demographic factors, near the mouth of the funnel, is party identification. Attachments to parties are reflective of citizens' memberships of social groups and when party attachments are anchored in social identities they tend to be stronger (Campbell et al., 1960; Mason and Wronski, 2018). As a consequence, a decline of the political effects of socio-demographic factors can be expected to trickle down to affect citizens' attachments with parties.

Much in line with what holds for socio-demographic characteristics, the prevailing narrative about how party attachments have fared over time is one of decline. The idea that the attachments between citizens and political parties are weakening is in fact a common theme in the comparative literature on public opinion and voting behaviour. References to a trend of dealignment date back to at least the 1970s (Crewe, Sarlvik, and Alt, 1977). The premise of this work is that the psychological attachments that citizens feel towards political parties, are eroding (Dalton and Wattenberg, 2002; Dalton, 2013; Garzia, Ferreira da Silva, and De Angelis, 2022). The effects of this decline for voters' choices and their stability are straightforward. Given the powerful role of party identifications in shaping citizens' electoral choices, either directly or by means of coloured perceptions of the political reality (Bartels, 2002; Campbell et al., 1960; Lewis-Beck et al., 2008), a weakening of party attachments would result in an electorate that is less 'anchored' and more volatile.

Dalton and Wattenberg (2002) have previously shown evidence of a decrease of the share of partisans in European electorates and in the United States. A comparative analysis of partisanship in six European democracies by Berglund et al. (2005) similarly shows indications of a decline in partisanship between 1960 and 2000, while Önnudóttir and Harðarson(2020) show that in a majority of the sixteen European countries included in their analysis, the share of partisans trends downwards. Relying on a pooled sample of longitudinal election survey data from fourteen West European countries, Garzia, Ferreira da Silva, and De Angelis (2022: 7) also observe 'a decrease of about 40 percentage points in the share of people reporting to feel close/very close to a political party over the last six decades'. While average trends hint at a decline in the share of citizens who identify with a party, it has also been shown that the decline in partisanship is particularly stark among the youngest generations (Dalton and Wattenberg, 2002), which is indicative of a continued future decline of party attachments.

Rather than simply assuming that this prevailing narrative is correct and that the decline in party attachments explains the surge in electoral volatility, in this chapter, I carefully scrutinize the empirical evidence for partisan dealignment as well as its connection to volatility. Chapter 3 has shown that the impact of long-term socio-demographic factors has weakened, but only moderately so. Given that feelings of belonging to certain socio-demographic groups shape party attachments (Campbell et al., 1960; Garzia, 2013), the altogether limited amount of change in terms of the political role of socio-demographic variables likely implies that party attachments have not weakened drastically either. Furthermore, a number of publications cast doubt on the party decline thesis (Hetherington, 2001) and on the idea that party attachments have weakened, or continue to weaken, over time. Focusing on the presence and effects of party attachments among voters in US elections, for example, Green, Palmquist, and Schickler (2004: 14) conclude that the 'rumors of partisanship's death' are 'exaggerated'. Furthermore, in the United States (Iyengar et al., 2019) but also elsewhere (Hobolt, Leeper, and Tilley, 2021), scholars have shown indications of growing partisan polarization. These findings are suggestive of an increased—and perhaps even a renewed—political impact of citizens' partisan identifications.

A first goal of this chapter is therefore to provide an updated answer on the question whether party attachments have indeed weakened over time and to what extent. In addition, I move beyond trends in levels of partisanship and their strength and also evaluate how party attachments structure the vote—and whether the connection between partisanship and volatility has changed over time.

4.1 The nature and measurement of party attachments

Party identification, as originally defined by Campbell et al. (1960), refers to the psychological attachment of a citizen to a political party. Conceived in this way, party attachment strongly influences voters' choices. Party identification not only serves as a 'standing decision' when deciding whom to vote for, but it also shapes citizens' views of the political world. Through these mechanisms, party attachment stabilizes the vote. Campbell et al. (1960), for example, report that 82 per cent of the strong partisans in their 1956 survey indicated that they mostly or always vote for the same party. In contrast, only 16 per cent of the independents did so.

The idea that citizens have psychological attachments to parties and that these attachments structure their electoral behaviour is not uncontested. At a conceptual level, scholars of partisanship are divided on the question whether party attachments are exogenous to citizens' political preferences or whether they are endogenous to them. From a comparative perspective, there are concerns that partisanship is a concept that applies mostly to the United States and does not travel to many other settings.

First, the conceptual debate opposes scholars who think of party attachments as an exogenous social identity (Huddy and Bankert, 2017) as well as a political identification that shapes citizens' views of the political world (Campbell et al., 1960; Green, Palmquist, and Schickler, 2004) and those arguing that party attachments are nothing more than a running tally of citizens' political preferences and evaluations (Fiorina, 1981). This debate about the very nature of partisanship has taken the form of a vigorous methodological discussion on how to assess the stability of partisanship and how best to estimate the causal links between party attachments, on the one hand, and political preferences, on the other (Bartels, 2002; Green and Palmquist, 1990; Green and Baltes, 2016). The truth is probably somewhere in between, with partisanship being both 'a pervasive dynamic force shaping citizens' perceptions of, and reactions to, the political world' (Bartels, 2002: 138) and, to some extent, a reflection of citizens' evaluations of political events and actors (Garzia, 2013). The nature of party attachments likely differs between individuals as well, with some having a partisan attachment that is identity-based and others having attachments that are more evaluation-like. Whiteley and Kölln (2019), for example, refer to the socialization-based partisanship as 'type-1 partisanship' and label partisanship that reflects citizens' policy evaluations as 'type-2 partisanship'. Along the same lines, Kroh and Selb (2009) argue that different experiences of political socialization might explain why individuals develop one or the other 'type' of party attachment.

While this is an important conceptual and empirical debate, I would argue that regardless of whether party attachments are profound political identities or running tallies, the trend in partisanship offers a valuable indicator of change in electoral behaviour. From an identity perspective, a decline in party attachments would signify that the anchoring identities that structure citizens' vote choices are eroding. If party identification is more evaluation-based, in contrast, a weakening of party attachments would signify a less fundamental change. Even so, a decreased willingness to report attachments to parties would be informative and also indicative of citizens' own assessment of how loyal to a specific party they are.

A second important debate surrounding party attachments relates to the extent to which party attachments are present and influencing voters' choices in countries other than the United States—where the concept was first introduced. To some extent, systematic differences between countries are to be expected. Under proportional electoral rules, with more parties to choose from, party attachments will arguably be weaker (Bowler, Lanoue, and Savoie, 1994; Huber, Kernell, and Leoni, 2005). The ideological polarization of the party system is also of importance; more partisans are found when polarization is higher (Lupu, 2015). In addition, it has been argued that in federal countries like Canada, where the party systems differ depending on the level of government, citizens tend to have weaker attachments to parties (Clarke and Stewart, 1987).

More fundamentally, some have questioned the very presence of party attachments in a number of European countries (Bartle and Bellucci, 2009). In the Netherlands, for example, it has been shown that many citizens indicate that they identify with more than one party (van Der Eijk and Niemöller, 1983), while Thomassen (1976) has pointed out that there is more variation in reported party attachments than in Dutch voters' electoral choices. Clearly, such observations are not consistent with conceptions of party identification as an unmoved mover (Thomassen and Rosema, 2009). It has also been argued that electorates in some European countries identify not with parties but with the left or the right (Fleury and Lewis-Beck, 1993; Lewis-Beck, Stubager, and Nadeau, 2013).

To some extent, the debates about the validity and importance of party identifications in multiparty contexts are a result of the difficulties in measuring party identification in such contexts (Budge, Crewe, and Farlie, 1976). For the US context, Campbell et al. (1960) suggested capturing party attachments by asking respondents: 'Generally speaking, do you usually think of yourself as a Republican, a Democrat, an Independent, or what?' Translating this item to other contexts is not straightforward. In particular, mentioning all the parties is difficult when there are (many) more than two parties competing in an election (Thomassen and Rosema, 2009). At the same time, not naming parties drastically reduces the number of respondents who indicate that they have a party attachment (Castro Cornejo, 2019; Kaase, 1976). Other elements of the Michigan measure of party identification have been adapted in different ways in different countries too, such as whether or not to prompt independence as an option (Johnston, 1992). Each of these changes influences what percentage of the respondents reports a party identification—and ultimately the extent to which party identifications are accurately captured in a survey. When studying partisanship comparatively, and levels of partisanship in particular, it therefore has to be kept in mind that 'the image of voters' attachment to parties that is conveyed by election studies hinges to a good extent on how one goes about measuring people's identification (or lack thereof) with the parties' (Blais et al., 2001: 17).

Discussions on how best to capture party identifications cross-nationally, in multiparty contexts in particular, are ongoing. Large comparative projects such as the Comparative Study of Electoral Systems (CSES) have shifted to capturing 'closeness' to a party (Thomassen and Rosema, 2009). Others have argued that the propensity-to-vote items that are included in many European election studies can be used to construct an alternative measure of party identification (Paparo, De Sio, and Brady, 2020). There are also efforts to measure party identifications in multiparty contexts while simultaneously staying close to the original conception of party attachments as a social identity (Bankert, Huddy, and Rosema, 2017), though such measures are a complement to rather than a replacement of a general partisanship question. Importantly, these are all fairly recent developments, which are partly stimulated by a trend towards more comparative research and cross-national data-collection efforts. For most of the time period that is covered in this book, the available measures of party attachments are country-specific adaptations of the item that Campbell et al. (1960) introduced.

These considerations are important for a comparative longitudinal study of the presence and strength of party attachments. First, it seems that comparing levels of party identification between countries is only possible when the exact same question wording is used to capture party attachment. Second, an examination of levels of party identification within countries over time is only possible when the wording of the party identification measure is stable across surveys. With this in mind, I now turn to an analysis of over-time trends in party attachments in Australia, Canada, Denmark, Germany, Great Britain, the Netherlands, Sweden, and the United States.

4.2 Are there fewer partisans now?

Despite debates about the presence and importance of party attachments outside the United States, each of the eight countries that is considered here incorporated some version of a party identification measure in their election studies. In several countries, however, the wording changes over time. To limit the impact of such over-time variation, and to avoid differences in measurement driving the trends, I restrict the analyses to the party identification question that is included in the largest number of surveys in a country—with only small changes, such as the inclusion or exclusion of a particular party as an option. For the United States, I focus only on presidential election years. That way, the variation in levels of partisanship between congressional and presidential election years (Bartels, 2000) does not affect the overall time trend.

Table 4.1 gives an overview of the standard question wording[1] to capture party identification in each of the eight countries. Elections denoted with an asterisk included a short version of the partisanship question.[2] While some countries have stayed close to the question from the *American National Election Study*, other countries rely on measures that differ more strongly. With the exception of Germany and the Netherlands, all questions include references to the main political parties, as well as a prompt to indicate whether one is an independent. Most importantly, all questions clarify in one way or another that a party identification is more profound than simply voting for a party. That is done by means of words like 'generally speaking' for countries that follow the US model of measuring party identification, by indicating explicitly that attachment is different from voting (as in Germany) or by means of the word 'adherent'. Most surveys also tap the strength of party attachments by means of follow-up questions. For this element of the measurement of partisanship as well, measures and question wordings vary between countries and over time (see Appendix G).

As a first step, I focus on the share of partisans in each country. In a second step, I provide more nuance and examine trends in the strength of party attachments.

As I have indicated in section 4.1, wording differences in party identification questions likely have an impact on reported levels of partisanship in different countries. The variations in question wording thus make it impossible to compare levels of partisanship between countries. However, the relative consistency of question wordings within countries allows examining whether party attachments have weakened over time. In line with work from the early 2000s (Berglund et al., 2005; Dalton and Wattenberg, 2002), I expect to observe a decline in the percentage of the population that identifies with a

---

[1] Self-evidently, the precise parties that are mentioned in the question vary over time.
[2] More specifically, these surveys only asked 'Do you think of yourself as an adherent or not as an adherent to a political party?'

Table 4.1 Wording and coverage of the party identification measures

Country	Question	Elections
Australia	Generally speaking, do you usually think of yourself as Liberal, Labor, National, or what?	1987, 1990, 1993, 1996, 1998, 2001, 2004, 2007, 2010, 2013, 2016, and 2019
Canada	In federal politics, do you usually think of yourself as a Conservative, Liberal, NDP, Bloc Quebecois, Green, or none of these?	1988, 1993, 1997, 2000, 2004, 2006, 2008, 2011, 2015, and 2019
Denmark	Many consider themselves adherents of a particular party. There are also many who don't feel they are adherents of any party. Do you consider yourself to be, for example, a Social Democrat, a Conservative, a Social Liberal, a Liberal supporter, a Socialist People's Party supporter, a Communist, or something else? Or don't you feel as though you are an adherent of any party?	1971, 1973, 1975, 1977, 1979, 1984, 1990, 1994, 2001, 2005, 2007, 2011, and 2015
Germany	Many people in Germany feel close to a particular party for a longer period of time even if they occasionally vote for another party. What about you? In general terms, do you feel attached to a particular political party?	1972, 1976, 1980, 1983, 1987, 1990, 1994, 2002, 2005, 2009, 2013, and 2017
Great Britain	Generally speaking, do you think of yourself as Conservative, Labour, Liberal Democrat, [if Scot: SNP; if Wales: Plaid Cymru], or what?	1964, 1966, 1970, feb. 1974, oct. 1974, 1979, 1983, 1987, 1992, 1997, 2001, 2005, 2010, 2015, 2017, and 2019
The Netherlands	Many people think of themselves as adherent to a particular political party, but there are also people who do not think of themselves as an adherent to a political party. Do you think of yourself as an adherent or not as an adherent to a political party?	1971, 1972, 1977, 1982, 1986, 1989, 1994, 1998, 2002, 2006, 2010*, 2012*, and 2017*
Sweden	Many people consider themselves as adherents of a specific party. But there are also many others who do not have any such attachment to any of the parties. Do you usually think of yourself as, for example, a folkpartist, socialdemokrat, moderat, centerpartist, vänsterpartist, miljöpartist, or kristdemokrat? Or do you have no such attachment to any of the parties?	1968, 1970, 1973, 1976, 1979, 1982, 1985, 1988, 1991, 1994, 1998, 2002, 2006, 2010, and 2014
United States	Generally speaking, do you usually think of yourself as a Republican, a Democrat, an Independent, or what?	1952, 1956, 1960, 1964, 1968, 1972, 1976, 1980, 1984, 1988, 1992, 1996, 2000, 2004, 2008, 2012 and 2016

party. This observation would be consistent with the idea that electorates have become less 'anchored' over time.

Figures 4.1 and 4.2 plot the percentage of the survey samples that can be categorized as partisan in each of the elections listed in Table 4.1. It can be noted, first, that the percentage of partisans in the most recent election study is lower than the percentage of partisans in the first election study, for which there is data in seven of the eight countries. In Australia, the percentage of partisans has dropped from 94 per cent in 1987 to 84 per cent in 2019. In Denmark, the percentage of partisans has declined from 53 per cent in 1971 to 40 per cent in 2015. The German data only show a slight drop, from 78 per cent partisans in 1972 to 75 per cent partisans in 2017. In Great Britain, the percentage of partisans in the population declined from 95 per cent in 1964 to 87 per cent partisans in 2019. In the Netherlands, the percentage of partisans was 37 per cent in 1971 and 28 per cent in 2017. In Sweden, the percentage of partisans fell from 65 per cent in 1968 to 27 per cent in 2014.[3] Finally, in the United States, there were 77 per cent partisans in 1952 and 63 per cent in 2016. The exception to this pattern is Canada, as the percentage of partisans has increased during the time period for which there are data, from 68 per cent in 1988 to 76 per cent in 2019. It should be noted, however, that the Canadian time series is the shortest for which partisanship is measured consistently.[4]

When only considering the percentage of partisans at the start and the end of the time series, however, a lot of variation gets lost. Looking at the trends in each of the countries in Figures 4.1 and 4.2 more closely, it is obvious that few countries have witnessed a systematic and continuous decline of the share of partisans over time. The Swedish trend is most in line with the idea of a gradual but consistent over-time decline in the percentage of partisans. With the exception of the 1976 and 1982 elections, the share of partisans in an election survey is systematically lower than that in the previous survey. The British data also show a gradual decline of the percentage of partisans over time, though the decline is much less sharp than what holds for Sweden— which might be a function of the different question wording used to capture party identification in the two countries. Furthermore, this decline appears to

---

[3] For Sweden, at the time of writing, the data on the 2018 election study is available for the CSES module only, which uses a general closeness question rather than the standard partisanship question included in Table 4.1. For that reason, 2018 is not included in Figure 4.2.

[4] This is due to a change in the question wording from 1988 onwards. Previously, the measure was the same as that used in Australia and Great Britain. From 1988 onwards, the survey item prompts independence in the question by means of the option 'or none of these'.

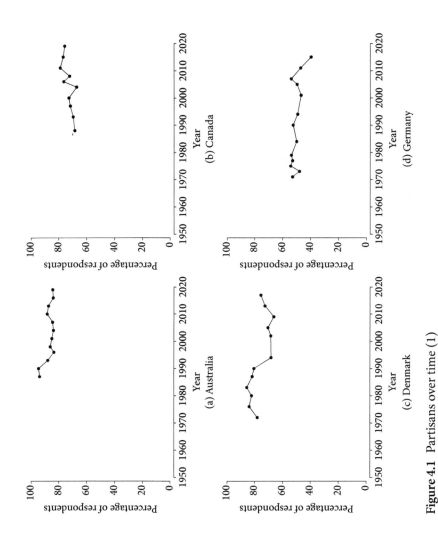

Figure 4.1 Partisans over time (1)

Note: Percentage of partisans in each election. Partisanship is measured as indicated in Table 4.1.

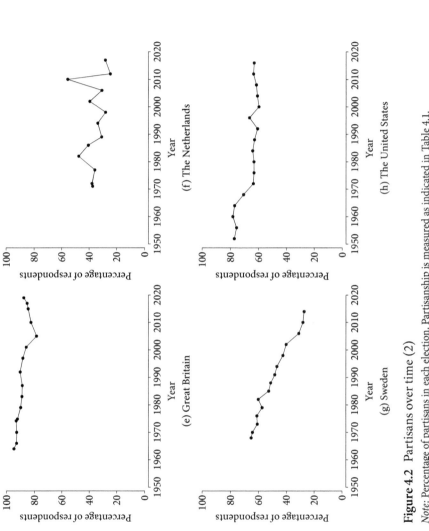

Figure 4.2 Partisans over time (2)
Note: Percentage of partisans in each election. Partisanship is measured as indicated in Table 4.1.

have been reversed in recent British elections. Since 2005, each election survey systematically reports a somewhat higher level of partisanship than the previous one.

In Australia, Denmark, Germany, and the United States, a decline in the percentage of partisans is clearly noticeable, but it is not continuous. The drop in the share of the population that identifies with a party in these five countries occurred at a specific point in time and has remained at a lower level since that decrease. In Australia, the decline occurred around 1990; in Denmark, the decline is more recent and seems to have started in the late 2000s only. In Germany, the decline coincides with the unification of Germany—and the inclusion of respondents from East Germany in the samples.[5] The most recent period, much in line with what can be observed for Great Britain, even suggests an increase of the percentage of partisans in Germany. This supports the findings of Arzheimer (2017), who drew attention to an uptick in partisanship in recent German elections.

In the United States, the decline of party attachments mostly occurred in the 1960s, which previous work has linked to the Vietnam war and a series of political scandals (Dalton and Wattenberg, 2002; Nie, Verba, and Petrocik, 1974). In the Netherlands, even though the percentage of partisans is smaller at the end of the time series than at the start, the trend can best be described as erratic. The share of the Dutch electorate which indicates that they are partisan fluctuates strongly from one election to another, with ups and downs that do not seem systematic and that are—at first sight—not linked to particular political events either. Perhaps the wording of the partisanship item in the Netherlands, which does not stress the identity aspect of partisanship (e.g. no use of 'think of yourself as') and does not stress the more general character of party attachments (e.g. no use of the words 'generally' or 'usually') explains at least part of the instability of party attachments in the Netherlands.

In summary, in seven of the eight countries that are considered, the percentage of partisans is lower at the end of the time series than at the start. The exception is Canada, where levels of partisanship have seemingly remained stable, and might even have increased somewhat, since 1988. But even though the most recent surveys in the other countries include fewer partisans than the early surveys, there are few contexts where partisanship has decreased strongly and consistently. In fact, in both Germany and Great Britain, the trend in partisanship appears to have reversed in recent elections. The Swedish context offers the strongest case for theories of dealignment; the share of partisans in

---

[5] Part of the decline is indeed due to the inclusion of respondents from the East in the samples. However, there remains a drop in partisanship between the 1990 and 1994 surveys, even when focusing only on Länder in the West. This can be seen from the graph that is included in Appendix E.

Sweden has decreased strongly in a near-linear fashion. In other settings, the decline is not only more limited, but the weakening of party attachments also seems time-specific.

It could be argued that even though the share of partisans has not declined dramatically in several of the countries that are studied here, the number of citizens who *strongly* identify with a party is in decline. To account for the possibility that the trends in Figures 4.1 and 4.2 hide a more important decline in the strength of party attachments, it is important to break down the group of partisans into strong and weak partisans. Figures 4.3 and 4.4 therefore show the share of strong partisans in election surveys in each of the eight countries over time. Details on the operationalization and the wording of the measures of partisan strength can be found in Appendix G.[6]

Figures 4.3 and 4.4 show that there is much variation between countries in the share of respondents who report being strong partisans. The graphs also indicate that there are important between-country differences in the over-time trends in strong partisanship. For a number of countries, the trend lines suggest a strong drop in the share of the electorate that can be categorized as strong partisans. Notably, in Australia, Germany, Sweden, and especially in Great Britain the percentage of strong partisans is substantially lower in recent surveys than at the start of the time period. In line with what the trends in overall partisanship suggested, however, in several of these countries that decline appears to be halted, and even reversed, in recent times. Specifically, in Australia, Germany, and Great Britain, the share of strong partisans has increased in recent years.

In Denmark, the share of strong partisans has remained stable until about 2010, after which it has started to decline somewhat. In the Netherlands, much like what holds for partisanship overall, a clear trend in the percentage of strong partisans cannot be discerned. Finally, for both Canada and the United States, the trend lines that are included in Figures 4.3 and 4.4 are indicative of a growth in the share of strong partisans over time.

Hence, looking at strong partisans rather than partisanship overall, does not fundamentally alter the conclusions that could be drawn based on Figures 4.1 and 4.2 There is evidence of change, but there are few contexts where the empirical pattern of change is both strong and continues in recent times.

Overall, the data indicate that fewer people now feel attached to a party than was the case in the 1960s or 1970s. The decline, however, is limited in many countries, absent in Canada, and in most instances cannot be characterized as systematic. Furthermore, these trends do not appear to obfuscate a more important decline in the share of strong partisans. Though there is evidence

---

[6] An alternative way of visualizing over-time changes in the strength of partisanship that allows assessing the stacked distribution of non-partisans, weak partisans, and strong partisans is provided in Appendix H.

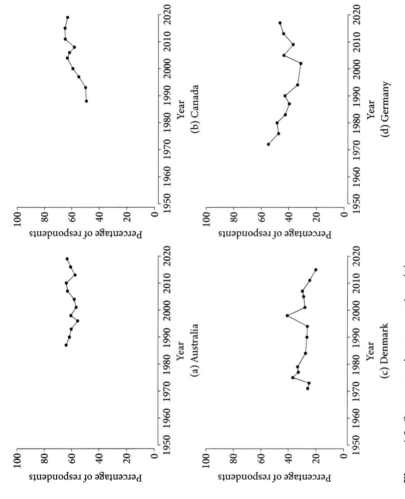

Figure 4.3 Strong partisans over time (1)

Note: Percentage of strong partisans in each election. Partisanship is measured as indicated in Appendix G.

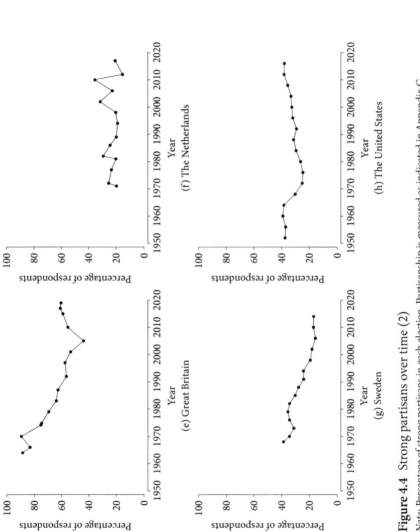

Figure 4.4 Strong partisans over time (2)

Note: Percentage of strong partisans in each election. Partisanship is measured as indicated in Appendix G.

that the group of strong partisans has grown smaller over time, this trend is not continuous. In this regard, the contrast between the continued surge in volatility and an increase in the share of partisans in recent years is particularly noteworthy. Of course, the absence of a strong decrease in partisanship might, at least in part, be a function of measurement. It is hard to capture the deep-seated identifications of citizens with parties in survey research. And even the original Michigan item is limited in that regard (Greene, 2002). Taken at face value, however, these trends seem insufficient to explain the increase in electoral volatility in established democracies.

4.3 Is partisanship a weaker anchor now?

Even if the percentage of partisans has not fallen dramatically or continuously in most countries, as section 4.2 has shown, the role of party attachments as an 'anchor' of the vote might well have weakened over time.

That would be the case if the nature of party identification is changing over time, from a more Michigan-style identity that functions as an unmoved mover to a reflection of more short-term political attitudes and evaluations. According to Garzia (2013, 2014), such as change has taken place in Western Europe. In particular, he states that 'partisan loyalties have shifted from largely reflecting long-term social and ideological identities to the result of individual attitudes towards more visible political objects, such as the party leaders' (Garzia, 2013: 68). If the very nature of party attachments changes over time and party identification increasingly reflects citizens' evaluations of party leaders or issue positions, then those attachments will constrain the vote less strongly. The implication would be that even those who indicate that they feel attached to a political party are increasingly volatile.

In order to test whether the anchoring role of party attachments has weakened over time, I use the survey data to examine the connection between partisanship and volatility in each election by means of linear probability models. In doing so, the focus is on the extent to which party attachments structure voters' choices and stabilize their party preferences. As a dependent variable, I use the indicator of switching that was also presented in Chapter 1. The indicator relies on information on citizens' vote choices in the election that is the focus of the election study and their recalled vote choice in the previous election. Such recall questions suffer from important limitations,

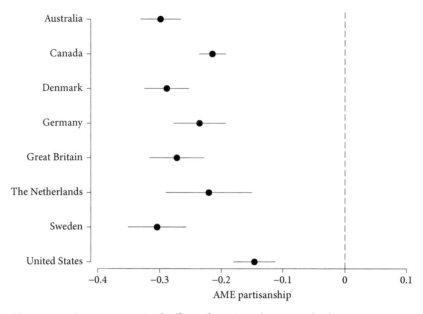

Figure 4.5 Average marginal effect of partisanship on volatility

Note: Estimates from eight country-specific linear probability models with partisanship as the only independent variable. Spikes indicate 95 per cent confidence intervals.

however, and I therefore complement the main comparative analyses with an analysis of British and Swedish panel data. As an independent variable, I include a dichotomous variable that distinguishes between those who identify with a party, and those who do not—based on the questions that are listed in Table 4.1.

Before studying change over time, it is useful to verify the connection between partisan attachments—as measured in each of the eight countries—and volatility. To that end, Figure 4.5 shows, for each country, the pooled bivarite estimated effect of partisanship on volatility. Not surprisingly, the estimates are consistently negative and significant. Partisans, across countries, are substantially less likely to switch parties from one election to the next than non-partisans. Furthermore, Figure 4.5 shows that the association between partisanship and volatility is quite strong. In the United States, partisans are about fifteen percentage points less likely to switch parties than non-partisans. In the other countries, effects are stronger, varying from a twenty-one-percentage-points effect in Canada to an effect of thirty percentage points in Sweden.

Partisans are thus substantially less likely to switch parties, which is indicative of the anchoring role that party attachments play for voting behaviour. The question, however, is whether this stabilizing effect of partisanship is stable over time or whether there are indications that partisans as well are increasingly volatile. To provide an answer to this question, I still focus on country-pooled individual-level survey data. For each country, I estimate a linear probability model to explain party-switching, by means of partisanship, the election year, and a partisan × election year interaction.

Figures 4.6 and 4.7 plot the predicted likelihood of switching in each election in the data set—for non-partisans and partisans, respectively. The white circles show the likelihood that a non-partisan switches parties between elections, while the black circles show this likelihood for those identifying with a party. First, note that for every single election survey, those who identify with a party are systematically less likely to switch parties from one election to another than those who do not have a party attachment. This observation, which testifies of the anchoring role of party attachments, holds across countries and over time. In fact, when estimating the interaction between partisanship and a linear time trend, there are only three countries for which the difference in the likelihood of switching between partisans and non-partisans is significantly reduced over time. These countries are Germany, Sweden, and the United States.

To evaluate the *changing* role of party attachments, however, it is crucial to evaluate not just the difference in the likelihood that partisans and non-partisans switch parties but also levels of switching over time. These figures in fact replicate the trends in individual-level volatility presented in Chapter 1 but for partisans and non-partisans separately. If partisanship were consistently 'protecting' voters from switching parties, levels of party switching among partisans (the black circles) would be low and fairly stable over time. That is not what Figures 4.6 and 4.7 show. Even if non-partisans are substantially more likely to switch than partisans, the increase of volatility does not appear to be driven by the behaviour of non-partisans only. Instead, the trend lines for the two groups are remarkably parallel.

Focusing on change among partisans, Figures 4.6 and 4.7 allow comparing the behaviour of partisans in the most recent time period with their behaviour at the start of the time series. A close look at the black circles in these graphs does not offer much evidence of change in Australia, Canada, and the United States. The former two countries are the two for which the time period that is covered is the shortest, however, with data available from 1987 or 1988 onwards. For the United States, where the data allow tracing back the likelihood that partisans and non-partisans switch parties since 1952, there is

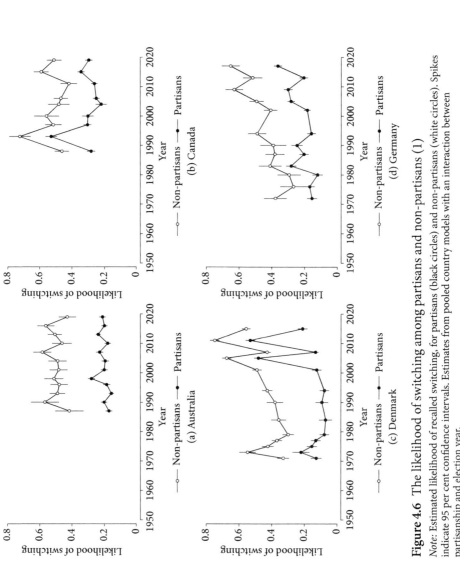

Figure 4.6 The likelihood of switching among partisans and non-partisans (1)

Note: Estimated likelihood of recalled switching, for partisans (black circles) and non-partisans (white circles). Spikes indicate 95 per cent confidence intervals. Estimates from pooled country models with an interaction between partisanship and election year.

no indication that the structuring role of party attachments has changed. If anything, partisans are less likely to change parties now than they were previously—which could reflect an increased polarization among partisans in the United States (Lelkes, 2016). In Denmark, Germany, Great Britain, the Netherlands, and Sweden, in contrast, partisans in the 2010s are more likely to switch in elections than partisans were in the 1970s. The slope is definitely steeper in some countries than in others, though. While we see a moderate increase in partisans' likelihood to switch parties in Sweden and Great Britain, the surge is in fact quite strong in Denmark and Germany.

Importantly, Figures 4.6 and 4.7 clarify that party attachments are not and have never been a guarantee to a voter remaining loyal to a party. It is not exceptional that between 15 per cent and 20 per cent of partisans switch parties. But what happens in high-volatile elections is particularly noteworthy. Take, for example, the Canadian 1993 election,[7] the Danish 2011 election, or the Dutch 1971 and 2010 elections. In these elections, volatility was not driven by non-partisans only; in each of these cases, more than 40 per cent of those who indicate that they feel attached to a party admitted having switched parties. This holds, furthermore, despite the fact that recall questions are relied on to estimate party switching. Those who indicate that they are a partisan of a specific party in particular might feel more pressured to (falsely) report stable voting behaviour to appear more consistent. Thus, despite the likely presence of such a consistency bias, high shares of partisans still admit to having switched parties from one election to the next.

Overall, these analyses hint at the limitations to the anchoring role of party attachments on voters' choices. Identifying with a party does not mean always sticking to this party when voting, a point that Campbell et al. (1960) already made. The high level of switching among partisans in high-volatility elections in particular is quite remarkable. In some instances, more than half of those who say they feel attached to a party change their votes from one election to the next. Most importantly, this longitudinal analysis of the connection between partisanship and switching offers suggestive evidence for party attachments constraining the vote less over time. In five of the eight countries, and in five of the six countries for which we can trace behaviour since at least the early 1970s, partisans change parties more now than before.

Figures 4.6 and 4.7 offer a broad view of patterns of change; they rely on data from eight different countries and cover a time period of several decades

---

[7] Two new regionalist parties emerged in this election, explaining the high level of party switching for this particular election (Bélanger, 2004).

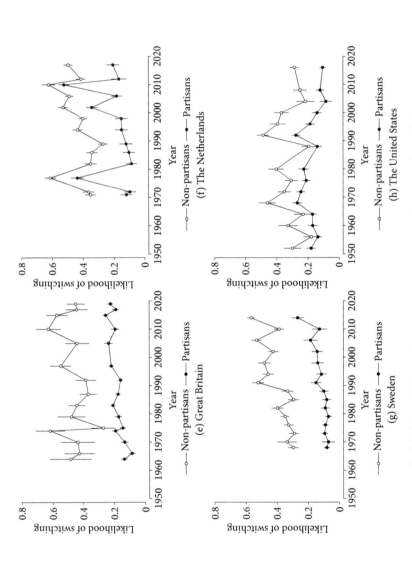

Figure 4.7 The likelihood of switching among partisans and non-partisans (2)

Note: Estimated likelihood of recalled switching, for partisans (black circles) and non-partisans (white circles). Spikes indicate 95 per cent confidence intervals. Estimates from pooled country models with an interaction between partisanship and election year.

in each of the countries. This broad perspective comes at a cost in terms of the available measures, however. In particular, to get insights on over-time changes in the stability of the vote choices of partisans and non-partisans, they rely entirely on citizens' recalled vote choice in the previous election. Such questions, as has been mentioned before, likely introduce error due to memory problems and bias because of citizens' desire for consistency (Dassonneville and Hooghe, 2017b; van Der Eijk and Niemöller, 2008; Waldahl and Aardal, 2000).

Replicating the same analyses with election panel data would eliminate these effects of recall questions on the estimated levels of switching of partisans and non-partisans. And while few countries have multiple election surveys with a panel component, the British and the Swedish data allow assessing a fairly long-term trend in levels of panel volatility among partisans and non-partisans.

First, I take a look at the British case by making use of the 1963–1970 Political Change in Britain panel study, the 1987–1992, 1992–1997, 1997–2001, and the 2005–2009 British Election Panels, and the 2014–2023 British Election Study Internet Panel.[8]

Table 4.2 lists the percentage of switchers in each of these election panels among the group of non-partisans and partisans, respectively. Partisanship is measured in the first survey of each panel, using the question listed in Table 4.1. That is: 'Generally speaking, do you think of yourself as Conservative, Labour, Liberal Democrat, SNP, Plaid Cymru or what?' In line with how I proceeded before, switching is operationalized as changing parties between elections, and the panel structure allows relying on the reported vote choices immediately following each election. Those who abstain from voting in at least one of the elections are excluded from the analyses. The panel-based information in Table 4.2 is consistent with the information from recall questions in also showing that non-partisans are more likely to switch parties than partisans. Importantly, Table 4.2 shows further evidence of the weakening effect of a partisan anchor on voters' choices. While 12 per cent of partisans switched parties between 1964 and 1966, and 16 per cent did so between 1966 and 1970, since the 1990s, around one in four British partisans changes parties from one

---

[8] Using these data sets, I can trace what share of partisans and non-partisans changed parties between the 1964 and 1966 elections, between the 1966 and 1970 elections, between the 1987 and 1992 elections, between the 1992 and 1997 elections, between the 1997 and 2001 elections, between the 2005 and 2009 elections, between the 2015 and 2017 elections, and between the 2017 and 2019 elections. For details on these panel surveys, see Appendix A.

Table 4.2 The percentage of switchers among partisans and non-partisans in British panel studies

Elections	Non-partisans (%)	Partisans (%)
1964–1966	23.1	12.1
1966–1970	50.0	15.9
1987–1992	32.0	23.6
1992–1997	45.6	28.3
1997–2001	46.8	22.6
2005–2009	55.2	26.7
2015–2017	37.6	25.7
2017–2019	36.5	22.9

election to the next. Even those who still self-identify as partisans thus have grown increasingly volatile over time.

The Swedish data also allow verifying whether the surge in partisans' likelihood to switch parties from one election to the next holds when analysing panel data. More specifically, from 1979 onwards Swedish election studies consistently have a panel component whereby half of the sample is re-interviewed in the following election study and the other half of the sample consists of a fresh cross-section of respondents. To ensure comparability with the other countries, in the preceding analyses I operationalized volatility in Sweden by means of a recall question. As Table 4.3 shows, however, a very similar pattern emerges when focusing on the panel component of the Swedish election studies.

More specifically, Table 4.3 clarifies that over time, the share of respondents who switched parties from one election to the next has increased among both non-partisans and partisans. Of course, non-partisans are consistently more likely to switch parties than partisans. However, the over-time increase in individuals' likelihood to switch parties is much stronger among partisans than it is among non-partisans. For non-partisans, their likelihood to switch parties has increased from 39 per cent in the early 1980s to 54 per cent in 2014. This corresponds to an increase of 15 percentage points, or a 38 per cent increase for the full time period. While this is a fairly strong increase already, the surge in volatility is even more stark when focusing on partisans. As shown in Table 4.3, their likelihood to switch parties increased from 9 per cent to 26 per cent, corresponding to an increase of 184 per cent. As a result, while non-partisans were more than four times more likely to switch parties between subsequent

Table 4.3 The percentage of switchers among partisans and non-partisans in Swedish panel studies

Elections	Non-partisans (%)	Partisans (%)
1979–1982	39.4	9.1
1982–1985	38.3	10.5
1985–1988	38.0	8.8
1988–1991	43.8	14.8
1991–1994	45.9	13.9
1994–1998	41.0	15.4
1998–2002	44.5	16.8
2002–2006	57.9	23.9
2006–2010	45.7	21.3
2010–2014	54.3	25.8

elections than partisans at the start of the time series, their likelihood to switch is 'only' twofold that of partisans for the last election for which we have panel data.

In short, these results indicate that even though partisans are still and consistently less likely to switch parties than non-partisans, the extent to which being a partisan stabilizes voters' choices appears to be in decline. The over-time increase in volatility is not driven exclusively by voters who lack party attachments. Partisans also increasingly switch parties from one election to the next.

4.4 Summary and implications

The rise in electoral volatility is often linked to a trend towards dealignment. Work along these lines argues that the attachments between citizens and parties have weakened and without this powerful heuristic of the vote choice, which also serves as a 'standing decision', it should not come as a surprise that voters' choices have grown more volatile.

The evidence that is presented in this chapter, however, shows a picture that is more nuanced. Of the eight countries for which I have analysed the trend in the percentage of partisans over time, there is only one—Sweden—that has witnessed a sharp and continuous decline of the share of the population identifying with a party. In other countries, the decline is more limited, often bound to a specific period in time, and sometimes characterized by a noteworthy increase in partisanship in recent elections. Trends in levels of partisanship, therefore, seem insufficient to explain the changes that can be observed across established democracies. In particular, the increase in levels of volatility is more systematic than the observed pattern of decline in partisanship. When focusing on the strong partisans more specifically there are also few indications that the share of strong partisans has dropped strongly and consistently over time.

The connection between party attachments and the vote choice, however, *is* changing—at least in the European countries considered here. In those five settings, not only non-partisans but also partisans are increasingly likely to change parties from one election to the next. This change is suggestive for a pattern that Garzia (2013, 2014) has already drawn attention to: that the nature of party attachments in Europe might well be changing from an 'unmoved mover' to an attitude that reflects citizens' more short-term political evaluations.

More generally, the analyses that are presented in this chapter also point out that reporting a party identification is no guarantee to stable vote choices. Highly volatile elections stand out in this regard. Even in countries that have not seen a clear trend of weakening party attachments or a weakening of the anchoring role of party identification, partisans are not immune to change. Over 50 per cent of partisans in Canada reported having switched parties between 1988 and 1993. And a majority of partisans in Denmark reported a change in their vote between 2007 and 2011. Even in Germany, which, according to Figure 4.1, has seen a growth in the percentage of respondents who indicate that they feel attached to a parties over the past decade, close to 40 per cent of those who identify as partisan has switched parties between 2013 and 2017.

In short, there is no evidence of an across-the-board decline of the share of the population that identifies as partisan, partisans also are often volatile, and they seem to increasingly switch votes in European democracies. Evidently, the downward slope in partisanship alone is insufficient to explain the surge in electoral volatility in established democracies. But the results are indicative of partisanship becoming a less effective 'anchor' over time. Whether this weakening of the structuring effect of partisanship results in an increased impact of short-term factors is the question to which I turn in Chapter 5.

5
Increasingly short term?

One of the most influential interpretations of the changes in electoral behaviour in established democracies portrays long- and short-term determinants of the vote as communicating vessels. The argument then holds that the weakening role of long-term determinants is counterbalanced by short-term factors increasingly guiding voters' choices (Dalton, 2020). Franklin, Mackie, and Valen (1992: 400), for example, argued that the decline of cleavage politics that they observed across Western Europe would be 'compensated' by a rise of issue voting.

The idea is simple and straightforward and has great intuitive appeal. As a result, the idea of short-term factors gaining weight has motivated students of elections to scrutinize their impact on the vote, with particular attention being paid to the effects of issues, performance evaluations, and candidates or leaders on the vote (Costa Lobo, 2006). Each of these factors, which are situated close to the tip of Campbell et al. (1960)'s funnel of causality, are thought to have become increasingly important for understanding how voters choose parties.

Work that has studied in depth over-time changes in the effect and weight of short-term determinants, however, is more scarce. The few studies that have examined the role of short-term factors over time, furthermore, generally fail to offer strong support for this expectation that short-term factors are increasingly guiding voters' choices (Dassonneville, 2016; Dassonneville and Lewis-Beck, 2019; Thomassen, 2005).

This lack of evidence, I argue in this chapter, should not come as a surprise. First, as the previous chapters have shown, the decline of long-term factors is perhaps more limited than some assume. Levels of partisanship in particular have not declined much in several of the established democracies that are studied in this book. Second, by theorizing about long- and short-term factors as communicating vessels, one overlooks an important insight from Campbell et al. (1960: 128): that, inside the funnel of causality, an individual's party identification 'has a profound influence across the full range of political objects to which the individual voter responds'. A weakening of party identifications, from this perspective, would lead citizens to have less pronounced opinions on political issues, the candidates, or the state of the economy.

Voters Under Pressure. Ruth Dassonneville, Oxford University Press. © Ruth Dassonneville (2023).
DOI: 10.1093/oso/9780192894137.003.0005

In what follows, I first review the existing empirical evidence on over-time changes in the effects of short-term factors on citizens' electoral choices. I then elaborate in more depth on the implications of the inter-connectedness of long- and short-term factors within the funnel. Finally, I empirically assess over-time trends in the effects of three sets of short-term determinants on the vote in Australia, Canada, Denmark, Germany, Great Britain, the Netherlands, Sweden, and the United States. For these analyses, I focus on the role of economic evaluations and party leaders.

5.1 Partisanship, short-term determinants, and change over time

The idea that long- and short-term determinants should be thought of as communicating vessels is widespread. Indeed, a common reading of the changes in electoral behaviour in established democracies holds that (1) partisanship has weakened; and (2) by implication, short-term determinants of the vote have gained weight. Take, for example, the following quote from Bankert, Huddy, and Rosema (2017: 126)'s work:

> Levels of partisanship have declined in Europe in recent decades (...). And this decline in partisanship has led to greater electoral volatility, an increase in personality-centred elections, and heightened economic voting.

But what is the evidence supporting the view that short-term factors compensate for the decline of partisanship? Research that focuses on the question whether a decline of partisanship is associated with an increased importance of short-term factors and studies that specifically analyse over-time changes in the weight of short-term factors are in fact few and far between.

Kayser and Wlezien (2011) offer one of the few studies that has examined in depth the connection between levels of partisanship and short-term determinants of the vote. Focusing on the role of the economy, they theorize and evaluate whether 'declining partisanship implies a greater weight for performance in the vote' (Kayser and Wlezien, 2011: 366). Relying on the data from the Eurobarometer surveys, they test at the individual and the aggregate levels whether the effect of the economy on support for the incumbent is strengthened when partisanship is weak. Their analyses offer support for this expectation, leading Kayser and Wlezien (2011: 387) to conclude that 'people at the partisan margin are more susceptible to short-term forces such as the economy'. Reflecting on the implication of their findings for long-term trends in electoral behaviour, Kayser and Wlezien (2011: 387) argued that '[i]f party attachment is indeed declining, performance should matter more and policy should matter less to voters'.

Chapter 4 showed some evidence of a decline in levels of partisanship, though it also clarified that the decline remains limited. To get a grasp of changes in voters' behaviour, therefore, it might be useful to more directly assess the weight of short-term factors over time. Work that has done so, and that has examined over-time changes in the effect of different types of short-term factors on the vote, is less conclusive. Thomassen (2005) edited what is probably the most comprehensive analysis of the over-time effects of long- and short-term determinants to date. Studying the determinants of voters' choices in six countries of Western Europe (Denmark, Germany, the Netherlands, Norway, Sweden, and the United Kingdom) until the early 2000s, the collaborators of this edited volume scrutinized trends in the roles of value orientation and of three types of short-term determinants of the vote: issues, retrospective evaluations, and party leaders. The wealth of data and systematic analyses of the determinants of voters' choices over time by the *The European Voter* team, however, did not show evidence of a growing weight of short-term factors. Thomassen (2005: 263) summarized the evidence as follows:

> The conclusion with regard to all short-term factors, issues, retrospective judgements, and leaders is simple and straightforward: We did not find the slightest evidence in support for the hypothesis that the effect of these factors on party choice would increase over time.

Analysing generational differences to get a glimpse of over-time changes in the determinants of voters' choices, Walczak, van der Brug, and de Vries (2012) also did not find support for the expectation that short-term factors increasingly matter. In fact, they found that among younger generations of voters in Europe, performance evaluations and economic conditions matter *less*. My own analyses of change in the economic vote over time, which I conducted jointly with Michael S. Lewis-Beck, also failed to show evidence of an increased impact of the economy on the vote (Dassonneville and Lewis-Beck, 2019). Using individual-level survey data from election studies in seven European countries, and using an aggregate-level approach to study the connection between economic indicators and the vote for the incumbent in democracies in Western Europe, we found great stability in the economic vote over time.

Several other large-scale comparative studies furthermore confirm Thomassen's (2005) conclusions that the effects of leaders on the vote has remained stable over time. Even if leaders arguably matter for voters' choices (Aarts, Blais, and Schmitt, 2011; Garzia, 2012), other longitudinal analyses that scrutinize the impact of leaders on voters' electoral choices also dismiss the argument that leaders increasingly matter (Bittner, 2018; Karvonen, 2010).[1] Analysing over-time changes in the effect of leaders on the vote in six established democracies, Holmberg and Oscarsson (2011: 50) found that:

> [t]he trend for party leader effects is increasing somewhat in two countries, decreasing somewhat in one country, shows trendless fluctuations in two countries, and remains the same over time in one country.

Based on this evidence, Holmberg and Oscarsson (2011) concluded that the hypothesis that leader effects are growing over time is in fact 'a myth'.

There has been less work on over-time changes that has focused on the role of issues in particular, perhaps because measures of issue voting—taking a proximity or valence perspective or focusing on issue ownership—are more diverse and vary more over time. The few studies that have touched upon this topic fail to show evidence of an issue voting growing stronger over time (see, in particular, the chapter by Aardal and van Wijnen in Thomassen (2005)). In an analysis of Dutch election survey data that distinguishes between the role of age, period, and cohort effects, van der Brug and Rekker (2021) shed light on over-time changes in the effects of specific issues. More specifically, they examine age, period, and cohort differences in the effects of citizens' attitudes towards redistribution, their immigration attitudes, and their views on European unification. Their analyses show a mixed picture of change in the role of issues between 1994 and 2017. For redistribution, the period effects suggest a decline in the effects, while the effect of citizens' views about European unification appear to have increased over time. For immigration, finally, the effect fluctuates but there is 'little evidence that the immigration issue has structurally become more important over time' (van der Brug and Rekker, 2021: 794).

---

[1] Arguably, the debate on whether or not there is evidence of a personalization in electoral behaviour is in part a methodological one. And it is argued that studying over-time changes in the effects of individual leaders who come and go is particularly challenging (McAllister, 2012).

5.2 The connections between long- and short-term determinants and implications for change

Clearly, empirical support for the expectation that short-term determinants are gaining weight over time is scant. Given that the decline of socio-structural factors on the vote is altogether limited (cf. Chapter 3), and since party attachments have not weakened strongly over time either (cf. Chapter 4), that is perhaps not entirely surprising.

There is, however, another—more substantive—reason why we should not expect short-term factors to compensate for the weakened role of long-term determinants on the vote. As Campbell et al. (1960) pointed out, the different factors of the vote that have a place within the metaphorical funnel of causality are inter-connected. Long-term factors, and partisanship in particular, play a key role in that regard. These variables not only have a direct effect on voters' electoral choices, but they also colour voters' perceptions of the state of the economy, of the candidates, and of the issues of the day. A wealth of empirical evidence supports this key insight from *The American Voter*, showing that partisan attachments shape citizens' perceptions of how the government performs (Bartels, 2002; Tilley and Hobolt, 2011), their views about how governments handle crises (Pickup, Stecula, and Van Der Linden, 2020), their attribution of responsibility (Bisgaard, 2015), their evaluations of party leaders (Bittner, 2015; Garzia, 2013), and the positions they hold on specific issues (Broockman and Butler, 2017; Lenz, 2012).

To understand why this matters, take a voter v, whose choice is determined by long-term determinants L and short-term determinants S. If we conceive of the role of different determinants of the vote choice as additive explanatory variables, then the choice of voter v can be expressed as follows:

$$\text{Party choice}_v = L + S. \tag{5.1}$$

According to this equation, a voter's choice for a party or candidate is the result of both long-term considerations and how they evaluate the candidates and parties in terms of short-term factors such as the economic performance of incumbents, their position on issues, or how much they like the leader of a party. Research on electoral behaviour traditionally assumed that long-term factors had most weight, thus:

$$L > S. \tag{5.2}$$

Now consider what happens when long-term factors lose weight, if one conceives of the role of long- and short-term factors as additive. If we hypothesize that the impact of long-term factors has halved, the party choice of voter v can be expressed as follows:

$$\text{Party choice}_v = (0.50 \times L) + S. \tag{5.3}$$

As a mere function of the weakened impact of long-term factors, the relative weight of short-term determinants on the vote has increased, and it is not implausible that for many voters S now matters as much or even more than $0.50 \times L$.

Things are different when we do not conceive of long- and short-term factors as simply additive but when we take into account the structuring role of long-term factors on citizens' short-term political evaluations. Based on work on the role of partisanship, for example, as a lens, it is probably more correct to think of S as partly a function of L:

$$S = L + (L \times s) + s \tag{5.4}$$

where S are the short-term evaluations that we measure in, for example election surveys that ask voters to evaluate the state of the economy or the competence of party leaders and s are citizens' 'true' evaluations that are independent of their long-term partisan biases. As equation 5.4 suggests, there is a difference in intercepts when measuring S (captured by the first L) that results from citizens' long-term characteristics. Taking economic evaluations as an example, partisans of the incumbent will consistently evaluate the economy as in better shape than partisans of the opposition. Furthermore, citizens' party identifications can also bias to what extent they take into account changes in the objective economy, which is captured by $L \times s$.

Taking into account the inter-connections between long- and short-term determinants of the vote, the choice of voter v is expressed as follows:

$$\begin{aligned}\text{Party choice}_v &= L + S \\ &= L + (L + (L \times s) + s).\end{aligned} \tag{5.5}$$

If now we consider what happens when long-term factors lose weight, it is obvious that the relative weight of S, as measured in survey research, does not automatically increase as the weight of L decreases. In fact, if the weight of long-term factors (L) decreases, this will also weaken the impact of S because a smaller L implies a smaller shift in the intercept of short-term attitudes based on partisanship, for example, but also a reduced bias ($L \times s$). As a result, when long-term factors matter less, citizens' observed short-term attitudes towards political objects (S) will be less polarized, and their effect on the vote will be reduced as well.

Hypothesizing again that the effect of long-term factors has halved, this reduction in its effect necessarily reduces S too (see equation 5.6). The extent to which S decreases when L weakens obviously depends on the initial values of L and s, but what is certain is that the connections between long- and short-term factors imply that a decline in the impact of long-term factors leads to a decline in the impact of short-term factors too.

$$\begin{aligned} \text{Party choice}_v &= (0.50 \times L) + S \\ &= (0.50 \times L) + ((0.50 \times L) + ((0.50 \times L) \times s) + s). \end{aligned} \quad (5.6)$$

To illustrate this point, I take the data from one particular election study—the 2016 American National Election Study[2]—and examine the role of long- and short-term determinants of the vote by focusing on partisanship and economic evaluations, respectively.

The data confirm the structuring role of partisanship on respondents' short-term political evaluations. As can be seen from Figure 5.1, the distribution of respondents' answers to the question whether and how much better or worse the economy has become in the past year differs meaningfully depending on whether respondents are independent, partisan of the opposition (i.e. Republican in 2016) or partisan of the incumbent party (i.e. Democrat in 2016). More specifically, 11 per cent of the opposition partisans thought the economy had become somewhat or much better, compared to 24 per cent of the independents and 47 per cent of the incumbent partisans. At the other end of the scale, 46 per cent of the opposition partisans thought the economy had become either somewhat or much worse, compared to 31 per cent of the independents and 13 per cent of the incumbent partisans. Clearly, there is more polarization of the state of the economy among partisans than there is among independents. Given the connection between partisanship and short-term attitudes (in this case, economic evaluations), the assumption of simple additive effects between long- and short-term factors (cf. equation 5.1) appears invalid.

These sociotropic retrospective evaluations of the economy correlate in meaningful ways with respondents' vote choices. In line with the expectations

---

[2] I focus on the US context because the bipartisan nature of US politics simplifies the example. In addition, we know that party attachments are strong in the United States, allowing for a focus on the role of a single and strong long-term factor. The principle, however, should generalize to contexts where other long-term factors structure the vote and where more than two parties compete.

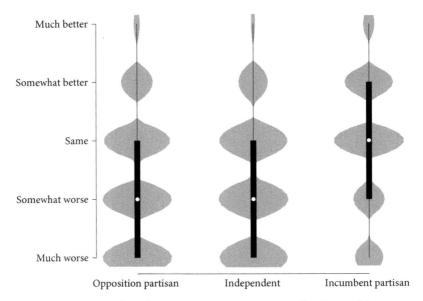

Figure 5.1 Violin plot of sociotropic retrospective evaluations of the economy by partisan group, ANES 2016

Note: Graph shows distribution of responses to questions asking respondents to indicate whether they thought that the economy had got better or worse (and how much better/worse) in the past year. The category of independents includes both pure independents and independents who lean towards a party.

from work on economic voting (Lewis-Beck and Stegmaier, 2007), the more positively an individual evaluates the state of the economy, the higher their likelihood of supporting the incumbent party. This is evident from Model 1 in Table 5.1, which shows the results of a linear probability model to explain voting for the incumbent (the Democratic candidate in the 2016 US presidential elections), with respondents' economic evaluations as the only independent variable.

Not taking into account any other determinant of the vote choice, the estimates of Model 1 suggest that a one-unit increase in economic evaluations (measured on a scale from 1 to 5), is associated with a twenty-four-percentage-point increase in the probability of supporting the incumbent.

What I am most interested in here, however, is how economic evaluations affect voters' choices when long-term factors matter a lot versus when they do not matter much. To gain insights into this question, Models 2 and 3 in Table 5.1 focus on partisans and independents, respectively. Partisans have long-term attachments to parties, and these attachments colour their perceptions of the state of the economy—as shown in Figure 5.1. As a result, their short-term political attitudes—in this case, their economic evaluations—strongly correlate with their vote choice. The coefficient for economic evaluations in Model 2 of Table 5.1 indeed suggests a strong association of 0.25.

What happens when voters are not guided by long-term attachments to parties to structure their vote choice but also to structure how they perceive political objects? In Model 3, I proxy such a situation by focusing only on respondents who indicate that they do not identify with a party. This group still includes respondents who can be categorized as leaners, that is, respondents who do not spontaneously identify with a party but who admit that they feel closer to one party than the other when pushed. As can be seen from the coefficient on economic evaluations in Model 3, it is *smaller*, not larger, when long-term factors are not at play. Model 4 goes a step further and only focuses on 'true' independents, which further limits the estimation sample. As shown in Table 5.1, among this group, which claims to be free from partisan attachments, the association between short-term economic evaluations and the vote is further reduced. The coefficient of economic evaluations among this group is a mere 0.14 compared to the 0.25 among partisans.

When estimating a single model and interacting respondents' economic evaluations with the strength of their partisanship (i.e. whether they are independent, leaner, or partisan), the interaction terms reach statistical significance.[3] The differences in the strength between the different groups are clarified in Figure 5.2, which shows the average marginal effect of a one-unit change in economic evaluations on the likelihood to vote for the incumbent,

Table 5.1 Economic evaluations and support for the incumbent, ANES 2016

	All respondents	Only partisans	Independents and leaners	Only independents
Economic evaluation	0.235***	0.247***	0.199***	0.136***
	(0.006)	(0.007)	(0.013)	(0.028)
Intercept	−0.213***	−0.221***	−0.174***	−0.016
	(0.020)	(0.022)	(0.040)	(0.074)
N	2798	1908	887	237
R^2	0.245	0.287	0.160	0.080

Note: Robust standard errors in parentheses. *$p < 0.05$, **$p < 0.01$, ***$p < 0.001$.

[3] At the 0.05 level for the contrast between leaners and partisans and the 0.001 level for the contrast between pure independents and partisans. Estimates can be consulted in Appendix I.

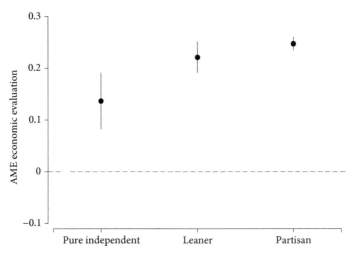

Figure 5.2 Effect of sociotropic retrospective evaluations of the economy by partisan group, ANES 2016

Note: Graph shows average marginal effect and 95 per cent confidence intervals of sociotropic economic evaluations on the likelihood to vote for the incumbent. Estimates are based on a linear probability model to explain voting for the incumbent, by means of economic evaluations, partisanship status, and their interaction. Full results are reported in Appendix I.

by partisan groups. For each group, the sociotropic retrospective economic evaluations[4] are positively associated with voting for the incumbent. However, there are important differences in the strength of this effect between the partisan groups. The impact of economic evaluations on the likelihood to vote for the incumbent is somewhat weaker for leaners than for partisans, but it is strongly reduced among pure independents.

The patterns that are presented in Figure 5.1, Table 5.1, and Figure 5.2 are fully in line with what we know about the role of long-term factors, and partisanship in particular, as a lens through which citizens view political objects (Bartels, 2002; Campbell et al., 1960). While not showing anything new, the example is important as it illustrates that if long- and short-term factors of the vote are not simply additive determinants of voters' choices but inter-connected (cf. equation 5.5), a decline of the role of long-term factors will not automatically give more weight to short-term factors.

---

[4] That is, backward-looking evaluations about the national economy.

5.3 The evidence: Short-term factors over time

Having discussed the connection between long- and short-term factors at a theoretical level and its implications for the expected consequences of a decline of long-term factors on the vote, I now turn to an empirical analysis of over-time trends in the effects of short-term factors on citizens' electoral choices.

I focus on two short-term factors: evaluations of the economy and like/dislike ratings of the party leaders. For these two short-term determinants, unlike what holds for issues, the survey data include measures that are fairly consistent—both between countries and within countries over time.

5.3.1 Empirical strategy

To assess change in the role of short-term factors in the eight established democracies on which I focus in this book, I proceed in a similar way to what I did for assessing the role of socio-demographic factors over time; that is, I estimate a series of election-specific models, in each country, and visually assess change over time.

First, to study the role of economic evaluations over time, I focus on a binary dependent variable, which distinguishes between parties that were in office before the election (coded as 1) and parties that were in opposition (coded as 0). The quantity of interest is limited to a single coefficient in each election-specific model, allowing a visual presentation of the effects of economic evaluations rather than the R^2. Note, however, that focusing on changes in the added explanatory power of economic evaluations leads to the same conclusions (these results are reported in Appendix J). The models that test the impact of economic evaluations on the vote choice include controls for respondents' long-term socio-demographic characteristics and partisanship. The latter variable is coded as a categorical variable distinguishing between partisans of the incumbent, non-partisans, and partisans of opposition parties.

For assessing the role of leader evaluations, all parties are taken into consideration. To estimate the impact of leaders on voters' choices, I hence rely on a series of multinomial logit estimations. Rather than looking at the coefficients for each specific party, I assess over-time change in the role of leader evaluations through a focus on their contribution to explaining voters' choices. In particular, in line with what I did in Chapter 3, I decompose the pseudo-R^2 statistic of the estimations to obtain an estimate of the marginal contribution of leader evaluations for explaining variation in citizens' vote choices. Besides measures of respondents' evaluations of party leaders, in line with how I proceed for examining the impact of economic evaluations, the models account for individuals' socio-demographic characteristics (cf. Chapter 3) and their party identification—which is operationalized as a categorical measure of whether and what party a respondent reports identifying with.

In order to evaluate whether the impact of economic evaluations and that of ratings of the party leaders have changed over time in each of the eight countries, it is of foremost importance that these short-term factors are measured in the same or similar ways over time. To capture economic evaluations, I rely on sociotropic retrospective evaluations, that is, survey items that ask respondents to evaluate the state of the national economy by looking at the past. A large majority of the election studies includes such items. The only country for which no such items are available is Germany, but in this case measures of the current state of the national economy could be relied on. Even when sociotropic retrospective items are available, there is some variation in wording and in the time frame that is mentioned when asking voters to assess changes in economic conditions. Most studies include questions that use the standard reference to the state of the economy twelve months ago (Lewis-Beck and Stegmaier, 2013). But in Denmark, for example, the items generally ask respondents to evaluate the state of the economy in comparison to three years ago. Within countries, however, there is less variation. Furthermore, whenever there were several items included in a single survey, consistency with the measures in other years was prioritized. There is also some variation in the answer options for respondents, with some surveys only offering a choice between worse, same, and better, and other surveys allowing further nuance for those indicating that the economic situation is improving or deteriorating. For consistency, I recode all the items to distinguish three answer options; worse (deteriorating), same (stable), and better (improving).

Turning to the role of party leaders, most of the election surveys that are analysed in this book include some measures that capture how respondents evaluate the leaders of different parties. To enhance the comparability of the analyses, I only consider items that asked respondents to rate how much they like or dislike leaders or to rate them on a thermometer scale. More specific measures of leaders' traits, in contrast, while available in some countries and surveys, were not included.[5] Respondents' ratings of different leaders were included as independent variables in election-specific multinomial logit estimations. In a few surveys, more than one politician of the same party was rated;

---

[5] Because such measures are less common, a longitudinal analysis of their effects was not possible.

in such cases, only one leader was included in the analyses—with a focus on the individual that was the party's leader or their *Spitzenkandidat* at the time of the election. In countries where certain parties only appeal to voters in one specific region, only respondents living in that region are typically asked to rate that party's leader. This holds, for example, for the leader of the Bloc Québecois in Canada or for the leader of the Scottish National Party in Great Britain. To maximize the number of observations for the estimation, in such instances I excluded the leader thermometers for regional party leaders from the models.

Details on the question wording of the measures that were included in each of the election surveys, and their operationalization, can be found in Appendix K.

5.3.2 Results

I start by assessing over-time changes in the impact of economic evaluations on the vote. The focus for these analyses is on voting for the incumbent, and the expectation from the economic voting literature is that those who evaluate the state of the economy more positively will reward the incumbent for its performance by voting for it (Duch and Stevenson, 2008). For settings where the government was composed of a coalition of parties, I consider as an incumbent all parties that were in government before the election, without distinction between the party of the prime minister and junior coalition parties. Given that it has been argued that the economy affects the vote share of the party of the prime minister more strongly than that of other parties in the coalition (Giuliani and Massari, 2019; Larsen, 2016), however, I also verified whether similar patterns emerge when taking as a dependent variable the vote for the party of the prime minister in settings of coalition government. As can be seen from the results in Appendix J, doing so does not substantively change the conclusions.

Figures 5.3 and 5.4 summarize the results of eighty-two election-specific logistic regression models to explain the vote for an incumbent party. As indicated earlier, each of the models includes controls for all socio-demographic predictors that were also relied on in Chapter 3 as well as a measure of partisanship. The focus is on the effect of respondents' economic evaluations on their likelihood of supporting an incumbent party. As mentioned in section 5.3.1, economic evaluations were measured by means of an economic evaluation scale with three values; worse (deteriorating), same, or better (improving). Figures 5.3 and 5.4 show, for each election, the average marginal

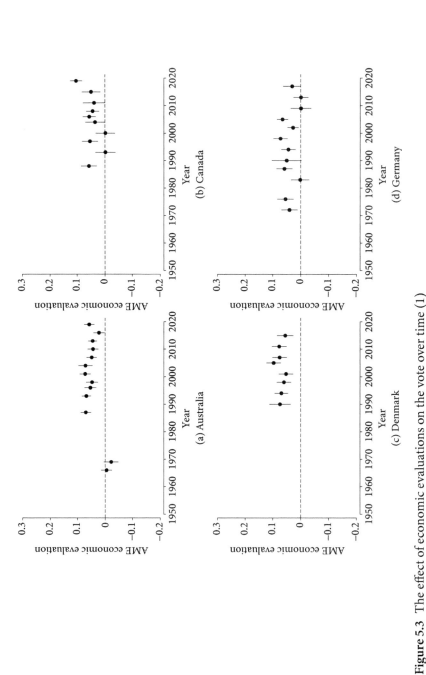

Figure 5.3 The effect of economic evaluations on the vote over time (1)

Note: Average marginal effect of retrospective sociotropic economic evaluation on voting for the incumbent. Estimates from election-specific models. Details on the wording of the economic measures can be found in Appendix K.

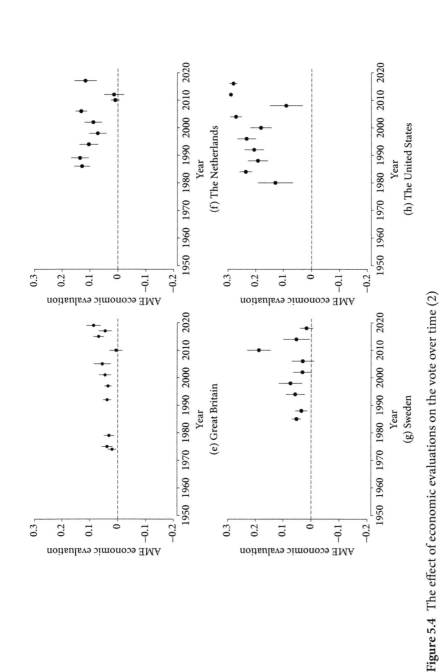

Figure 5.4 The effect of economic evaluations on the vote over time (2)

Note: Average marginal effect of retrospective sociotropic economic evaluation on voting for the incumbent. Estimates from election-specific models. Details on the wording of the economic measures can be found in Appendix K.

effect of a one-unit shift in terms of economic evaluations on the likelihood of supporting an incumbent party. The effect thus captures the difference between evaluating the economy as stable rather than deteriorating or the effect of evaluating economic conditions as improving rather than stable.[6]

The results show strong support for economic voting theory. Out of eighty-two estimates, there are only two that do not suggest a positive association between respondents' economic evaluation and their likelihood to support an incumbent party. Furthermore, no less than sixty-eight out of eighty-two estimates show a positive and significant association between evaluations of the state of the economy and support for an incumbent party—implying a success rate of 83 per cent.

The key question, however, is how the impact of citizens' evaluations of the state of the economy on the vote has fared over time. In that regard, the country-specific plots in Figures 5.3 and 5.4 show very few indications of an increased role of economic evaluations over time. Out of the eight countries that are analysed here, there are only three for which the marginal effect of economic evaluations on the vote seems to be increasing somewhat: Canada, Great Britain, and the United States. In Australia and also in Denmark, the estimates are very stable over time. In Sweden, there is some fluctuation, but a clear trend cannot be discerned. Finally, in the two remaining countries, Germany and the Netherlands, the over-time trend is in fact one of economic evaluations being less and less strongly associated with the vote. As can be seen from the country-specific graphs in Figures 5.3 and 5.4, even though there are some elections in these countries for which economic evaluations seemed to matter more, the underlying trend appears to be negative. In failing to show a clear trend in the effect of economic evaluations on the vote, the results that are presented in Figures 5.3 and 5.4 are fully in line with earlier work on over-time changes in the economic vote in European democracies, which also concluded that 'the strength of the economic vote remains unchanged' (Dassonneville and Lewis-Beck, 2019: 100). This visual assessment of the over-time trend in the effect of economic voting is also supported by a more formal estimation of these time trends. As can be seen from the results that are presented in Appendix L, there is not a single country for which the coefficient of economic evaluations has increased significantly over time.

Importantly, when assessing over-time trends in the amount of explanatory power that is added when economic evaluations are included in models of

---

[6] In additional analyses, which are reported in Appendix J, I also estimate the effect of improving and deteriorating economic conditions separately—leading to the same substantive conclusions.

the vote choice (through a decomposition of the pseudo-R^2), the picture is essentially the same. As can be seen in Appendix J, this alternative approach to assessing change over time does not offer evidence of an increased importance of economic evaluations either. In addition, for countries where coalition governments are an option, using a vote for the party of the prime minister as the dependent variable instead of a vote for any party in the coalition does not substantively alter the results either (see Appendix J).

The economy is one of the most studied short-term determinants of the vote, and citizens' evaluations of the state of the economy are consistently related to their likelihood to support an incumbent party. In contrast to what much scholarly work suggests, however, there is virtually no evidence of economic evaluations gaining weight in citizens' vote-choice calculus. Hence, a rise of economic considerations or performance evaluations on the vote does not appear to be a main cause of the surge of electoral volatility that we are witnessing across established democracies.

Next, I assess the role of leaders on the vote and how the impact of leader evaluations has changed over time. To examine the effect of leaders on the vote, I estimate multinomial logistic regression models, in which all major parties are included as options for the vote. Given this set-up and the fact that the models include as independent variables respondents' ratings of multiple party leaders, I summarize the results with respect to the explanatory power of the leader variables rather than their effect on the vote.

More specifically, Figures 5.5 and 5.6 show the results for the decomposition of the pseudo-R^2 statistic, with a focus on the total R^2 (solid lines) and the part of the R^2 that is due to the inclusion of the leader evaluation variables in the models (dashed lines) versus the socio-demographics and measure of partisanship. As can be seen from the country-specific plots in Figures 5.5 and 5.6, leader evaluations generally add a great deal of explanatory power to a model of the vote choice. The explained variation that is due to the inclusion of leadership variables is generally between 0.2 and 0.4, which is a considerable amount in vote-choice models where the total pseudo-R^2 is between 0.6 and 0.8.

While the graphs in Figures 5.5 and 5.6 consistently point to leader evaluations contributing a great deal to explaining voters' choices, there are few indications of change over time. Focusing specifically on the dashed lines, which indicate the variation that can be explained by the leadership variables, the United States is the only country where a clear increase in the explanatory power of voters' ratings of the leaders can be discerned. There is also a hint of an increase in the role of leaders in recent British elections and also

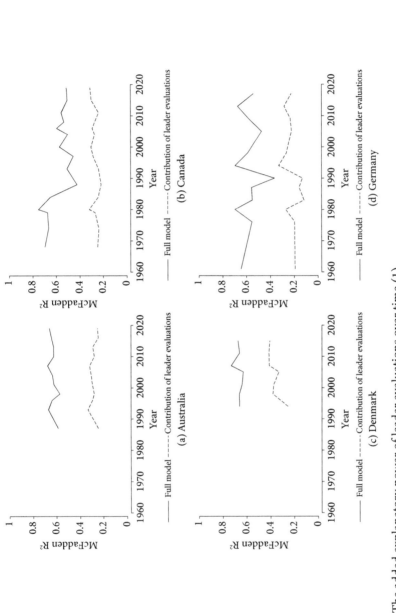

Figure 5.5 The added explanatory power of leader evaluations over time (1)

Note: Difference in the McFadden R^2 statistic of a model with leader evaluations and socio-demographic variables and partisanship versus a model with only socio-demographic variables and partisanship. Details on the wording of the leader variables can be found in Appendix K.

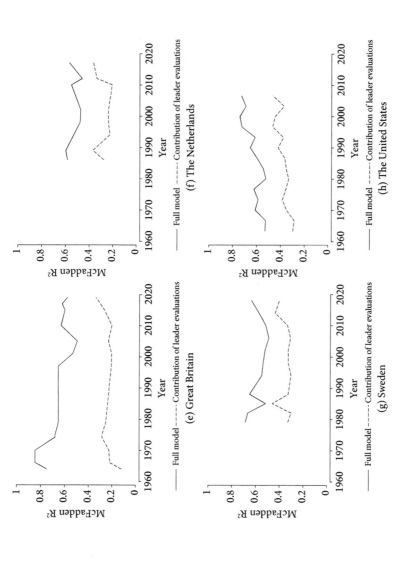

Figure 5.6 The added explanatory power of leader evaluations over time (2)

Note: Difference in the McFadden R^2 statistic of a model with leader evaluations and socio-demographic variables and partisanship versus a model with only socio-demographic variables and partisanship. Details on the wording of the leader variables can be found in Appendix K.

in Denmark, but the time period for the latter country is fairly short. In the five remaining countries (Australia, Canada, Germany, the Netherlands, and Sweden), the explanatory power of the leader variables fluctuates over time. In some of these countries, the effect of leaders appears to be somewhat more important in recent elections (e.g. the Netherlands and Sweden), but in Australia, the reverse holds. Overall, in none of these countries does a clear time trend emerge from the graphical summary of the results.

This lack of strong evidence for an increase in the extent to which leader variables explain variation in the vote choice is further confirmed by the results that are presented in Appendix L. These additional analyses show that there are only two countries where the underlying time trend that is visualised in Figures 5.5 and 5.6 is positive and significant: Denmark and the United States. Even in those two countries, however, the change is substantively limited and covers a short time period in the Danish case.

Many earlier studies have examined whether the effect of leaders on the vote increases over time, in specific countries (Bittner, 2018) or by means of comparative analyses (Holmberg and Oscarsson, 2011; Karvonen, 2010). In line with this work, I find that there are no strong indications of a trend towards personalization of electoral behaviour in established democracies. Even though party leaders matter a great deal for explaining vote choices, the evidence for the idea that leaders increasingly matter is fairly limited overall, with perhaps the exception of the United States and, to some extent, Great Britain. These results are more in line with the conclusions of Holmberg and Oscarsson (2011), who stated that the idea of a personalization in voters' choices is largely 'mythical'. Citizens' evaluations of the party leaders, one of the chief examples of a short-term determinant of the vote choice, do not appear to have gained much weight over time. The increase in electoral volatility that can be discerned across established democracies, therefore, is unlikely to be strongly driven by an increased focus on party leaders.

5.4 Summary and implications

A recurrent claim in studies of electoral behaviour holds that the weakening of long-term structural determinants of the vote has given more room for short-term factors to guide voters' choices. This argument is based on a conception of long- and short-term factors of the vote acting as communicating vessels. More specifically, if the role and impact of long-term factors weakens, it is assumed that this will be compensated by a greater role for short-term determinants of the vote (Dalton, 2020).

In this chapter, I have argued that such a conception of the role of long- and short-term factors overlooks the strong connection between long- and short-term determinants of the vote. Long-term factors, such as one's class identity, religious affiliation, or partisanship, not only have an independent effect on the vote, but they also shape how citizens view political objects. As a consequence, the estimated effect of short-term factors on the vote is, at least in part, driven by the structuring role of long-term identities. When the impact of long-term determinants weakens, then the variation in citizens' evaluations of the state of the economy, of party leaders, or their position on certain issues will be reduced, weakening their effect on voters' choices.

Given the inter-connectedness between long- and short-term determinants of the vote, it should in fact not come as a surprise that previous work has failed to find strong support for the idea that short-term factors increasingly guide voters' choices. The empirical analyses that are presented in this chapter do not offer strong evidence of change in the role of short-term factors. The effects of the economy and of leaders is mostly stable over time in established democracies. The main exception is perhaps the United States, but this is precisely one of the countries where partisan attachments have remained mostly stable and where there are hardly any indications of an increase in volatility (see Chapter 1). For understanding the rise in electoral volatility, the role of short-term factors thus seems to be limited.

This chapter, but also Chapters 3 and 4, show that existing explanations fall short of explaining the remarkable rise of electoral volatility and instability in electoral behaviour that can be observed in many established democracies. On the one hand, the decline of long-term factors on the vote, while present, remains limited. On the other, the impact of short-term factors on the vote has not strongly increased in countries that have witnessed a surge in electoral volatility. To truly understand the sources of the rise in volatility in many democracies, alternative explanations are needed. In the second part of this book, I propose an alternative explanation, which explicitly takes into account the inter-connections between different determinants of the vote choice.

PART II
A NEW FRAMEWORK FOR EXPLAINING CHANGE

Group-based Cross-pressures and voter volatility

6
Sources of instability

Cross-pressures and unconstrained vote choices

In the first part of this book, I reviewed previous arguments that connect the factors that influence voters' decision-making process to electoral volatility. I also evaluated what the empirical evidence is for these arguments.

At an empirical level, the weight of the evidence that is presented in Chapters 3, 4, and 5, is limited. Indications of change are definitely more mixed than is suggested when authors state rather conclusively that 'long-term determinants of electoral behavior have decreased in explanatory power over the past decades' (Oscarsson and Oskarson, 2019: 275), that '[partisanship's] chief role in explaining vote choice been replaced by short-term forces such as evaluations of party leaders' (Ferreira da Silva, Garzia, and De Angelis, 2021: 221), or that 'the decline in partisanship has led to (…) an increase in personality-centered elections, and heightened economic voting' (Huddy, Bankert, and Davies, 2018: 195), to give just some examples.

At a theoretical level, I challenge an assumption that is present in many studies which argue that change is driven by a shift from long- to short-term determinants: that long-term determinants always stabilize voters' choices, and that short-term determinants are always a source of volatility. Instead, I theorize that long-term factors, and individuals' socio-demographic characteristics in particular, can either be a source of stability or of instability of the vote. More specifically, whether socio-demographic characteristics stabilize vote choices depends on the connections between them and whether individuals are *cross-pressured*, based on their group-memberships, or not. I furthermore theorize that short-term factors are not always a source of instability. Instead, I argue that whether short-term factors stabilize or destabilize the vote depends on whether individuals' short-term preferences are constrained by and therefore in line with pre-existing party preferences that result from their socio-demographic characteristics.

In this chapter, I expand on this theoretical argument. In a first step, I lay out in more detail the intuition behind my argument. In a second step I discuss the theoretical mechanisms that underpin the argument. Finally, I zoom in on the role of long-term socio-demographic factors and discuss under which conditions group-based cross-pressures are more likely and how these conditions have changed over time.

6.1 The argument

A large number of different factors, including citizens' personal characteristics and environmental and contextual factors, are known to influence and explain voters' choices. Scholars who have studied the sources of electoral volatility and who have sought explanations for the increase in voter volatility in voters' decision-making process have mostly focused on the importance and weight that different determinants hold in that decision process.

The theoretical argument that I present and empirically test in this book shifts the focus away from the weight of specific (groups of) determinants of the vote towards the connections between them. More specifically, I argue that what is key is whether different determinants of the vote lead to support with one specific party or instead have cross-cutting influences, that is, whether a voter's decision process is constrained or not. I use the term 'constraint' here to refer to the extent to which different determinants of the vote choice are connected and hence—much like Converse (1964: 66)—as a synonym for 'interrelatedness' or 'interconnectedness'. A fully constrained decision-making process would be one in which different determinants all push a voter to prefer one specific party, while an unconstrained vote-choice process would imply that different determinants are associated with preferences for different parties.

I furthermore theorize that the extent to which a voting-decision process is constrained is driven in large part by the connections between factors at the front end of the metaphorical funnel of causality. Given that different determinants of the vote are interrelated (Campbell et al., 1960), what happens near the mouth of the funnel of causality should trickle down and influence the role of more short-term determinants as well.

The idea is that when socio-demographic characteristics all push an individual in the same direction, the voting-decision process is anchored from the start and strongly guided towards one party in particular. Figure 6.1 illustrates, by means of a stylized example, what a decision process that is strongly constrained looks like. In this example, the individual voter's socio-demographic characteristics all push them to support one specific party: Party A. Given that this voter's socio-demographic characteristics, and therefore their positions on social cleavages (e.g. the class cleavage, religious cleavage, or the rural–urban cleavage) all push them to support party A, they develop an attachment to this party. Their party attachment pushes this voter to vote for party A on election day. In addition, given that the voter has developed a party attachment and for reasons on which I elaborate in section 6.2, that identification will also colour their views with respect to more short-term factors. For example, the voter's attachment with party A leads them to support the positions of party A on different issues and to like the candidates and leaders of party A; and, depending on whether party A is in government or in opposition, this voter will evaluate the state of the economy differently too. As a result, this voter's views regarding different short-term determinants of the vote are, to a large extent, constrained by their socio-demographic characteristics and partisanship, implying that these short-term factors further strengthen the voter in their support for party A.

For the voter in this hypothetical example, their socio-demographic characteristics have a stabilizing impact on their vote. But so do the short-term factors. Given that they are influenced and constrained by the voter's socio-demographic and/or partisan predispositions, the voter's short-term opinions can thus also be expected to stabilize their vote choice, leading them to consistently support party A.

A strongly constrained vote-choice process, like the one depicted in Figure 6.1, contrasts with a decision-making process that lacks constraint—and where different determinants of the vote push an individual to support different parties. Depending on what specific socio-demographic characteristics citizens weigh more heavily, for example, they can prefer different parties. Due to the cross-cutting influences of their social group memberships, these

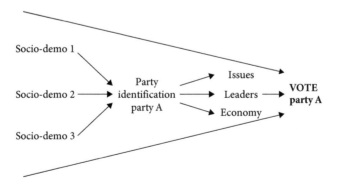

Figure 6.1 A strongly constrained voting decision

voters will not develop strong partisan predispositions. This lack of a strong party attachment also has implications for the role of short-term determinants because it implies that voters' short-term attitudes and evaluations are not influenced and constrained by a party preference either.

To clarify the idea of an unconstrained voting-decision process, and by way of contrast to the constrained voting-decision process in Figure 6.1, Figure 6.2 presents a stylized example of a largely unconstrained decision-making process. Starting with the role of the voter's socio-demographic characteristics, they do not consistently push the voter towards preferring one party. Based on their social class, sex, or level of education, for example, this voter has a preference for party C, party B, or party A. These are not conditions that foster the development of an attachment to a specific party. As a result, this voter's positions on issues, their evaluation of the candidates and leaders, and how they evaluate the state of the economy are not coloured by a preference for one party in particular. In the end, this voter is *cross-pressured* between different parties and, from one election to another, their vote can switch from one to another party. Note that the illustration of an unconstrained vote-choice process in Figure 6.2 takes into account a larger number of socio-demographic characteristics than the constrained-decision process in Figure 6.1. The number of cleavages that are politically relevant is one factor that likely contributes to the social characteristics pushing a voter in different partisan directions—a point on which I elaborate in section 6.3.

The main difference between a voting decision along the lines of Figure 6.1 and the one depicted in Figure 6.2 lies in the level of constraint and the extent to which different determinants of the vote push a voter in the same—or in different—directions. These examples also illustrate that the source of this difference in constraint is situated at the front end of the funnel, that is, in the role that long-term determinants play in shaping citizens' preferences for parties and in the extent to which their decision will be anchored by their social characteristics. To describe and study the presence or lack of strong social anchors,

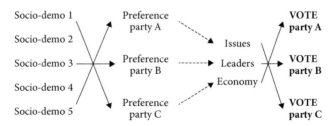

Figure 6.2 An unconstrained voting decision

I borrow the concept of *group-based cross-pressure* of the Columbia school scholars (Berelson, Lazarsfeld, and McPhee, 1954; Lazarsfeld, Berelson and Gaudet, 1944) and others who have studied this phenomenon (Brader, Tucker and Therriault, 2014). The core idea is that when citizens' positions on different social cleavages cross-cut, they will be cross-pressured between parties. The alternative is that citizens' group memberships have a cumulative effect because they are all associated with support for the same party (Powell, 1976). These group-based cross-pressures, I argue, fundamentally alter how a voter decides what party or candidate to support and have important consequences for the level of loyalty that a voter feels towards a party.

Note that in both Figure 6.1 and 6.2, there is place for long- as well as short-term factors to influence voters' choices. The main contrast between these two ideal types of how voting decisions can be made is therefore not about *which* factors influence voters' choices. What contrasts them is whether the different determinants push a voter towards one party or instead have cross-cutting influences on their vote. In other words, in one case, both long- and short-term factors stabilize voters' choices, and in the other case, the cross-pressures from long- and short-term determinants both destabilize the vote. In Figure 6.1, because all determinants strengthen support for one specific party, the different long- and short-term factors have a reinforcing and stabilizing impact on the voter's choice. In Figure 6.2, in contrast, the effects of some factors are undermining the effects of others—and the expectation is that this destabilizes their vote choice.

Having presented the intuition behind the argument that I empirically test in this book, in section 6.2 I expand on the theoretical mechanisms that connect cross-pressure to instability in voting and on the mechanisms that result in group-based cross-pressures affecting the role of more short-term determinants as well.

6.2 (In)stability of long- and short-term factors

Figures 6.1 and 6.2 depict voting-decision processes with varying levels of constraint. The difference in constraint between these two examples already starts at the mouth of the funnel, in the ways in which voters' socio-demographic characteristics shape their party preferences. More specifically, in Figure 2.1, the voter's socio-demographics consistently push them to prefer one party, while in Figure 6.2, the voter's social characteristics have cross-cutting influences and are associated with support for different parties. I theorize that these differences are consequential as they imply that, in one case, the long-term socio-demographic variables have a stabilizing effect on the electoral choices the individual makes, and, in the other case, long-term socio-demographic determinants are a source of instability.

But how come the socio-demographic characteristics of some voters are all pushing them in one direction while for others there are cross-cutting influences? First, it is important to keep in mind that not all socio-demographic variables strongly shape voters' choices. Social characteristics that constitute opposite ends of a political cleavage, however, are shaping voter's choices. Powell (1976: 2) describes these as 'an objective demographic division, such as class, ethnicity, or religion, in which particular membership categories are strongly associated with a particular political party'. Individuals, however, 'each hold multiple identities at one time' (Klar, 2013: 1108), and these identities can be associated with different political cleavages. For individuals who hold social group memberships that are associated with different political cleavages, then, their influence can either be cumulative or it can be cross-cutting (Berelson, Lazarsfeld, and McPhee, 1954; Powell, 1976). In the former case, the position of the individual on the different political cleavages is consistently associated with support for one particular party. In the latter, their positions on different cleavages are associated with support for different parties.

When the different group memberships and social identities of an individual are cross-cutting, the expectation is that this will reduce the likelihood that an individual will develop an attachment with a party or will weaken the attachments they hold. Cross-cutting group memberships are also expected to increase the likelihood of switching. Previous work that has studied the connections between citizens' social identities and political parties provides evidence that is in line with this intuition. Berelson, Lazarsfeld, and McPhee (1954), for example, drew attention to the role of the cross-cutting influences of class and religion. In their panel analysis of voting behaviour in Erie County, they observed that the groups who were cross-pressured based on their religion and class—such as white-collar Catholics or labour union Protestants—were more likely to switch parties than voters for whom religion and class had a cumulative influence. These behavioural differences are likely driven by the fact that cumulative group memberships strengthen party attachments, while cross-cutting cleavages weaken them. More recent empirical evidence on this question also comes from the United States, where there is a renewed focus on the connection between voters' social identities and partisanship. This work shows evidence of the continued relevance of social characteristics and the extent to which they are a source of cross-pressure. Notably, Mason and Wronski (2018) have shown that when different partisan groups are more socially sorted, implying there is a strong alignment between their partisan attachment and their different social identities (Mason, 2016), this results in stronger party attachments. These differences are also found to have implications for citizens' political behaviour, with less socially sorted and therefore more cross-pressured individuals having a higher likelihood of engaging in split-ticket voting (Davis and Mason, 2016). Evidence of a connection between group-based cross-pressures and partisanship is not limited to the US context. In the German case, for example, Mayer and Schultze (2019) have found that higher levels of group-based cross-pressure are associated with a tendency for citizens to identify with multiple parties.

In summary, depending on whether socio-demographics are connected to cumulative or cross-cutting cleavages, long-term determinants either stabilize or destabilize the vote.

Much in the same way as socio-demographic factors, which can either stabilize or destabilize voters' choices, depending on whether different determinants push a voter towards the same or to different parties, short-term determinants can also be theorized to have either a stabilizing or a destabilizing impact on the vote. For short-term factors as well, what is key is whether they pull a voter towards one specific party or whether their impacts are cross-cutting instead.

More specifically, if a voter's evaluation of the state of the economy pulls them towards one party, but their issue preferences foster support for another party, and their evaluations of the leaders would lead them to vote for yet another party, this voter is cross-pressured based on their short-term preferences. Lacking constraint, the short-term preferences of this voter thus destabilize their voting decision—which will likely result in volatility. In contrast, if a voter's evaluations of the state of the economy, their issue positions, and their evaluations of the leaders all lead them to conclude that they should vote for one party in particular, these factors stabilize their vote.

Crucially, I theorize that the extent to which short-term political preferences are cross-cutting depends on the level of constraint among variables closer to the mouth of the funnel of causality, that is, temporally and causally prior to short-term attitudes. As we know from the work of Campbell et al. (1960), and as illustrated in Figures 6.1 and 6.2, long-term socio-demographic variables shape citizens' party attachments, and these party attachments can subsequently colour individuals' views about more short-term political objects. These connections are important as they imply that constraint due to long-term factors can trickle down to constrain the role of short-term determinants as well.

The mechanisms that connect citizens' long-term preferences with their more short-term preferences and evaluations of political objects have been studied in depth by scholars examining the role of partisanship in opinion formation. This work highlights two separate mechanisms that can act as a source of bias in terms of citizens' short-term political attitudes: selective exposure and motivated reasoning.

First, selective exposure refers to a tendency of citizens to opt for media sources that share their partisan predispositions and to consult information that they expect to agree with (Bolsen and Leeper, 2013; Stroud, 2010). The underlying psychological mechanism that is argued to spur such behaviour is a preference for cognitive consistency (Iyengar and Hahn, 2009). Citizens, in other words, want to protect their underlying preferences from dissonant information and therefore avoid exposure to information that might contradict their partisan predispositions. If citizens are successful in limiting exposure to information that contradicts their long-term preferences, the information that they see will simply reinforce their partisan leanings (Iyengar and Hahn, 2009; Klapper, 1960). For voters who are not cross-pressured based on their socio-demographic characteristics and group identities, and who prefer one particular party, selective exposure implies that the short-term information that they see further confirms their party preference. As a result of this process, the evaluations of the state of the economy, of the leaders, and views on specific issues further strengthen the support for the party non-cross-pressured voters were already pulled to—based on long-term factors.

Selective exposure to information is usually thought of as a consequence of citizens' deliberative efforts to avoid contradictory information. The strength of these motivations, furthermore, varies as a function of other factors—such as how important a citizen finds a specific topic (Mummolo, 2016). But a bias in the information that individuals are exposed to can also occur in a non-deliberate fashion, as a consequence of the bubble within which an individual lives and the social context and individuals with whom they interact. By way of contrast with motivated exposure, Iyengar and Hahn (2009: 21) refer to this mechanism as a 'de facto exposure'. Even if it is not deliberate, such exposure can also contribute to long-term predispositions trickling down and constraining the more short-term views of citizens.

Second, we know that partisan-motivated reasoning colours citizens' political attitudes and preferences (Bolsen and Palm, 2019; Leeper and Slothuus, 2014). More specifically, when exposed to information, and when evaluating this information, a biased way of processing this information helps citizens in 'maintaining and protecting identity orientations towards a political party' (Bolsen and Palm, 2019). Such identity-protective motivated reasoning, which leads voters to reject information that threatens their identity (Druckman and McGrath, 2019), is especially relevant for my theoretical argument. There is ample empirical evidence that confirms the role of motivated reasoning in public opinion formation. This work shows, for example, that citizens' support for specific policy proposals is shaped by their partisan identity (Peterson, 2019), that partisans adjust their position on issues in line with cues from party elites (Brader and Tucker, 2012), that partisans 'turn a blind eye' when a member of their party is corrupt (Anduiza, Gallego, and Muñoz, 2013) or shift whom they attribute responsibility for bad performance to as a way to protect their partisan preferences (Bisgaard, 2015). This process of biased information processing, as a mechanism to protect one's pre-existing identities, has important implications for the connections between long- and short-term determinants within the funnel of causality and for the extent to which the voting-decision process will be characterized by constraint. Specifically, for voters who do not have cross-cutting identities and develop an attachment with one specific party, this partisanship subsequently leads them to disregard information that is at odds with their partisan predisposition. As a result, it becomes more likely that this voter's issue opinions or their evaluations of performance and of the candidates and leaders are in line with and therefore only further confirm one's long-term predispositions.

In summary, I theorize that short-term determinants of the vote choice, like citizens' issue positions, performance evaluations, or how much they like specific candidates or party leaders, do not *always* destabilize voters' electoral choices. Whether determinants of the vote are a source of stability or of instability depends on whether they push a voter towards one specific party or instead provide conflicting information and are a source of cross-pressure. Importantly, I have argued that the extent to which short-term factors are a source of cross-pressure and therefore instability depends on the constraining influence of more long-term determinants. Mechanisms of selective exposure and motivated reasoning result in short-term attitudes that are both more in line with one's long-term predisposition and more consistent between each other (because the different short-term attitudes are all coloured by the same predispositions). Ultimately, this should result in a voting decision that is very much constrained overall, which is expected to result in voting choices that are less volatile.

6.3 Conditions that foster or limit group-based cross-pressure

So far, I have argued that the connections between different determinants of the vote choice, and more specifically whether they all pull a voter towards one party or are a source of cross-pressure, is key to explaining the stability of voters' choices. I have also theorized that group-based cross-pressures are a main driver of constraint in the voting-decision process and that their effects trickle down in the funnel of causality through mechanisms of selective exposure and motivated reasoning. To serve as a compelling theoretical framework for explaining the surge in electoral volatility that is observed in many democracies, however, these cross-pressures should have increased over time.

To evaluate whether that is plausible, it is insightful to think more about the conditions that foster and limit group-based cross-pressures, that is, what factors can explain variation in the extent to which citizens are cross-pressured between parties, based on their socio-demographic characteristics. Two factors in particular can be thought of: (1) the number of socio-demographic cleavages that are politically salient and (2) the importance that an individual voter attaches to these different cleavages and aspects of their social identity. In terms of both these factors, there are good reasons to expect change over time that would result in more cross-cutting cleavages overall.

6.3.1 The number of cleavages

In Chapter 3, I introduced a distinction between 'old' and 'new' cleavages. With the former, I refer to the cleavages that Lipset and Rokkan (1967) identified and found to structure party politics in established democracies. With 'new' cleavages, I refer to cleavages that some scholarly work argues are gaining in importance in recent decades, such as the gender, education, and age cleavages (Ford and Jennings, 2020). The empirical results in Chapter 3 indicate that these new cleavages contribute less to explaining voters' electoral choices than old cleavages. Still, their emergence and the politicization of gender, age, and education-based cleavages in some countries implies that the number of politically relevant group memberships increases. With more groups being politically relevant, the implication is that the likelihood of cross-cutting group memberships increases. This expectation that the number of relevant group identities has increased over time is also present in other work, as evident from the following quote from Klar (2013: 1108):

> [I]ndividuals each hold multiple identities at one time that are, on occasion, associated with competing interests—and this may be more true now than it ever has been before. Detachment from traditional, overarching social structures are setting individuals free to identify with new and multiple social and political groups.

The expectation that an increase in the number of politically salient cleavages increases the likelihood of citizens finding themselves in cross-cutting social groups is based on simple mathematics. For the sake of illustration, consider a party system with two parties (party A and party B) in a society that is characterized by two political cleavages. Based on an individual's group membership on the first cleavage, they would either be pushed to support party A or party B. And the same holds for the second cleavage. As can be seen in Table 6.1, this results in four possible combinations of cleavage-based party preferences. Of those four combinations, two combinations reflect situations in which an individual's position on the two cleavages leads them to prefer the same party (A, A and B, B), while two combinations result in cross-pressure. If individuals' positions on the cleavages were determined fully randomly, half of the respondents would thus be cross-pressured and the other half would not. As the number of politically salient cleavages increases, the chance that an individual is cross-pressured increases accordingly. As shown in the second column in Table 6.1, with four cleavages and still two parties, the number of possible combinations increases to sixteen. Of these sixteen combinations, only two result in a complete absence of cross-pressure (four × A and four × B). As a result, if individuals were randomly assigned their positions on the four cleavages, seven out of eight would be at least somewhat cross-pressured.

Moving from mathematics to voters, take—as an example—a young Catholic woman living in the state of Baden-Württemberg in Germany and earning an above-average income. If only the 'old' cleavages are politically relevant and structuring voters' choices, this woman's choice is straightforward; she will support a right-wing party. Because of her religious background, she casts a vote for the Christian Democratic Union (CDU). Her group memberships do not lead her to feel cross-pressured between the CDU and other

Table 6.1 The connection between the number of cleavages and the likelihood of being cross-pressured

	Party preference based on position on cleavage	
	Context with two cleavages	Context with four cleavages
Option 1	**A, A**	**A, A, A, A**
Option 2	A, B	A, A, A, B
Option 3	B, A	A, A, B, A
Option 4	**B, B**	A, B, A, A
Option 5		B, A, A, A
Option 6		A, A, B, B
Option 7		A, B, B, A
Option 8		B, B, A, A
Option 9		B, A, A, B
Option 10		A, B, B, B
Option 11		B, A, B, B
Option 12		B, B, A, B
Option 13		B, B, B, A
Option 14		A, B, A, B
Option 15		B, A, B, A
Option 16		**B, B, B, B**
	1/2 cross-pressured	7/8 cross-pressured

parties. Things change when her age and gender identity become politically relevant group memberships. Now, while her income and religious affiliation would still lead her to prefer the CDU, the fact that she is young and female would push her to parties on the left. The more cleavages structure voting behaviour, and the more group memberships become politically relevant, the more citizens will feel cross-pressured based on at least two of their multiple group memberships.

The number of cleavages that are politically salient and that could structure citizens' vote choices can increase because new groups emerge and become politically mobilized. But another possibility is that factors gain or lose salience because the connection between socio-demographic variables is changing over time. A good example in this regard relates to the roles of income and education. The work of Gethin, Martínez-Toledano, and Piketty (2022), for example, points out that income and education traditionally had a similar effect on the vote choice—with both being positively associated with voting for right-of-centre parties. Over time, however, the effect of education has become distinct from that of income, with higher education increasing the odds of voting for left-wing parties (Gethin, Martínez-Toledano, and Piketty, 2022; Piketty, 2019) and parties that are green or left-libertarian in particular (Abou-Chadi and Hix, 2021). As a result of such a change, a sociodemographic characteristic that was already present in society becomes a distinctive determinant of the vote—and can act as a source of cross-pressure.

In summary, if the number of different group identities that are politicized has indeed increased over time, as some work has argued, this should result in more citizens feeling group-based cross-pressured between parties overall.

6.3.2 Cleavage-based encapsulation

A second factor that can influence whether citizens will—based on their social characteristics—come to prefer a single party or instead will be cross-pressured between parties relates to the relative political importance of these socio-demographic characteristics. Turning back to the illustration of an unconstrained voting-decision process in Figure 6.2, based on their different socio-demographic characteristics, the hypothetical voter in this example prefers party A, party B, or party C. These cross-cutting influences disappear, however, if the voter really cares about one of their social identities only.

What is key is thus whether and how many social characteristics are politically salient for the individual. Voters can attach greater weight to some aspects of their identity than others. And if the voter mainly thinks of themselves and their political interests in terms of their class identity, for example, the cross-cutting impacts of other identities, such as their sex or education, become irrelevant, leading to the development of an attachment with one party only. Even though an individual is a member of cross-cutting identity groups, therefore, this does not automatically lead to a feeling of cross-pressure. An example in this regard is provided by how different groups reacted to Trump in the context of the 2016 US presidential election. The analyses of Cassese (2020: 178) indicate that 'white evangelical Republican women are not ambivalent partisans', suggesting that their religious and gender identities had a limited impact overall.

The importance that individuals attach to their identities is thus important, but this importance can be shaped by contextual factors. In this regard, it should be kept in mind that socio-demographic factors and membership of social groups are not, by themselves, factors that are sufficient to push voters to support a particular party (Zuckerman, Valentino, and Zuckerman, 1994). These group memberships should be made politically relevant, and it should be obvious for the members of a group which party defends their interest. Parties play an active role in this process and can reduce the influence of cross-cutting identities by priming one identity specifically (Klar, 2013).

One specific way in which parties can generate a strong link with a sociodemographic section of the electorate and ensure that this characteristic becomes politically relevant and dominates other—potentially conflicting—identities is by means of 'encapsulation'. Katz (1990: 144) describes this phenomenon, which was historically important in European democracies, as follows:

> [T]he continued cohesion of social groups provided a solid basis for a virtual party monopoly on political linkage; parties represented coherent programmes (in a social if not necessarily in a logical or ideological sense) and were supported by a variety of ancillary organizations that could effectively encapsulate supporters in a socially and politically homogeneous and all-embracing network.

In order to 'encapsulate' sections of the electorate, as (Katz, 1990) describes it, and to foster homogeneity through a focus on one particular cleavage group, the presence of organizations ancillary to the political parties is crucial. Mass parties on the left traditionally relied on an alliance with labour unions, while right-wing parties sometimes counted on close ties with organized religion. Organizations like labour unions or churches, in other words, helped to ensure these parties' control over groups of voters that could easily be mobilized (Bartolini and Mair, 1990) and that stably and loyally voted for the mass party (Katz, 1990; Rokkan, 1977). Ultimately, these organizations acted as 'reliable anchors for stable exchange relationships with political parties' (van Biezen and Poguntke, 2014: 210).[1]

This process of encapsulation is directly relevant for the level of constraint in voters' decision-making processes. In particular, for voters that are fully encapsulated based on their position on one specific cleavage, their other—potentially competing—group memberships become irrelevant to their vote choice. Lacking cross-cutting influences, therefore, the decision process of encapsulated voters should be strongly constrained.

Trade unions are a prime example of 'collateral' or 'ancillary' societal organizations. They are mostly allied with left-of-centre parties and link their members to these parties (Bartolini and Mair, 1990; van Biezen and Poguntke,

---

[1] The role of these organizations is also central in theories about how consociationalism can ensure democratic stability in divided societies (Andeweg, 2000).

2014). The ties between labour unions and left-wing parties historically helped those parties to maintain a stable electoral base through their efforts to mobilize their members or by campaigning for the party or candidates (Piazza, 2001). In connecting their members to particular parties, the unions hence contributed to strengthening political cleavages and stabilizing electorates. It could be argued, however, that the connection between labour unions and left-of-centre parties is indicative of a wider societal presence of organizational connections between different interest groups and particular parties. In terms of the mobilizing effects of labour unions, for example, Gray and Caul (2000: 1004) contend that their efforts 'spur a countermobilization by organizations across the ideological spectrum'.

Previous work offers indications of the role that encapsulation by trade unions plays for stabilizing electoral behaviour. Bartolini and Mair (1990), for example, showed a negative correlation between a country's trade union density and levels of electoral volatility. More recent work confirms the connection between the strength of trade unions and volatility. Martin, de Lange, and van der Brug (2022: 359), for example, use aggregate-level data on elections between 2005 and 2017 to show that parties in fourteen West European democracies that have 'lower shares of trade union member support experience higher levels of volatility'. A decline in the presence of labour unions, it seems, has implications for the stability of election outcomes. Organized religion, much like trade unions, has been argued to play an anchoring role, strengthening the linkage between religious identity and the vote but for parties on the right of the ideological spectrum (van Biezen and Poguntke, 2014).

There are strong indications, however, that parties' hold on sections of the electorate, through mechanisms of encapsulation that are fostered by their collaboration with ancillary organizations, is in decline. Previous work has already documented a decline in trade union density in a number of countries, at least for the most recent time period (Scruggs and Lange, 2002; Visser, 2002). And for religion as well, there are indications of a decline. Patterns of secularization in advanced democracies are well established, in particular as far as the Christian churches are concerned (Kenis and Pasture, 2010; Knutsen, 2004a; van Biezen and Poguntke, 2014). Studying religion and religiosity across the world, Inglehart (2021) even shows an acceleration of the secularization trend in recent years. In what follows, I take a closer look at the evidence of change in the strength of trade unions and organized religion in the eight countries that are analysed in this book.

114   SOURCES OF INSTABILITY

I start by looking at change in terms of the strength of trade unions. More specifically, in Table 6.2, I show levels of trade union density by decade in each of the eight countries. The data on trade union density are retrieved from the Organisation for Economic Co-operation and Development (OECD).[2] This measure captures the percentage of salary earners that are member of a trade union. The change scores reflect the over-time change in percentage points.

As can be seen in Table 6.2, the decline is particularly pronounced in recent decades. When comparing levels of trade union density in the 1990s with those in the 2010s, the data show a decline in trade union density in each of the eight countries. This is not the case when contrasting levels of trade union density in the 1960s and 2010s. That is a consequence of the fact that until the 1990s, levels of trade union membership either remained stable or increased—contributing to the stabilization of European electorates as described by Bartolini and Mair (1990). The past two decades, however, show a picture that is rather different and is suggestive of the weakening of the strength of class-based encapsulation in these eight countries.

The data on trade union density that are presented in Table 6.2 are suggestive of a weakening of socio-organizational bondedness from around the 1980s and 1990s onwards. Incidentally, that is also when we see that levels of net volatility start to surge across democracies. These patterns are consistent with the idea that a change in levels of group-based encapsulation—which prevented the cross-cutting influence of different social identities—has contributed to the increase in volatility.

Turning to organized religion, I assess the role of the organizational strength of religion and over-time variation in the eight countries analysed in this book by means of measures of church attendance. Such information, in particular in countries that are mostly dominated by Christian denominations, should reflect to what extent churches have a large membership and can reach out to them to organize politically or to exert political influence. Survey data allow light to be shed on differences in church attendance between countries and change over time. In some of the election studies analysed in this book, information on church attendance is available. However, answer options vary quite a lot between countries and even within countries over time. As an alternative, I make use of comparable data from large-scale comparative survey projects. More specifically, the World Values Survey (WVS) has included a question on

---

[2] The data are available at https://stats.oecd.org/BrandedView.aspx?oecd_bv_id=lfs-data-en&doi= data-00371-en. I used administrative data when available, and relied on survey estimates when those were not available. For country-years when both are available, their correlation is 0.99. I also imputed data from missing country-years using linear to interpolation.

Table 6.2 Trade union density by decade

	1960s(%)	1970s(%)	1980s(%)	1990s(%)	2000s(%)	2010s	Change since 1960s	Change since 1990s
Australia	47.5	47.9	46.2	33.9	21.2	15.9	−31.6	−18.0
Canada	29.1	33.7	34.7	34.0	30.4	29.6	0.5	−4.4
Denmark	59.6	68.2	77.4	75.6	71.2	67.0	7.4	−8.6
Germany	33.1	33.8	34.2	30.0	21.7	17.7	−15.4	−12.3
Great Britain	40.4	46.8	47.2	35.1	27.9	24.9	−15.5	−10.2
The Netherlands	40.3	37.5	28.8	24.6	21.2	18.0	−22.3	−6.6
Sweden	66.4	74.1	83.7	92.1	78.9	67.9	1.5	−24.2
United States	28.6	25.2	18.2	14.5	12.2	10.7	−17.9	−3.8

Note: Data show average level of trade union density by decade, as reported by the OECD. Administrative data are relied on most of the time, complemented with information from survey estimates that the OECD provides when administrative information is missing. The measure reflects the percentage of salary earners that are members of a trade union. Change is indicated in percentage points.

church attendance in its survey since its first wave (1981), and the International Social Survey Program (ISSP) has done the same for its 1991, 1998, 2008, and 2018 surveys. I rely on these two projects to obtain estimates of church attendance in Australia, Canada, Denmark, Germany, Great Britain, the Netherlands, Sweden, and the United States.

Table 6.3 shows the trends in church attendance for the eight countries studied here. A decline in the share of the population that attends church at least monthly can be clearly discerned in each of the countries for which the data set includes multiple entries. The decline is weakest in the Danish case, but levels of church attendance were low even at the start of the time series (i.e. in the 1980s) in Denmark. For the seven countries for which there are multiple entries on the share of the population attending church regularly, the data show a decline between 23 per cent (in Denmark) and 67 per cent (in Sweden). The data that are summarized in Table 6.3 suggest that the share of the population that attends a religious service at least once a month has plummeted. As a consequence, the structuring role that organized religion can play in citizens' lives, and in their political choices in particular, has weakened too.

Trade union density and church attendance are just two examples of societal organizations. Their decline, however, is important because these are the typical organizations that had strong links with political parties and that could mobilize and structure voters' behaviour through a mechanism of encapsulation. These organizations were crucial in the building of 'pillars' in societies that would encapsulate citizens and ensure their loyalty to one party (Rokkan,

Table 6.3 Trends in church attendance

Country	1980s(%)	1990s(%)	2000s(%)	2010s(%)
Australia	39.6	24.6	19.0	19.2
Canada			36.6	
Denmark	10.7	11.2	9.4	7.5
Germany		19.2	23.0	14.8
Great Britain		41.5	27.2	22.1
The Netherlands		26.6	19.9	16.9
Sweden	23.2	9.5	6.6	7.6
United States	70.4	54.3	46.3	43.3

Note: Data show the average percentage of respondents in surveys indicating they attend church once a month or more often. Data from the World Values Surveys 1981–2016 longitudinal file, the ISSP 1991, 1998, 2008, and 2018 surveys on religion. For Denmark, data are taken from the Danish values studies cumulative files, which include the European and World Values Surveys.

1977; van Biezen and Poguntke, 2014). When these organizations are closely linked to political parties, the organization's members 'cast their vote according to their leaders' recommendation even if they disagree with individual elements [of a party's program] because their prime loyalty is to the organisation' (Poguntke, 2002: 8). These ancillary—or collateral—organizations hence provide parties with a reservoir of stable electoral support and limit electoral volatility.

Importantly, collateral organizations like trade unions and churches play a rather unique role in stabilizing electorates for parties in this way. Other social organizations, like new social movements, can also establish connections with parties (Hutter, Kriesi, and Lorenzini, 2018). However, because these organizations generally lack a formal organization, are not coordinating their members to the same extent, and are generally more politically independent and autonomous, these movements should not be expected to link their membership to certain parties in a stable way. Instead, new social movements offer 'structurally weak social anchorage' (Poguntke, 2002: 10). In terms of linkage between citizens and parties, in other words, the weakening role and presence of more traditional collateral organizations such as trade unions and churches is not compensated by a growing role of newer organizations and social movements. As a result, the decline in membership of trade unions and organized religion is indicative of a weakening of the structural links between citizens and political parties.

If voters are no longer encapsulated to vote for the party defending their class interests or the interests of their religious groups, their other identities can influence their choice too—increasing the odds that they will feel cross-pressured between parties, based on their socio-demographic characteristics.

In summary, long-term determinants—and citizens' socio-demographic characteristics in particular—can either have a stabilizing or a destabilizing impact on the vote. If few cleavages are politically relevant, and those cleavages are the basis of efforts to 'encapsulate' sections of the electorate and link them to specific parties, the impact of cross-cutting cleavages is reduced and the impact of socio-demographics on the vote will be stabilizing. However, as the number of politically relevant cleavages increases, and as encapsulation is lessened, it becomes more likely that individuals are influenced by cross-cutting identities. And when they are cross-pressured, citizens' socio-demographic characteristics are a source of instability for their vote choice.

6.4 Summary and implications

Rather than assuming that long-term determinants of the vote always stabilize voters' choices while short-term determinants are always a source of instability, I argue that both long- and short-term determinants can act as sources of stability or as a breeding ground for unstable vote choices. When different determinants of the vote—both long- and short-term—push voters towards different parties, this results in a vote-choice process that lacks constraint and that leads to instability in voting choices.

I have also theorized that an important source of a lack of constraint is to be found near the front end of the funnel. In particular, the presence of group-based cross-pressures implies that party attachments are not formed. And lacking a strong partisan predisposition, the psychological mechanisms that help citizens to protect their group identities from information that is inconsistent with their identity are not at play for cross-pressured voters. As a result, their short-term preferences are not coloured and constrained by long-term predispositions. In the end, the voting-decision process of group-based cross-pressured voters is one in which different factors—both long- and short-term—can push the individual in different partisan directions. The outcome of that decision process, therefore, is more volatile.

Having laid out the main argument, I turn to empirics—starting with the question of how we can operationalize the extent to which different determinants push a voter in one or in different partisan directions. In order to do so, in Chapter 7, I elaborate on the concept of cross-pressures, with a focus on group-based cross-pressures. I also introduce the empirical approach that I rely on to operationalize cross-pressure.

7
Cross-pressured voters

The core argument that is laid out in this book is that to understand the increased volatility of voters' electoral behaviour, a focus on the interconnections between variables within the funnel of causality has more promise than conceiving of different sets of predictors as compensating or counterbalancing for the role of others. In particular, key to understanding whether voters' electoral choices will be either stable or volatile is capturing the extent to which voters' choices and their political views more generally are 'constrained'. That constraint, I argue, can be captured by considering the extent to which different determinants of the vote 'point in the same direction', and all lead to a preference for a certain party.

In Chapter 6, I theorized that both long- and short-term determinants of the vote can push a voter towards one particular party or have cross-cutting influences on a voter's choice. However, I also contended that cross-cutting influences based on voters' socio-demographic characteristics—and thus at the front end of the funnel of causality—are key; that is, their effects trickle down and ultimately determine whether a voter's decision process will be largely constrained or unconstrained. I have also argued that a larger number of social cleavages, and a lack of encapsulation based on one specific cleavage identity, have the potential to spur group-based cross-pressure—which I theorize has contributed to the rise in electoral volatility. In Chapter 8, I test whether that is indeed the case. To do so, however, I require an empirical measure that can capture how cross-pressured voters are.

More specifically, I need a measure that captures to what extent variables are constraining voters' support for one particular party. In what follows, I elaborate on the concept of being 'cross-pressured'—which I will use as a tool to assess constraint in voters' choices. I then give more details on the empirical approach that is used to operationalize cross-pressure and validate the measure in a number of ways. That way, this chapter sets the stage for the empirical chapters that examine change over time in levels of cross-pressure and their connection with volatility.

7.1 The concept of cross-pressure

The idea that voters can be cross-pressured and that being cross-pressured between parties affects citizens' political behaviour is not new. Studying voters' decision-making processes and following voters throughout the campaign, the Columbia school scholars were the first to introduce the concept of cross-pressure. Their survey data suggested that voters who were cross-pressured were less likely to turn out to vote and more likely to change their party preference over the course of an election campaign (Berelson, Lazarsfeld, and McPhee, 1954; Lazarsfeld, Berelson and Gaudet, 1944).

In this initial work, but also in later studies on the topic, the idea of cross-pressure has been conceived of and operationalized in three main ways. Lazarsfeld (1944: 328–329) describes these different origins of citizens' feelings of cross-pressure and their influence on the stability of the vote as follows:

> We saw, for instance, that well-to-do people and Protestants were much more likely to vote Republican than poor people and Catholics. A well-to-do Catholic, therefore, was under cross-pressures. Another index of cross-pressure can be developed by dividing the respondents into those whose family members are all in agreement and those with a political deviate or, at least, someone who has not yet made up his mind. Another type of cross-pressure exists around a citizen who intends to vote for a party but does not agree with all its tenets.

First, there are cross-pressures that arise from multiple group memberships, that conflict in their impact on the vote. Lazarsfeld (1944) cites the example of a well-to-do Catholic whose economic situation should guide them to support the Republican candidate while their Catholic identity pushes the voter towards the Democrats. Others have built on these insights to study the role of conflicting group memberships on electoral participation and the vote choice (Mutz, 2002; Zuckerman, Valentino, and Zuckerman, 1994). Powell (1976) in particular linked the emergence of cross-pressures to the cleavage structure in a society. With knowledge of the political cleavages in a society, according to Powell (1976), we can assess whether an individual either takes 'cumulative cleavage positions' or 'cross-cutting cleavage positions'. In the first case, an individual's 'group memberships are all commonly associated with the same party'. For those in the 'cross-cutting' category, in contrast, 'one group membership is commonly associated with one party, while a second membership is associated with another party' (Powell, 1976: 2). There is some evidence to the effect that such group-based cross-pressures are associated with instability in the vote. Powell (1976), for example, shows that—in the Austrian context—whether citizens are in a cumulative cleavage position or a cross-cutting cleavage position is predictive of the strength of their party attachments. Furthermore, Zuckerman, Valentino, and Zuckerman (1994) find a strong relationship between what they refer to as the 'structuration of social and political networks' and voting stability.

A second and related source of cross-pressure can be found in an individual's immediate social environment. The quote from Lazarsfeld (1944) contrasts individuals whose family members are all in agreement with them and those for whom that is not the case. In their study of changes in vote preferences over the course of a campaign, Berelson, Lazarsfeld, and McPhee (1954) indeed find that the partisan composition of a voter's family correlates with their likelihood to change parties. In particular, while 73 per cent of respondents whose family shared their party preference reported a stable party preference, only 47 per cent of those whose family preferred the other party did (Berelson, Lazarsfeld, and McPhee, 1954: 120–121). The role of shared party preferences in this study was also shown to extend beyond the immediate family. Sharing parties with friends and even with co-workers, the authors show, is also associated with a more stable party preference—though to a lesser extent than what holds for the family. Such findings are suggestive of the important role that social interactions play as a mechanism to explain the emergence of cross-pressures and their impact on the vote (Mutz, 2002). Further evidence of the role of individuals' social environment comes from work that tries to map individuals' discussion networks and how political information flows within such networks (Beck et al., 2002; Huckfeldt et al., 1995; Huckfeldt and Sprague, 1995). When such networks are cohesive, it appears, they remain 'largely unaffected by the larger climate of opinion' (Huckfeldt et al., 1995: 1049)—which arguably stabilizes their vote.

Finally, there are the cross-pressures that emerge from citizens' opinions on the issues, candidates, and the parties. Berelson, Lazarsfeld, and McPhee (1954: 19) argued that 'people with "cross-pressured" opinions on the issues or candidates or parties—that is, opinions or views simultaneously supporting different sides—(...) are more likely to be unstable in their voting position during the campaign'. Campbell et al. (1960) picked up on such attitudinal sources of cross-pressures for their study of the determinants of voters' choices. In line with the findings of the Columbia school, they found that conflicting political attitudes led voters to delay their voting decision. Much of the recent work that studies cross-pressures and their impact on the vote has focused on this attitudinal source of conflict between parties. Hillygus and Shields (2008) in particular, focusing on the US context, argue that inconsistencies between individuals' partisanship and their positions on key issues are crucial for understanding which voters are 'persuadable' and hence likely to change their vote over time. Using observational and experimental data, they show that cross-pressured partisans decide later, are more volatile during the campaign, and are more likely to eventually defect from their party. Furthermore, Endres and Panagopoulos (2019: 1094) show that when exposing cross-pressured partisans to information that 'highlights issue disagreement' they 'waver in their support for their parties' candidate'. While most previous work focuses on the US context, there is also comparative work on the topic. He (2016), who uses election survey data from Germany, the Netherlands and Great Britain, shows that having policy preferences that push an individual in different partisan directions is strongly associated with late deciding.

Overall, there is strong evidence that holding conflicting political attitudes or policy preferences, interacting with individuals who hold different party preferences, and having conflicting group memberships all influence voting behaviour in important ways. In particular, citizens who are cross-pressured are more often late deciders and switch parties more often. Thus, cross-pressures are a critical source of political instability. Importantly, while most previous work on the role of cross-pressure for voters' choices focuses on the dynamics of voters' decision process over the course of an election campaign, I argue that such cross-pressures also contribute a great deal to explaining volatility in party preferences between elections and to the increase in volatility over time—as we will see in Chapters 8 and 9.

The concept of cross-pressure can thus arise from different sources. My theoretical argument that the extent to which multiple determinants of the vote push a voter in one or in different partisan directions is key to explaining volatility and informs my focus on cross-pressures that originate in citizens' socio-demographic characteristics, as well as their more short-term attitudes and political opinions. Even though cross-pressures that emanate from conflicting influences in one's social environment might be at play as well, I therefore only focus on the first and the third type of cross-pressure, that is, on cross-pressures that arise from multiple group memberships, on the one hand, and cross-pressures that result from short-term influences, such as issue opinions or candidate evaluations, on the other.

7.2 How to capture cross-pressures?

The main concept, and the first mover in my theory of why voters are volatile, is group-based cross-pressure, that is, a feeling of cross-pressure that emerges from citizens' memberships of different social groups. To capture such cross-pressures, I use an indicator of 'cross-pressure scores' that was developed by Brader, Tucker and Therriault (2014). He (2016) also adapted this measure in her work on issue cross-pressures in multiparty democracies. The cross-pressure score measure was specifically designed to 'capture the cumulative impact of pressures (...) that arise from one's social strata or group memberships' (Brader, Tucker and Therriault, 2014: 25). In line with the concept of cross-pressures, the measure taps whether an individual's membership of different social groups results in reinforcing or conflicting influences. In the former instance, the cross-pressure score will be low, while many conflicting influences will be reflected in a high cross-pressure score.

To introduce the measure and how it is constructed, I focus on group-based cross-pressure and thus stay close to Brader and colleagues' (2014) measure of cross-pressure. In Chapter 9, I adapt this measure to also account for the cross-cutting influence of other determinants of the vote, and more short-term factors in particular.

To calculate cross-pressure scores by means of survey data, Brader, Tucker and Therriault (2014: 30–32) propose a four-step process:

1. Estimate a regression model to obtain estimates of the relationships between socio-demographic characteristics and the vote choice.
2. Use the regression estimates to obtain the predicted probabilities of supporting each of the parties or candidates in the election.
3. Calculate the variance in predicted probabilities across parties or candidates.
4. Rescale the number to ensure that higher values of the cross-pressure (CP)-score indicator correspond to higher cross-pressure (which empirically corresponds to low variance in the predicted probabilities).

In the first step, one estimates a regression model to assess the associations between the independent variables that are the source of cross-pressure (in my case, socio-demographic variables) and a dependent variable. Like Brader, Tucker and Therriault (2014), I focus on the reported vote choice as a dependent variable, thus assessing cross-pressure with respect to citizens' vote choices. Brader, Tucker and Therriault (2014), who operationalize group-based cross-pressure in different countries and partisan settings, use logistic regression to estimate a vote-choice model in a two-party context and rely on multinomial logit models in cases of multiparty competition. I proceed in the same way and estimate logistic regression models for the United States and multinomial logistic regression models in the other seven countries. Furthermore, in line with how I proceeded for the estimation of vote-choice models in the first part of this book, I restrict the choice options to parties that received the support of at least 2 per cent of the respondents in an election sample.

Important decisions in the estimation step have to be taken in terms of what variables to include and which to exclude from the regression model. In this regard, Brader, Tucker and Therriault (2014) warn that when researchers want to use the indicator to draw comparisons between countries or to conduct longitudinal analyses, the question of which demographic variables to include in the estimation is in fact the question that is 'most acute.' In particular, they caution that 'when major social cleavages that are highly relevant to politics are omitted, the reliability of the measure is compromised' (Brader, Tucker and Therriault, 2014: 14). I take these concerns seriously and include in the estimations all socio-demographic variables that were also used in Chapter 3. This implies that I rely on a combination of old and new cleavages, accounting for the role of class or income, religion, urbanization, gender, age, and education.[1] And, in line with how I proceeded in Chapter 3, regional cleavages are accounted for in countries that are marked by a strong regional divide. In the United States, furthermore, I account for the role of race. Within each country, the same variables are relied on for each election over time. Given that indicators—but also what cleavages are politically salient—vary between countries, the estimates cannot be directly compared across contexts. My interest, however, is in documenting changes in cross-pressures over time and the correlates of these CP scores within each of the eight democracies analysed here.

As a second step, the estimations from the regression models are used to obtain the predicted probabilities associated with each outcome option; that is, when estimating a multinomial logit model predicting voting for parties A,

---

[1] It could be theorized that several of these socio-demographic characteristics should be interacted to account for the possibility that the effects of different identities interact. Because the number of parties included in the estimation is sometimes large and the number of respondents in each cell is limited, however, I mostly focus on main effects. The exception is the interaction between income and education, which is systematically included for estimations in countries where no measure of self-identification with a social class is available. Previous work has shown that the interaction between income and education approximates class differences (Kitschelt and Rehm, 2019).

B, and C, one subsequently obtains—for each respondent—the probabilities, based on the estimation, of voting for parties A, B, and C.

The third step is to assess the variance in individuals' predicted probabilities to support different parties. This can be done in different ways, with a focus on the full distribution of predicted probabilities to voting for each outcome option or a more restricted number of parties. Brader, Tucker and Therriault (2014: 35) point out that this choice boils down to 'a conceptual question: which parties truly matter to the respondent's decision making process?' As a general approach, I focus on variation between the two highest predicted probabilities—which corresponds to the 'top-2 variance' method of Brader, Tucker and Therriault (2014). I do so because, conceptually, as soon as a voter hesitates between two parties they should be more likely to switch votes. Furthermore, focusing on the top two parties only should limit the impact of supply-side change, and an increase in the number of parties in particular, on the measure. Empirically, Brader, Tucker and Therriault (2014) also show that cross-pressures that rely on different approaches to examine variance (i.e. considering all parties or different levels of selectivity) are all highly correlated. I also validate that the main results that are presented in this book hold when making a different coding decision for the calculation of variance. As shown in Appendix M, the results are substantively similar when considering all parties.

When the variation between predicted probabilities is calculated, the final step that Brader, Tucker and Therriault (2014) propose is to rescale the measure to enhance its interpretation. In line with Brader, Tucker and Therriault (2014), I scale the measure in such a way that it ranges between 0 and 1, with 1 corresponding to the highest level of cross-pressure. Note that I estimate vote-choice models and calculate variances for each election study separately; to allow for assessing trends in the CP score over time, the scaling is done at the country level.

Brader, Tucker and Therriault (2014) verify the validity of the CP score measure and indicate that groups that we would expect to be more cross-pressured indeed obtain a higher cross-pressure score.[2] To assess the validity of the measure used in this book, and to illustrate this method for obtaining individual-level measures of respondents' group-based cross-pressure, I focus on one election in particular. I select a US election, where the two-party competition simplifies the illustration, and focus on the 2008 presidential election. Table 7.1 shows the results of a logistic regression estimation, with

[2] Focusing on the US context, they confirm—for example—that evangelicals in union households have a higher score on the cross-pressure index than evangelicals in non-union households.

voting for the Democratic presidential candidate Barack Obama versus the Republican candidate John McCain. The estimates in Table 7.1 indicate which socio-demographic groups are more likely to vote for the Democratic candidate than for the Republican. Focusing on the estimates for which the effects are significant, it can be seen that women are significantly more likely to vote for the Democrats, that age has a significant negative effect, that Protestants are less likely to vote Democratic than all other denominational groups, and that Latinos, and especially Black respondents, have a much higher likelihood of voting for Obama than White respondents.

These estimates are then used to obtain individual respondents' predicted probabilities of voting for the different parties, and the difference between these probabilities is used to generate the CP score measure, which is scaled to range between 0 and 1, with higher values corresponding to more cross-pressure. For respondents who have characteristics that consistently push them to vote for either Obama or for McCain, the CP score measure should be close to 0. In contrast, for respondents who have some characteristics that are associated with a vote for the Democrats but other characteristics that pull them to support the Republicans, the value of the CP score should be closer to 1.

Table 7.2 includes information on the socio-demographic profile of a select number of respondents in the 2008 American National Election Studies (ANES) survey, who were included in the estimation in Table 7.1. Respondents have been selected to cover a range of different values on the CP score index, from low, over medium, to a high CP score. The information on the socio-demographic profile of these respondents, and the associated CP scores, indicate that the measure is behaving as we would expect. For example, the respondent on the first row is female, young, falls in the 'No/other religious denomination' category, lives in the North and is Black, all characteristics that consistently push her to vote for the Democratic party. Given this high level of consistency in the different elements of her social profile, the estimate for the CP score for this respondent is close to zero. On the other hand, the respondent in the penultimate row has a socio-demographic profile that leads to cross-pressure. On the one hand, she is female and Catholic, factors that Table 7.1 associates with a higher likelihood to vote for the Democrats. But she also lives in the South and is White, which are indicators that push towards a vote for the Republican Party. These conflicting influences are reflected in the value of the CP score of this individual, which is close to 1.

The example of the US 2008 presidential election illustrates how the CP score is obtained and what it measures. The indicator, it seems, captures

Table 7.1 Explaining vote choice in the US 2008 presidential election, socio-demographic determinants

	Vote for Democrat
Female	0.295*
	(0.140)
Age	−0.015***
	(0.004)
Income percentile	−0.794
	(0.462)
High school (ref: grade school or less)	−0.724
	(1.256)
Some college (ref: grade school or less)	−2.297
	(1.266)
College (ref: grade school or less)	−1.093
	(1.293)
High school × Income	0.216
	(0.479)
Some college × Income	0.679
	(0.478)
College × Income	0.389
	(0.481)
Catholic (ref: Protestant)	0.434*
	(0.173)
Jewish (ref: Protestant)	2.252***
	(0.669)
Other or none (ref: Protestant)	0.779***
	(0.174)
Lives in a state in the South	−0.636***
	(0.142)
Black (ref: White)	5.602***
	(0.718)
Latino (ref: White)	1.333***
	(0.177)
Intercept	2.737*
	(1.261)
N	1,419
Pseudo-R^2	0.306

Note: Standard errors in parentheses. *$p < 0.05$, **$p < 0.01$, ***$p < 0.001$.

the dynamics of long-term demographics having cross-cutting influences on a voter's choice quite well. I therefore rely on this measure and obtain individual-level estimates of group-based cross-pressures in all elections that are analysed in this book, covering eight countries and spanning several decades of survey data in each country.

Table 7.2 Examples of respondents' socio-demographic profile and their CP score

Sex	Age	Income	Religious denomination	Education	South	Race	Vote choice	CP score
Female	21	0–16 percentile	Other and none	High school	0	Black	DEM	0.0008148
Female	48	34–67 percentile	Jewish	College	0	White	DEM	0.1859461
Male	60	68–95 percentile	Catholic	Some college	1	White	REP	0.5016213
Male	38	34–67 percentile	Protestant	Some college	1	White	REP	0.5019344
Female	66	17–33 percentile	Catholic	High school	1	White	DEM	0.9954302
Male	46	68–95 percentile	Protestant	Some college	1	Hispanic	REP	0.9959439

Note: Estimations of group-based CP score indicator for a selection of respondents in the ANES 2008.

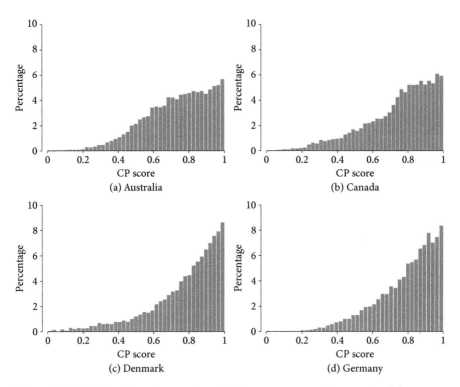

Figure 7.1 Distribution of group-based CP score measure by country (1)

Note: Group-based CP score from election-specific vote-choice models. Details on the variables included in the estimation can be found in Appendix C.

Figures 7.1 and 7.2 show the distributions of this indicator for each of the eight countries analysed and for the full, pooled data sets of surveys in each country. The histograms clarify that there is substantial variation in levels of group-based cross-pressure, with respondents across the range of the scale in each country. It is important to note, however, that the distributions are consistently skewed to the right, indicating that there are more high cross-pressured individuals than low cross-pressured respondents. In terms of the differences between countries, it is not surprising to note that there are more high cross-pressured respondents in countries with more parties. With more parties, it is more likely that two or more parties will appeal to voters with a similar socio-demographic profile, which should logically translate in similar predicted probabilities to vote for these parties—and thus to a higher CP score. In Chapter 8 I use this measure, which captures group-based cross-pressures, to evaluate whether levels of cross-pressure have increased over time. In Chapter 9, I also use it to verify whether group-based cross-pressures affect

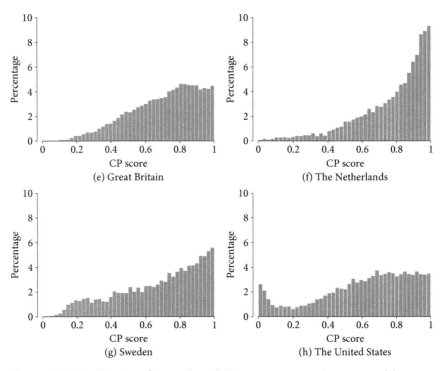

Figure 7.2 Distribution of group-based CP score measure by country (2)

Note: Group-based CP score from election-specific vote-choice models. Details on the variables included in the estimation can be found in Appendix C.

the role of other variables in the funnel of causality. For that test, I additionally construct a similar measure of cross-pressure based on respondents' short-term political preferences; that is, I follow the same steps to estimate an individual's level of cross-pressure but include different independent variables in the estimation stage (i.e. not respondents' socio-demographic group characteristics). Before proceeding with the main empirical analyses, however, I examine the CP score measure in a bit more depth, with a focus on the main measure of group-based cross-pressures.

Brader, Tucker and Therriault (2014), who study group-based cross-pressures, conducted a series of important additional analyses to validate their measure. They show that the measure is useful in the two-party setting of the United States as well as in the multiparty Polish context. They also present evidence that methodological choices—such as the decision how many parties to include in the estimation of the vote-choice model—do not strongly influence the scores. Furthermore, they find that their cross-pressure scores correlate with the partisan heterogeneity of a respondent's social network. Finally, their measure of cross-pressure appears to correlate in expected ways with indicators of political participation and engagement. These empirical analyses all strengthen the confidence in the applicability of the measure. In the following sections, I take some additional steps and present the results of a series of analyses that serve to clarify what it means to be cross-pressured based on one's socio-demographic characteristics.

7.3 How cross-pressured voters motivate their vote

In a first step, I verify whether the measure indeed taps the extent to which voters' choices are bound by structures and their membership of specific social groups.

To do so, I examine whether citizens who are more cross-pressured provide different reasons to motivate their choice for a party. I specifically want to find out whether being cross-pressured correlates with voters indicating that their membership of particular social groups motivates their vote choice. The expectation is that those who are more cross-pressured, based on their socio-demographic characteristics, receive less 'guidance' from their membership of social groups.

To shed light on this issue, I rely on open-ended questions asking voters to indicate the main reasons for their vote choice. Such questions are not widely relied on in electoral research, and critics of this type of questions argue that citizens are not aware and able to identify the real motivations of their behaviour (Nisbett and Wilson, 1977). However, other work indicates that this type of open-ended question provides useful and complementary information to that of closed-ended questions and is helpful for identifying different subgroups of voters (Blais, Martin, and Nadeau, 1998; Blumenstiel and Plischke, 2015; Lefevere, 2011; Marien, Dassonneville, and Hooghe, 2015).

Here, I use the information from such open-ended questions to cross-validate the measure of group-based cross-pressure. If the CP score index that is used in this book indeed taps the extent to which voters' choices are bound by their membership of social groups, the expectation is that voters who motivate their choices by specifically referring to social groups are less cross-pressured than those who do not.

For this analysis, I focus on the German case, which provides—for different election years—information on citizens' self-reported reasons for voting for the party of their choice. In particular, I make use of the 2002, the 2009, and the 2013 German Election Study data sets, which each include a similar set of precoded variables summarizing respondents' answers to the following open-ended question:

> And why did/will you vote for this party? Please tell me the reasons most important to you.

Respondents' answers were coded and categorized, in between three (in 2009 and 2013) and ten (in 2002) separate variables that capture the different motivations respondents indicate guided their party choice. These categories include a variety of motivations, relating to specific policies, local candidates, leaders, strategic considerations, or performance evaluations. From the list of precoded motivations, I selected the reasons listed in Table 7.3 as indicative of voters being bound by structure. These motivations relate to the different cleavages, including class differences, religion, and place of living—such as the contrast between East and West.

To test whether voters who motivate their choice by mentioning heuristics that reflect that they are 'bound by structure' are less cross-pressured, I create—for each of the three German data sets—a dichotomous variable that captures whether or not a respondent mentions one of the motivations in Table 7.3 when asked for the reason of their vote choice. That way, I distinguish between respondents who motivated their decision by referencing a group or structure (coded as 1) and those who do not (coded as 0). In each election survey, between 5 and 10% of all respondents motivate their vote choice by referring to one of the reasons listed in Table 7.3. In 2002, 196 (8.0 per cent) of respondents are coded as group deciders; in 2009, 249 (5.8 per cent) are

Table 7.3 Selected vote-choice motivations

Reason	Year(s) included
Party represents workers/trade unions	2002
Represents workers/trade unions/common people	2009
Represents workers/simple citizens	2013
Party supports the middle class	2002, 2013
Party supports business people	2002
Supports middle class/small and medium-sized businesses	2009
Party of the Eastern part	2002, 2009
Regional political party	2013
Christian	2002
Christian/religious	2009, 2013

coded as group deciders, and in 2013, there are 99 (6.7 per cent) coded as group deciders.

I then calculated respondents' cross-pressure score, following the steps presented in section 7.2. The set of demographic variables used to construct the measure of cross-pressure are: religious denomination, urban–rural character of the place of living, gender, age, level of education, and a dummy variable to distinguish between East and West.[3] For each election survey, the CP score measure was standardized to run from 0 (least cross-pressured) to 1 (most cross-pressured). On average, the CP score of respondents in these three election surveys is 0.522 in 2002, 0.566 in 2009, and 0.614 in 2013.

If the CP-score indicator indeed captures the extent to which voters' choices are bound by their membership of social groups, we should see that, on average, the category of self-motivated group deciders are less cross-pressured than those who do not motivate their voting choice by referencing a specific group. Figure 7.3 offers support for this expectation. In each of the three election surveys that are analysed here, respondents who motivate their voting decision by mentioning one of the heuristics listed in Table 7.3, on average, have a lower CP score than those who do not offer a group motivation for their vote choice.

Admittedly, Figure 7.3 shows a correlation between the indicator of group-based cross-pressures and the self-reported measure of group motivations for electoral choices that is far from perfect. And the difference between the two groups is not significant in 2013. That is not entirely surprising, given the limitations of open-ended questions as well as the limited number of precoded answer options that fit the idea of group-based voting decisions. Still, the association between the two indicators is in the expected direction. These results offer suggestive evidence of the CP score measure tapping the extent to which voters' choices are bound by their membership of social groups. The CP score measure, these analyses suggest, has face validity.

7.4 How cross-pressured voters evaluate parties

Having introduced the CP score measure, and having shown that the measure correlates with the extent to which voters motivate their choice by referring to specific social groups, I now explore in more detail how the CP score correlates with different types of attitudes towards parties. By doing so, I gain more insights in the meaning of feeling cross-pressured for voters.

---

[3] Given that much information is missing on the income variable in 2009, income or its interaction with education are not included in the estimations.

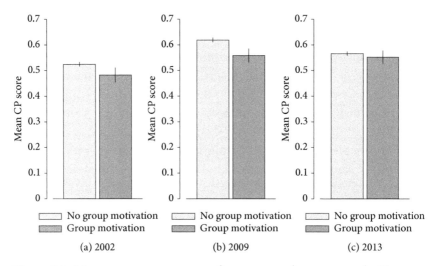

Figure 7.3 Mean cross-pressure score for group- and non-group-deciders

Note: Bars indicate the mean CP score by group. The light grey bars indicate the mean for the group not motivating their vote by referring to groups, the dark grey bars indicate the group that does motivate their vote through references to groups. The spikes on top of the bars indicate 95 per cent confidence intervals.

The purpose of the indicator of Brader, Tucker and Therriault (2014: 28) is to capture the distinction between individuals whose 'intersecting social identities combine to push them largely in one political direction while others' social identities leave them buffeted by conflicting impulses'. By considering the extent to which individuals' socio-demographic characteristics are predictive of their vote choice, the measure indeed taps whether their membership of different social groups leads them to support one party in particular.

A feeling of cross-pressure between parties and not being pushed to support one party in particular, however, can correspond to rather different empirical realities. A first option is that voters do not prefer any of the parties. Lacking a party preference, their socio-demographic characteristics will not discriminate between their support for the parties on offer. A second option is that cross-pressured voters consider voting for multiple parties. In this case, their lack of decidedness between parties is driven by multiple parties appearing as valid options to support.

Both options of what it means to be cross-pressured are plausible and might, to some extent, be at play, but the implications of these two options are rather different. In the first case, a feeling of cross-pressure between parties results in alienation of the political parties; that is, voters who lack a preference generally evaluate all parties less favourably, and their undecidedness thus reflects a lack of enthusiasm towards the party offer in general. In the latter case, a feeling of cross-pressure does not lead to a rejection of all parties but is consistent with voters positively evaluating multiple parties at the same time; that is, voters are ambivalent between multiple parties. In both cases, their socio-demographic characteristics do not push a voter towards one specific party, but their feelings about the other parties differ. Either they have no party preference at all or they prefer multiple parties.

The relative importance of these two options can also shed light on the sources of changes in levels of cross-pressure over time. Observing that cross-pressured voters are more alienated and do not prefer any of the parties would be consistent with their social identities (completely) losing political relevance. If cross-pressured voters are mostly ambivalent, in contrast, and positively rate multiple parties, that would be more in line with the idea that different social identities become political salient, resulting in voters equally considering different parties.

In other words, feeling cross-pressured can mean that citizens are alienated from all parties or that they are ambivalent between two or multiple options. These two types of attitudes towards the parties—alienation and ambivalence—have been thoroughly studied in the literature, mostly in connection to voter turnout (Adams, Dow, and Merrill, 2006; Johnston, Matthews, and Bittner, 2007; Yoo, 2010). These attitudes are often conceptualized in terms of the spatial positions of voters and parties (Adams and Merrill III, 2003; Plane and Gershtenson, 2004; Navarrete, 2020), though there is also work that relies on party evaluations, thermometer ratings, or like/dislike ratings of the parties to measure citizens' alienation from parties and ambivalence (Çakır, 2022; Dassonneville and Hooghe, 2018; Johnston, Matthews, and Bittner, 2007). Here, I rely on this latter strategy to verify whether and to what extent cross-pressured voters are alienated from the parties on offer or ambivalent between multiple parties.

For this analysis, I rely on the data from the European Election Study (EES) voter surveys. This implies that the analyses only focus on a subset of five European democracies (Denmark, Germany, Great Britain, the Netherlands, and Sweden). But for these five countries, the EES provides comparable measures of respondents' ratings of the different parties in seven election surveys between 1989 and 2019.[4] In particular, since 1989, the EES voter surveys include a battery of items asking respondents to indicate their probability of

---

[4] The exception is Sweden, which has only been a part of the EES since 1999 and which thus provides data for five elections.

ever voting for the different parties on offer. The items are commonly referred to as PTV-measures (i.e., measures of respondents' self-reported 'propensity to vote' for a specific party) (Paparo, De Sio, and Brady, 2020; van der Eijk, 2002). The question reads as follows:

> Some people always vote for the same party. Other people make up their minds each time. Please tell me for each of the following how probable it is that you will ever vote for this party in general elections.

The answer options on this question range between 0 and 10,[5] and respondents were asked to rate about eight different parties on average. Using respondents' answers on these questions, I create two different indicators of their answer patterns, which are related to respondents' levels of alienation and ambivalence, respectively.

As a first indicator, I use the maximum rating that a respondent gives to any of the parties. Alienation refers to 'how far the respondent is from his or her closest party' (Johnston, Matthews, and Bittner, 2007: 737). To ease the interpretation of the effects, I focus on the maximum PTV, which reflects how convinced they are about their most preferred party, and which can thus be interpreted the reverse of their alienation. The maximum PTV score that respondents give to a party is generally quite high. For the five countries analysed here, the average PTV score given to the best-rated party is 8.49, and the median score given to that party is 9. If feelings of cross-pressure reflect a lack of enthusiasm about parties more generally, the expectation is that cross-pressured voters will give a lower PTV score to their most preferred party.

The second indicator serves as an operationalization of how ambivalent respondents are between multiple parties. To capture whether and to what extent voters indicate hesitation between at least two parties, I focus on the difference in ratings between respondents' highest rated parties. Conceptually, the measure thus captures the reverse of ambivalence. There is quite some variation in the extent to which voters differentiate between their first and second most preferred parties. On average, the difference between the highest- and second-highest-rated party in the sample is 2.79 (on 0–10 scales); the median difference is two points. If feelings of cross-pressure mostly result in voters considering multiple parties (rather than a single party), we should see that

---

[5] In 1989, 1999, and in 2004, for all countries but Sweden, answer options ranged between 1 and 10. These scales have been recoded to range from 0 to 10 as well.

the difference between the first- and second-highest-rated party is smaller for high cross-pressured voters.

To test these expectations, I first have to operationalize cross-pressures in the EES data. Luckily, all surveys include the necessary information on respondents' socio-demographic characteristics to capture their level of group-based cross-pressure. I follow the approach presented earlier, starting with the estimation of multinomial regressions of the vote choice. As a dependent variable, I focus on respondents' reported vote in the most recent legislative election in their country.[6] To operationalize group-based cross-pressures, I estimate vote-choice models that account for respondents' gender, age, level of education, self-reported social class, religious denomination, and the level of urbanization of their place of living. Appendix N offers details on the operationalization of all socio-demographic variables.

I examine the associations between group-based cross-pressures, the maximum rating, and the difference between the first and second most preferred party. I estimate ordinary least-squares (OLS) models and focus on one country at a time. I account for differences over time by including year fixed effects in the models.

In a first set of OLS models, I explain the maximum PTV rating respondents give to parties. The independent variable of interest is an individual's cross-pressure score—coded from 0 (the least cross-pressured) to 1 (the most cross-pressured). The results of these analyses are visually presented in Figure 7.4. The results indicate that in three of the five countries, higher levels of cross-pressure are associated with significantly lower ratings of voters' most preferred party. In Great Britain and Sweden, the difference between low and high cross-pressured voters is not statistically different from zero. But even in Denmark, Germany, and the Netherlands, where effects are significant, the substantive size of the effects is very small. Compared to the least cross-pressured voters, the most cross-pressured in Denmark, Germany, and the Netherlands on average rate their most preferred party about 0.3 points lower. Considering that ratings range between 0 and 10, this is a small effect. Overall, these results offer few indications that a feeling of cross-pressure leads to a general lack of enthusiasm about the parties on offer.

Turning to the connection between cross-pressure and ambivalence, I estimate a second set of models, again using OLS. The dependent variable in these models is the difference, in scale points, between a respondent's first- and second-most-preferred party. The main independent variable is again respondents' cross-pressure score. The models include year fixed effects and, to account for floor and ceiling effects based on how positively respondents

---

[6] In line with how I proceeded for the longitudinal analysis, I restrict the choice options to parties that received the support of at least 2 per cent of the respondents in an election sample.

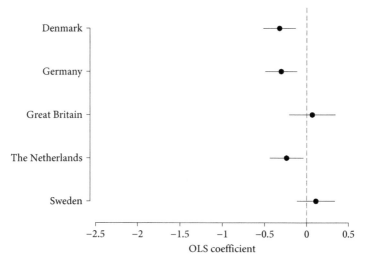

Figure 7.4 Cross-pressures and the most preferred party

Note: Estimates from five country-specific OLS models. Estimated effect of group-based cross-pressure and 95 per cent confidence intervals are shown. The models also include year fixed effects. For the full results, see Appendix N.

generally evaluate parties, I also include respondents' maximum PTV score in the models.[7] Figure 7.5 summarizes the results by focusing on the coefficient for the effect of the CP score measure.

The results are indicative of a strong connection between cross-pressured scores and the extent to which voters differentiate between parties. In each of the five countries, the most cross-pressured distinguish significantly less between their most-preferred and second-most-preferred party than the least cross-pressured. These effects, furthermore, are substantively quite important. In Great Britain, the most cross-pressured rate their most-preferred and second-most-preferred party almost a full point closer than the least cross-pressured. In the other countries, the effects are even larger, exceeding 1.5 points in Denmark and Germany.

Combined, the results of these analyses are suggestive of group-based cross-pressures leading voters to consider more than one party. Voters' appreciation for their most preferred party is not substantively different for the least or the most cross-pressured. But the latter group does consider more parties. Cross-pressured voters' multiple identities thus make it harder for them to identify which is 'their' party.

---

[7] Not including this control leads to the same substantive results.

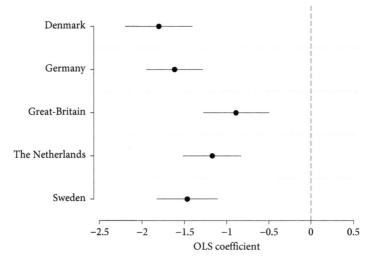

Figure 7.5 Cross-pressures and differences between parties
Note: Estimates from five country-specific OLS models. Estimated effect of group-based cross-pressure and 95 per cent confidence intervals are shown. The models also include year fixed effects and a control for the maximum PTV score. For the full results, see Appendix N.

7.5 Summary and implications

The strong and continued increase in electoral volatility is suggestive of a rather fundamental change in the ways citizens vote and decide what parties and candidates to support. The first part of this book has shown that this change cannot be characterized as a consequence of a shift in importance from long-term to short-term determinants of the vote. As an alternative explanation, I argue that we should turn back to the cleavages that used to guide voters choices and study the weakening of group memberships that traditionally bound voters' choices. In short, I theorize that voters' choices are less constrained by group memberships now, and this change accounts for the surge in electoral volatility in many democracies.

Constraint in voters' political choices, I argue, is provided by individuals' memberships of different socio-demographic groups and how closely those groups are associated with specific political parties. If group memberships do not strongly guide voters' choices, they will be more cross-pressured between parties, resulting in more volatile political behaviour. To capture this concept, I propose relying on the CP-score indicator that Brader, Tucker and Therriault (2014) introduced. This indicator provides an empirical estimate of the extent to which voters—based on their social characteristics—discriminate between parties.

In this chapter, I provided more information on how this indicator is constructed before examining the validity of the indicator as a tool to test my theoretical argument. First, I verified whether the CP score index correlates with how citizens motivate their vote choice when asked to do so. Encouragingly, I find that voters who refer to the party of their choice representing the interests of specific social groups are less cross-pressured than those who indicate that their choice is motivated by other reasons.

Using EES data, I also showed that these cross-pressures are not strongly associated with a lack of enthusiasm towards parties, meaning cross-pressures do not lead to alienation from institutional political parties. Rather, cross-pressured citizens evaluate multiple parties more similarly, suggesting they are truly considering more parties than voters who do not feel cross-pressured based on their socio-demographic characteristics. The socio-demographic characteristics and social identities of cross-pressured voters, in other words, results in them being available to be swayed to vote for multiple parties.

Having introduced the measure that will be used to capture group-based cross-pressures, and having shed more light on what the measure captures, in Chapter 8 I examine over-time change in levels of cross-pressures. I seek an answer to the question of whether feelings of cross-pressure have increased over time—as I theorize.

8
Increasingly cross-pressured

Having introduced the concept of group-based cross-pressures, and having presented the measure that is used to capture cross-pressures, I now turn to using this measure to test the implications of my theoretical argument.

I suggest that changes in electoral behaviour, and the trend towards higher levels of electoral volatility in particular, result from a change in the extent to which voters' choices are bound by their membership of social groups. That decline in the extent to which voters' choices are constrained should lead to an increase in electorates' levels of group-based cross-pressure. I also expect that such a change will have implications for the roles of other determinants of the vote choice, which will be less anchored by citizens' socio-demographics.

This chapter focuses on the first expectation and examines whether there is evidence of an over-time change in the constraining role of individuals' social characteristics on their voting decisions. Using the cross-pressure (CP)-score indicator that was introduced in Chapter 7, I assess change over time in voters' levels of group-based cross-pressure. For doing so, I again use longitudinal election survey data from the eight established democracies that are the focus of this book.

In a first step, I simply examine the bivariate association between group-based cross-pressures and time. Given that change over time can be the result of period effects that affect all voters roughly to the same extent or by the entry of younger generations that differ in their level of cross-pressure, I then seek to disentangle these two dynamics. In a next step, I try to isolate changes at the voter level from a simultaneous change at the demand-side level; the increase in the number of parties. Finally, I complement the analyses using a CP score measure with an assessment of change in levels of ambivalence—which I have shown in Chapter 7 correlates strongly with group-based cross-pressure.

8.1 Cross-pressures over time

To serve as a plausible source of the rise in electoral volatility, levels of cross-pressure should have increased over time—in particular, in those countries that have seen a strong surge in levels of party switching. To study change over time, I focus on describing trends in levels of group-based cross-pressure in Australia, Canada, Denmark, Germany, Great Britain, the Netherlands, Sweden, and the United States.

For each survey that could be included, I followed the steps outlined in Chapter 7 in order to obtain a group-based cross-pressure score for each individual respondent in the survey. I repeat the steps for each election and 8 countries, for a total of 124 election years. As indicated in Chapter 7, I calculate respondents' CP score with a focus on the role of their socio-demographic characteristics.

As a first way to examine change over time, I summarize the results by means of a series of graphs that show the distribution in the group-based CP score in each election sample by means of a ridgeline plot, showing the densities of the distribution in the CP score measure for each election. The density plots also include a vertical line—which indicates the median value for that specific survey. In each country graph, as one moves from the bottom to the top, the distributions for more recent elections are shown. These plots allow change in the median CP score in each of the countries over time to be visually assessed, while also indicating how much variation there is in the extent to which citizens' social group memberships cause conflict between different parties.

Figures 8.1, 8.2, 8.3, and 8.4 present the ridgeline plots. Each of these figures includes the distributions of two of the eight countries. This visualization of the distributions of the CP score measure by election illustrates over-time change. To interpret these figures, I invite readers to look at the results for one country at a time. Take, for example, the ridgeline plot for Denmark (panel c in Figure 8.2). The bottom graph in this plot shows the density distribution of CP score measure for the 1971 survey. For this survey, the distribution is fairly flat, with respondents across the range of the CP score measure. As one moves up and assesses the distribution of the CP score measure for more recent elections, the shape of the distribution changes. In the Danish case, this change is reflected in a shift of the median value (i.e. the vertical lines) to higher levels and distributions that become more skewed towards higher values. Each of these eight plots thus summarizes how group-based cross-pressures are distributed within surveys and how these distributions have changed over time.

The results that are summarized in Figures 8.1, 8.2, 8.3, and 8.4 are generally in line with my expectations. First, with the exception of the United States, in all countries, a trend can be discerned whereby the median CP score moves

CROSS-PRESSURES OVER TIME 143

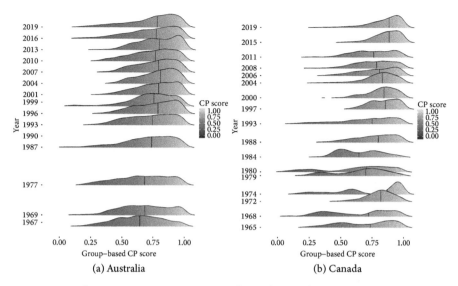

Figure 8.1 Change in CP scores in Australia and Canada

Note: Group-based CP score measures are calculated as explained in chapter 7. Details on the variables included in the estimation can be found in Appendix C.

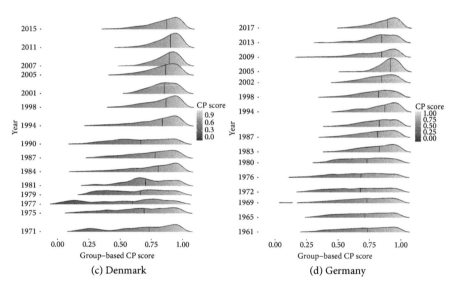

Figure 8.2 Change in CP scores in Denmark and Germany

Note: Group-based CP score measures are calculated as explained in chapter 7. Details on the variables included in the estimation can be found in Appendix C.

144 INCREASINGLY CROSS-PRESSURED

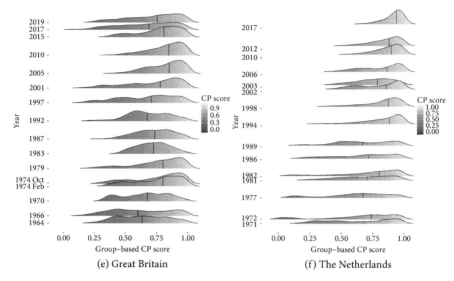

Figure 8.3 Change in CP scores in Great Britain and the Netherlands

Note: Group-based CP score measures are calculated as explained in chapter 7. Details on the variables included in the estimation can be found in Appendix C.

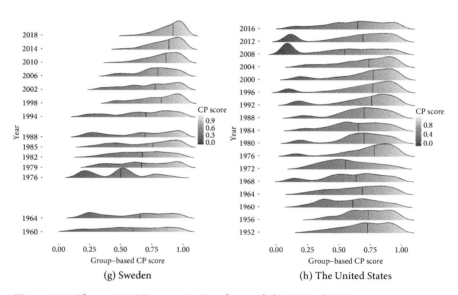

Figure 8.4 Change in CP scores in Sweden and the United States

Note: Group-based CP score measures are calculated as explained in chapter 7. Details on the variables included in the estimation can be found in Appendix C.

to the right. This indicates that the median CP score of respondents in these election surveys increases over time.

The increase is smaller in the majoritarian countries than in the proportional European democracies. Still, even in Australia and Canada, the average CP score is about 0.1 points higher in recent elections than in the early elections for which the scores can be calculated. Looking at the lines that indicate the median CP score value for Australia in Figure 8.1, it increases from 0.65 in 1967 to 0.78 in 2019. Assessing the distribution more generally, it is also clear that there are more respondents with a high CP score in recent elections (light colours in the plots) than in elections in the 1960s and 1970s. For Canada as well, the distribution of the CP scores in Figure 8.1 are clearly more skewed to the right in recent elections than at the start of the time series. For Canada, the median CP score in 1965 was 0.74, which increased to 0.88 in 2019. In Great Britain, CP scores in recent elections are at a higher level than in elections in the 1960s (see the left-hand plot in Figure 8.3). The median value for the 1964 election was 0.62, while it was 0.74 in the 2019 election sample. The trend is clearly not linear, however, and in 2017, for example, CP scores were lower than in elections in the 2000s. This is perhaps not entirely surprising, given that the 2017 UK general election was marked by a reversal of a long-term decline in the dominance of the Conservative and Labour parties (Fieldhouse et al., 2020).

The increase in citizens' estimated level of cross-pressure between countries is strongest in the four countries in continental Europe: Denmark, Germany, the Netherlands, and Sweden. In each of these countries, the ridgeline plots suggest a gradual but consistent shift towards higher levels of group-based CP scores over time. In Denmark, the median CP score increases from 0.74 in 1971 to 0.87 in the most recent election included. The plot for Denmark in Figure 8.2 also clarifies that low CP scores are only found in elections before the mid-1990s. In Germany (right-hand plot in Figure 8.2), CP scores rose from 0.73 on average for elections in the 1960s to 0.89 in the 2017 election. The skew of the distributions also clearly shifts to the right in Germany, which indicates that there are many more high cross-pressured respondents in recent election surveys. In the Netherlands, cross-pressures were at their lowest levels in the late 1970s and early 1980s, with median CP scores of 0.68 and 0.72 for the 1977 and 1981 elections, respectively (see the right-hand plot in Figure 8.3). This contrasts sharply with the median CP score for the 2017 election, which is 0.94—corresponding to a 0.26-point increase in the CP score. Assessing the distributions, the ridgeline plot for the Netherlands shows a shift from CP scores across the range of values in the early elections to a concentration of high CP scores in recent elections. Finally, median CP scores consistently increased in Sweden as well. Panel g in Figure 8.4 shows a sharp difference between CP scores for elections in the 1960s (median value of 0.60) and elections in the 2010s (median value of 0.87). Here as well, the distribution changes from a fairly even distribution across the range of values to a distribution that is skewed towards high CP scores.

In other words, in the four continental European countries, where the surge in median levels of cross-pressure is the strongest, the ridgeline plots also show a decrease in variation in CP scores. Not only are voters in these countries generally more cross-pressured between parties, but the CP scores from all voters are also more clustered around the higher median level. This is mostly a result of the fact that there are hardly any voters left with a very low CP score.

The ridgeline plots in Figures 8.1–8.4 are not only suggestive of a trend towards more group-based cross-pressures over time, but the differences between countries also map well onto the differences in levels and increases in volatility observed in Chapter 1 (in particular, Figures 1.2 and 1.3). The countries where electoral behaviour has grown more volatile over time, as captured by a strong increase in the reported level of party switching between elections—are also the countries where the CP scores have increased most strongly. Simultaneously, the United States, which is the only country where there is no discernible trend in CP scores over time, is also the country where there was no growth in party switching between elections. That the increase in CP scores is more moderate in Australia and Canada than what holds for the European countries is also in line with the trends of change in voters' behaviour that were presented in Chapter 1. While trends in between-election switching or campaign deciding were shown to be upwards in these two countries too, the slope of the increase clearly was more moderate than what holds for countries like Germany or Sweden.

The strong similarities in the time trends of party switching, on the one hand, and group-based cross-pressure, on the other, translates in high correlations between the percentage of switchers in an election survey and the median value of the group-based CP score of respondents in that survey. In fact, with the exception of the United States (0.05) and Canada (0.21), the correlations coefficients range between 0.39 and 0.89.[1] The resemblance in over-time trends in voter switching and levels of group-based cross-pressure offer a first indication of the connection between these two concepts.

---

[1] The Pearson correlation coefficient is 0.61 in Australia, 0.59 in Denmark, 0.77 in Germany, 0.61 in Great Britain, 0.39 in the Netherlands, and 0.89 in Sweden.

Overall, the results in Figures 8.1–8.4 are in line with my expectations. They show an increase in levels of group-based cross-pressures in countries characterized by an increase in volatility. This implies that in those countries, based on their socio-demographic characteristics and membership of social groups, voters are increasingly undecided between parties. For seven out of the eight countries analysed here, the trend is upwards, and it is particularly pronounced in the four continental European countries. In these contexts, the patterns depicted in the ridgeline plots are indicative of a rather fundamental change in voters' behaviour. Electoral choices nowadays are less anchored by voters' memberships of social groups and their position on different social cleavages. The fact that trends in CP scores track over-time change in levels of party switching quite well is indicative of the potentially powerful role that group-based cross-pressures play in explaining the rise in electoral volatility that can be observed in many democracies. To offer more than indications, Chapter 10 will more systematically examine the connection between cross-pressures and volatility. Before doing so, however, I tease out the observed increase in cross-pressure a little more.

8.2 Disentangling time effects: Period or generation effects?

Figures 8.1–8.4 indicate that in most countries, the median value of the CP score is at a higher level in recent elections than it was at the start of the time series in the respective countries. This increase can be a result of different time dynamics. In particular, it might be that electorates as a whole have become more cross-pressured over time or that the change is mostly driven by younger generations of voters—who make their voting decisions in a different way than generations before them.

Previous work that has studied changes in voting behaviour, in terms of the importance of long-term determinants or the effects of ideology and issues, has identified generational change as the likely 'engine of change' (van der Brug and Franklin, 2018). This expectation is based on the intuition that citizens' political attitudes and preferences are formed during a formative period of their lives and remain largely stable afterwards (Hooghe, 2004). This period, which is sometimes referred to as citizens' 'impressionable years', is usually traced back to late adolescence or early adulthood (van der Brug and Rekker, 2021). If citizens' political attitudes, values, and their preferences for certain parties indeed are largely stable once they are formed, the expectation would be that the increase in levels of group-based cross-pressures is mostly the result of younger generations—who are more cross-pressured—entering the electorate. Older generations, in contrast, would continue to make choices under considerably lower levels of cross-pressure if change was entirely driven by new generations.

The idea that change is driven by generational replacement implies that it is gradual. Change can be more abrupt, however, if all voters—irrespective of their generation—are affected by it. In this case, differences from one election to the next, from year to year, and from decade to decade are more important than the contrasts between members of different generations. Empirically, such across-the-board changes that affect all voters roughly to the same extent can be described as a change that is driven by period effects.

Few studies have examined empirically to what extent changes in the determinants of voters' choices reflect period or generational effects. To be sure, attention has been given to cohort and generational differences in what determines voters' choices (see, in particular, the special issue edited by van der Brug and Kritzinger, 2012). Franklin, Mackie, and Valen (1992), for example, show that the role of class and religion on the vote is stronger among the oldest generations. Along the same lines, based on an analysis of 'propensity-to-vote' (PTV) measures in the European Election Studies, van der Brug (2010: 599) concludes that 'older generations tend to vote more strongly on the basis of their social position than younger generations'. The findings of Walczak, van der Brug, and de Vries (2012) are also suggestive of differences between generations as they find that socio-demographic variables have more explanatory power on the vote choices of older generations. It should be noted, however, that the observed decline in the predictive power of structural determinants in their analysis is mostly due to a decline in the effect of religion. For the roles of social class and urbanization, Walczak, van der Brug, and de Vries (2012) find more stability across generations. The most comprehensive analysis of generational differences in the determinants of voters' choices is that by van der Brug and Rekker (2021). As they indicate, their study—which focuses on the Dutch case—is the first to disentangle the effects of all three time-related effects in over-time changes in voting behaviour: age, period, and generation. In doing so, their study departs from earlier studies that either could not distinguish between all time effects because of the cross-sectional nature of the data that were employed (Wagner and Kritziger, 2012; Walczak, van der Brug, and de Vries, 2012) or did not account for life-cycle effects when examining differences between generations (Franklin, Mackie, and Valen, 1992; van der Brug and Kritzinger, 2012). Van der Brug and Rekker (2021: 782) argue that this omission is likely to be important because it could imply that generational and life-cycle effects are confounded:

> It is theoretically possible that, as people grow older, socio-structural factors become more important factors in their party choice. The observed differences between cohorts could thus reflect life-cycle effects, rather than generational differences.

The results of van der Brug and Rekker (2021) do not offer strong evidence of the generational change perspective. For religion as well as class, they find no indications that their effects are stronger for the oldest generations. This lack of strong evidence for the idea that structural changes in electoral behaviour are driven by generational replacement aligns well with my earlier work on the Dutch case. Focusing on the roles of age, period, and cohort effects for explaining the increase in volatility in the Netherlands, I also found few indications of cohort effects (Dassonneville, 2013). The Netherlands, however, is just one case. And the trends in the effects of socio-demographic variables in Chapter 3 pointed out that the Netherlands is somewhat of an outlier. In fact, the Netherlands stands out as a case where the decline in the explanatory effect of socio-demographics was particularly strong and sharp. It is therefore important to study the contribution of generational change in a larger number of countries.

It is also important to stress that previous work has focused on change in the effects of specific socio-demographic variables on the vote choice, not on the extent to which the effects of these variables lead voters to feel cross-pressured between parties. In this regard, it is important to point out that van der Brug and Rekker (2021) find that the effect of citizens' level of education on their party preferences is stronger for the youngest generations. Even if the effects of religion or social class on the vote are not weaker for the youngest generations than they are for generations before them, the stability of these effects in combination with the fact that education seemingly affects their vote more—implying that an additional cleavage structures their vote—might cause higher levels of cross-pressure.

With this in mind, I proceed with an analysis that aims to disentangle the role of period and generation effects in the trend in cross-pressure scores in each of the eight countries that is scrutinized in this book. In line with van der Brug and Rekker (2021), these analyses also account for life-cycle effects, which otherwise risk being confounded with differences between younger and older generations. Disentangling age, period, and generation or cohort effects is somewhat of a challenge because of the perfect linear dependency between the two variables (Glenn, 2003; Neundorf and Niemi, 2014). More specifically, with information on the time of a survey and the age of a respondent, we know which birth cohort they are born in (Period − Age = Cohort). This linear dependency of the three time-related variables also implies that their effects cannot be estimated without restricting some parameters. One way to do so is to include a categorical variable instead of estimating effects in a continuous way (Neundorf and Niemi, 2014).

In the analyses that follow, I break the linear dependency by categorizing age and birth cohorts. To capture the effect of age, I distinguish between four age groups; the eighteen to twenty-nine-year-olds, the thirty to forty-nine-year-olds, the fifty to sixty-four-year-olds, and those aged sixty-five and over. To capture the effects of birth cohorts, I distinguish between six groups that capture a common categorization of individuals in the Greatest generation (1910–1924), the Silent generation (1925–1945), Baby-boomers (1946–1964), Generation X (1965–1980), Generation Y (1981–1996) and Generation Z (1997–). The concept of a generation refers to individuals from the same birth cohort or group of cohorts that lived through the same events and that are influenced by these events (Mannheim, 1928). Therefore, the definition and grouping of individuals in certain generations is best done while taking into account the historical and political context in which individuals live. This implies that generations are country-specific. Previous work that focuses on over-time change in specific countries has hence defined generations based on country-specific events (Grasso et al., 2019; van der Brug and Rekker, 2021). To increase the comparability of the estimates between countries, however, here I rely on a common definition of generations across countries. To account for the fact that these generations are not necessarily meaningful or equally meaningful across countries, I also verify whether results hold when not creating large categories but rather focusing on a distinction between five-year birth cohorts instead (see Appendix O).

I use pooled data by country, and estimate ordinary least-squares (OLS) models to explain an individual respondent's group-based CP score. The models include a linear effect for year (i.e. election years), the categorical age variable, and the categories to distinguish between generations. It should be noted that Sweden is excluded from these analyses because detailed information on the age and birth year of respondents is only included in a limited number of the Swedish election surveys.[2]

Before proceeding with the results of the analysis of the effects of age, periods, and generations, I invite readers to take another look at the patterns of change that are shown in Figures 8.1–8.4. These show quite some variation from one election to the next. Furthermore, in the countries that are characterized by an increase in levels of cross-pressure, the increase is often quite sharp. The strength of the increase in levels of cross-pressure over time is also evident from the OLS models in Table 8.1. In these initial models, I only include a continuous year measure as an independent variable, which provides an estimate of how much the group-based CP score—on average—changes each year in the eight countries for which I have data. In line with the trends that could be observed in Figures 8.1–8.4, the estimates in Table 8.1 show no indications of a growth in cross-pressures in the United States. In the other countries, the coefficient on the year variable suggests a significant increase in levels of cross-pressure over time. There are indications of a substantially small increase in levels of cross-pressure in Great Britain. The increase is also rather modest in Australia and Canada, where the CP score is estimated to increase by 0.02 and 0.03, respectively each decade. The estimated increase in cross-pressure is more sizeable in Germany. More specifically, the coefficient of 0.004 implies that cross-pressure on average increases by 0.1 every twenty-five years. In line with what the ridgeline plots suggested, the surge in cross-pressure is strongest in Denmark, the Netherlands, and Sweden. In these countries, the CP score—which has a theoretical minimum of 0 and a maximum of 1—increases by almost 0.1 every fifteen years. These patterns do not mesh well with the idea of a gradual process of change that is driven by younger generations. It is, of course, possible that even though not every subsequent generation is more cross-pressured, specific generations have contributed to meaningful changes in levels of cross-pressure.

To disentangle to what extent the changes over time are the result of generational change or of more general period effects affecting all voters, Table 8.2 presents the results of a series of models that use OLS estimation and that include as independent variables a continuous year variable, a categorical age variable, and a series of generation dummies. As indicated before, Sweden is

---

[2] The publicly available data sets of the Swedish Election Studies generally include a precoded variable of respondents' age group rather than a continuous age variable. This implies not only that the age groups cannot be constructed in a similar way as for the other countries but also that many respondents cannot be categorized to the different generations based on their estimated birth cohort either.

Table 8.1 Explaining CP score, change over time

	Australia	Canada	Denmark	Germany	Great Britain	The Netherlands	Sweden	United States
Year	0.002***	0.003***	0.006***	0.004***	0.001***	0.006***	0.006***	−0.001***
	(0.000)	(0.000)	(0.000)	(0.000)	(0.000)	(0.000)	(0.000)	(0.000)
Intercept	−3.465***	−6.076***	−11.228***	−6.223***	−1.058***	−10.269***	−11.208***	2.900***
	(0.154)	(0.139)	(0.218)	(0.146)	(0.145)	(0.184)	(0.146)	(0.162)
N	23,434	26,934	20,214	17,886	30,936	20,466	29,168	22,620
R^2	0.035	0.089	0.162	0.132	0.005	0.172	0.173	0.008

Note: Robust standard errors in parentheses. * $p < 0.05$, ** $p < 0.01$, *** $p < 0.001$.

Table 8.2 Explaining CP score, age, period, and generation effects

	Australia	Canada	Denmark	Germany	Great Britain	The Netherlands	United States
Year	0.002***	0.004***	0.005***	0.004***	0.000	0.005***	−0.002***
	(0.000)	(0.000)	(0.000)	(0.000)	(0.000)	(0.000)	(0.000)
18–29 (ref.)							
30–49	0.026***	0.015***	0.003	−0.006	0.009*	−0.038***	−0.002
	(0.005)	(0.004)	(0.005)	(0.004)	(0.004)	(0.005)	(0.007)
50–64	0.025***	0.018**	0.002	−0.008	0.022***	−0.068***	0.003
	(0.007)	(0.006)	(0.007)	(0.006)	(0.006)	(0.007)	(0.010)
65+	−0.019*	0.013	−0.026**	−0.010	−0.022*	−0.092***	0.047**
	(0.009)	(0.008)	(0.009)	(0.008)	(0.008)	(0.009)	(0.014)
Greatest generation (ref.)							
Silent generation	0.005	−0.010	0.009	0.005	0.007	0.036***	0.004
	(0.006)	(0.005)	(0.008)	(0.006)	(0.005)	(0.007)	(0.007)
Baby-boomers	0.019*	−0.006	−0.013	0.019*	0.039***	0.070***	0.031**
	(0.008)	(0.007)	(0.010)	(0.008)	(0.007)	(0.009)	(0.011)
Generation X	0.047***	−0.012	0.003	0.022**	0.067***	0.067***	0.001
	(0.010)	(0.009)	(0.011)	(0.009)	(0.009)	(0.011)	(0.016)
Generation Y	0.086***	−0.009	0.023	0.017	0.050***	0.020	−0.024
	(0.012)	(0.012)	(0.014)	(0.012)	(0.012)	(0.013)	(0.021)
Generation Z	0.098***	−0.049*	−0.117**	−0.009	0.017	0.024	0.019
	(0.025)	(0.021)	(0.040)	(0.019)	(0.024)	(0.017)	(0.057)
Intercept	−2.621***	−6.972***	−9.265***	−6.730***	0.505	−9.733***	3.914***
	(0.349)	(0.314)	(0.462)	(0.351)	(0.333)	(0.370)	(0.533)
N	22,576	24,837	13,104	14,604	28,803	18,444	19,997
R^2	0.058	0.107	0.141	0.125	0.023	0.214	0.015

Note: Robust standard errors in parentheses. *$p < 0.05$, **$p < 0.01$, ***$p < 0.001$.

excluded from these analyses. Turning to the estimates in Table 8.2, note that the coefficients on the year variable are very similar to those in Table 8.1. That the estimated annual change in cross-pressure is only slightly affected when life-cycle and generational effects are accounted for in the models implies that the over-time increase in levels of cross-pressure is affecting all voters and is not restricted to the youngest generations.

The estimates capturing age differences in cross-pressure are in expected directions for most countries; that is, the estimates are suggestive of the older—on average—being somewhat less cross-pressured than younger age groups. The negative coefficients are in line with earlier work which argues that there is a pattern of habituation in voters' choices. As voters grow older and participate in more elections, they are increasingly likely to vote for a party they supported previously (Dinas, 2014; Gomez, 2013). Such habituation effects should reduce the extent to which older voters feel cross-pressured between parties. While the sign of the coefficients—for the oldest age group in particular—is in the expected direction in most countries, it only reaches significance in the Netherlands. Furthermore, the exact opposite pattern is found in the United States, where it appears that the oldest age group is *more* cross-pressured than the youngest.

Finally, the estimates in Table 8.2 only offer weak evidence for the expectation that change is driven by generational replacement. Australia is the only country where each new generation appears to be more cross-pressured than the previous one. The estimates for Australia suggest that younger generations are significantly more cross-pressured than the Greatest generation—which serves as the reference category. Furthermore, the size of the coefficients gradually increases with each new generation. In the other countries, there are sometimes important generational differences between generations. The estimates, however, are not consistent with the expectation of a gradual increase in cross-pressure that is driven by generational replacement; that is, some generations have levels of cross-pressure that differ significantly from that of the reference category (the Greatest generation), but there are no indications of each new generation being more cross-pressured than the previous generation. This lack of a clear pattern of generational replacement does not appear to be driven by the definition and operationalization of generations. As shown in Appendix O, focusing on five-year birth cohorts does not show strong evidence of a pattern that corresponds to a process of generational change either. Australia is still the only country where younger cohorts are quite systematically more cross-pressured than older birth cohorts. In addition, even when focusing on the main contrast between older (baby-boomers and older) and newer generations (the generations born after the baby-boom generations), there is not much evidence of generational differences in levels of group-based cross-pressure. More precisely, while there are three countries where young generations are significantly more cross pressured than old generations, the exact opposite pattern is found in two countries (see Appendix O).

Levels of cross-pressure have increased over time in several established democracies. Electorates have grown especially more cross-pressured in the continental European countries that are analysed in this book. Disentangling to what extent this trend towards higher levels of cross-pressure is the result of more general period effects or instead the result of a process of generational replacement offers more evidence for the former type of change. Even though there are differences in cross-pressure between the members of different generations, there are few countries where the surge in cross-pressures appears to be driven by increasingly high levels of cross-pressure in each new generation. That period effects remain present and have a significant effect when accounting for generational differences suggests that the trend towards higher levels of cross-pressure is affecting all voters. Even older generations, who have been socialized in a time when cross-pressures were lower overall, have been affected by the change and are now somewhat more cross-pressured.

The fact that all generations seem to be affected to some extent by a trend towards more cross-pressure suggests that contextual factors are likely to be important in shaping the conditions that lead electorates to feel more cross-pressured. One important contextual source of change that is logically connected to how cross-pressured voters feel is the number of parties a voter can choose from. As party system fragmentation increases, and as the number of viable parties on the ballot increases, the likelihood that a voter will feel cross-pressured between at least two parties should increase. To disentangle to what extent such changes in the supply-side versus changes in voters' attitudes and preferences contribute to the increase in cross-pressure, in section 8.3, I study change over time, while accounting for the role of party system fragmentation.

8.3 Change in cross-pressures and change in supply

The core argument that I make in this book is that the increase in volatility is driven by a change in the extent to which voters' party preferences and electoral choices are anchored in group memberships. The over-time increase in levels of cross-pressure in several countries, especially those where volatility has surged, fits this argument. The extent to which voters will feel cross-pressured between parties, however, is likely not to depend on voters' characteristics only but also on supply-side factors. In particular, in settings where more parties compete for voters' electoral support, the likelihood that an individual will be cross-pressured on average should be higher; that is, the more parties a voter can choose from, the higher the odds that there will be at least two parties that are somewhat close to the voter or that the voter likes for some reason.

Over time, party system fragmentation has increased in Western democracies (for more details, see Appendix P). Such a supply-side change is expected to lead to an increase in electorates' levels of cross-pressure. Of course, the increase in the number of parties that gain representation in parliaments is in part a result of the fact that voters' loyalties to specific parties have decreased. In particular, the increase in cross-pressure and the subsequent decrease in party loyalty may have served as a breeding ground for more party system fragmentation. Still, to isolate the effect of voter-driven change from change that results from a change in the party offer, in Table 8.3, I estimate the effect of time while controlling for the effective number of parties, in terms of vote shares (the Effective number of electoral parties (ENEP) variable in the table).[3]

The estimates in Table 8.3 show that the CP indicator is generally higher when party system fragmentation increases (i.e. the effect of ENEP). The strength of this association varies quite a lot between countries, however, and is only positive and significant in three countries. In Great Britain, the effect of party system fragmentation is particularly strong. For the United States, accounting for a measure of party system fragmentation does not alter the conclusions with regard to the absence of a meaningful trend in group-based CP scores.

In the other countries, and thus in six of the seven countries for which Table 8.1 showed indications of a significant increase in levels of cross-pressure over time, I find continued evidence of an increase in cross-pressure even when accounting for the increasingly varied party offer. In these countries, there is thus evidence of an increase in group-based cross-pressure net of the increase in party system fragmentation—that is, arguably in part driven by voter-level changes. These findings are suggestive of the importance of structural societal changes for explaining changes in electoral behaviour.

---

[3] Information on the effective number of parties, in terms of vote shares, in each election is retrieved from Gallagher's electoral systems website (Gallagher, 2021). For recent elections, the information comes from Döring and Manow (2021).

Table 8.3 Explaining CP score, change over time and the effective number of parties

	Australia	Canada	Denmark	Germany	Great Britain	The Netherlands	Sweden	United States
Year	0.003***	0.002*	0.006***	0.003**	−0.001	0.005***	0.004*	−0.001
	(0.000)	(0.001)	(0.001)	(0.001)	(0.001)	(0.000)	(0.002)	(0.001)
ENEP	−0.040*	0.072	−0.025	0.002	0.131***	0.013*	0.057*	0.065
	(0.015)	(0.035)	(0.020)	(0.016)	(0.026)	(0.005)	(0.025)	(0.050)
Intercept	−5.816***	−3.782*	−11.499***	−6.045**	1.626	−8.979***	−6.645*	3.024*
	(0.822)	(1.514)	(1.882)	(1.719)	(1.021)	(0.753)	(2.924)	(1.188)
N	23,434	26,934	20,214	17,886	30,936	20,466	29,168	22,620
R^2	0.042	0.101	0.165	0.132	0.043	0.179	0.179	0.011

Note: Robust standard errors in parentheses. * $p < 0.05$, ** $p < 0.01$, *** $p < 0.001$.

8.4 Increasingly ambivalent electorates

The trends in cross-pressure scores provide evidence that is in line with my expectations. In several countries, especially in settings where electoral volatility is on the rise, electorates appear to be increasingly cross-pressured between parties.

The CP score measure that is used to study change is empirically constructed and is based on the connection between individuals' socio-demographic characteristics and their likelihood to support different parties. To gain more confidence in the trends, and to verify that the trend in the CP score index reflects real changes in how voters perceive parties and in how determined they are about their choice for one party, I also study change over time while relying on a more direct measure of cross-pressure.

More specifically, I make use of voters' PTV ratings of parties to assess to what extent they clearly prefer a single party or are instead ambivalent between multiple options. In Chapter 7, I showed that the CP score measure is strongly associated with such a measure of ambivalence; that is, for respondents who are more cross-pressured, the difference in ratings of their first- and second-most-preferred parties is significantly smaller. Here, I verify whether, in line with the trends in the CP score measure, we also observe that the difference in PTV scores between voters' first- and second-highest-rated parties decreases over time. Such a trend would be indicative of voters having a harder time distinguishing between the parties on offer, which would be in line with the idea that they are less 'bound' to one party in particular.

In line with how I proceeded in Chapter 7, I rely on data from the European Election Study (EES) voter surveys to examine ambivalence because these surveys measured respondents' attitudes towards parties in a consistent way over time. In particular, EES surveys asked respondents to indicate their probability to vote for each of the parties on a 0–10 scale.[4] The reliance on EES data limits the analyses to the European democracies, hence including the countries where there is most evidence of an increase in group-based cross-pressure.

To capture party ambivalence, I focus on the difference in respondents' ratings of their first and most-preferred party (i.e. the reverse of ambivalence). This variable has a theoretical range between 0 (if a respondent gives the same score to their two most-preferred parties) and 10 (if a respondent gives the maximum rating to one party and scores all other parties at 0).

Table 8.4 shows, for each country and EES survey-year, the mean difference between respondents' first and second-most-preferred parties. Even though the time period that is covered by the EES data is considerably shorter than

---

[4] As indicated previously, sometimes the PTV measures ranged between 1 and 10. For comparability, all measures were rescaled to range between 0 and 10.

Table 8.4 Trend in party ambivalence, EES data

	1989	1994	1999	2004	2009	2014	2019	Trend
Denmark	3.27	2.63	2.70	3.11	2.53	3.12	2.47	↓
Germany	3.76	2.64	3.48	2.96	2.64	3.49	2.71	↓
Great Britain	4.28	2.99	3.01	3.24	2.41	3.59	2.49	↓
The Netherlands	4.00	2.21	2.35	2.54	1.72	2.21	1.88	↓
Sweden	–	–	2.81	1.17	2.45	2.60	2.59	↓

Note: Entries show the average difference between the rating of the top two parties of respondents in survey-years.

the longitudinal election surveys that I used to study trends in group-based cross-pressure, the data point to a reduction in the differences between party evaluations over time. Focusing on the difference between the first and the last year for which there is data, the gap between the first- and the second-most-preferred party shrank by 0.8 points in Denmark, 1.1 points in Germany, 1.8 points in Great Britain, and 2.1 points in the Netherlands. These are quite sizeable differences and are reflective of voters increasingly considering multiple options when deciding whom to vote for. The only country for which there is hardly any evidence of citizens growing increasingly ambivalent is Sweden, but this is also the country for which the EES allows studying change only since 1999.

8.5 Summary and implications

Voters are growing more volatile in many established democracies. While this trend is well documented, there is more uncertainty about the reasons why voters' electoral choices have become more unstable. Previous work has argued that the increase in volatility is due to an overall decline in the explanatory power of long-term factors or due to short-term determinants gaining weight in voters' electoral calculus. As an alternative framework to explain these changes, I draw attention to the connections between different determinants of the vote choice; that is, are different determinants of the vote all pushing a voter towards one specific party or is a voter—based on these determinants—cross-pressured between parties?

A main source of cross-pressure, I have argued in Chapter 7, comes from individuals' memberships of different social groups and hence their positions on the main cleavages in a society. When voters are in a position of cross-cutting cleavages, they lack a group anchor, leading their voting decision to be less constrained overall—increasing the odds of volatility.

To be a plausible explanation of the changes in electoral volatility that are observed, we ought to see a similar trend in the extent to which voters are cross-pressured. The results that are presented in this chapter indeed indicate that voters are more cross-pressured, based on their socio-demographic characteristics, than was the case a few decades ago. There is important variation between countries, however, and it is only in the proportional European countries that there is evidence of a strong increase in group-based cross-pressures.

The increase in cross-pressure, where it occurs, appears to be a phenomenon that is affecting all generations. While members of different generations can be somewhat more or less cross-pressured, there are few countries where the data suggest that the increase in group-based cross-pressure is driven by new generations of highly cross-pressured voters. Even voters who were politically socialized in a time when cross-pressures were low, it seems, now are more cross-pressured between parties. Furthermore, in all countries but Great Britain and the United States, there is evidence of voters being increasingly cross-pressured even when accounting for varying levels of party system fragmentation. While the trend towards more party system fragmentation contributes to electorates growing more cross-pressured, the increase in group-based cross-pressure cannot be explained away by such supply-side changes.

That voters nowadays are more likely to consider multiple options—rather than being bound to a single party—is also a conclusion that can be drawn from trends in voter ambivalence. Over time, it seems, voters differentiate less between their most- and second-most-preferred party, which is consistent with the idea that they are more cross-pressured—at least in the European countries analysed.

In this chapter, I focused mostly on feelings of cross-pressure that arise from voters' socio-demographic characteristics and hence their positions on social cleavages. Theoretically, I argue that group-based cross-pressures matter because they have trickle-down effects throughout the funnel of causality; that is, a voter whose socio-demographic characteristics do not offer them guidance to choose between parties will also lack guidance in terms of their partisanship or in terms of how they evaluate more short-term factors such as issues, leaders, or the economy. The voting decision of a cross-pressured voter, in other words, will be largely unstructured. In Chapter 9, I focus on this part of the theory and study in more depth how factors further down the funnel of causality influence the choices of cross-pressured voters.

9

The impact of cross-pressures

Less constraint

The rise in electoral volatility, I posit, is to a large extent a consequence of the fact that citizens' vote choices have become less 'constrained' over time; that is, there has been a weakening of the extent to which different factors that affect voters' electoral choices all point in the same direction. In Chapter 8, I focused on a major source of this change: an increase in group-based cross-pressures.

The upward trend in citizens' group-based cross-pressures implies that, based on their socio-demographic characteristics, citizens increasingly consider different political parties and are less socially bound to one party in particular. In other words, the direct effects of individuals' socio-demographics are no longer consistently pushing them to one party in particular and instead have cross-cutting influences on their party preference. I have theorized that this change in the role of socio-demographic characteristics, which can be situated at the front end of the metaphorical funnel of causality, is key to explaining volatility. Importantly, however, given the connections between long- and short-term determinants of the vote within a funnel of causality, an increase in group-based cross-pressure should also provoke other changes in the ways in which voters choose parties; that is, the trend towards more group-based cross-pressures at the front end of the funnel should also impact the roles of party attachments and of more short-term determinants on the vote.

More specifically, a lack of constraint in the front end of the funnel of causality will trigger a lack of constraint further down the funnel of causality. First, voters who are cross-pressured, based on their socio-demographic characteristics, should be less likely to develop an attachment with a party. Second, lacking an attachment to a party, these voters' evaluations of short-term influences, such as the state of the economy, party leaders, or specific issues, should be less constrained as well. As a result, these short-term determinants are also less likely to all line up to lead to support for one specific party.

This chapter focuses on the extent to which there is constraint in the role of vote-choice determinants further down the funnel of causality. It specifically

Voters Under Pressure. Ruth Dassonneville, Oxford University Press. © Ruth Dassonneville (2023).
DOI: 10.1093/oso/9780192894137.003.0009

seeks to show that a lack of constraint in terms of voters' socio-demographic group membership leads to less constraint further down the funnel as well. To do so, I examine the association between group-based cross-pressures and partisanship, as well as cross-pressure based on citizens' short-term political attitudes, including their evaluations of the economy, their evaluations of leaders, and their issue positions.

9.1 Cross-pressured voters lack party attachments

One way in which the lack of constraint due to group-based, cross-pressured voters trickles down within the funnel of causality is through its connection with party attachments; that is, for those whose group memberships do not lead to a feeling of cross-pressure, it should be easy to identify which party is 'theirs'. Thus, those voters should more easily identify a political party as being close to them and develop a stronger attachment to that party. Furthermore, in the absence of cross-cutting cleavages, in-group and out-group dynamics—which feature prominently in the work of scholars who conceive of partisanship as a social identity—should be strengthened as well. In contrast, for voters who feel strongly group-based cross-pressures, different parties are considered, leading to lower levels of partisanship and weaker attachments to parties.

To evaluate the association between group-based cross-pressures and party attachments, I make use of the information on individuals' levels of group-based cross-pressure, operationalized as explained in Chapter 7, and connect this to whether or not they identify with a party. As indicated in Chapter 4, party attachments are measured by means of different questions in each of the countries, with some being closer to the original Michigan-style conception of a psychological attachment than others. Furthermore, the measure of group-based cross-pressure is country-specific as well, accounting for cleavages that are important in a particular setting. I therefore analyse the connection between cross-pressure and party attachments within countries and estimate country-specific regression models.

Here, I focus on explaining whether a respondent indicates that they identify with a party (coded as 1) or not (coded as 0). In Appendix Q, I report the results for an alternative measure of partisanship, which also takes into account the strength of party attachments. The results of both sets of analyses are very similar.

To ease the interpretation of the effects, I estimate linear probability models. For each country, I estimate two models, a first model only includes a linear time trend (year) as an independent variable, and a second model additionally accounts for individuals' group-based cross-pressure (CP) score. That way, I control for the gradual decline in levels of partisanship in some countries (cf. Chapter 4), and the comparison between the models allows the extent to which cross-pressures can account for the over-time decline in party attachments to be evaluated.

Tables 9.1 and 9.2 show the results of these estimations. Note, first, that the linear time trend is negatively signed in all countries—hinting at a decrease in the share of the electorate that identifies with a party. However, the size of the effect varies and only reaches significance in four countries (Canada, Denmark, Great Britain, and the United States). This is consistent with what I showed in Chapter 4, indicating that there are signs of a trend of decreasing partisanship across countries but that the decline remains weak. Turning to the effect of group-based cross-pressures, the results in Table 9.1 and 9.2 show that the association between cross-pressures and partisanship is consistently negative. The strength of this association is moderate to strong in six of the countries analysed, and significant at conventional levels.[1] The exceptions are Canada and Germany, countries where the data on party attachment showed either no decline or a rather atypical pattern of growing levels of partisanship in recent elections (see Figures 4.1 and 4.2). In all other countries, the analyses suggest that those who feel more cross-pressured—based on their socio-demographic characteristics—are significantly less likely to indicate that they have an attachment to a party. The results that are reported in Appendix Q indicate a strong connection between group-based cross-pressure and partisan strength[2] as well. In fact, the negative association between group-based cross-pressure and partisan strength only fails to reach a conventional level of significance in Germany.

The coefficients on the CP score measure, as they are reported in Tables 9.1 and 9.2, vary quite a lot. The strongest association is found for Sweden, where the coefficient suggests that the most cross-pressured (a score of 1 on the CP score variable) are twenty-one percentage points less likely to be a partisan than the least cross-pressured (score of 0 on the CP score variable). In Denmark, the effect is strong as well, with eighteen percentage points difference in the likelihood of being a partisan as respondents move from being the least to

---

[1] Readers will note that the R^2 is consistently low in these models, despite the inclusion of the measure of group-based cross-pressure. This highlights that the cross-pressures and partisanship, while related, are empirically distinct concepts.
[2] Coded to range from non-partisan to strong partisan, where 0 = non-partisan, 1 = weak partisan, and 2 = strong partisan.

Table 9.1 Cross-pressures and partisanship (1)

	Australia	Australia	Canada	Canada	Denmark	Denmark	Germany	Germany
Year	−0.000**	−0.000	−0.002***	−0.002***	−0.003***	−0.002***	−0.003***	−0.003***
	(0.000)	(0.000)	(0.000)	(0.000)	(0.000)	(0.000)	(0.000)	(0.000)
Group-based CP score	–	−0.068***	–	−0.052***	–	−0.175***	–	−0.024
		(0.011)		(0.013)		(0.022)		(0.021)
Constant	1.549***	1.315***	4.806***	4.483***	6.602***	4.537***	6.106***	5.953***
	(0.241)	(0.242)	(0.277)	(0.285)	(0.566)	(0.624)	(0.359)	(0.384)
N	23,315	23,315	22,416	22,416	16,717	16,717	15,949	15,949
R^2	0.000	0.002	0.009	0.009	0.007	0.011	0.010	0.010

Note: Robust standard errors in parentheses. * $p < 0.05$, ** $p < 0.01$, *** $p < 0.001$.

Table 9.2 Cross-pressures and partisanship (2)

	Great Britain	Great Britain	The Netherlands	The Netherlands	Sweden	Sweden	United States	United States
Year	−0.001*** (0.000)	−0.001*** (0.000)	−0.002*** (0.000)	−0.001*** (0.000)	−0.004*** (0.000)	−0.002*** (0.000)	−0.001*** (0.000)	−0.001*** (0.000)
Group-based CP score	–	−0.050*** (0.007)	–	−0.156*** (0.021)	–	−0.211*** (0.013)	–	−0.128*** (0.011)
Constant	2.712*** (0.180)	2.673*** (0.180)	4.816*** (0.522)	3.152*** (0.569)	7.599*** (0.360)	5.243*** (0.390)	2.634*** (0.276)	3.002*** (0.279)
N	29,267	29,267	16,529	16,529	27,784	27,784	22,507	22,507
R^2	0.003	0.005	0.004	0.008	0.014	0.023	0.002	0.008

Note: Robust standard errors in parentheses. * $p < 0.05$, ** $p < 0.01$, *** $p < 0.001$.

Table 9.3 Levels of partisanship among the least and most cross-pressured

Country	CP score = 0 (%)	CP score = 1 (%)
Australia	94.3	87.6
	(92.8–95.7)	(86.9–88.3)
Canada	87.1	81.9
	(85.2–89.0)	(81.1–82.7)
Denmark	66.3	48.8
	(62.9–49.7)	(47.6–50.0)
Germany	79.6	77.1
	(76.2–82.9)	(76.1–78.2)
Great Britain	95.8	90.8
	(94.8–96.8)	(90.2–91.3)
The Netherlands	51.7	36.1
	(48.4–54.9)	34.9–37.2)
Sweden	66.0	44.9
	(64.1–67.8)	(43.9–46.0)
United States	79.6	66.8
	(78.2–80.9)	(65.7–67.8)

the most cross-pressured. In the Netherlands, the effect is sixteen percentage points. The effects are more moderate in the other countries, though differences of thirteen percentage points (the United States), seven percentage points (Australia), and five percentage points (Canada and Great Britain) are still meaningful.

Given that average levels of partisanship differ quite a lot between countries, it is useful not only to look at the estimated effect but also to examine predicted levels of partisanship across the range of the CP score variable. To clarify the association between cross-pressure and partisanship, Table 9.3 shows, for each country, the predicted level of partisanship—based on the linear probability models—for respondents at the lowest and highest CP score levels, respectively.

Table 9.3 shows that with the exception of the German case, higher levels of cross-pressure are associated with a substantively important decline in partisanship. Look, in particular, at the strong effects in Sweden. As can be seen from the entries in Table 9.3, respondents who are least cross-pressured (CP score of 0), have a 66 per cent likelihood of reporting a partisan attachment. This likelihood drops to 45 per cent for those who are most cross-pressured. In the Netherlands, the reported levels of partisanship are the lowest of all countries. Here as well, however, the association between group-based cross-pressures and the likelihood of having a party attachment is fairly strong. More specifically, the likelihood of having a party attachment drops from 52 per cent to 36 per cent as respondents move from the lowest to the highest level of group-based cross-pressure. Even in the countries where the effects are more limited, such as Australia, Canada, Great Britain and the United States, Table 9.3 suggests a non-negligible drop in the share of respondents who are partisan as the level of cross-pressure increases.

When comparing the two models for each country in Tables 9.1 and 9.2, it also becomes clear that shifts in levels of cross-pressure explain part of the over-time decline in partisanship. In Denmark, the Netherlands, and Sweden, the coefficients on the year trend weaken when accounting for group-based cross-pressures. This pattern is not consistent, however. In countries like Great Britain, for example, group-based cross-pressures are related as expected with lower partisanship but do not account for over-time changes in levels of partisanship.

Overall, the results in this section are in line with the expectation that a lack of constraint—based on individuals' socio-demographic characteristics—weakens the likelihood that voters indicate that they identify with one party in particular. Importantly, the results also show that the association between group-based cross-pressures and partisanship is far from perfect. This suggests that the indicator of citizens' group-based cross-pressures is not a simple alternative for existing measures of party identification. I would even argue that group-based cross-pressures are a more useful concept to capture the extent to which citizens' vote choices are bound by structures and guided by group memberships. Reported party attachments capture whether citizens feel close to a party at the time of the survey. But how strong that 'anchor' of their partisanship is varies between individuals and depends on their reading and interpretation of the survey question that serves to capture partisanship. Measures of group-based cross-pressures, in contrast, because they do not rely on individuals reporting how much their party preferences are 'bound', are more objective indicators of the role of structure in citizens' choices.

9.2 Group-based cross-pressures and short-term cross-pressures

A second expectation which follows from the argument that a lack of guidance stemming from citizens' social characteristics trickles down in the funnel of causality is that citizens' more short-term preferences and opinions will also constrain their vote less than what holds for low cross-pressured individuals. In other words, the expectation is that group-based cross-pressures will serve as a breeding ground for a lack of constraint in terms of citizens' political attitudes and preferences and ultimately result in a feeling of cross-pressure based on their political views and preferences too.

To assess the validity of this expectation, I continue to rely on the longitudinal election study data from the eight countries analysed in this book. As an independent variable, I use the indicator of a respondent's group-based cross-pressure that was presented in Chapter 7 and used in Chapter 8 to study change over time. In addition, I create a second measure of cross-pressure, this time using information on respondents' political attitudes and preferences. In particular, I rely on information on the two short-term determinants of the vote choice that were also used in Chapter 5; that is, I account for respondents' evaluations of the state of the economy and their evaluations of the party leaders.

Using information on these two sets of indicators, I estimate vote-choice models to predict respondents' party preference through a multinomial regression or a logistic regression in the United States. I then follow the steps laid out in Chapter 7 to calculate a measure of respondents' CP score, which is scaled to run from 0 (the minimum value observed in a country) to 1 (the maximum value observed in a country).[3] Given the input that is used to calculate this indicator, I refer to this second measure of cross-pressure as 'short-term cross-pressure'.

The two indicators—group-based CP score and short-term CP score—are thus supposed to capture the extent to which voters consider different parties. But the variables that are used to predict voters' choices and to assess to what extent choices are predictable differ. For group-based cross-pressure, only socio-demographic information is included, while for short-term cross-pressure, only information on economic evaluations and evaluations of leaders is included. The expectation, however, is that both indicators of cross-pressure will be correlated. If a lack of structure at the front end of the funnel of causality trickles down, we should see that citizens scoring high on group-based cross-pressures will, on average, have a higher level of short-term cross-pressure too.

---

[3] In line with how I proceeded for the group-based cross-pressure score, I focus on the variation in predicted probabilities between the two parties for which a respondent has the highest probability of voting, according to the estimation. This is the approach that Brader, Tucker and Therriault (2014) label the 'top 2-variance' method.

For seventy-five elections, the country-specific surveys include the necessary information to operationalize both the group-based CP score and the short-term CP score. I analyse the association between the two measures within countries to account for the fact that the indicators that are available and relied on in each country differ somewhat. I estimate the connection between the two types of CP scores through ordinary least-squares (OLS) models. I estimate two sets of OLS estimations. A first set of models, which is summarised in Table 9.4, shows the overall association between group-based and short-term cross-pressures in the pooled country-specific data sets. As a second step, I add to the models election-fixed effects, implying that the coefficient on the group-based cross-pressure variable captures the association between the two types of cross-pressure *within* election samples. These results, which are shown in Table 9.5, are important because they account for over-time factors that have simultaneously affected different types of cross-pressure.

Looking at the overall association between group-based and short-term cross-pressures in Table 9.4 first, it can be seen that the association between the two types of cross-pressure is not only positive in each case, but it is also significant at conventional levels in seven of the eight countries. The fact that the indicators of cross-pressure are scaled to run from 0 to 1 eases the interpretation of the effect sizes. More specifically, with the exception of the models for Australia and the United States, the country-specific coefficients are larger than 0.15 and often larger than 0.20. These effect sizes imply that a shift from the lowest to the highest group-based CP score (from 0 to 1) is associated with an increase of more than fifteen percentage points in short-term cross-pressure. In Germany and Sweden, the increase amounts to about twenty-five percentage points, and in the Netherlands even to thirty-five percentage points. These are substantively important associations. In Australia, the estimated coefficient of the group-based CP score is smaller than in the other countries. In fact, those who are most cross-pressured, based on their socio-demographic characteristics, have a short-term CP score that is about six percentage points higher than the least group-based cross-pressured. In the United States, the coefficient that is reported in Table 9.4 is not only insignificant but its size is also a fraction of the effect sizes that are found in most other countries. In the United States, therefore, there is not only no evidence of a change in the extent to which voters are group-based cross-pressured (cf. Chapter 8), but these cross-pressures also do not seem to have trickle-down effects in the funnel of causality.

The estimates in Table 9.4 are essentially bivariate estimates of the association between the two types of cross-pressure. Because both group-based and short-term cross-pressures can be influenced by the same contextual variables, a more conservative approach to evaluating the strength of the association between the two is to assess the connection between the two variables within elections. Therefore, the estimates in Table 9.5 show the results of estimations that include election-fixed effects. The inclusion of these election-specific intercepts reduces the strength of the association between group-based and short-term cross-pressure in several countries. In Germany, for example, the within-election coefficient is 0.05 (it was 0.23 in Table 9.4). In other countries, however, the association is in fact strengthened when assessing it within election samples, as a comparison of the coefficients for Australia highlight. As was the case for the estimations without election-fixed effects, the United States is the only case where the association between the two types of cross-pressure is indistinguishable from zero. Overall, the results in Table 9.5 show that group-based and short-term cross-pressures in electorates not only correlate over time but also that within election surveys as well, individuals who are more group-based cross-pressured tend to be more cross-pressured based on short-term determinants.

In summary, the results in Tables 9.4 and 9.5 suggest that citizens who, based on their socio-demographic characteristics, are cross-pressured between parties and uncertain what party to choose also hold short-term political preferences that lead them to feel cross-pressured between parties. The uncertainty that is instilled in voters based on their socio-demographic characteristics is thus not compensated by short-term factors structuring their choices more. Instead, the lack of guidance from long-term factors translates into vote choices that are less structured by political preferences as well.

9.3 Group-based cross-pressures and issue-based cross-pressures

The results that are presented in section 9.2 suggest that voters who feel more cross-pressured, based on their socio-demographic characteristics, also feel more cross-pressure based on a number of more short-term determinants of the vote. In particular, their evaluation of the state of the economy and their ratings of the party leaders are also a source of cross-pressure for the group-based cross-pressured. I focus on these two indicators mostly because of data restrictions. Given the comparative and longitudinal scope of the analyses,

Table 9.4 Explaining short-term cross-pressure

	Australia	Canada	Denmark	Germany	Great Britain	The Netherlands	Sweden	United States
Group-based CP score	0.065***	0.164***	0.159***	0.233***	0.165***	0.345***	0.257***	0.021
	(0.012)	(0.022)	(0.025)	(0.016)	(0.012)	(0.020)	(0.013)	(0.014)
Intercept	0.366***	0.357***	0.420***	0.327***	0.319***	0.352***	0.333***	0.237***
	(0.009)	(0.018)	(0.021)	(0.013)	(0.009)	(0.016)	(0.010)	(0.010)
N	18,430	10,158	8,744	11,644	13,877	7,807	11,116	6,791
R^2	0.002	0.006	0.005	0.018	0.012	0.045	0.037	0.000

Note: Robust standard errors (in parentheses) are clustered by election. * $p < 0.05$, ** $p < 0.01$, *** $p < 0.001$.

Table 9.5 Explaining short-term cross-pressure, within-election effects

	Australia	Canada	Denmark	Germany	Great Britain	The Netherlands	Sweden	United States
Group-based CP score	0.151***	0.191***	0.168***	0.054**	0.141***	0.217***	0.245***	0.022
	(0.011)	(0.022)	(0.025)	(0.018)	(0.013)	(0.022)	(0.014)	(0.014)
Election FE	✓	✓	✓	✓	✓	✓	✓	✓
N	18,430	10,158	8,744	11,644	13,877	7,807	11,116	6,791
R^2	0.129	0.015	0.009	0.103	0.046	0.095	0.053	0.022

Note: Robust standard errors (in parentheses) are clustered by election. * $p < 0.05$, ** $p < 0.01$, *** $p < 0.001$.

economic evaluations and leader evaluations are essentially the only items that are measured fairly consistently between countries and over time. This implies that an important type of short-term predictor of the vote—issue preferences—is not accounted for in the analysis.

To address this limitation, and to explore whether group-based, cross-pressured individuals also feel cross-pressured based on their positions on specific issues, I again make use of data from the European Election Study (EES). More specifically, I use data from the 1979 and the 2019 EES voter surveys. These constitute the first and the most recent voter surveys within the framework of the EES project, and both surveys included measures of citizens' positions on a varied set of issues (see also Dalton, 2018). I limit the analysis to the countries that are part of the EES and that are also analysed in depth in this book. For the 1979 EES, this limits the analyses to Denmark, Germany, Great Britain, and the Netherlands. The 2019 survey includes information on these same countries and Sweden.

The 1979 EES voter survey measured respondents' issue positions by means of thirteen items on which respondents were asked to indicate their level of agreement (agree strongly, agree, disagree, or disagree strongly). The items capture positions on topics related to the economy, inequality, law and order, defence, abortion, the environment, and foreign policy, among others. The exact question wording for the items is reported in Appendix N.

In the 2019 EES voter survey, a smaller number of items was included to capture respondents' issue preferences. The six items that were included, however, covered a broad set of issues, including the economy, redistribution, same-sex marriage, civil liberties, immigration, and the environment (see Appendix N for the question wording). Respondents were asked to indicate their position on the issues on a scale from 0 to 10.

To correlate group-based cross-pressures with cross-pressure based on issue preferences, I again construct two sets of respondent-specific measures of their CP score. First, to operationalize group-based cross-pressures in the EES surveys, I follow the approach explained in Chapter 7 using the indicators of respondents' socio-demographic characteristics that are available in the EES. In other words, I first estimate multinominal vote-choice models that account for respondents' socio-demographic characteristics. I then obtain the predicted probabilities of voting for different parties based on these models and calculate the CP score indicator by means of information on the top two predicted probabilities. As measures of respondents' socio-demographic characteristics, the EES allows including in the estimation respondents' gender, age, level of education, religious denomination, and the level of urbanization of their place of living. In the 1979 survey, I also account for family income (and its interaction with education) and in the 2019 survey for respondents' reported social class. Appendix N offers details on the operationalization of all socio-demographic variables.

In line with how I proceeded for the analyses that draw on longitudinal election surveys in each country, for the EES analyses as well the group-based CP-scores were calculated for each country-year separately, and scaled to run from 0 to 1. Thus, within each country-year, the least cross-pressured individuals receive a score of 0 and the most cross-pressured individuals get a score of 1.

The goal of the EES analysis is to verify whether individuals who are more group-based cross-pressured are also more issue-based cross-pressured. To examine whether that is indeed the case, I examine the association between the group-based cross-pressure scores and an analogous measure that uses respondents' issue positions as a source of cross-pressure. To operationalize such issue-based cross-pressures, I again proceed by estimating multinomial logistic regressions to predict the vote choice and then follow the steps outlined earlier to obtain a measure of an individual's CP score. For the 1979 voter survey, the regression models include as independent variables respondents' level of agreement on the thirteen issue items. For the 2019 survey, the six available issue items were included as independent variables. These models include no other control variables.

To assess the connection between group-based and issue-based cross-pressure scores in the 1979 and 2019 EES voter surveys, I estimate year-pooled regression models. The dependent variable in these models is a respondent's issue-based CP score, which has also been scaled to range from 0 to 1 within a country-year. The independent variable is a respondent's group-based CP score, scaled in the same way.

Table 9.6 summarizes the results of these analyses. For both survey-years, the results show a positive and statistically significant association between citizens' group-based CP score and the extent to which they are cross-pressured based on their issue positions. The coding of both CP score variables from 0 to 1 eases the interpretation of the effect size. More precisely, the estimated effects suggest that respondents who obtain the highest score on the group-based CP index (coded as 1) on average have an issue-based CP score that is 14 per cent (in 1979) or 6 per cent (in 2019) higher than that of those with the lowest group-based CP score (coded as 0).

The association between group-based and issue-based cross-pressures is only moderately strong, but the direction of the effect is in line with what

Table 9.6 Group-based and issue-based cross-pressure, EES data

	1979	2019
Group-based CP score	0.137***	0.059**
	(0.029)	(0.018)
Denmark (ref.)	–	–
Germany	0.001	−0.049***
	(0.017)	(0.011)
Great Britain	−0.062**	−0.128***
	(0.020)	(0.013)
The Netherlands	−0.120***	−0.009
	(0.019)	(0.011)
Sweden	–	−0.094***
	–	(0.012)
Intercept	0.573***	0.750***
	(0.025)	(0.016)
N	1,479	2,947
R^2	0.068	0.064

Note: Robust standard errors in parentheses.
*$p < 0.05$, **$p < 0.01$, ***$p < 0.001$.

was found for the more general 'short-term cross-pressures' index. Thus, quite consistently, I find that respondents who—based on their socio-demographic characteristics—lack guidance to choose a party are also more undecided based on their short-term political preferences and their positions on specific issues.

9.4 Summary and implications

The key claim that I make in this book is that a weakening of the guidance that citizens' group memberships provide is a main source for the growing levels of electoral volatility in many established democracies. While Chapter 8 has offered evidence of an increase in group-based cross-pressures, such a trend does not necessarily imply more volatile voting behaviour. After all, as the results in Chapter 3 pointed out, socio-demographic characteristics—by themselves—only explain a small part of the variation in citizens' electoral choices.

The results that are presented in this chapter, however, suggest that a lack of political guidance coming from citizens' socio-demographic characteristics trickles down further in the funnel of causality. Citizens who are less bound by their social group memberships are also less likely to develop attachments to parties and, on average, hold political attitudes and positions that help them less to discriminate between parties in the polling booth.

The implication is that citizens whose socio-demographic characteristics do not push towards a specific party miss an anchor when considering the state of the economy, party leaders, or political issues. As a result, they hold political preferences that are not pushing them strongly towards one specific party either. Overall, the short-term attitudes and preferences of voters who are cross-pressured, based on their membership of socio-demographic groups, are less constrained—and help them less to choose a party.

Voters who feel cross-pressured, based on their socio-demographic characteristics, clearly do not compensate this lack of structure by finding more guidance in other, more short-term determinants on the vote. On the contrary, the results in this chapter show a positive correlation between group-based cross-pressures and other, more short-term sources of cross-pressure. The implication is that voters who feel strong group-based cross-pressures are not 'bound by structure'. The expectation, therefore, is that group-based cross-pressures are a strong indicator of electoral volatility and uncertainty. Chapter 10 tests this expectation.

10
Cross-pressures, late deciding, and volatility

A growing share of the electorate in many established democracies feels cross-pressured between parties, based on their membership of different social groups. This group of voters, whose socio-demographic characteristics provide less political guidance, also make choices that appear to be less constrained in terms of other—more short-term—political attitudes. Group-based cross-pressured voters, hence, are not 'bound by structure' when choosing what party or candidate to support.

I posit that this decline of constraint based on individuals' social group memberships and identities is key to explaining the increased undecidedness of voters and the surge in electoral volatility. That voters whose socio-demographic characteristics do not provide them with guidance cast votes that are more volatile was also the intuition of former Belgian Prime Minister Dehaene (cf. Chapter 1). The crucial test of the argument therefore consists of an analysis of the association between the extent to which voters' choices are constrained by their socio-demographic characteristics and the instability of their choices.

This chapter presents the results of such a test. To capture how much individuals' socio-demographic characteristics constrain their choices, I rely on the measure of individuals' group-based cross-pressure (CP) score that was presented and relied on in the previous chapters. To examine whether such cross-pressures are associated with instability of voters' choices, I study the association between cross-pressures and two dependent variables: the reported timing of an individual's voting decision and whether or not they switched parties between elections.

For both dependent variables, I rely on the longitudinal election study data from the eight countries that are the focus of this book. Given that measures of party switching that rely on recall questions are prone to error, I also use panel data from the British Election Studies to verify whether results replicate when using information from election panels.

Finally, it is important to point out that the individual sources of electoral volatility have already received considerable attention in the literature and have been explained with reference to different theories. To isolate the effect of group-based cross-pressures, and to assess their impact in comparison to alternative explanations for the rise in volatility, I also conduct a series of tests in which theories of volatility—relating to partisan dealignment, citizens' increased cognitive mobilization, and their dissatisfaction with politics—are accounted for.

10.1 Theoretical expectations

Before proceeding with the analyses that test the main theoretical argument, it is useful to recap my expectations concerning the role of group-based cross-pressures, partisanship, and the impact of more short-term determinants of the vote on electoral instability.

My argument, as elaborated in Chapter 6, makes two crucial points about the connection between the nature of a voter's decision-making process, on the one hand, and the instability of the outcome of that decision process, on the other. First, I have argued that whether vote choices are stable or unstable depends on the connections between different variables in a funnel of causality—which I conceptualize in terms of how constrained voters' decision-making processes are. Second, I theorize that constraint based on citizens' group memberships and their social identities are the key driver and source of constraint. I argue that such cleavage-based constraint—which I operationalize by means of a measure of group-based cross-pressure—trickles down in the funnel of causality. The analyses that are presented in Chapter 9 provide evidence that is in line with the idea of trickle-down effects.

My expectations with respect to the role of constraint are thus twofold: (1) I expect that levels of constraint—overall—determine the stability of voters' choices and (2) theorize that the main source for constraint comes from the connections between socio-demographic characteristics. Given my focus on group-based cross-pressure as the driver of change, in this chapter, I focus on empirically testing the second expectation; that is, I examine the behavioural consequences of group-based constraint and test the expectation that respondents who are more cross-pressured based on their group memberships make vote choices that are more unstable. For readers who want to see a test of the link between overall constraint and vote instability, I refer to Appendix R.

10.2 Group-based cross-pressured voters decide later

As a first indicator of instability in voters' choices, I focus on a measure of the timing of the voting decision. For group-based cross-pressured voters, their social characteristics and group membership do not push them to prefer one party in particular. Given that their group memberships are not constraining their preferences, these voters are likely to enter the campaign without knowing what party to vote for and are expected to decide later.

To verify whether this expectation is indeed borne out by the data, I examine the association between respondents' group-based CP score and the timing of their vote choice. More specifically, I regress respondents' reported time of their voting decision on their group-based CP score—calculated as explained in Chapter 7. I operationalize the reported timing of vote choices as in Chapter 1, implying that I distinguish between all answer options that reflect deciding whom to vote for during the campaign (coded as 1) or having decided before the campaign (coded as 0). Using these variables, I estimate a series of country-specific linear probability models to explain late deciding.

Figure 10.1 visually summarizes the results of these country-specific and bivariate regression models. As can be seen from the estimates that are plotted in this figure, in each of the eight countries there is a positive and significant association between being more group-based cross-pressured and deciding late. The association between cross-pressures and late deciding is in fact quite strong and varies between an effect of nine percentage points in the United States to fifty-four percentage points in the Netherlands.

Given that levels of campaign deciding differ strongly between countries, it is also useful to examine how respondents' overall likelihood of being a campaign decider varies as a function of how much they are group-based cross-pressured. In Australia, the likelihood of deciding late increases from 21 per cent among the least cross-pressured to 34 per cent among the most cross-pressured. In Canada, more voters decide late, but here as well levels of cross-pressure matter. More specifically, the likelihood that a Canadian voter decides late increases from 38 per cent to 50 per cent as they move from the lowest to the highest CP score. In Denmark, the likelihood of late deciding increases from 9 per cent to 37 per cent as we move from the least to the most cross-pressured. In Germany, the probability of deciding during the campaign increases from essentially 0 per cent among the least cross-pressured to 27 per cent among the most cross pressured. In Great Britain, the likelihood of being a campaign decider ranges from 10 per cent among the least cross-pressured to 29 per cent among the most cross-pressured. The Netherlands is

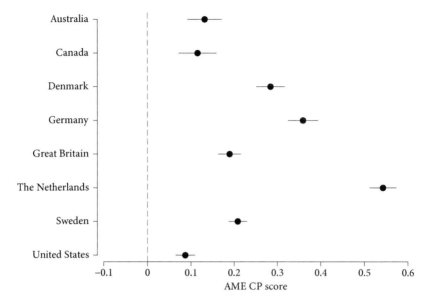

Figure 10.1 Marginal effect of cross-pressure on likelihood to decide late

Note: Marginal effect of shifting the group-based cross-pressure score from the minimum (0) to the maximum (1) value on the likelihood of switching. Estimates from country-specific bivariate linear probability models.

the case where cross-pressures are most strongly associated with late deciding. In particular, practically 0 per cent of the least cross-pressured and 52 per cent of the most cross-pressured decide during the campaign. In Sweden, the likelihood of deciding during the campaign increases from 14 per cent to 35 per cent when moving from the least to the most cross-pressured voters. Finally, there is weak evidence of a connection between group-based cross-pressures and deciding late in the United States. Overall, very few Americans decide during the campaign, though their proportion increases somewhat as group-based cross-pressures increase (from 11 per cent among the least cross-pressured to 19 per cent among the most cross-pressured).

The estimates that are presented in Figure 10.1 are the result of a series of bivariate regression models. It could be argued that given that both campaign deciding and group-based cross-pressures are on the rise, the association simply reflects that both increase over time rather than a meaningful connection between the two. To address this possibility, Table 10.1 shows the results of country-specific models that include a linear time trend. As can be seen from the estimates in Table 10.1, in most countries there has been a linear increase in individuals' likelihood to decide late what party to vote for. In several countries, the association between the indicator of group-based cross-pressures and late deciding is also substantially weakened when the linear time trend is added. Notably, in the Netherlands the strength of the association between group-based cross-pressure and campaign deciding is halved. Even so, the estimates in Table 10.1 still show consistently positive, significant, and meaningfully strong associations between group-based cross-pressures and late deciding.

Furthermore, as can be seen from the results that are reported in Table 10.2, even when I include election-fixed effects in the models, and hence shift the focus to analysing the association between group-based cross-pressures and late deciding *within* election-years, there is strong evidence that higher levels of group-based cross-pressures are associated with a significantly higher likelihood of making one's voting decision during the campaign (versus before the start of the campaign).

Overall, the analyses of the association between group-based cross-pressure and late deciding offer strong evidence that voters whose socio-demographic characteristics offer little guidance to choose between parties are more undecided. As this group has not arrived at a firm voting decision before the start of the election campaign, they can arguably be swayed more easily over the course of the election campaign and switch parties in response to specific campaign events or debates (Fournier et al., 2004; Johann et al., 2018).

Even though cross-pressured voters decide later, it is important to keep in mind the findings of Chapter 9. These results suggested that voters who are more cross-pressured, based on their socio-demographic characteristics, are also more cross-pressured based on other—more short-term—determinants of the vote choice. Cross-pressured voters are thus simultaneously more easily influenceable by what happens during a campaign, because they are less likely to have decided what party to support before the start of the campaign, and less constrained by short-term campaign factors. Group-based cross-pressured voters enter the campaign without a fixed idea who to support. But without the anchors from socio-demographic group memberships, the issues, leaders, or topics that are covered during the campaign are also helping them less to discriminate between parties.

Table 10.1 The association between group-based cross-pressure and campaign deciding, accounting for linear time trend

	Australia	Canada	Denmark	Germany	Great Britain	The Netherlands	Sweden	United States
Group-based CP score	0.136***	0.111***	0.125***	0.120***	0.158***	0.260***	0.117***	0.088***
	(0.020)	(0.023)	(0.018)	(0.018)	(0.013)	(0.017)	(0.012)	(0.011)
Year	−0.003***	0.000	0.005***	0.006***	0.003***	0.009***	0.003***	0.001***
	(0.000)	(0.000)	(0.000)	(0.000)	(0.000)	(0.000)	(0.000)	(0.000)
Intercept	6.453***	−0.195	−10.480***	−12.198***	−6.722***	−18.318***	−6.707***	−1.292***
	(0.821)	(0.562)	(0.543)	(0.416)	(0.404)	(0.508)	(0.378)	(0.279)
N	17,504	15,772	17,658	14,230	24,716	19,426	26,382	16,395
R²	0.006	0.002	0.034	0.078	0.019	0.102	0.024	0.005

Note: Robust standard errors in parentheses. * $p < 0.05$, ** $p < 0.01$, *** $p < 0.001$.

Table 10.2 The association between group-based cross-pressure and campaign deciding, within-election effects

	Australia	Canada	Denmark	Germany	Great Britain	The Netherlands	Sweden	United States
Group-based CP score	0.162*** (0.020)	0.085*** (0.023)	0.164*** (0.019)	0.071*** (0.019)	0.129*** (0.014)	0.248*** (0.018)	0.139*** (0.012)	0.085*** (0.012)
Election FE	✓	✓	✓	✓	✓	✓	✓	✓
N	17,504	15,772	17,658	14,230	24,716	19,426	26,382	16,395
R^2	0.015	0.014	0.044	0.111	0.024	0.110	0.043	0.016

Note: Robust standard errors in parentheses. $^* p < 0.05$, $^{**} p < 0.01$, $^{***} p < 0.001$.

10.3 Group-based cross-pressured voters are more volatile

10.3.1 Group-based cross-pressure and volatility

As a second indicator of the instability in voters' choices, I analyse voter volatility. I again study the role of group-based cross-pressures by means of the longitudinal election study data from eight established democracies—with party switching as a dependent variable and a respondent's group-based cross-pressure score as the independent variable. To substantiate the argument that an increase of group-based cross-pressures is part of the reason why we are witnessing a surge in electoral volatility in many democracies, it is important to verify whether—at an individual level—cross-pressures indeed predict party switching.

To maximize the coverage of the analyses, I operationalize switching by means of information on respondents' reported vote choice and their recalled voting behaviour in the previous election. Those who report to have voted for the same party are coded as stable voters (0), while those who indicate a different party for the current and the previous election are coded as switchers (1). Respondents who indicate to have abstained in one of the two elections and those who were not eligible in the first election are dropped from the analyses.

Figure 10.2 visually summarizes the results of a series of country-specific linear probability models to explain party switching. As for the association between cross-pressures and late deciding, as an initial step I estimate the bivariate association between the two variables. The estimates in Figure 10.2 show the expected positive association between group-based cross-pressures and volatility. In each of the eight democracies analysed, the coefficient has a positive sign, and the strength of the association between the cross-pressure score and volatility is often quite strong. The smallest coefficient is found for the United States, where the results suggest that moving from the lowest to the highest level of group-based cross-pressures increases the likelihood that an individual will switch parties by about eleven percentage points. In Denmark and in the Netherlands, the effect is almost 0.30. In Sweden, finally, the effect is about thirty-three percentage points.

Given that levels of party switching vary considerably between countries (cf. Chapter 1), it is again useful to translate these effects to changes in the predicted probability of party switching in each context. In Australia, the likelihood of switching parties between elections increases from 8 per cent among the least cross-pressured to 24 per cent among the most cross-pressured. In

Canada, the estimated probability of party switching is 16 per cent among the least cross-pressured, while it is 33 per cent for the most cross-pressured. In Denmark, the likelihood of switching parties increases from 10 per cent among the least cross-pressured to 39 per cent among the most cross-pressured. In Germany, 6 per cent of the least cross-pressured are estimated to switch parties, while this increases to 29 per cent for the most cross-pressured. Turning to the estimates for Great Britain, the estimates in Figure 10.2 correspond to an increased likelihood of party switching from 12 per cent to 24 per cent as the cross-pressure score moves from the lowest to the highest value. In the Netherlands, the corresponding estimates are 8 per cent for the least cross-pressured and 38 per cent for the most cross-pressured. Figure 10.2 shows the strongest association in Sweden. This coefficient corresponds to the likelihood of party switching increasing from roughly 2 per cent among the least group-based cross-pressured to 35 per cent among the most cross-pressured. Finally, the eleven percentage points effect in the United States corresponds to a 12 per cent likelihood of switching among the least cross-pressured and a 22 per cent likelihood among the most cross-pressured.

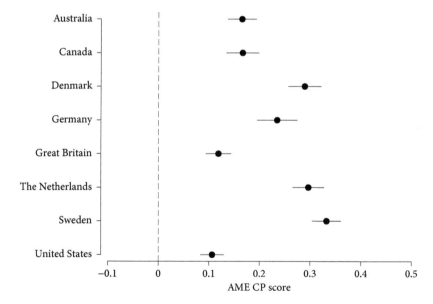

Figure 10.2 Marginal effect of cross-pressure on likelihood to switch parties

Note: Marginal effect of shifting the group-based cross-pressure score from the minimum (0) to the maximum (1) value on the likelihood of switching. Estimates from country-specific bivariate linear probability models.

As holds for the association between group-based cross-pressures and campaign deciding, the association between cross-pressures and party switching as well could be spurious and driven by the fact that the two happen to increase over time in most countries. To account for this possibility, Table 10.3 presents the results of country-specific models that include a linear time trend. Including this control reduces the strength of the association between group-based cross-pressures and voter volatility. Even though reduced in size, however, the estimates in Table 10.3 still indicate that there is a consistently positive, significant, and substantively important association between levels of group-based cross-pressure and voter volatility. Furthermore, as can be seen from the estimates in Table 10.4, even when entirely removing over-time variation from the data sets by the inclusion of election-fixed effects, higher levels of group-based cross-pressures are associated in expected ways with individuals' likelihood of party switching. This implies that within a specific election study as well, those who are more cross-pressured are significantly more likely to report having switched parties between elections.

The results that are presented in this section show strong evidence that in elections in these eight countries, those who are more cross-pressured between parties, based on their socio-demographic characteristics, are significantly and substantially more likely to switch parties between elections. Even though the evidence is correlational, it does suggest that citizens whose decision-making process lacks constraint, because their socio-demographic characteristics have cross-cutting influences, are more likely to be party switchers.

10.3.2 Cross-pressures or partisanship?

While suggestive, the results that are presented in Figure 10.2 can be challenged in a number of ways. In particular, to firmly claim that levels of cross-pressure are key to explaining party switching it is important to account for the role of a number of alternative sources of volatility.

The role of partisanship is a particularly important variable in this regard. As indicated in Chapter 9, I theorize that those who are more cross-pressured are also less likely to develop an attachment to a party. Party identification, therefore, can be thought of as a mediating variable. At the same time, I do not expect the effects of group-based cross-pressures to be fully mediated by partisan attachments. If that was the case, theories of partisan dealignment would be sufficient to explain the increase in electoral volatility.

Table 10.3 The association between group-based cross-pressure and volatility, accounting for linear time trend

	Australia	Canada	Denmark	Germany	Great Britain	The Netherlands	Sweden	United States
Group-based CP score	0.154***	0.113***	0.107***	0.110***	0.107***	0.202***	0.105***	0.100***
	(0.015)	(0.017)	(0.018)	(0.022)	(0.013)	(0.017)	(0.015)	(0.012)
Year	0.001***	0.002***	0.006***	0.003***	0.002***	0.003***	0.006***	−0.001***
	(0.000)	(0.000)	(0.000)	(0.000)	(0.000)	(0.000)	(0.000)	(0.000)
Intercept	−1.868***	−3.521***	−12.359***	−6.146***	−3.591***	−5.870***	−11.250***	2.581***
	(0.376)	(0.375)	(0.559)	(0.420)	(0.303)	(0.518)	(0.429)	(0.292)
N	20,846	20,154	17,291	14,434	24,206	16,728	10,693	14,329
R^2	0.007	0.009	0.042	0.023	0.009	0.025	0.107	0.009

Note: Robust standard errors in parentheses. * $p < 0.05$, ** $p < 0.01$, *** $p < 0.001$.

Table 10.4 The association between group-based cross-pressure and volatility, within-election effects

	Australia	Canada	Denmark	Germany	Great Britain	The Netherlands	Sweden	United States
Group-based CP score	0.141*** (0.015)	0.101*** (0.018)	0.137*** (0.018)	0.097*** (0.022)	0.089*** (0.013)	0.218*** (0.017)	0.109*** (0.016)	0.112*** (0.012)
Election FE	✓	✓	✓	✓	✓	✓	✓	✓
N	20,846	20,154	17,291	14,434	24,206	16,728	10,693	14,329
R^2	0.016	0.031	0.100	0.034	0.014	0.060	0.110	0.021

Note: Robust standard errors in parentheses. * $p < 0.05$, ** $p < 0.01$, *** $p < 0.001$.

Mediation should be imperfect for two main reasons. First, citizens' socio-demographic characteristics (and hence group-based cross-pressure)—in addition to influencing the vote through their impact on partisanship—can also have a more direct effect on the vote choice. Second, we know that party attachments are not perfectly predicted by individuals' social characteristics either. There is even work which argues that partisan attachments increasingly reflect citizens' more short-term political attitudes, and their evaluations of the leaders in particular (Garzia, Ferreira da Silva, and De Angelis, 2022).

To gain insights into the mediating role of partisan attachments, but also to show the added value of a focus on group-based cross-pressures for explaining volatility compared to work which has argued that the surge in electoral volatility results from a decline in partisan attachments, it is therefore important to verify whether group-based cross-pressures remain a significant predictor of volatility when partisanship is controlled for.

The results in Tables 10.5 and 10.6 summarize the results of a series of country-specific linear probability models. The tables include two sets of regression estimates for each country. For each country, the first model replicates the analyses from Figure 10.2, focusing on the bivariate association between group-based cross-pressures and party switching. In contrast to the estimates in Figure 10.2, however, the samples are restricted to respondents for which the data include information on whether or not they are a partisan. Doing so enhances the comparison with the second set of estimates in each country, which adds to the regression model a control for whether or not an individual respondent identifies with a party (0 = non-partisan, 1 = partisan).

A number of conclusions can be drawn from the estimates in Tables 10.5 and 10.6. First, not surprisingly, the results show that partisans are significantly and substantially less likely to switch parties than non-partisans. The coefficient on the partisanship variable is consistently negative, significant, and quite substantial. Second, controlling for partisan attachments reduces the estimated coefficient of respondents' group-based cross-pressure. Importantly, however, even when accounting for whether individuals report being a partisan of a specific party, the extent to which their socio-demographic characteristics lead them to feel cross-pressured between parties continues to have a significant and meaningful effect on their likelihood to switch parties. In fact, the effect of the CP score variable is only somewhat reduced when a control for partisanship is added to the models. This implies that the mediation effect of partisanship is altogether limited. It also signals that the CP score is not simply an alternative measure that taps partisanship, but that it also provides additional—and I would argue causally deeper—information on the likelihood that an individual will switch parties.

10.3.3 Cross-pressure and volatility: Panel evidence

A reliance on recall questions allows light to be shed on the dynamics of party switching in a large number of countries and elections. However, recall questions also have a number of disadvantages. In particular, memory problems and a bias towards consistency are known to cause an underestimation of the true amount of party switching when recall questions are relied on (Dassonneville and Hooghe, 2017b; Waldahl and Aardal, 2000). Furthermore, the lack of a time lag between the measure of cross-pressure and the measure of party switching render the estimates purely correlational; that is, the estimates cannot be taken to suggest that having a high group-based CP score leads voters to *subsequently* switch parties.

To address these limitations, I complement the examination of the association between group-based cross-pressure and voter volatility with a panel analysis of the association between group-based cross pressure and party switching. In particular, I rely on British panel study data to operationalize party switching in consecutive elections and to examine the association between group-based cross-pressure (at election e) and subsequently switching parties (i.e. from election e to $e+1$).

I make use of six different panel studies from the British context that allow operationalizing switching between consecutive elections and focus on a change in the reported vote choice in the post-election waves of the panel surveys. More specifically, I capture party switching between 1964 and 1966, 1983 and 1987, 1987 and 1992, 1992 and 1997, 1997 and 2001, and between 2015 and 2017 using the panel data that were also employed in Chapter 4.[1]

Using these panel data, I seek an answer to the questions of whether party switching is driven by group-based cross-pressures and whether cross-pressured voters are more likely to subsequently switch parties. I pool the data from the six panel studies and estimate a linear probability model to predict party switching. The main independent variable is respondents' group-based CP score, measured at election e. I also include panel-fixed effects to account for between-panel differences in volatility but also in the measures

---

[1] For details on these panel studies, see Appendix A.

Table 10.5 The association between group-based cross-pressure and volatility, control for partisanship (1)

	Australia	Australia	Canada	Canada	Denmark	Denmark	Germany	Germany
Group-based CP score	0.166***	0.147***	0.177***	0.155***	0.293***	0.224***	0.235***	0.207***
	(0.015)	(0.014)	(0.017)	(0.017)	(0.017)	(0.016)	(0.022)	(0.022)
Partisan	–	−0.259***	–	−0.221***	–	−0.306***	–	−0.227***
		(0.011)		(0.010)		(0.007)		(0.011)
Intercept	0.078***	0.325***	0.149***	0.353***	0.105***	0.325***	0.065***	0.275***
	(0.011)	(0.015)	(0.013)	(0.016)	(0.014)	(0.014)	(0.018)	(0.021)
N	20,737	20,737	17,598	17,598	15,707	15,707	12,857	12,857
R^2	0.006	0.043	0.006	0.036	0.015	0.119	0.008	0.046

Note: Robust standard errors in parentheses. $^*p < 0.05$, $^{**}p < 0.01$, $^{***}p < 0.001$.

Table 10.6 The association between group-based cross-pressure and volatility, control for partisanship (2)

	Great Britain	Great Britain	The Netherlands	The Netherlands	Sweden	Sweden	United States	United States
Group-based CP score	0.113***	0.102***	0.289***	0.247***	0.335***	0.293***	0.106***	0.093***
	(0.013)	(0.013)	(0.017)	(0.017)	(0.015)	(0.014)	(0.012)	(0.012)
Partisan	–	−0.266***	–	−0.198***	–	−0.222***	–	−0.118***
		(0.013)		(0.007)		(0.008)		(0.008)
Intercept	0.120***	0.377***	0.097***	0.214***	0.018	0.173***	0.118***	0.213***
	(0.009)	(0.016)	(0.013)	(0.014)	(0.009)	(0.011)	(0.008)	(0.010)
N	22,939	22,939	14,286	14,286	10,425	10,425	14,272	14,272
R^2	0.003	0.030	0.016	0.060	0.043	0.109	0.005	0.023

Note: Robust standard errors in parentheses. * $p < 0.05$, ** $p < 0.01$, *** $p < 0.001$.

available for constructing the group-based CP scores. Therefore, the estimates should be interpreted as indicating the within-panel effects of group-based cross-pressures on party switching.

Model 1 in Table 10.7 suggests that higher levels of group-based cross-pressures are indeed positively and significantly associated with subsequent party switching. In terms of marginal effects, moving from the lowest to the highest level on the measure of CP score is associated with a nine-percentage-point increase in the likelihood of switching to another party in the next election. This effect is hardly reduced when accounting for whether or not respondents reported being a partisan in the first panel wave, again indicating that partisan attachments do not entirely mediate the impact of group-based cross-pressure (see Model 2 in Table 10.7). It is also noteworthy that the strength of the association between group-based cross-pressures and subsequent party switching in these panel data is very similar to the within-election effects for British election reported in Table 10.4.

Given that more than half of the respondents in the pooled data set are respondents from the British Election Study Internet Panel, I also verify whether results hold when excluding observations from this large panel study. As evident from the estimates of Models 3 and 4 in Table 10.7, when only focusing on the five oldest panel studies, I still find a positive and statistically significant association between the CP score and party switching. The size of the effect, furthermore, is essentially the same as what I found in the pooled panel data set.

Table 10.7 Explaining party switching in UK panel studies

	All panels		Excluding 2015–2017	
Group-based CP score	0.093***	0.075***	0.093**	0.083**
	(0.015)	(0.015)	(0.029)	(0.031)
Partisan	–	−0.150***	–	−0.163***
	–	(0.009)	–	(0.030)
Panel FE	✓	✓	✓	✓
N	21,541	20,266	4,913	4,125
R²	0.009	0.024	0.016	0.027

Note: Robust standard errors in parentheses. $^*p < 0.05$, $^{**}p < 0.01$, $^{***}p < 0.001$.

10.4 Cross-pressures or alternative explanations for volatility?

So far, the results that are presented in this chapter offer strong evidence of an association between citizens' feelings of group-based cross-pressure and their likelihood to switch parties between elections. However, to confidently claim that group-based cross-pressures are key to explaining volatility, and that a rise in group-based cross-pressure has contributed to the surge in volatility, it is important to validate whether the role of cross-pressures holds when accounting for alternative explanations for the rise in electoral volatility.

Previous work that studies the determinants of volatility, and causes for rising levels of volatility in particular, points to two important alternative explanations. A first body of work conceives of the rise in electoral volatility as a consequence of the cognitive mobilization of the electorate. Dalton (2012, 2013) in particular has argued that as a result of the expansion of higher education across democracies and the multiplication of information sources, citizens are now better prepared to 'deal with the complexities of politics' (Dalton, 2012: 37). This results in the emergence and growth of a new group of highly politically sophisticated non-partisans, who are a 'primary source of the fluidity and volatility observed in recent (...) elections' (Dalton, 2012: 37).

According to this thesis, the rise in volatility is—at least in part—a result of the growing cognitive mobilization of the electorate. Building on the work of Dalton (2012, 2013), much research that seeks to identify the sources of electoral volatility—from one election to another or in the context of an election campaign—has studied the connection between indicators of cognitive mobilization, political sophistication, or political knowledge and party switching. The findings of this literature can best be described as mixed. Some work finds no evidence of a strong connection between indicators such as education, political interest, or political knowledge and party switching (Geers and Strömbäck, 2019; Söderlund, 2008) or reports that these factors are negatively correlated to party switching (Dassonneville, 2012). Others have qualified the connection between measures of political sophistication and party switching, and argue that neither the least nor the most sophisticated should be expected to switch parties. This argument is particularly relevant for the study of party switching over the course of an election campaign as it is argued that switching is a function of both the exposure to political information and openness to change (Converse, 1962). Only those who have a certain level of political sophistication will be exposed to information that could sway their partisan preferences. The most politically sophisticated, however, are very resistant to changing their attitudes (Zaller, 1992). Several studies confirm the curvilinear relationship between indicators of political sophistication and party switching during election campaigns, with the highest odds of switching among those with medium levels of political interest, knowledge, or education (Lachat, 2007; van der Meer et al., 2015). Furthermore, there are indications that a similar pattern appears when studying party switching between elections (Dassonneville and Dejaeghere, 2014; Kuhn, 2009), in particular when switching between ideological blocks is focused on (Lachat, 2007).

Even though the evidence of the cognitive mobilization thesis is somewhat mixed and has been qualified in a number of ways, to isolate the role of cross-pressures it is important to account for the role of citizens' political sophistication as a determinant of electoral volatility.

A second group of studies consider party switching not as a result of heightened levels of political sophistication but instead as an expression of dissatisfaction or discontent with the party one previously voted for and with party politics more generally. The connection between dissatisfaction and volatility was first observed by Carsten Zelle (1995), who proposed a model of 'frustrated floating voters'. Based on an analysis of German election survey data, he concluded that party switchers were 'somewhat less satisfied with the political system, less trusting in parties, and less happy about their favoured party' (Zelle, 1995: 340). Other work has confirmed the role of dissatisfaction with a party's performance as a trigger of party switching (Söderlund, 2008). More fundamental political attitudes such as political efficacy, political trust, or democratic satisfaction have also been shown to be negatively associated with volatility (Dassonneville, 2012; Dassonneville and Dejaeghere, 2014; Voogd, van der Meer, and van der Brug, 2019). However, work that studies trends in political trust (van der Meer, 2017) or satisfaction with democracy (van Ham et al., 2017) finds that those attitudes have remained largely stable over time, making changes in citizens' level of 'frustration' an unlikely candidate to explain the surge in electoral volatility. Still, I account for the role of democratic attitudes in order to single out the unique contribution of cross-pressures for explaining party switching.

To examine the role of group-based cross-pressures while controlling for these alternative sources of volatility, I focus on four countries for which election surveys regularly include measures that can be used to proxy the effects of cognitive mobilization and of 'frustration': Australia, Germany, the Netherlands, and the United States.

Table 10.8 shows the estimations of nine linear probability regression models to predict whether a respondent switched parties. Each model includes the indicator of the extent to which a respondent is cross-pressured (group-based

CP score), a linear time trend, and the linear and squared terms for a proxy of cognitive mobilization: political interest. Five of the models also include indicators that capture respondents' satisfaction with democracy or political trust.[2] To ease the interpretation of the effects, the measures of political interest, satisfaction with democracy, and political trust were all scaled to range between 0 and 1—with higher values corresponding to higher levels of interest, satisfaction, or trust. Information on the question wording of these measures is reported in Appendix S.

The results in Table 10.8 offer some evidence of the connection between indicators of cognitive mobilization and political frustration, on the one hand, and volatility, on the other. The coefficients for political interest and its squared term mostly show the expected curvilinear pattern. More precisely, the positive main effect and the negative squared term are suggestive of respondents with medium levels of political interest being most likely to switch parties. There are only few instances where this pattern seems to be significant, however, and significance levels drop when indicators of political frustration are added to the model. The coefficients for satisfaction with democracy are all in the expected negative direction and significant, suggesting that the most dissatisfied switch most—though significance levels vary. For political trust, the results show the expected negative and significant effect in Australia but not in the United States.

The most important take-away from the results in Table 10.8, however, is that the coefficient of the CP-score variable in these models consistently remains a strong indicator of volatility.

10.5 Summary and implications

The surge in electoral volatility across established democracies is well established. And while much work has studied the individual-level sources of party switching, the more deep-seated causes of the over-time surge in voters' tendencies to switch parties are still largely unknown. In particular, the ways in which voters' decision processes have changed, which leads them to switch more often and to be more uncertain about their vote choice, are not entirely clear. A commonly invoked argument links the rise in volatility to a growing role of short-term factors like issues, the economy, or party leaders in the

---

[2] I do not include satisfaction with democracy and trust in a single model because the availability of consistent indicators of dissatisfaction is much more limited than what holds for political interest.

Table 10.8 Explaining party switching in Australia, Germany, the Netherlands, and the United States, alternative explanations

	Australia	Australia	Australia	Germany	Germany	The Netherlands	The Netherlands	United States	United States
Group-based CP score	0.148***	0.136***	0.125***	0.105***	0.115***	0.202***	0.348***	0.098***	0.104***
	(0.015)	(0.016)	(0.020)	(0.025)	(0.028)	(0.017)	(0.044)	(0.012)	(0.016)
Political interest	0.090*	0.092	0.073	0.049	0.087	0.082*	0.019	−0.001	0.005
	(0.046)	(0.051)	(0.063)	(0.049)	(0.056)	(0.033)	(0.060)	(0.039)	(0.049)
Political interest^2	−0.106**	−0.104**	−0.085	−0.040	−0.063	−0.124***	−0.093	−0.066*	−0.067
	(0.035)	(0.038)	(0.046)	(0.043)	(0.048)	(0.031)	(0.053)	(0.032)	(0.040)
Satisfaction with democracy	–	–	−0.112***	–	−0.135***	–	−0.067**	–	–
			(0.015)		(0.018)		(0.025)		
Political trust	–	−0.066***	–	–	–	–	–	–	−0.029
		(0.008)							(0.022)
Year	0.001***	0.002***	−0.002***	0.003***	0.003***	0.003***	0.003***	−0.001***	−0.002***
	(0.000)	(0.000)	(0.000)	(0.000)	(0.000)	(0.000)	(0.001)	(0.000)	(0.000)
Intercept	−2.090***	−3.931***	4.253***	−5.487***	−4.870***	−5.915***	−6.160**	2.363***	4.410***
	(0.380)	(0.440)	(0.961)	(0.506)	(0.661)	(0.549)	(1.900)	(0.300)	(0.652)
N	20,736	17,847	14,166	12,601	11,159	15,958	6,825	13,747	8,664
R^2	0.008	0.013	0.009	0.016	0.016	0.026	0.015	0.014	0.012

Note: Robust standard errors in parentheses. $^*p < 0.05$, $^{**}p < 0.01$, $^{***}p < 0.001$.

vote choice. As Chapter 5 has indicated, however, there is very little empirical evidence to support this claim.

This book makes the argument that a more promising explanation of the change lies in the implications of change near the front end of the funnel of causality on the extent to which voters' choices are structured and guided by their memberships of different social groups. Voters' choices, I argue, increasingly lack structure and are made by means of a decision process that is more unconstrained, implying that different factors and determinants do not all point towards a single party. To capture this lack of constraint, I rely on a measure of group-based cross-pressure. I argue that such group-based cross-pressures, which emanate from the cross-cutting influence of citizens' social characteristics are a key determinant of unstable voting behaviour.

Chapter 8 showed that electorates in many established democracies, especially the proportional European countries studied here, are increasingly cross-pressured—based on their socio-demographic characteristics. In addition, the results from Chapter 9 pointed out that group-based cross-pressures weaken party attachments and strengthen a feeling of cross-pressure based on other, more short-term, determinants of the vote. These patterns are suggestive of the anchoring role that socio-demographic characteristics can play in voters' decision-making processes. Lacking such anchors, I argue, voters will be more uncertain what party to vote for and switch parties more often.

The results presented in this chapter lend support to this argument. Voters who are, based on their social characteristics, more cross-pressured between parties make their voting decisions later and switch parties more often. What is more, the connection between group-based cross-pressures and party switching is rather strong. This is clear from the cross-sectional analyses, and an analysis of panel data suggests that a high degree of cross-pressure is also predictive of switching later on.

Furthermore, the results that are presented in this chapter indicate that the impact of such group-based cross-pressures is not well captured by measures of partisanship. Even though I theorized in Chapter 6 that group-based cross-pressures should weaken the development of strong attachments to parties, accounting for survey-based measures of whether individuals identify with a party does not strongly reduce the estimated effect of group-based cross-pressures. These group-based cross-pressures, therefore, are not a mere proxy measure of partisanship.

Overall, the results offer more evidence for the argument that the rise in electoral volatility is, at least in part, a consequence of voters being increasingly cross-pressured between parties.

11
Conclusion

Electoral behaviour is growing more volatile over time, with increasingly large sections of the electorate making their voting decision late in the campaign and a surge in the proportion of voters that switches parties between elections. While these trends are well established, we know less about the individual-level behaviour that underpins the instability in voters' electoral choices. The key motivation for this book was therefore to find what it is that has changed in the ways in which voters choose parties or candidates that results in voting decisions that are more unstable.

Much previous work has asked the exact same question. That work has pointed to the role of different types of vote-choice determinants and has argued that a shift in the weight of different factors is a key cause of change. In particular, an assumption that guides research on this question is that the impact of long-term factors has declined while short-term determinants of the vote increasingly guide voters' choices. As I have shown, the empirical evidence to support it is remarkably weak and inconsistent.

With this observation as a starting point, this book had three main goals: (1) to scrutinize the available evidence for existing theories of change in the voting decision process; (2) to propose an alternative theory of change, which differs from existing theories by shifting the focus away from the weight of different determinants of the vote to their inter-connections; and (3) to empirically test the validity of this new theory of change.

To recap, the theoretical argument that I make is that the instability in electoral choices is not driven by whether or not specific types of vote choice determinants (e.g. long-term or short-term) shape the vote but by the connections between factors of the vote choice. More specifically, if different vote-choice determinants all push a voter in one direction, that should stabilize their vote. In contrast, when different determinants of the vote pull voters towards different parties, voters are cross-pressured and ultimately more volatile.

In this concluding chapter, I first review the main conclusions and findings of the previous chapters. In a second section, I expand on the heterogeneity of the patterns between countries and what factors could contribute to these

Voters Under Pressure. Ruth Dassonneville, Oxford University Press. © Ruth Dassonneville (2023).
DOI: 10.1093/oso/9780192894137.003.0011

differences. Having dedicated an entire book to studying change over time, I then turn to the question how things might (or might not) further change in the future. In a further section, I highlight the limitations the book and point to directions for future research on electoral volatility and its sources. I conclude with a discussion of the main implications of the findings for electoral democracies.

11.1 Summary of the book

The goal of this book was to gain insights in the sources for the rise in electoral volatility, with specific attention given to the connection between how voters choose and how stable the outcome of their decision process is. To answer that question, I employed individual-level survey data from eight established democracies: Australia, Canada, Denmark, Germany, Great Britain, the Netherlands, Sweden, and the United States. Each of these countries has a long tradition of fielding election surveys, and there is a great deal of continuity in the measures that are included in these election surveys, as well as a fair amount of overlap in survey measures between the different countries. In a few instances, I complemented the analyses of historical election survey data with other surveys, in particular those from the European Election Studies project. I also complemented the cross-sectional analysis with a test with panel data. My analyses of this wealth of data provide important insights in the individual-level sources of volatility and offer evidence that is in line with my argument that voting decisions that are characterized by a high level of group-based cross-pressure are key to explaining electoral volatility.

As Chapter 1 has shown, there is much evidence of change. Aggregate-level election results show that parties' vote shares are increasingly unstable between elections, and individual-level survey data also provide evidence of change. Of the eight established democracies for which I analyse survey data, there are five countries where the percentage of campaign deciders has substantially increased and seven where the share of party switchers has grown over time. In the countries where there is evidence of change, furthermore, the indicators of instability in voters' electoral behaviour point to a rather stark surge in instability.

Given the strength and the nature of this change, it should not come as a surprise that much research has already been conducted on the topic of volatility. Several authors, furthermore, have theorized about the connections between determinants of the vote and the instability of voters' choices. In Chapter 2, I summarized the main arguments that can be found in previous work, with specific attention given to theories about the decline of long-term determinants of the vote and a counterbalancing increase in the effect of short-term factors. I also pointed out that this work—either explicitly or implicitly—assumes that factors which are thought of as long-term determinants always stabilize voters' choices while short-term determinants are always thought of as a source of instability. The key argument that is made in this chapter is that this assumption overlooks the strong connections between different determinants of the vote, both long- and short-term. As a consequence of these connections, long-term determinants of the vote can sometimes be a source of instability. And short-term factors can sometimes stabilize choices.

To further convince readers of the need for rethinking the link between changes in voters' decision-making processes and electoral volatility, Chapters 3–5 offered a systematic examination of the empirical evidence for different theories of change. In Chapter 3, I examined the impact of individuals' socio-demographic characteristics on their vote choice. This chapter clarified that scholarly work is very much divided on the question of whether the effect of social characteristics on the vote is in decline or not. The empirical evidence that is presented in this chapter focuses on the explanatory power of socio-demographic variables over time in each of the eight countries studied in this book. The analyses offer further evidence to suggest that the decline in the impact these variables has been limited overall.

In Chapter 4, I examined the role of partisanship and the possibility that dealignment drives the increase in electoral volatility. This chapter points out that even though there are indications of a decline in the proportion of partisans in several countries, the trend is fairly moderate in most contexts and often linked to a specific time period rather than being continuous. In addition, the analyses that are presented in this chapter indicate that the increase in volatility is not limited to non-partisans but that those who report being a partisan as well have become more likely to switch parties.

In the final chapter of the first part of the book, Chapter 5, I focused on the role of short-term determinants of the vote, with particular attention given to the effects of evaluations of the state of the economy and of party leaders. In line with previous work that has studied the effects of such short-term factors longitudinally, my analyses do not show strong evidence of change. Instead, I find that the impact of economic evaluations on the vote choice has remained largely stable in each of the eight established democracies analysed. Furthermore, the explanatory power of citizens' leader ratings also appears to have remained largely stable over time—especially in those countries where electoral volatility has increased strongly.

Given that the empirical evidence for alternative theories of change is rather thin overall, in the second part of the book I developed and tested a new theory of change. In Chapter 6, I presented a theoretical argument that is based on two key claims. First, I argued that depending on the connections between different determinants of the vote choice and whether they all pull a voter towards one party or are associated with support for different parties, a voter's decision-making process is either constrained or unconstrained. Voting decisions that are characterized by much constraint, I further theorized, should result in more stability than unconstrained decision-making processes. Second, I posited that the presence of cross-pressures emanating from citizens' socio-demographic characteristics are crucial to determining whether or not a voter's decision process will be constrained. When the influences of different social characteristics are cross-cutting, feelings of cross-pressure trickle down in the funnel of causality, resulting in a voting decision process that lacks constraint. In a final section of this chapter, I elaborated on the conditions under which group-based cross-pressures become more likely. I specifically indicated that both the number of cleavages that are salient and the extent to which cleavages are encapsulated are likely important factors. And given overtime trends with respect to both of these items, it is quite plausible that the extent to which voters are cross-pressured, based on their group memberships and social characteristics, has increased over time.

In Chapter 7, then, I turned to empirics and presented a measure that allows—at an individual level—to what extent voters are cross-pressured to be captured. I built on the work of Brader, Tucker and Therriault (2014) to present a measure of group-based cross-pressure and also explored the meaning of this measure in more depth. Notably, I showed that those who report that their vote choice is driven by their group memberships are less cross-pressured on average. An analysis of patterns in the reported propensities to vote for different parties offered further face validity to the measure of cross-pressures. More specifically, I found that those who score higher on the empirically constructed measure of cross-pressure rate their propensity to vote for different parties more equally—suggesting that they effectively feel more ambivalent between parties.

Having introduced a measure that is well suited to test my theoretical argument, I next turned to testing the implications of the theory. In particular, three expectations were tested: (1) that levels of group-based cross-pressure in established democracies have increased over time, (2) that group-based cross-pressures trickle down to affect other determinants of the vote, and (3) that higher levels of group-based cross-pressure are associated with more instability in the vote. The analyses that I presented show support for each of these three expectations.

In Chapter 8, I showed that in seven of the eight countries that are analysed, levels of group-based cross-pressure have increased over time—the exception being the United States. These trends are particularly strong in the proportional European countries that are studied, though there are also hints of change in Australia, Canada, and Great Britain. These patterns of change, I also found, are not driven by a process of generational replacement. With the exception of Australia, the over-time patterns suggest that all generations have been affected by change and have grown more cross-pressured over time.

The consequences of group-based cross-pressure for other determinants of the vote choice were examined in Chapter 9. Specifically, I tested the expectation that group-based cross-pressures imply that citizens lack an anchor and that a lack of constraint therefore trickles down in the funnel of causality. The results that I reported in this chapter offer evidence that is in line with these expectations. First, I found that those who are more cross-pressured, based on their socio-demographic characteristics, are less likely to report being a partisan. The association between group-based cross-pressure and partisanship is far from perfect, however, suggesting that the two concepts are related but conceptually and empirically distinct. A second set of results that was presented in this chapter shows that respondents who are more cross-pressured, based on their socio-demographics, are also more cross-pressured because of their short-term political attitudes, such as their economic and leader evaluations or their positions on issues.

The final and main empirical test of my theoretical argument consists of an examination of the connection between group-based cross-pressure and indicators of instability in voters' choices. In Chapter 10, I provided such a test, with a focus on two indicators of instability: the timing of the voting decision and party switching. For both indicators, I found evidence of a significant and substantively important association with group-based cross-pressure. The more cross-pressured individuals are, based on their socio-demographic characteristics, the higher are their chances of deciding whom to vote for during the campaign (rather than before) and the higher their likelihood of switching parties between elections. I furthermore complemented the correlational analyses based on cross-sectional election surveys with an analysis of British panel data. This test suggests that individuals who are more cross-pressured between parties in one election are more likely to subsequently change parties.

In summary, I have argued that to understand whether a voter's choice is stable or unstable we have to look at the extent to which their voting decision process is constrained. I furthermore theorized that a main source of constraint originates in the role of socio-demographic characteristics and the extent to which these are a source of cross-pressure. The results of my empirical analyses are largely in line with the theory, showing that group-based cross-pressures have become more widespread over time, that these cross-pressures are connected to other determinants of the vote choice, and that individuals who are more cross-pressured, based on their socio-demographics, report electoral behaviour that is characterized by more instability. Even though the patterns are broadly in line with my expectations, the analyses also showed important differences between countries. In section 11.2, I elaborate on these differences and expand on likely sources of the between-country heterogeneity in the data.

11.2 The role of context

I started this book manuscript with the observation that electoral behaviour in many established democracies is growing more volatile and unstable over time. Aggregate-level indicators, such as the Pedersen index of net volatility, provide evidence of such a change. Furthermore, individual-level data—when they are available—show evidence of change at the voter level. While there is thus much evidence of change, this does not mean that all established democracies are witnessing an increase in volatility or that the surge is equally strong across settings.

Just focusing on the eight countries that are studied in depth in this book, the data suggest important differences in levels of volatility. The time trends of the percentage of switchers in election studies over time that were presented in Chapter 1 are telling in this regard (see, in particular, Figures 1.2 and 1.3). These graphs show a strong increase in volatility in Denmark, Germany, the Netherlands, and Sweden; a more moderate increase in Australia, Canada, and Great Britain; and no evidence of an increase in party switching in the United States. To some extent, these differences were to be expected. Naturally, under less permissive electoral rules, and when the number of viable parties that voters could consider switching to is smaller, we should expect less volatility (Bischoff, 2013; Dassonneville and Hooghe, 2017*a*). The majoritarian electoral systems that are used in Australia, Canada, Great Britain, and the United States, in other words, should result in lower *levels* of volatility. Furthermore, such institutional rules can be expected to moderate the impact of voter-driven change. Even if voters in these countries are less anchored over time, the impact of this change can be expected to be muted because majoritarian rules 'set severe constraints on voter choice, limiting expressive voting in favour of more strategic behaviour' (Mair, 2008: 43).[1] Under majoritarian rules, in other words, the behavioural consequences of changes in voters' anchoring to parties and in the ways in which voters choose parties should be more limited.

Information on electoral rules, however, is not helpful for explaining why there is evidence of more volatility in Australia, Canada, and Great Britain but no evidence of change in the United States. The US case, therefore, deserves more discussion. In terms of the main results that are presented in this book, there is evidence that in the United States, as in the other countries, individuals who are more group-based cross-pressured between parties are more likely to decide late and to switch parties. Thus, the connection between group-based constraint and volatility is present in the United States as well. However, and crucially, the time trends that were presented in Chapter 8 offered no indications that individuals in the United States have grown more cross-pressured over time. If anything, the patterns suggest that a growing part of the US electorate has very low group-based cross-pressure (CP) scores.

Admittedly, in contrast to the other majoritarian systems that are studied in this book, the United States is a true two-party system. This should further reduce the likelihood of switching and also the likelihood that one considers another party—and therefore cross-pressure. However, the United States have been a two-party system throughout the period of observation, leaving the *declining* trend in individuals' CP score unaccounted for.

Analysing the reasons for difference in sources of cross-pressures between countries, and in particular between the United States and the other countries, is outside the scope of this manuscript. But work that studies the US case specifically offers a few indications of what might lead Americans to grow less group-based cross-pressured over time. On the one hand, there is much evidence of an ideological polarization of the political elite in the United States (Layman et al., 2010; McCarty, Poole, and Rosenthal, 2016). Much like having few options to choose between, having options that diverge strongly in terms of what they offer and the politics they stand for should reduce citizens' willingness to switch parties but also the likelihood that they would consider different parties. There is not only evidence of polarization at the elite level but also of

---

[1] Though other work argues that strategic voting is as high in majoritarian systems as it is under proportional rules (Abramson et al., 2010).

mass polarization. In terms of their ideological positions, and also in terms of how Americans feel about the other party, there are indications of a strongly polarized and divided public opinion (Iyengar et al., 2019). At the individual level as well, having more polarized and extreme ideological views and feeling negative affect towards the other party should substantially decrease the extent to which voters are drawn to multiple parties. Potentially even more important to understanding the decline in group-based cross-pressures in the United States is the observation that the US electorate is socially sorting (Mason, 2016; Mason and Wronski, 2018). Specifically, there are indications that Americans' group identities are increasingly in line with their partisan preferences. For example, religion (Layman, 2001) and race (Mason, 2016), but also where one lives (Brown and Enos, 2021) have become more closely connected to partisanship over time, to a point where race and partisanship, for example, are seen as 'inseparable' (Westwood and Peterson, forthcoming). This process of social sorting and the increasingly strong connection between specific group identities and partisanship can be expected to substantially reduce cross-pressure. As Mason (2016) points out, when specific social identities—such as race or religion—become strongly aligned with party support, other identities that could have a cross-cutting influence matter less. When social identities are strongly connected to partisanship thus, it is those identities that structure citizens' political views and behaviour. Because of social sorting, regardless of one's gender, level of education, or income, for example, a Black voter will identify with the Democratic party and vote for its candidates.

Given these insights, it should not come as a complete surprise that the results that are presented in Chapter 8 show a decline in levels of group-based cross-pressures in the United States. In contexts where partisans are strongly socially sorted, multiple group identities should not lead to a feeling of cross-pressure.

11.3 What comes next?

The observation that there are important differences in the over-time trends between countries not only highlights that the processes that are described in this book are to some extent context-dependent but also serves as a reminder that the increase in electoral volatility could at some point be halted, or even reversed.

Of course, only in hindsight will we be able to tell whether the current time period and present levels of volatility are exceptional or a new normal. However, the results that are presented in this book do provide insights on what it would take for electoral volatility to increase further or for electoral instability to decline again. Having identified group-based cross-pressures as a key source of volatility, the strength of peoples' social identities and connections between social group memberships and parties are key. In what follows, I walk through a number of ways in which the political role of socio-demographic characteristics and group memberships might (further) change in the future. Each of these changes has different implications for the presence of group-based cross-pressures and consequently for electoral volatility.

A first possibility is that dynamics of group-based encapsulation, which matter especially for identities based on religion and social class, further weaken. In Chapter 6, I presented time series data of trade union membership and church attendance that are consistent with the idea of a decline of encapsulation across countries—though in varying degrees. If these trends continue in the future, the implication would be that an even smaller share of the electorate will be 'encapsulated' based on their class identity or their religious denomination. If these trends continue, that should result in a further growth of group-based cross-pressures in the electorate, leading to more volatility. This possibility is not restricted to the role of 'old' cleavages. In theory, all types of group memberships and social identities might lose political importance, weakening their connection to party preferences. Parties can, to some extent, contribute to such a change by positioning themselves as parties for broad categories of people rather than specific groups such as those based on class (on this point, see the work of Thau, 2018).

A second scenario is one in which even more social characteristics and types of group memberships gain political relevance. There are in fact many group identities and characteristics for which recent scholarship shows that they shape voting behaviour but that are not accounted for in this book. For example, there is work which points out that those who are employed in the public sector have different attitudes and political preferences than individuals who work in the private sector (Abou-Chadi and Hix, 2021). Other research draws attention to the association between sexuality and voting (Turnbull-Dugarte, 2020*b*, *a*). In addition, there are good reasons to assume that the increasing ethnic diversity of the electorate in many established democracies provides conditions that are prosperous for the development and strengthening of an ethnic or racial cleavage in electoral behaviour (Ford and Jennings, 2020). Due to data limitations, the analyses that I present in this book account for the role of race in the United States only, but there are indications that race and racial identities matter in other settings as well (Beauvais, 2022). If these and other group identities gain in political relevance, while other group memberships and social characteristics still matter, this potentially increases the number of cleavages. And with more cleavages, the expectation is that more citizens are members of cross-cutting cleavage groups and therefore, on average, more cross-pressured between parties. Under this type of change, therefore, electoral volatility could be expected to increase further.

Third, even when holding constant the number of group characteristics that are linked to political cleavages in a particular setting, change could be driven by variation in the share of the electorate for which these different group memberships really matter and shape their voting behaviour. For example, if, for a growing group of individuals, their educational background or their gender develop into political identities that shape voting behaviour, that could lead to higher levels of cross-pressure on average—resulting in more volatility.

Finally, there is a type of change under which group-based cross-pressures would decrease, resulting in lower electoral volatility too. For such a change to happen, we should see a decrease in the number of group memberships that guide people's party preferences or a substantial strengthening of the role of one or a limited number of group identities. The idea is that if one or a limited number of group identities are particularly salient, the role of other and potentially cross-cutting group memberships weakens, therefore reducing cross-pressure (Mason, 2016). In other words, if—through a process of sorting or in some other way—one specific identity becomes strongly aligned with party preferences, the outcome will resemble a situation of 'encapsulation', whereby that identity entirely anchors citizens' party preferences and their political behaviour. As indicated in section 11.2, there are indications of partisan social sorting in the United States. But in other countries as well it is not implausible that, at some point, cross-pressures will decline again because specific identities become particularly salient and dominate voters' choices. If we are in a process of a fundamental realignment of party competition, whereby, for example, the universalism–particularism divide will eventually become the main cleavage in voting behaviour (Bornschier et al., 2021), the characteristics that are related to that cleavage could end up dominating and overcrowding the role of other and potentially cross-cutting group memberships.

Which of these different scenarios will materialize is hard to predict. But the key insight from this book is that social characteristics and group memberships are important factors in the trajectory of electoral volatility. We are not seeing a surge in volatility because individuals' socio-demographics and other long-term determinants of the vote have become irrelevant to their vote choice. Rather, volatility rises when individuals' group memberships are a source of conflict and cross-pressure. Change in the cross-cutting influences of those socio-demographic characteristics could thus well change the over-time trend and bring back electoral volatility to somewhat lower levels.

11.4 Future research directions

The objective of this book project was to shed light on sources of the strong increase in electoral volatility that can be observed in many established democracies. In particular, the question that guided my research is what has changed in the ways in which voters choose parties to result in electoral choices that have become less certain and less stable.

The nature of this question, which concerns change over an extended period over time, informed the methodological choices that I made and the decision to rely on historical and cross-sectional election study data. In addition, because the trend in electoral volatility is present and visible in many established democracies, I opted for a comparative analysis, using data from eight different countries. I am convinced that this approach offers the best *possible* way to study change in voters' behaviour over time and if I were to restart this project, I would proceed in the same way. Still, my approach comes with a number of limitations, and alternative designs and approaches should therefore be relied on in future research studying the connections between group-based cross-pressure and voter volatility.

First, in an effort to increase the comparability of the analyses, both within countries over time and between countries, the empirical tests that are presented in this book rely on a limited number of fairly standard indicators of citizens' socio-demographic characteristics. This implies that several characteristics and group identities are not accounted for at all in the measures of cross-pressure. Racial identities, for example, are only consistently measured in US election surveys. In light of rises in migration rates and the growing ethnic and racial diversity of electorates in many countries, not taking into account how these identities contribute to or lessen cross-pressure in recent elections can be thought of as an important omission. For other variables and group identities, the measures that are used are not very refined. To capture the role of class, for example, I either rely on respondents' subjective identifications with social class groups or I proxy the role that occupational classes play by interacting respondents' income and level of education (by doing so, I follow an approach that was proposed by Kitschelt and Rehm, 2019). We know, however, that more detailed measures of, for example, individuals' occupational class are better suited to track changes in class structure and their impact on the vote (Oesch, 2006). Similarly, a focus on a distinction between men and women is only a blunt measure for capturing the role that gender identities play in shaping citizens' political opinions and preferences (Bittner and Goodyear-Grant, 2017). To comprehensively study the ways in which individuals' social characteristics and group identities structure their party preferences, and the ways in which these different identities are a source of cross-pressure or not, future research should disentangle as much as possible the broad categories of individuals' group memberships. Work that does not specifically aim to study change in cross-pressures over time or that does not seek to compare across countries could make most of the rich data that have been collected in public opinion surveys and election studies in several contexts to discern group memberships more and to obtain a more precise measure of group-based cross-pressure.

Building on this point, in studying the connections between group-based cross-pressures and volatility, I decided to rely on a measure of how much individuals are group-based cross-pressured overall. These cross-pressures, however, deserve to be disentangled more in future research. In particular, it would be insightful to examine more specifically whether some characteristics and identities provoke stronger feelings of cross-pressure than others when they cross-cut with other cleavages. Research from the United States points in this direction, with Cassese (2020), for example, showing that gender did not have a cross-cutting influence among White Evangelical women. Subsequent research could evaluate in particular whether some characteristics are especially prone to cross-pressure individuals and whether there is change in the main socio-demographics and identities that lead voters to feel cross-pressured. Furthermore, to gain insights in differences in cross-pressures between individuals, it would be insightful to think about and develop measures of cross-pressure that combine information on individuals' group memberships and the strength of their identification with those groups. The measures that are relied on in this manuscript only include information on group membership; extending this framework to consider identity strength as well seems like a logical next step to take.

As an important limitation, the results that are presented in this book manuscript are based on analyses of observational data and are mostly correlational in nature. I complement the purely cross-sectional analyses of historical election survey data with panel analyses as a way to give more credence to the argument that group-based cross-pressures are a source of, and hence precede, volatility. When the goal is not to study change over an extended period of time but instead to gain insights into the causal mechanisms that connect group-based cross-pressures and electoral behaviour, researchers could make use of experimental methods. Such work could rely on designs that prime different identities in respondents to generate a feeling of cross-pressure (Klar, 2013) in order to subsequently evaluate how this affects certainty of the vote choice. Insights on the mechanisms behind the role of cross-pressures could also be gained from work that manipulates the connection between parties or candidates and identity groups by means of treatments that include cues or appeals that target specific groups (Adida, Davenport, and McClendon, 2016; Holman, Schneider, and Pondel, 2015). Such appeals can generate cross-pressure in some participants, which can then have an incidence on the certainty of their preference for one party or candidate over another. Of course, such experimental approaches would not provide information on how the voting decision process has changed over time to spur more volatility and would not allow examining over-time change in levels of cross-pressure. But experimental designs along these lines could provide important insights into the ways in which cross-pressures influence voters' decision making and their electoral choices, as well as helping to disentangle the relative importance that different types of group identities have for generating feelings of cross-pressure.

Another point that deserves further scrutiny is the connection between cross-pressure and partisanship. At a theoretical level, I argued that individuals who are cross-pressured—based on their socio-demographic characteristics—are less likely to develop an attachment with a party. The empirical results confirm that there is a negative association between cross-pressure and partisanship, but it remains weak. To some extent, the lack of a strong connection between partisanship and group-based cross-pressures might reflect the difficulties of measuring party attachments in survey research. Another possibility is that the meaning of partisanship—as measured in surveys—changes over time. The results that are presented in this book hint at such a change with, for example, evidence that partisans are more likely to switch parties in recent elections than at the start of the time series. More work is needed, however, to disentangle the role of partisanship and dealignment in the process of change that I have described in this book.

Finally, I decided to study the sources of electoral volatility at an individual level and with a focus on voters' behaviour. The results of my analyses show evidence of a connection between individuals' attitudes and their voting decision process, on the one hand, and levels of electoral volatility, on the other. At the same time, we know that voters do not make their choices in a void and that their voting decision reflect the options on the ballot. Much work has already shown that the effects of socio-demographic characteristics on the vote vary as a function of the party offer. Class voting, for example, has been shown to be strengthened when it is clearer for voters which parties defend the interests of specific classes, signalled by their ideological positions (Evans and Tilley, 2012; Evans and De Graaf, 2013), by the class backgrounds of MPs (Heath, 2015), or by means of programmatic and symbolic group appeals (Robison et al., 2021; Thau, 2021). Future studies should examine whether parties' behaviour, the positions they take, and the appeals they make affect not only the impact of specific socio-demographic characteristics on the vote but also whether they influence cross-pressures. Such work could help to disentangle the role and importance of demand- and supply-side factors in generating electoral change. It would be particularly interesting to explore whether over-time changes in parties' behaviour are linked to the increase in voters' cross-pressure in several democracies. For example, is there evidence to show that the social group signals and appeals that parties send have become less distinctive over time? Or is there evidence that parties appeal to a larger number of different groups, politicizing more cleavages and consequently increasing the chances of cross-pressure at the voter level? Work along these lines could make use of party platforms or media information and conduct content analyses of these materials over an extended period of time to identify change. Similar analyses have already been conducted with a focus on class and economic appeals in some countries but could be extended both geographically and thematically (Thau, 2018, 2019).

11.5 Concluding thoughts

The strong increase in electoral volatility that can be observed in many established democracies is one of the most remarkable changes in modern democratic politics. As a result of this change, the electoral context in which parties and candidates compete for votes differs starkly from electoral competition in the 1960s. By switching parties more frequently and in larger numbers, present-day voters introduce a great deal of instability in election outcomes and create more uncertainty for politicians and parties. On the one hand, the fact that party loyalty has waned in many established democracies can be thought of as a good thing because the need to convince voters over and over can serve as an incentive for parties to govern well, deliver on their promises, and be responsive to public opinion (Dassonneville, 2018). At the same time, high levels of volatility and electoral uncertainty arguably reduce the time horizon under which politicians can operate and push them to be immediately responsive to public opinion—even if doing so conflicts with responsible decision making (Mair, 2013).

Given the huge implications that volatility has for governing and governability, it is important that we understand its sources. If we know why voters are more or less uncertain about their choice, we can also think about factors that could bring down volatility. With this book, I attempted to clarify the sources of volatility by focusing specifically on the connections between different determinants of voters' choices rather than on the overall effect of (groups of) determinants that are assumed to have a stabilizing or destabilizing effect on the vote. I proposed a theoretical framework around the notion of cross-pressure, whereby the key distinction is whether different vote-choice determinants pull a voter towards one party (which should stabilize the vote) or instead have cross-cutting influences that destabilize choices. I have further theorized that cross-pressures emanate from individuals' socio-demographic characteristics and group memberships and subsequently trickle down to affect other determinants of the vote too.

The results broadly support my theoretical expectations, showing that group-based cross-pressures have become more widespread in many countries and that group-based cross-pressures make for more unconstrained voting-decision processes and are associated with late deciding and party switching. Group-based cross-pressures, this suggests, are an important source of electoral volatility. The implication is that volatility levels can decline again if the cross-cutting influences of individuals' different group memberships and social identities can be reduced. Such a change is not completely inconceivable, as I indicated in section 11.3.

Ultimately, this book shows that long-term determinants of the vote matter. Group characteristics were not only important to explain the vote in a time of 'frozen cleavages'. Even in contexts of high electoral volatility and party system change, this book shows, long-term socio-demographic characteristics explain people's choices—and crucially the stability of their choices. The connection between socio-demographics and volatility is explained by the fact that individuals' group characteristics can be a source of volatility if their influences cross-cut. I hope that this research can serve as a starting point for more work on the connection between group-based cross-pressure, voters' decision-making processes, and volatility—there is much still to be explored.

Bibliography

Aarts, Kees, André Blais, and Hermann Schmitt. 2011. *Political Leaders and Democratic Elections*. Oxford: Oxford University Press.

Abendschön, Simone and Stephanie Steinmetz. 2014. 'The gender gap in voting revisited: Women's party preferences in a European context'. *Social Politics* 21(1): 315–344.

Abou-Chadi, Tarik and Simon Hix. 2021. 'Brahmin Left versus Merchant Right? Education, class, multiparty competition, and redistribution in Western Europe'. *British Journal of Sociology* 72(1): 79–92.

Abramson, Paul R., John H. Aldrich, André Blais, et al. 2010. 'Comparing strategic voting under FPTP and PR'. *Comparative Political Studies* 43(1): 61–90.

Adams, James and Samuel Merrill III. 2003. 'Voter turnout and candidate strategies in American elections'. *Journal of Politics* 65(1): 161–189.

Adams, James, Jay Dow, and Samuel Merrill. 2006. 'The political consequences of alienation-based and indifference-based voter abstention: Applications to presidential elections'. *Political Behavior* 28(1): 65–86.

Adida, Claire L., Lauren D. Davenport, and Gwyneth McClendon. 2016. 'Ethnic cueing across minorities: A survey experiment on candidate evaluation in the United States'. *Public Opinion Quarterly* 80(4): 815–836.

Alford, R. 1962. 'A suggested index of the association of social class and voting'. *Public Opinion Quarterly* 26: 417–425.

Andeweg, Rudy B. 2000. 'Consociational democracy'. *Annual Review of Political Science* 3(1): 509–536.

Anduiza, Eva, Aina Gallego, and Jordi Muñoz. 2013. 'Turning a blind eye: Experimental evidence of partisan bias in attitudes toward corruption'. *Comparative Political Studies* 46(12): 1664–1692.

Arzheimer, Kai. 2017. 'Another dog that didn't bark? Less dealignment and more partisanship in the 2013 Bundestag election'. *German Politics* 26(1): 49–64.

Arzheimer, Kai and Elisabeth Carter. 2009. 'Christian religiosity and voting for West European Radical Right Parties'. *West European Politics* 32(5): 985–1011.

Bailey, Jack. 2019. 'The fact remains: Party ID moderates how voters respond to economic change'. *Electoral Studies* 61: 102071.

Bankert, Alexa, Leonie Huddy, and Martin Rosema. 2017. 'Measuring partisanship as a social identity in multi-party systems'. *Political Behavior* 39(1): 103–132.

Bartels, Larry M. 2000. 'Partisanship and voting behavior, 1952–1996'. *American Journal of Political Science* 44(1): 35–50.

Bartels, Larry M. 2002. 'Beyond the running tally: Partisan bias in political perceptions'. *Political Behavior* 24(2): 117–150.

Bartle, John and Paolo Bellucci, eds. 2009. *Political Parties and Partisanship: Social Identity and Individual Attitudes*. London: Routledge.

Bartolini, Stefano and Peter Mair. 1990. *Identity, Competition and Electoral Availability. The Stability of European Electorates 1885–1985*. Cambridge: Cambridge University Press.

Beauvais, E. 2022. 'The Political Consequences of Indigenous Resentment'. *Journal of Race, Ethnicity, and Politics* 7(1), 37–64.

Beck, Paul A., Russell J. Dalton, Steven Greene, and Robert Huckfeldt. 2002. 'The social calculus of voting: Interpersonal, media, and organizational influences on presidential choices'. *American Political Science Review* 96(1): 57–73.

Bélanger, Éric. 2004. 'The rise of third parties in the 1993 Canadian federal election: Pinard revisited'. *Canadian Journal of Political Science* 37(3): 581–594.

Benedetto, Giacomo, Simon Hix, and Nicola Mastrorocco. 2020. 'The rise and fall of social democracy, 1918–2017'. *American Political Science Review* 114(3): 928–939.

Berelson, Bernard R., Paul F. Lazarsfeld, and William N. McPhee. 1954. *Voting. A Study of Opinion Formation in a Presidential Campaign*. Chicago, IL/London: University of Chicago Press.

Berglund, Frode, Sören Holmberg, Hermann Schmitt, and Jacques Thomassen. 2005. 'Party identification and party choice'. In *The European Voter: A Comparative Study of Modern Democracies*, ed. Jacques Thomassen. Oxford: Oxford University Press, pp. 105–123.

Best, Robin E. 2011. 'The declining electoral relevance of traditional cleavage groups'. *European Political Science Review* 3(2): 279–300.

Bischoff, Carina S. 2013. 'Electorally unstable by supply or demand?—An examination of the causes of electoral volatility in advanced industrial democracies'. *Public Choice* 156(3–4): 537–561.

Bisgaard, Martin. 2015. 'Bias will find a way: Economic perceptions, attributions of blame, and partisan-motivated reasoning during crisis'. *Journal of Politics* 77(3): 849–860.

Bisgaard, Martin. 2019. 'How getting the facts right can fuel partisan-motivated reasoning'. *American Journal of Political Science* 63(4): 824–839.

Bisgaard, Martin and Rune Slothuus. 2018. 'Partisan elites as culprits? How party cues shape partisan perceptual gaps'. *American Journal of Political Science* 62(2): 456–469.

Bittner, Amanda. 2015. 'Leader evaluations and partisan stereotypes: A comparative analysis'. In *Personality Politics? The Role of Leader Evaluations in Democratic Elections*, ed. Marina Costa Lobo and John Curtice. Oxford: Oxford University Press, pp. 17–37.

Bittner, Amanda. 2018. 'Leaders always mattered: The persistence of personality in Canadian elections'. *Electoral Studies* 54: 297–302.

Bittner, Amanda and Elizabeth Goodyear-Grant. 2017. 'Sex isn't gender: Reforming concepts and measurements in the study of public opinion'. *Political Behavior* 39(4): 1019–1041.

Blais, André, Pierre Martin, and Richard Nadeau. 1998. 'Can people explain their own vote? Introspective questions as indicators of salience in the 1995 Quebec referendum on sovereignty'. *Quality and Quantity* 32(4): 355–366.

Blais, André, Elisabeth Gidengil, Richard Nadeau, and Neil Nevitte. 2001. 'Measuring party identification: Britain, Canada and the United States'. *Political Behavior* 23(1): 5–22.

Blumenstiel, Jan Eric and Thomas Plischke. 2015. 'Changing motivations, time of the voting decision, and short-term volatility—the dynamics of voter heterogeneity'. *Electoral Studies* 37: 28–40.

Bolsen, Toby and Thomas J. Leeper. 2013. 'Self-interest and attention to news among issue publics'. *Political Communication* 30(3): 329–348.

Bolsen, Toby and Risa Palm. 2019. 'Motivated reasoning and political decision making'. In *Oxford Research Encyclopedia of Politics*. Oxford: Oxford University Press. https://doi.org/10.1093/acrefore/9780190228637.013.923.

Bornschier, Simon, Silja Häusermann, Delia Zollinger, and Céline Colombo. 2021. 'How "us" and "them" relates to voting behavior—social structure, social identities, and electoral choice'. *Comparative Political Studies* 54: 2087–2122.

Bowler, Shaun, David J. Lanoue, and Paul Savoie. 1994. 'Electoral systems, party competition, and strength of partisan attachment: Evidence from three countries'. *Journal of Politics* 56(4): 991–1007.

Brader, Ted and Joshua A. Tucker. 2012. 'Following the party's lead: Party cues, policy opinion, and the power of partisanship in three multiparty systems'. *Comparative Politics* 44(4): 403–403.

Brader, Ted, Joshua A. Tucker, and Andrew Therriault. 2014. 'Cross pressure scores: An individual-level measure of cumulative partisan pressures arising from social group memberships'. *Political Behavior* 36(1): 23–51.

Broockman, David E. and Daniel M. Butler. 2017. 'The causal effects of elite position-taking on voter attitudes: Field experiments with elite communication'. *American Journal of Political Science* 61(1): 208–221.

Brooks, Clem, Paul Nieuwbeerta, and Jeff Manza. 2006. 'Cleavage-based voting behavior in cross-national perspective: Evidence from six postwar democracies'. *Social Science Research* 35(1): 88–128.

Brown, Jacob R. and Ryan D. Enos. 2021. 'The measurement of partisan sorting for 180 million voters'. *Nature Human Behaviour* 5: 998–1008.

Budge, Ian. 1982. 'Electoral volatility: Issue effects and basic change in 23 post-war democracies'. *Electoral Studies* 1(2): 147–168.

Budge, Ian, Ivor Crewe, and Dennis Farlie, eds. 1976. *Party Identification and Beyond: Representations of Voting and Party Competition*. New York: Wiley.

Campbell, Angus, Philip E. Converse, Warren E. Miller, and Don E. Stokes. 1960. *The American Voter*. New York: John Wiley and Sons.

Caramani, Daniele. 2004. *The Nationalization of Politics: The Formation of National Electorates and Party Systems in Western Europe*. Cambridge: Cambridge University Press.

Casal Bertoa, Fernando, Kevin Deegan-Krause, and Tim Haughton. 2017. 'The volatility of volatility: Measuring change in party vote shares'. *Electoral Studies* 50: 142–156.

Cassese, Erin C. 2020. 'Straying from the flock? A look at how Americans' gender and religious identities cross-pressure partisanship'. *Political Research Quarterly* 73(1): 169–183.

Castro Cornejo, Rodrigo. 2019. 'Partisanship and question-wording effects: Experimental evidence from Latin America'. *Public Opinion Quarterly* 83(1): 26–45.

Çakır, Semih. 2022. 'Does party ambivalence decrease voter turnout? A global analysis'. *Party Politics* 28(4): 713–726.

Chiaramonte, Alessandro and Vincenzo Emanuele. 2017. 'Party system volatility, regeneration and deinstitutionalization in Western Europe (1945–2015)'. *Party Politics* 23(2): 376–388.

Clark, Terry Nichols and Seymour Martin Lipset. 1991. 'Are social classes dying'. *International Sociology* 6(4): 397–410.

Clark, Terry Nichols, Seymour Martin Lipset, and Michael Rempel. 1993. 'The declining political significance of social class'. *International Sociology* 8(3): 293–316.

Clarke, Harold D. and Marianne C. Stewart. 1987. 'Partisan inconsistency and partisan change. Partisan inconsistency in federal states: The case of Canada'. *American Journal of Political Science* 31(2): 383–407.

Converse, Philip E. 1962. 'Information flow and the stability of partisan attitudes'. *Public Opinion Quarterly* 26(4): 578–599.

Converse, Philip E. 1964. 'The nature of belief systems in mass publics'. In *Ideology and Discontent*, ed. David E Apter. New York: Free Press, pp. 206–261.
Costa Lobo, Marina. 2006. 'Short-term voting determinants in a young democracy: Leader effects in Portugal in the 2002 legislative elections'. *Electoral Studies* 25(2): 270–286.
Cramer, Katherine J. 2016. *The Politics of Resentment: Rural Consciousness in Wisconsin and the Rise of Scott Walker*. Chicago, IL: University of Chicago Press.
Crewe, Ivor and David Denver. 1985. *Electoral Change in Western Democracies: Patterns and Sources of Electoral Volatility*. London: Croom Helm.
Crewe, Ivor, Bo Sarlvik, and James Alt. 1977. 'Partisan dealignment in Britain 1964–1974'. *British Journal of Political Science* 7(2): 129–190.
Dalton, Russell. 2020. *Citizen Politics: Public Opinion and Political Parties in Advanced Industrial Democracies*. Seventh edition. Thousand Oaks, CA: Sage.
Dalton, Russell J. 1984. 'Cognitive mobilization and partisan dealignment in advanced industrial democracies'. *Journal of Politics* 46(2): 264–284.
Dalton, Russell J. 1996. 'Political cleavages, issues, and electoral change'. In *Comparing Democracies: Elections and Voting in Global Perspective*, ed. Lawrence LeDuc, Richard G. Niemi, and Pippa Norris. Thousand Oaks, CA Sage, pp. 319–342.
Dalton, Russell J. 2012. 'Apartisans and the changing German electorate'. *Electoral Studies* 31(1): 35–45.
Dalton, Russell J. 2013. *The Apartisan American: Dealignment and Changing Electoral Politics*. Washington, DC: CQ Press.
Dalton, Russell J. 2018. *Political Realignment: Economics, Culture, and Electoral Change*. Oxford: Oxford University Press.
Dalton, Russell J. and Scott E. Flanagan, eds. 2017. *Electoral Change in Advanced Industrial Democracies: Realignment or Dealignment*. Princeton, NJ: Princeton University Press.
Dalton, Russell J. and Martin P. Wattenberg. 2002. *Parties without Partisans. Political Change in Advanced Industrial Democracies*. Oxford: Oxford University Press.
Dalton, Russell J., Ian McAllister, and Martin P. Wattenberg. 2002. 'The consequences of partisan dealignment'. In *Parties without Partisans. Political Change in Advanced Industrial Democracies*. Oxford: Oxford University Press, pp. 37–63.
Dassonneville, Ruth. 2012. 'Electoral volatility, political sophistication, trust and efficacy. A study on changes in voter preferences during the Belgian regional elections of 2009'. *Acta Politica* 47(1): 18–41.
Dassonneville, Ruth. 2013. 'Questioning generational replacement. An age, period and cohort analysis of electoral volatility in the Netherlands, 1971–2010'. *Electoral Studies* 32(1): 37–47.
Dassonneville, Ruth. 2016. 'Volatile voters, short-term choices? An analysis of the vote choice determinants of stable and volatile voters in Great Britain'. *Journal of Elections, Public Opinion and Parties* 26(3): 273–292.
Dassonneville, Ruth, and Michael S. Lewis-Beck. 2014. 'Macroeconomics, economic crisis and electoral outcomes: A national European pool'. *Acta Politica* 49(4): 372–394.
Dassonneville, Ruth. 2018. 'Electoral volatility and parties' ideological responsiveness'. *European Journal of Political Research* 57(4): 808–828.
Dassonneville, Ruth. 2021. 'Change and continuity in the ideological gender gap. A longitudinal analysis of left-right self-placement in OECD countries'. *European Journal of Political Research* 60(1): 225–238.
Dassonneville, Ruth and Yves Dejaeghere. 2014. 'Bridging the ideological space. A cross-national analysis of the distance of party switching'. *European Journal of Political Research* 53(3): 580–599.

Dassonneville, Ruth and Marc Hooghe. 2017a. 'Economic indicators and electoral volatility: Economic effects on electoral volatility in Western Europe, 1950–2013'. *Comparative European Politics* 15(6): 919–943.

Dassonneville, Ruth and Marc Hooghe. 2017b. 'The noise of the vote recall question: The validity of the vote recall question in panel studies in Belgium, Germany, and the Netherlands'. *International Journal of Public Opinion Research* 29(2): 316–338.

Dassonneville, Ruth and Marc Hooghe. 2018. 'Indifference and alienation: Diverging dimensions of electoral dealignment in Europe'. *Acta Politica* 53(1): 1–23.

Dassonneville, Ruth and Michael S. Lewis-Beck. 2019. 'A changing economic vote in Western Europe? Long-term vs. short-term forces'. *European Political Science Review* 11(1): 91–108.

Dassonneville, Ruth, Marc Hooghe, and Bram Vanhoutte. 2012. 'Age, period and cohort effects in the decline of party identification in Germany: An analysis of a two decade panel study in Germany (1992–2009)'. *German Politics* 21(2): 209–227.

Dassonneville, Ruth, André Blais, and Yves Dejaeghere. 2015. 'Staying with the party, switching or exiting? A comparative analysis of determinants of party switching and abstaining'. *Journal of Elections, Public Opinion and Parties* 25(3): 387–405.

Davis, Nicholas T and Lilliana Mason. 2016. 'Sorting and the split-ticket: Evidence from presidential and subpresidential elections'. *Political Behavior* 38(2): 337–354.

Debus, Marc, Mary Stegmaier, and Jale Tosun. 2014. 'Economic voting under coalition governments: Evidence from Germany'. *Political Science Research and Methods* 2(1): 49–67.

De Vries, Catherine and Sara Hobolt. 2020. *Political Entrepreneurs: The Rise of Challenger Parties in Europe*. Princeton, NJ: Princeton University Press.

Deegan-Krause, Kevin and Zsolt Enyedi. 2010. 'Agency and the structure of party competition: Alignment, stability and the role of political elites'. *West European Politics* 33(3): 686–710.

Dejaeghere, Yves and Ruth Dassonneville. 2017. 'A comparative investigation into the effects of party-system variables on party switching using individual-level data'. *Party Politics* 23(2): 110–123.

Deschouwer, Kris (2009). *The Politics of Belgium: Governing a Divided Society*. Basingstoke: Palgrave Macmillan.

Dinas, Elias. 2014. 'Does choice bring loyalty? Electoral participation and the development of party identification'. *American Journal of Political Science* 58(2): 449–465.

Dolezal, Martin. 2010. 'Exploring the stabilization of a political force: The social and attitudinal basis of green parties in the age of globalization'. *West European Politics* 33(3): 534–552.

Döring, Holger and Philip Manow. 2021. 'Parliaments and Governments Database (ParlGov): Information on Parties, Elections and Cabinets in Modern Democracies'. http://www.parlgov.org/.

Dow, Jay K. and James W. Endersby. 2004. 'Multinomial probit and multinomial logit: A comparison of choice models for voting research'. *Electoral Studies* 23(1): 107–122.

Druckman, James N. and Mary C. McGrath. 2019. 'The evidence for motivated reasoning in climate change preference formation'. *Nature Climate Change* 9(2): 111–119.

Duch, Raymond M. and Randolph T. Stevenson. 2008. *The Economic Vote: How Political and Economic Institutions Condition Election Results*. New York: Cambridge University Press.

Duncan, Fraser. 2015. 'Preaching to the converted? Christian democratic voting in six West European countries'. *Party Politics* 21(4): 577–590.

Endres, Kyle and Costas Panagopoulos. 2019. 'Cross-pressure and voting behavior: Evidence from randomized experiments'. *Journal of Politics* 81(3): 1090–1095.

Enyedi, Zsolt. 2008. 'The social and attitudinal basis of political parties: Cleavage politics revisited'. *European Review* 16(3): 287–304.

Erk, Jan. 2017. 'Is age the new class? Economic crisis and demographics in European politics'. *Critical Sociology* 43(1): 59–71.

Evans, Elizabeth and Meryl Kenny. 2019. 'The women's equality party: Emergence, organisation and challenges'. *Political Studies* 67(4): 855–871.

Evans, Geoffrey. 2010. 'Models, measures and mechanisms: An agenda for progress in cleavage research'. *West European Politics* 33(3): 634–647.

Evans, Geoffrey and Nan Dirk De Graaf, eds. 2013. *Political Choice Matters: Explaining the Strength of Class and Religious Cleavages in Cross-National Perspective*. Oxford: Oxford University Press.

Evans, Geoffrey and Ksenia Northmore-Ball. 2017. 'Long-term factors: Class and religious cleavages'. In *The Routledge Handbook of Elections*, ed. Justin Fisher, Edward Fieldhouse, Mark N. Franklin, Rachel Gibson, Marta Cantijoch, and Christopher Wlezien. London: Routledge.

Evans, Geoffrey and James Tilley. 2011. 'How parties shape class politics: Explaining the decline of the class basis of party support'. *British Journal of Political Science* 42(1): 137–161.

Evans, Geoffrey and James Tilley. 2012. 'The depoliticization of inequality and redistribution: Explaining the decline of class voting'. *Journal of Politics* 74(4): 963–976.

Evans, Jocelyn and Gilles Ivaldi. 2018. *The 2017 French Presidential Elections: A Political Reformation?* Basingstoke: Palgrave Macmillan.

Farrell, David M. *Electoral systems: 'A comparative introduction.'* Basingstoke: Palgrave MacMillan, 2001.

Ferreira da Silva, Frederico, Diego Garzia, and Andrea De Angelis. 2021. 'From party to leader mobilization? The personalization of voter turnout'. *Party Politics* 27(2): 220–233.

Fieldhouse, Edward, Jane Green, Geoffrey Evans et al. 2020. *Electoral Shocks. The Volatile Voter in a Turbulent World*. Oxford: Oxford University Press.

Fiorina, Morris P. 1981. *Retrospective Voting in American National Elections*. New Haven, CT: Yale University Press.

Fleury, Christopher J. and Michael S. Lewis-Beck. 1993. 'Anchoring the French voter: Ideology versus party'. *Journal of Politics* 55(4): 1100–1109.

Ford, Robert and Will Jennings. 2020. 'The Changing Cleavage Politics of Western Europe'. *Annual Review of Political Science* 23: 295–314.

Fournier, Patrick, Richard Nadeau, André Blais, Elisabeth Gidengil, and Neil Nevitte. 2004. 'Time-of-voting decision and susceptibility to campaign effects'. *Electoral Studies* 23(4): 661–681.

Franklin, Mark N., Thomas T. Mackie, and Henry Valen, eds. 1992. *Electoral Change: Responses to Evolving Social and Attitudinal Structures in Western Europe*. Cambridge: Cambridge University Press.

Gallagher, Michael. 2021. 'Electoral Systems Website. Election Indices'. http://www.tcd.ie/Political_Science/staff/michael_gallagher/ElSystems/.

Garzia, Diego. 2012. 'Party and leader effects in parliamentary elections: Towards a reassessment'. *Politics* 32(3): 175–185.

Garzia, Diego. 2013. 'Changing parties, changing partisans: The personalization of partisan attachments in Western Europe'. *Political Psychology* 34(1): 67–89.

Garzia, Diego. 2014. *Personalization of Politics and Electoral Change*. London: Palgrave Macmillan.

Garzia, Diego, Frederico Ferreira da Silva, and Andrea De Angelis. 2022. 'Partisan dealignment and the personalisation of politics in West European parliamentary democracies, 1961–2018'. *West European Politics* 45: 311–334.

Geers, Sabine and Jesper Strömbäck. 2019. 'Patterns of intra-election volatility: The impact of political knowledge'. *Journal of Elections, Public Opinion and Parties* 29(3): 361–380.

Gethin, Amory, Clara Martínez-Toledano and Thomas Piketty. 2022. 'Brahmin Left Versus Merchant Right: Changing Political Cleavages in 21 Western Democracies, 1948–2020'. *Quarterly Journal of Economics* 137(1), 1–48.

Giger, Nathalie. 2009. 'Towards a modern gender gap in Europe?' *Social Science Journal* 46(3): 474–492.

Gimpel, James G, Nathan Lovin, Bryant Moy, and Andrew Reeves. 2020. 'The urban–rural gulf in American political behavior'. *Political Behavior* 42(4): 1343–1368.

Gingrich, Jane and Silja Häusermann. 2015. 'The decline of the working-class vote, the reconfiguration of the welfare support coalition and consequences for the welfare state'. *Journal of European Social Policy* 25(1): 50–75.

Giuliani, Marco and Sergio Alberto Massari. 2019. 'The economic vote at the party level: Electoral behaviour during the Great Recession'. *Party Politics* 25(3): 461–473.

Glenn, Norval D. 2003. Distinguishing age, period, and cohort effects. In *Handbook of the Life Course*, ed. Mortimer, Jeylan T., Shanahan, Michael J. Boston, MA: Springer, pp. 465–476.

Goerres, Achim. 2008. 'The grey vote: Determinants of older voters' party choice in Britain and West Germany'. *Electoral Studies* 27(2): 285–304.

Goetz, Klaus. 2014. 'A question of time: Responsive and responsible democratic politics'. *West European Politics* 37(2): 379–399.

Goldberg, Andreas. 2020. 'The evolution of cleavage voting in four Western countries: Structural, behavioural or political dealignment?' *European Journal of Political Research* 59(1): 68–90.

Gomez, Raul. 2013. 'All that you can(not) leave behind: Habituation and vote loyalty in the Netherlands'. *Journal of Elections, Public Opinion & Parties* 23(2): 134–153.

Grasso, Maria Teresa, Stephen Farrall, Emily Gray, Colin Hay, and Will Jennings. 2019. 'Thatcher's children, Blair's babies, political socialization and trickle-down value change: An age, period and cohort analysis'. *British Journal of Political Science* 49(1): 17–36.

Gray, Mark and Miki Caul. 2000. 'Declining voter turnout in advanced industrial democracies, 1950 to 1997: The effects of declining group mobilization'. *Comparative Political Studies* 33(9): 1091–1122.

Green, Donald P. and Susanne Baltes. 2016. 'Party identification: Meaning and measurement'. In *The SAGE Handbook of Electoral Behaviour*, ed. Kai Arzheimer, Jocelyn Evans, and Michael S. Lewis-Beck. London: Sage, pp. 287–312.

Green, Donald Philip and Bradley Palmquist. 1990. 'Of artifacts and partisan instability'. *American Journal of Political Science* 34(3): 872.

Green, Donald P., Bradley Palmquist, and Eric Schickler. 2004. *Partisan Hearts and Minds: Political Parties and the Social Identities of Voters*. New Haven, CT: Yale University Press.

Greene, Steven. 2002. 'The social-psychological measurement of partisanship'. *Political Behavior* 24(3): 171–197.

Hagle, Timothy M. and Glenn E. Mitchell. 1992. 'Goodness-of-fit measures for probit and logit'. *American Journal of Political Science* 36(3): 762–784.

Harsgor, Liran. 2018. 'The partisan gender gap in the United States: A generational replacement?' *Public Opinion Quarterly* 82(2): 231–251.
Harteveld, Eelco and Elisabeth Ivarsflaten. 2018. 'Why women avoid the radical right: Internalized norms and party reputations'. *British Journal of Political Science* 48(2): 369–384.
Hayes, Bernadette C. 1995. 'The impact of class on political attitudes: A comparative study of Great Britain, West Germany, Australia and the United States'. *European Journal of Political Research* 27(1): 69–91.
He, QinqQian. 2016. 'Issue cross-pressures and time of voting decision'. *Electoral Studies* 44: 362–373.
Heath, Oliver. 2015. 'Policy representation, social representation and class voting in Britain'. *British Journal of Political Science* 45(1): 173–193.
Hetherington, Marc J. 2001. 'Resurgent mass partisanship: The role of elite polarization'. *American Political Science Review* 95: 619–631.
Hillygus, D. Sunshine and Todd G. Shields. 2008. *The Persuadable Voter: Wedge Issues in Presidential Campaigns*. Princeton, NJ: Princeton University Press.
Hobolt, Sara B. 2016. 'The Brexit vote: A divided nation, a divided continent'. *Journal of European Public Policy* 23(9): 1259–1277.
Hobolt, Sara, Thomas J. Leeper, and James Tilley. 2021. 'Divided by the vote: Affective polarization in the wake of the Brexit referendum'. *British Journal of Political Science* 51(4): 1476–1493.
Holman, Mirya R, Monica C Schneider, and Kristin Pondel. 2015. 'Gender targeting in political advertisements'. *Political Research Quarterly* 68(4): 816–829.
Holmberg, Soren and Henrik Oscarsson. 2011. 'Party leader effects on the vote'. In *Political Leaders and Democratic Elections*, ed. Kees Aarts, André Blais, and Hermann Schmitt. Oxford: Oxford University Press, pp. 35–51.
Hooghe, Marc. 2004. 'Political socialization and the future of politics'. *Acta Politica* 39(4): 331–341.
Huber, John D., Georgia Kernell, and Eduardo L. Leoni. 2005. 'Institutional context, cognitive resources and party attachments across democracies'. *Political Analysis* 13: 365–386.
Huckfeldt, R. Robert and John Sprague, eds. 1995. *Citizens, Politics and Social Communication: Information and Influence in an Election Campaign*. Cambridge: Cambridge University Press.
Huckfeldt, Robert, Paul A. Beck, Russell J. Dalton, and Jeffrey Levine. 1995. 'Political environments, cohesive social groups, and the communication of public opinion'. *American Journal of Political Science* 39(4): 1025–1054.
Huddy, Leonie and Alexa Bankert. 2017. 'Political partisanship as a social identity'. In *Oxford Research Encyclopedia of Politics*. Oxford: Oxford University Press. https://doi.org/10.1093/acrefore/9780190228637.013.250.
Huddy, Leonie, Alexa Bankert, and Caitlin Davies. 2018. 'Expressive versus instrumental partisanship in multiparty European systems'. *Political Psychology* 39(S1): 173–199.
Huettner, Frank and Marco Sunder. 2012. 'Axiomatic arguments for decomposing goodness of fit according to Shapley and Owen values'. *Electronic Journal of Statistics* 6: 1239–1250.
Huijsmans, Twan, Eelco Harteveld, Wouter van der Brug, and Bram Lancee. 2021. 'Are cities ever more cosmopolitan? Studying trends in urban–rural divergence of cultural attitudes'. *Political Geography* 86: 102353.
Hutter, Swen, Hanspeter Kriesi, and Jasmine Lorenzini. 2018. 'Social movements in interaction with political parties'. In *The Wiley Blackwell Companion to Social Movements*, ed.

David A. Snow Sarah A. Soule Hanspeter Kriesi Holly J. McCammon Hoboken, NJ: John Wiley and Sons Ltd'. pp. 322–337.

Immerzeel, Tim, Eva Jaspers, and Marcel Lubbers. 2013. 'Religion as catalyst or restraint of radical right voting?' *West European Politics* 36(5): 946–968.

Inglehart, Ronald F. 2021. *Religion's Sudden Decline: What's Causing It, and What Comes Next?* New York: Oxford University Press.

Inglehart, Ronald and Pippa Norris. 2000. 'The developmental theory of the gender gap: Women's and men's voting behavior in global perspective'. *International Political Science Review* 21(4): 441–463.

Inglehart, Ronald and Pippa Norris. 2003. *Rising Tide: Gender Equality and Cultural Change around the World.* Cambridge: Cambridge University Press.

Irvine, William P. and H. Gold. 1980. 'Do frozen cleavages ever go stale? The bases of the Canadian and Australian party systems'. *British Journal of Political Science* 10(2): 187–218.

Iversen, Torben and Frances Rosenbluth. 2006. 'The political economy of gender: Explaining cross-national variation in the gender division of labor and the gender voting gap'. *American Journal of Political Science* 50(1): 1–19.

Iyengar, Shanto and Kyu S Hahn. 2009. 'Red media, blue media: Evidence of ideological selectivity in media use'. *Journal of Communication* 59(1): 19–39.

Iyengar, Shanto, Yptach Lelkes, Matt Levendusky, Neil Malhotra, and Sean J. Westwood. 2019. 'The origins and consequences of affective polarization in the United States'. *Annual Review of Political Science* 22: 129–146.

Jacobs, Alan M. 2016. 'Policy making for the long term in advanced democracies'. *Annual Review of Political Science* 19: 433–454.

Jansen, Giedo, Nan Dirk de Graaf, and Ariana Need. 2012. 'Explaining the Breakdown of the Religion–Vote Relationship in the Netherlands'. *West European Politics* 35(4): 756–783.

Jansen, Giedo, Geoffrey Evans, and Nan Dirk de Graaf. 2013. 'Class voting and left-right party positions: A comparative study of 15 Western democracies, 1960–2005'. *Social Science Research* 42(2): 376–400.

Johann, David, Katharina Kleinen-von Königslöw, Sylvia Kritzinger, and Kathrin Thomas. 2018. 'Intra-campaign changes in voting preferences: The impact of media and party communication'. *Political Communication* 35(2): 261–286.

Johnston, Richard. 1992. 'Party identification measures in the Anglo-American democracies: A national survey experiment'. *American Journal of Political Science* 36(2): 542–559.

Johnston, Richard, J. Scott Matthews, and Amanda Bittner. 2007. 'Turnout and the party system in Canada, 1988–2004'. *Electoral Studies* 26(4): 735–745.

Kaase, Max. 1976. 'Party identification and voting behaviour in the West German election of 1969'. In *Party Identification and Beyond*, ed. Ian Budge, Ivor Crewe, and Dennis Farlie. London: Wiley, pp. 83–102.

Karvonen, Lauri. 2010. *The Personalisation of Politics: A Study of Parliamentary Democracies.* Colchester: ECPR Press.

Katz, Richard S. 1990. 'Party as linkage: A vestigial function?' *European Journal of Political Research* 18(1): 143–161.

Kayser, Mark Andreas and Christopher Wlezien. 2011. 'Performance pressure: Patterns of partisanship and the economic vote'. *European Journal of Political Research* 50(3): 365–394.

Kenis, Leo and Patrick Pasture. 2010. *The Transformation of the Christian Churches in Western Europe: 1945–2000*, Vol. 6. Leuven: Universitaire Pers Leuven.

Kitschelt, Herbert. 1988. 'Left-libertarian parties: Explaining innovation in competitive party systems'. *World Politics* 40(2): 194–234.

Kitschelt, Herbert and Philipp Rehm. 2018. 'Determinants of dimension dominance'. In *Welfare Democracies and Party Politics. Explaining Electoral Dynamics in Times of Changing Welfare Capitalism*, ed. Philip Manow, Bruno Palier, Hanna Schwander Oxford: Oxford University Press, pp. 62–88.

Kitschelt, Herbert P. and Philipp Rehm. 2019. 'Secular partisan realignment in the United States: The socioeconomic reconfiguration of white partisan support since the new Deal era'. *Politics & Society* 47(3): 425–479.

Klapper, Joseph T. 1960. *The Effects of Mass Communication*. New York: Free Press.

Klar, Samara. 2013. 'The influence of competing identity primes on political preferences'. *Journal of Politics* 75(4): 1108–1124.

Knutsen, Oddbjørn. 2004*a*. 'Religious denomination and party choice in Western Europe: A comparative longitudinal study from eight countries, 1970–97'. *International Political Science Review* 25(1): 97–128.

Knutsen, Oddbjørn. 2004*b*. *Social Structure and Party Choice in Western Europe: A Comparative Longitudinal Study*. Houndsmills: Palgrave Macmillan.

Knutsen, Oddbjørn. 2013. 'Structural determinants of party choice: The changing impact of socio-structure variables on party choice in comparative perspective'. In *Party Governance and Party Democracy*, ed. Wolfgang C. Müller and Hanne Marthe Narud. New York: Springer, pp. 175–203.

Kriesi, Hanspeter. 2010. 'Restructuration of partisan politics and the emergence of a new cleavage based on values'. *West European Politics* 33(3): 673–685.

Kriesi, Hanspeter. 2014. 'The populist challenge'. *West European Politics* 37(2): 361–378.

Kroh, Martin and Peter Selb. 2009. 'Inheritance and the dynamics of party identification'. *Political Behavior* 31(4): 559–574.

Kuhn, Ursina. 2009. 'Stability and change in party preference'. *Swiss Political Science Review* 15(3): 463–494.

Kuppens, Toon, Russell Spears, Antony S.R. Manstead, Bram Spruyt, and Matthew J. Easterbrook. 2018. 'Educationism and the irony of meritocracy: Negative attitudes of higher educated people towards the less educated'. *Journal of Experimental Social Psychology* 76: 429–447.

Laakso, Markku, and Rein Taagepera. '"Effective" number of parties: a measure with application to West Europe'. Comparative political studies 12(1): 3–27.

Lachat, Romain. 2007. *A Heterogeneous Electorate. Political Sophistication, Predisposition Strength and the Voting Decision Process*. Baden-Baden: Nomos.

Langsæther, Peter Egge and Rune Stubager. 2019. 'Old wine in new bottles? Reassessing the effects of globalisation on political preferences in Western Europe'. *European Journal of Political Research* 58(4): 1213–1233.

Larsen, Martin Vinæs. 2016. 'Economic conditions affect support for prime minister parties in Scandinavia'. *Scandinavian Political Studies* 39(3): 226–241.

Layman, Geoffrey. 2001. *The Great Divide: Religious and Cultural Conflict in American Party Politics*. New York: Columbia University Press.

Layman, Geoffrey C., Thomas M. Carsey, John C. Green, Richard Herrera, and Rosalyn Cooperman. 2010. 'Activists and conflict extension in American party politics'. *American Political Science Review* 104(2): 324–346.

Lazarsfeld, Paul F. 1944. 'The election is over'. *Public Opinion Quarterly* 8(3): 317–330.

Lazarsfeld, Paul F., Bernard R. Berelson, and Hazel Gaudet. 1944. *The People's Choice: How the Voter Makes Up His Mind in a Presidential Campaign*. New York: Duell, Sloan and Pearce.

Leeper, Thomas J. and Rune Slothuus. 2014. 'Political parties, motivated reasoning, and public opinion formation'. *Political Psychology* 35: 129–156.

Lefevere, Jonas. 2011. *Campaign Effects on Voter Decision Making*. PhD thesis. Antwerp: University of Antwerp.

Lelkes, Yphtach. 2016. 'Mass polarization: Manifestations and measurements'. *Public Opinion Quarterly* 80(S1): 392–410.

Lenz, Gabriel S. 2009. 'Learning and opinion change, not priming: Reconsidering the priming hypothesis'. *American Journal of Political Science* 53(4): 821–837.

Lenz, Gabriel, S. 2012. *Follow the Leader? How Voters Respond to Politicians' Policies and Performance*. Chicago, IL: University of Chicago Press.

Lewis-Beck, Michael S. and Mary Stegmaier. 2007. 'Economic models of voting'. In *The Oxford Handbook of Political Behavior*, ed. Russell J. Dalton and Hans-Dieter Klingemann. Oxford: Oxford University Press, pp. 518–537.

Lewis-Beck, Michael S. and Mary Stegmaier. 2013. 'The VP-function revisited: A survey of the literature on vote and popularity functions after over 40 years'. *Public Choice* 157(3–4): 367–385.

Lewis-Beck, Michael S. and Mary Stegmaier. 2016. 'The Hispanic immigrant voter and the classic American voter: Presidential support in the 2012 election'. *RSF: The Russell Sage Foundation Journal of the Social Sciences* 2(3): 165–181.

Lewis-Beck, Michael S., Rune Stubager, and Richard Nadeau. 2013. 'The Kramer problem: Micro–macro resolution with a Danish pool'. *Electoral Studies* 32(3): 500–505.

Lewis-Beck, Michael S., William G. Jacoby, Helmut Norpoth, and Herbert F. Weisberg. 2008. *The American Voter Revisited*. Ann Arbor, MI: University of Michigan.

Lipset, Seymour Martin and Stein Rokkan. 1967. *Party Systems and Voter Alignments: Cross-National Perspectives*. New York: Free Press.

Lupu, Noam. 2015. 'Party polarization and mass partisanship: A comparative perspective'. *Political Behavior* 37(2): 331–356.

Lyons, Jeffrey and Stephen M. Utych. Forthcoming. 'You're not from here!: The consequences of urban and rural identities'. *Political Behavior* 1–27.

Mair, Peter. 1993. 'Myths of electoral change and the survival of traditional parties'. *European Journal of Political Research* 24(2): 121–133.

Mair, Peter. 2007. 'The Challenge to Party Government'. EUI Working Papers SPS No. 2007/09.

Mair, Peter. 2008. 'Electoral volatility and the Dutch party system: A comparative perspective'. *Acta Politica* 43(2–3): 235–253.

Mair, Peter. 2013. *Ruling the Void: The Hollowing of Western Democracy*. London: Verso.

Mannheim, Karl. 1928. 'Das Problem der Generationen'. *Kolner Vierteljahrshefte fur Soziologie* 7(2): 309–330.

Marcinkiewicz, Kamil and Ruth Dassonneville. 2022. 'Do religious voters support populist radical right parties? Opposite effects in Western and East-Central Europe'. *Party Politics* 28(3): 444–456.

Marien, Sofie, Ruth Dassonneville, and Marc Hooghe. 2015. 'How second order are local elections? Voting motives and party preferences in Belgian municipal elections'. *Local Government Studies* 41(6): 898–916.

Martin, Nick, Sarah L. de Lange, and Wouter van der Brug. 2022. 'Holding on to voters in volatile times: Bonding voters through party links with civil society'. *Party Politics* 28: 354–364.
Mason, Lilliana. 2016. 'A cross-cutting calm: How social sorting drives affective polarization'. *Public Opinion Quarterly* 80(S1): 351–377.
Mason, Lilliana and Julie Wronski. 2018. 'One tribe to bind them all: How our social group attachments strengthen partisanship'. *Political Psychology* 39: 257–277.
Maxwell, Rahsaan. 2020. 'Geographic divides and cosmopolitanism: Evidence from Switzerland'. *Comparative Political Studies* 53(13): 2061–2090.
Mayer, Sabrina Jasmin and Martin Schultze. 2019. 'The effects of political involvement and cross-pressures on multiple party identifications in multi-party systems—evidence from Germany'. *Journal of Elections, Public Opinion and Parties* 29(2): 245–261.
McAllister, Ian. 2012. 'Lauri Karvonen, The Personalisation of Politics: A Study of Parliamentary Democracies'. *Australian Journal of Political Science* 47: 523–524.
McCarty, Nolan, Keith T. Poole, and Howard Rosenthal. 2016. *Polarized America: The Dance of Ideology and Unequal Riches*. Cambridge, MA: MIT Press.
Mummolo, Jonathan. 2016. 'News from the other side: How topic relevance limits the prevalence of partisan selective exposure'. *Journal of Politics* 78(3): 763–773.
Mutz, Diana C. 2002. 'The consequences of cross-cutting networks for political participation'. *American Journal of Political Science* 46(4): 838–855.
Mudde, Cas. 2013. 'Three decades of populist radical right parties in Western Europe: So what?.' *European Journal of Political Research* 52(1): 1–19.
Mudde, Cas. 2016. 'Europe's populist surge: A long time in the making'. *Foreign affairs* 95(6): 25–30.
Navarrete, Rosa M. 2020. 'Ideological proximity and voter turnout in multi-level systems: Evidence from Spain'. *Journal of Elections, Public Opinion and Parties* 30: 297–316.
Neundorf, Anja and Richard G. Niemi. 2014. 'Beyond political socialization: New approaches to age, period, cohort analysis'. *Electoral Studies* 33(1): 1–6.
Nie, Norman H., Sidney Verba, and John R. Petrocik. 1974. *The Changing American Voter*. Cambridge, MA: Cambridge University Press.
Nieuwbeerta, Paul and Wout Ultee. 1999. 'Class voting in Western industrialized countries, 1945–1990: Systematizing and testing explanations'. *European Journal of Political Research* 35(1): 123–160.
Nieuwbeerta, Paul, Nan Dirk de Graaf, and Wout Ultee. 2000. 'The effects of class mobility on class voting in post-war Western industrialized countries'. *European Sociological Review* 16(4): 327–348.
Nisbett, Richard E and Timothy D Wilson. 1977. 'Telling more than we can know: Verbal reports on mental processes'. *Psychological Review* 84(3): 231.
Norris, Pippa and Ronald Inglehart. 2001. 'Cultural Obstacles to Equal Representation'. *Journal of Democracy* 12(3): 126–140.
Oesch, Daniel. 2006. 'Coming to grips with a changing class structure: An analysis of employment stratification in Britain, Germany, Sweden and Switzerland'. *International Sociology* 21(2): 263–288.
Oesch, Daniel and Line Rennwald. 2018. 'Electoral competition in Europe's new tripolar political space: Class voting for the left, centre-right and radical right'. *European Journal of Political Research* 57(4): 783–807.
O'Grady, Tom. 2021. 'Is Ideological Polarisation by Age Group Growing in Europe?' https://osf.io/preprints/socarxiv/r8xbg/.

Önnudóttir, Eva H. and Ólafur Þ. Harðarson. 2020. 'Party identification and its evolution over time'. In *Research Handbook on Political Partisanship*, ed. Henrik Oscarsson and Sören Holmberg. Cheltenham: Edward Elgar Publishing, pp. 167–176.

Oscarsson, Henrik and Maria Oskarson. 2019. 'Sequential vote choice: Applying a consideration set model of heterogeneous decision processes'. *Electoral Studies* 57: 275–283.

Oshri, Odelia, Liran Harsgor, Reut Itzkovitch-Malka, and Or Tuttnauer. Forthcoming. 'Risk aversion and the gender gap in the vote for populist radical right parties'. *American Journal of Political Science.*

Oskarson, Maria. 2005. 'Social structure and party choice'. In *The European Voter*, ed. Jacques Thomassen. Oxford: Oxford University Press, pp. 83–104.

Otjes, Simon and André Krouwel. 2018. 'Old voters on new dimensions: Why do voters vote for pensioners' parties? The case of the Netherlands'. *Journal of Aging & Social Policy* 30(1): 24–47.

Paparo, Aldo, Lorenzo De Sio, and David W. Brady. 2020. 'PTV gap: A new measure of party identification yielding monotonic partisan attitudes and supporting comparative analysis'. *Electoral Studies* 63: 102092.

Pedersen, Mogens N. 1979. 'The dynamics of European party systems: Changing patterns of electoral volatility'. *European Journal of Political Research* 7(1): 1–26.

Peterson, Erik. 2019. 'The scope of partisan influence on policy opinion'. *Political Psychology* 40(2): 335–353.

Piazza, James. 2001. 'De-linking labor: Labor unions and social democratic parties under globalization'. *Party Politics* 7(4): 413–435.

Pickup, Mark, Dominik Stecula, and Clifton Van Der Linden. 2020. 'Novel coronavirus, old partisanship: COVID-19 attitudes and behaviours in the United States and Canada'. *Canadian Journal of Political Science/Revue canadienne de science politique* 53(2): 357–364.

Piketty, Thomas. 2019. *Capital et idéologie*. Paris: Éditions du Seuil.

Plane, Dennis L and Joseph Gershtenson. 2004. 'Candidates' ideological locations, abstention, and turnout in US midterm Senate elections'. *Political Behavior* 26(1): 69–93.

Poguntke, Thomas. 2002. 'Parties without firm social roots?: Party organisational linkage'. School of Politics, International Relations and the Environment (SPIRE), Keele University.

Powell, G. Binham Jr. 1976. 'Political cleavage structure, cross-pressure processes, and partisanship: An empirical test of the theory'. *American Journal of Political Science* 20(1): 1–23.

Putnam, Robert and David E. Campbell. 2010. *American Grace: How Religion is Reshaping our Civic and Political Lives.* New York: Simon & Schuster.

Raymond, Christopher. 2011. 'The continued salience of religious voting in the United States, Germany, and Great Britain'. *Electoral Studies* 30(1): 125–135.

Robison, Joshua, Rune Stubager, Mads Thau, and James Tilley. 2021. 'Does class-based campaigning work? How working class appeals attract and polarize voters'. *Comparative Political Studies* 54: 723–752.

Rokkan, Stein. 1977. 'Towards a generalized concept of Verzuiling: a preliminary note'. *Political Studies* 25(4): 563–570.

Rooduijn, Mathijs, Brian Burgoon, Erika van Elsas, and Herman G. van de Werfhorst. 2017. 'Radical distinction: Support for radical left and radical right parties in Europe'. *European Union Politics* 18(4): 536–559.

Schumacher, Ingmar. 2014. 'An empirical study of the determinants of Green party voting'. *Ecological Economics* 105: 306–318.

Scruggs, Lyle and Peter Lange. 2002. 'Where have all the members gone? Globalization, institutions, and union density'. *Journal of Politics* 64(1): 126–153.

Shorrocks, Rosalind. 2018. 'Cohort change in political gender gaps in Europe and Canada: The role of modernization'. *Politics & Society* 46(2): 135–175.

Sides, John, Michael Tesler and Lynn Vavreck. 2019. *Identity Crisis: The 2016 Presidential Campaign and the Battle for the Meaning of America*. Princeton, NJ: Princeton University Press.

Sloam, James and Matt Henn. 2017. *Youthquake 2017. The Rise of Young Cosmopolitans in Britain*. Cham: Palgrave Macmillan.

Söderlund, Peter. 2008. 'Retrospective voting and electoral volatility: A Nordic perspective'. *Scandinavian Political Studies* 31(2): 217–240.

Soroka, Stuart N. 2006. 'Good news and bad news: Asymmetric responses to economic information'. *Journal of Politics* 68(2): 372–385.

Stokes-Brown, Atiya Kai. 2006. 'Racial identity and Latino vote choice'. *American Politics Research* 34(5): 627–652.

Stroud, Natalie Jomini. 2010. 'Polarization and partisan selective exposure'. *Journal of Communication* 60(3): 556–576.

Stubager, Rune. 2009. 'Education-based group identity and consciousness in the authoritarian–libertarian value conflict'. *European Journal of Political Research* 48(2): 204–233.

Stubager, Rune. 2010. 'The development of the education cleavage: Denmark as a critical case'. *West European Politics* 33(3): 505–533.

Stubager, Rune. 2013. 'The changing basis of party competition: Education, authoritarian–libertarian values and voting'. *Government and Opposition* 48(3): 372–397.

Stubager, Rune, Kasper Hansen, Michael S. Lewis-Beck, and Richard Nadeau. 2021. *The Danish Voter: Democratic Ideals and Challenges*. Ann Arbor, MI: University of Michigan Press.

Thau, Mads. 2018. 'The demobilization of class politics in Denmark: The social democratic party's group-based appeals 1961–2004'. *World Political Science* 14(2): 169–188.

Thau, Mads. 2019. 'How political parties use group-based appeals: Evidence from Britain 1964–2015'. *Political Studies* 67(1): 63–82.

Thau, Mads. 2021. 'The social divisions of politics: How parties' group-based appeals influence social group differences in vote choice'. *Journal of Politics* 83: 675–688.

Thomassen, Jacques. 1976. 'Party identification as a cross-national concept: Its meaning in the Netherlands'. In *Party Identification and Beyond: Representations of Voting and Party Competition*, ed. Ian Budge, Ivor Crewe, and Dennis Farlie. London: John Wiley & Sons, pp. 63–79.

Thomassen, Jacques, ed. 2005. *The European Voter. A Comparative Study Of Modern Democracies*. Oxford: Oxford University Press.

Thomassen, Jacques and Martin Rosema. 2009. 'Party identification revisited'. In *Political Parties and Partisanship: Social Identity and Individual Attitudes*, ed. John Bartle and Paulo Bellucci. London: Routledge, pp. 42–59.

Tilley, James. 2015. '"We don't do God"? Religion and party choice in Britain'. *British Journal of Political Science* 45(4): 907–927.

Tilley, James and Sara B. Hobolt. 2011. 'Is the government to blame? An experimental test of how partisanship shapes perceptions of performance and responsibility'. *Journal of Politics* 73(2): 316–330.

Turnbull-Dugarte, Stuart J. 2020a. 'Cross-pressures and the European lavender vote: Testing the conditionality of the sexuality gap'. *Electoral Studies* 68: 102234.

Turnbull-Dugarte, Stuart J. 2020b. 'The European lavender vote: Sexuality, ideology and vote choice in Western Europe'. *European Journal of Political Research* 59(3): 517–537.

van Biezen, Ingrid and Thomas Poguntke. 2014. 'The decline of membership-based politics'. *Party Politics* 20(2): 205–216.

van der Brug, Wouter. 2010. 'Structural and ideological voting in age cohorts'. *West European Politics* 33(3): 586–607.

van der Brug, Wouter and Meindert Fennema. 2009. 'The Support Base of Radical Right Parties in the Enlarged European Union'. *European Integration* 31(5): 589–608.

van der Brug, Wouter and Mark N. Franklin. 2018. 'Generational replacement: Engine of electoral change'. In *Routledge International Handbooks*. London: Routledge, pp. 429–442.

van der Brug, Wouter and Sylvia Kritzinger. 2012. 'Generational differences in electoral behaviour'. *Electoral Studies* 31: 245–249.

van der Brug, Wouter and Roderik Rekker. 2021. 'Dealignment, realignment and generational differences in The Netherlands'. *West European Politics* 44(4): 776–801.

van der Brug, Wouter, Sara Hobolt, and Claes H. de Vreese. 2009. 'Religion and party choice in Europe'. *West European Politics* 32(6): 1266–1283.

van der Eijk, Cees. 2002. 'Design issues in electoral research: Taking care of (core) business'. *Electoral Studies* 21(2): 189–206.

van der Eijk, Cees and Broer Niemöller. 1983. *Electoral Change in the Netherlands*. Amsterdam: CT Press.

van der Eijk, Cees and Broer Niemöller. 2008. 'Recall Accuracy and Its Determinants'. In *Electoral Behavior. Volume 4: Debates and Methodology*, ed. Kai Arzheimer and Jocelyn Evans. Los Angeles, CA: Sage, pp. 232–280.

van der Meer, Tom W.G. 2017. 'Political trust and the "crisis of Democracy"'. In *Oxford Research Encyclopedia of Politics*. Oxford: Oxford University Press. https://doi.org/10.1093/acrefore/9780190228637.013.77.

van der Meer, Tom W.G., Erica V. Elsas, Rozemarijn Lubbe, and Wouter van der Brug. 2015. 'Are volatile voters erratic, whimsical or seriously picky? A panel study of 58 Waves into the nature of electoral volatility (the Netherlands 2006-2010)'. *Party Politics* 21(1): 100–114.

van der Waal, Jeroen, Peter Achterberg, and Dick Houtman. 2007. 'Class is not dead it has been buried alive: Class voting and cultural voting in postwar Western societies (1956-1990)'. *Politics & Society* 35(3): 403–426.

van Ham, Carolien, Jacques Jaques A. Thomassen, Kees Aarts, and Rudy B. Andeweg. 2017. *Myth and Reality of the Legitimacy Crisis: Explaining Trends and Cross-National Differences in Established Democracies*. Oxford: Oxford University Press.

Visser, Jelle. 2002. 'Why fewer workers join unions in Europe: A social custom explanation of membership trends'. *British Journal of Industrial Relations* 40(3): 403–430.

Voogd, Remko, Tom van der Meer, and Wouter van der Brug. 2019. 'Political trust as a determinant of volatile vote intentions: Separating within- from between-person effects'. *International Journal of Public Opinion Research* 31(4): 669–693.

Wagner, Markus and Sylvia Kritziger. 2012. 'Ideological dimensions and vote choice: Age group differences in Austria'. *Electoral Studies* 31(2): 285–296.

Walczak, Agnieszka, Wouter van der Brug, and Catherine Eunice de Vries. 2012. 'Long- and short-term determinants of party preferences: Inter-generational differences in Western and East Central Europe'. *Electoral Studies* 31(2): 273–284.

Waldahl, Ragnar and Bernt Aardal. 2000. 'The accuracy of recalled previous voting: Evidence from the Norwegian Election Study'. *Scandinavian Political Studies* 23(4): 373–389.
Westwood, Sean J. and Erik Peterson. Forthcoming. 'The inseparability of race and partisanship in the United States'. *Political Behavior*.
Whiteley, Paul and Ann-Kristin Kölln. 2019. 'How do different sources of partisanship influence government accountability in Europe?' *International Political Science Review* 40(4): 502–517.
Whitten, Guy D. and Harvey D. Palmer. 1996. 'Heightening comparativists' concern for model choice: Voting behavior in Great Britain and the Netherlands'. *American Journal of Political Science* 40(1): 231–260.
Wilkins-Laflamme, Sarah. 2016. 'The changing religious cleavage in Canadians' voting behaviour'. *Canadian Journal of Political Science/Revue canadienne de science politique* 49(3): 499–518.
Yoo, Sung-Jin. 2010. 'Two types of neutrality: Ambivalence versus indifference and political participation'. *Journal of Politics* 72(1): 163–177.
Zaller, J. 1992. *The Nature and Origins of Mass Opinion*. New York: Cambridge University Press.
Zelle, Carsten. 1995. 'Social dealignment versus Political Frustration: Contrasting Explanations of the Floating Vote in Germany'. *European Journal of Political Research* 27(3): 319–345.
Zuckerman, Alan S., Nicholas A. Valentino, and Ezra W. Zuckerman. 1994. 'A structural theory of vote choice: Social and political networks and electoral flows in Britain and the United States'. *Journal of Politics* 56(4): 1008–1033.

PART III
SUPPLEMENTARY MATERIALS

Appendix A
Data sets used for the analyses

A.1 Australia

- 1966: Aitkin, Donald, Kahan, Michael, and Stokes, Donald, 2019, Australian National Political Attitudes Survey, 1967, doi:10.26193/YKNUXT, ADA Dataverse, V2.
- 1969: Aitkin, Donald, Kahan, Michael, and Stokes, Donald, 2019, Australian National Political Attitudes Survey, 1969, doi:10.26193/OTUJCZ, ADA Dataverse, V2.
- 1977: Aitkin, Don, 2019, Australian National Political Attitudes Survey, 1979, doi:10.26193/AIOCOR, ADA Dataverse, V2
- 1987: McAllister, Ian, and Mughan, Anthony, 2017, Australian Election Study, 1987, doi:10.4225/87/PQFNYM, ADA Dataverse, V1.
- 1990: McAllister, Ian, Jones, Roger, Papadakis, Elim, and Gow, David, 2017, Australian Election Study, 1990, doi:10.4225/87/KPVA0F, ADA Dataverse, V1.
- 1993: Jones, Roger, McAllister, Ian, Denemark, David, and Gow, David, 2017, Australian Election Study, 1993, doi:10.4225/87/ZZ3NOB, ADA Dataverse, V1.
- 1996: Jones, Roger, McAllister, Ian, and Gow, David, 2017, Australian Election Study, 1996, doi:10.4225/87/NSDHWM, ADA Dataverse, V1.
- 1998: Bean, Clive, Gow, David, and McAllister, Ian, 2017, Australian Election Study, 1998, doi:10.4225/87/FFBWUU, ADA Dataverse, V2.
- 2001: Bean, Clive, Gow, David, and McAllister, Ian, 2017, Australian Election Study, 2001, doi:10.4225/87/CALXMK, ADA Dataverse, V1.
- 2004: Bean, Clive, McAllister, Ian, Gibson, Rachel, and Gow, David, 2017, Australian Election Study, 2004, doi:10.4225/87/G9ITIO, ADA Dataverse, V1.
- 2007: Bean, Clive, McAllister, Ian, and Gow, David, 2017, Australian Election Study, 2007, doi:10.4225/87/ZBUOW0, ADA Dataverse, V1.
- 2010: McAllister, Ian, Bean, Clive, Gibson, Rachel Kay, and Pietsch, Juliet, 2017, Australian Election Study, 2010, doi:10.4225/87/CYJNSM, ADA Dataverse, V2.

- 2013: Bean, Clive, McAllister, Ian, Pietsch, Juliet, and Gibson, Rachel Kay, 2017, Australian Election Study, 2013, doi:10.4225/87/WDBBAS, ADA Dataverse, V3.
- 2016: McAllister, Ian, Makkai, Toni, Bean, Clive, and Gibson, Rachel Kay, 2017, Australian Election Study, 2016, doi:10.4225/87/7OZCZA, ADA Dataverse, V2.
- 2019: McAllister, Ian, Bean, Clive, Gibson, Rachel, Makkai, Toni, Sheppard, Jill, and Cameron, Sarah, 2019, Australian Election Study, 2019, doi:10.26193/KMAMMW, ADA Dataverse, V2.

A.2 Canada

- 1965: Converse, Philip, Meisel, John, Pinard, Maurice, Regenstreif, Peter, and Schwartz, Mildred, Canadian National Election Study, 1965. [distributor], 1992, https://doi.org/10.3886/ICPSR07225.v1.
- 1968: Meisel, John, Canadian Federal Election Study, 1968 [distributor], 1992, https://doi.org/10.3886/ICPSR07009.v1.
- 1972: Market Opinion Research (Canada) Ltd, Canadian National Election Study, 1972, Ann Arbor, MI: Inter-University Consortium for Political and Social Research [distributor], 2006, https://doi.org/10.3886/ICPSR07410.v2.
- 1974, 1979, and 1980: Clarke, Harold D., Jenson, Jane, LeDuc, Lawrence, and Pammett, Jon H., The 1974–1979–1980 Canadian National Elections and Quebec Referendum Panel Study, Inter-University Consortium for Political and Social Research [distributor], 1992, https://doi.org/10.3886/ICPSR08079.v2.
- 1984: Lambert, Ronald D., Brown, Steven D., Curtis, James E., Kay, Barry J., and Wilson, John M., Canadian National Election Study, 1984, Inter-University Consortium for Political and Social Research [distributor], 1992, https://doi.org/10.3886/ICPSR08544.v1.
- 1988: Johnston, Richard, Canadian National Election Study, 1988, Inter-University Consortium for Political and Social Research [distributor], 1992, https://doi.org/10.3886/ICPSR09386.v1.
- 1993: Johnston, Richard, Blais, Andre, Brady, Henry E., Gidengil, Elisabeth, and Nevitte, Neil, Canadian Election Study, 1993: Incorporating the 1992 Referendum Survey on the Charlottetown Accord, Inter-University Consortium for Political and Social Research [distributor], 1995, https://doi.org/10.3886/ICPSR06571.v1.

- 1997: Blais, Andre, Gidengil, Elisabeth, Nadeau, Richard, and Nevitte, Neil, Canadian Election Survey, 1997, Ann Arbor, MI: Inter-University Consortium for Political and Social Research [distributor], 2000, https://doi.org/10.3886/ICPSR02593.v3.
- 2000: Blais, Andre, Gidengil, Elisabeth, Nadeau, Richard, and Nevitte, Neil, Canadian Election Survey, 2000, Ann Arbor, MI: Inter-University Consortium for Political and Social Research [distributor], 2004, https://doi.org/10.3886/ICPSR03969.v1
- 2004, 2006, 2008 and 2011: Fournier, Patrick, Stolle, Dietlind, Soroka, Stuart, Culter, Fred, Blais, André, Everitt, Joanna, Gidengil, Elisabeth, and Nevitte, Neil, Canadian Election Study, 2004–2011, https://ces-eec.arts.ubc.ca/english-section/surveys/.
- 2015: Fournier, Patrick, Cutler, Fred, Soroka, Stuart, and Stolle, Dietlind, Canadian Election Study, 2015, Telephone survey, https://ces-eec.arts.ubc.ca/english-section/surveys/.
- 2019: Stephenson, Laura B, Harell, Allison, Rubenson, Daniel, and Loewen, Peter John, 2020, 2019 Canadian Election Study—Phone Survey, https://doi.org/10.7910/DVN/8RHLG1, Harvard Dataverse, V1.

A.3 Denmark

- 1971: Borre Ole, Damgaard Erik, Nielsen Hands Jørgen, Sauerberg Steen, Tonsgaard Ole, and Worre Torben, Danish Pre- and Post-Election Study 1971, Dansk Data Arkiv Danish Data Archive, 1976, 1 data file: DDA-7, version: 1.0.0, http://dx.doi.org/10.5279/DK-SA-DDA-7.
- 1973: Borre Ole, Damgaard Erik, Nielsen Hans Jørgen, Sauerberg Steen, Tonsgaard Ole, and Worre Torben, Danish Election Study 1973, Dansk Data Arkiv Danish Data Archive, 1976, 1 data file: DDA-8, version: 1.0.0, http://dx.doi.org/10.5279/DK-SA-DDA-8.
- 1975: Borre Ole, Nielsen Hans Jørgen, Sauerberg, Steen, and Worre Torben, Danish Election Study 1975, Dansk Data Arkiv Danish Data Archive, 1976, 1 data file: DDA-16, version: 1.0.0, http://dx.doi.org/10.5279/DK-SA-DDA-16.
- 1977: Borre Ole, Nielsen Hans Jørgen, Sauerberg Steen, and Worre Torben, Danish Election Study 1977, Dansk Data Arkiv Danish Data Archive, 1978, 1 data file: DDA-166, version: 1.0.0, http://dx.doi.org/10.5279/DK-SA-DDA-166.
- 1979: Borre Ole, Glans Ingemar, Nielsen Hans Jørgen, Sauerberg Steen, Worre Torben, and Jørgen Andersen, Goul, Danish Election Study 1979,

Dansk Data Arkiv Danish Data Archive, 1981, 1 data file: DDA-287, version: 1.0.0, http://dx.doi.org/10.5279/DK-SA-DDA-287.
- 1981: Borre Ole, Glans Ingemar, Nielsen Hans Jørgen, Sauerberg Steen, Worre Torben, and Andersen Jørgen Goul, Danish Election Study 1981, Dansk Data Arkiv Danish Data Archive, 1983, 1 data file: DDA-529, version: 1.0.0, http://dx.doi.org/10.5279/DK-SA-DDA-529.
- 1984: Borre Ole, Glans Ingemar, Nielsen Hans Jørgen, Sauerberg Steen, Worre Torben, and Andersen Jørgen Goul, Danish Election Study 1984, Dansk Data Arkiv Danish Data Archive, 1986, 1 data file: DDA-772, version: 1.0.0, http://dx.doi.org/10.5279/DK-SA-DDA-772.
- 1987: Borre Ole, Elklit Jørgen, Glans Ingemar, Nielsen Hans Jørgen, Sauerberg Steen, Siune Karen, Svensson Palle, Togeby Lise, Tonsgaard Ole, Worre Torben, and Andersen Jørgen Goul, Danish Election Study 1987, Dansk Data Arkiv Danish Data Archive, 1996, 1 data file: DDA-1340, version: 1.0.0, http://dx.doi.org/10.5279/DK-SA-DDA-1340.
- 1990: Borre Ole, Nielsen Hans Jørgen, Sauerberg Steen, Worre Torben, and Andersen Jørgen Goul, Danish Election Study 1990, Dansk Data Arkiv Danish Data Archive, 1991, 1 data file: DDA-1564, version: 1.0.0, http://dx.doi.org/10.5279/DK-SA-DDA-1564.
- 1994: Andersen Jørgen Goul, Danish Election Study 1994, Dansk Data Arkiv Danish Data Archive, 2002, 1 data file: DDA-2210, version: 1.0.0, http://dx.doi.org/10.5279/DK-SA-DDA-2210.
- 1998: Borre Ole, Nielsen Hans Jørgen, and Andersen Jørgen Goul, and Andersen Johannes, Danish Election Study 1998, Dansk Data Arkiv Danish Data Archive, 2000, 1 data file: DDA-4189, version: 1.0.0, http://dx.doi.org/10.5279/DK-SA-DDA-4189.
- 2001: Borre Ole, Elklit Jørgen, Nielsen Hans Jørgen, Risbjerg Thomsen, Søren, Andersen Jørgen Goul, and Andersen Johannes, Danish Election Survey 2001, The main survey, Dansk Data Arkiv Danish Data Archive, 2004, 1 data file: DDA-12516, version: 1.0.0, http://dx.doi.org/10.5279/DK-SA-DDA-12516.
- 2005: Andersen Jørgen Goul, Danish Election Study 2005, Dansk Data Arkiv Danish Data Archive, 2007, 1 data file: DDA-18184, version: 1.0.0, http://dx.doi.org/10.5279/DK-SA-DDA-18184.
- 2007: Andersen Jørgen Goul, Danish Election Study 2007, Dansk Data Arkiv Danish Data Archive, 2012, 1 data file: DDA-26471, version: 1.0.0, http://dx.doi.org/10.5279/DK-SA-DDA-26471.
- 2011: Stubager Rune, Andersen Jørgen Goul, and Møller Hansen Kasper, Danish National Election Study 2011, Dansk Data Arkiv Danish Data

Archive, 2013, 1 data file: DDA-27067, version: 1.0.0, http://dx.doi.org/10.5279/DK-SA-DDA-27067.
- 2015: Møller Hansen Kasper, Danish National Election Study 2015, Dansk Data Arkiv Danish Data Archive, 2017, 1 data file: DDA-31083, version: 1.0.0, http://dx.doi.org/10.5279/DK-SA-DDA-31083.

A.4 Germany

- 1961: Scheuch, Erwin K., Wildenmann, Rudolf, and Baumert, Gerhard, 2014, Cologne Election Study (Federal Republic, November 1961), GESIS Data Archive, Cologne, ZA0057 Data file Version 2.0.0, doi:10.4232/1.11990.
- 1965: Kaase, Max, and Wildenmann, Rudolf, 1984, German Election Study, September 1965—Version 1, https://doi.org/10.3886/ICPSR07103.v1.
- 1969: Kaase, Max, Schleth, Uwe, Adrian, Wolfgang, Berger, Manfred, and Wildenmann, Rudolf, 1984, German Election Study, August–September 1969—Version 1, https://doi.org/10.3886/ICPSR07108.v1.
- 1972: Pappi, Franz U., 1973, Federal Parliament Election 1972 (1st and 2nd Follow-Up Survey), GESIS Data Archive, Cologne, ZA0633 Data file Version 1.0.0, https://doi.org/10.4232/1.0633.
- 1976: Berger, Manfred, Gibowski, Wolfgang G., Gruber, Edelgard, Roth, Dieter, Schulte, Wolfgang, Kaase, Max, Klingemann, Hans-Dieter, and Schleth, Uwe, 2015, Election Study 1976 (Panel: Initial Investigation, May–June 1976, August–September 1976; Follow-Up Survey, October–November 1976), GESIS Data Archive, Cologne, ZA0823 Data file Version 3.0.0, https://doi.org/10.4232/1.11982.
- 1980: Berger, Manfred, Gibowski, Wolfgang G., Fuchs, Dieter, Kaase, Max, Klingemann, Hans-Dieter, Roth, Dieter, Schleth, Uwe, and Schulte, Wolfgang, 1980, Election Study 1980 (Data Pool), GESIS Data Archive, Cologne, ZA1053 Data file Version 1.0.0, https://doi.org/10.4232/1.1053.
- 1983: Forschungsgruppe Wahlen (Mannheim), 1986, German Election Study, 1983—Archival Version, https://doi.org/10.3886/ICPSR08352.
- 1987: Berger, Manfred, Gibowski, Wolfgang G., Roth, Dieter, and Schulte, Wolfgang, 1989, Election Study 1987 (Trend Investigation), GESIS Data Archive, Cologne, ZA1536 Data file Version 1.0.0, https://doi.org/10.4232/1.1536.

- 1990: Forschungsgruppe Wahlen, Mannheim, 1981, Election Study 1990 (Trend Investigation), GESIS Data Archive, Cologne, ZA1920 Data file Version 1.0.0, https://doi.org/10.4232/1.1920.
- 1994: ZUMA, Mannheim, Berger, Manfred, Jung, Matthias, Roth, Dieter, Gibowski, Wolfgang G., Kaase, Max, Klingemann, Hans-Dieter, Küchler, Manfred, Pappi, Franz U., and Semetko, Holli A., 2012, Post-Election Study on the Federal Parliament Election 1994, GESIS Data Archive, Cologne, ZA2601 Data file Version 2.0.0, https://doi.org/10.4232/1.11460.
- 1998: Mannheimer Zentrum für Europäische Sozialforschung (MZES), Mannheim, Wissenschaftszentrum Berlin für Sozialforschung (WZB), Berlin, Zentralarchiv für Empirische Sozialforschung, Universität zu Köln, and ZUMA, Mannheim, 2013, German National Election Study—Post-Election Study 1998, German CSES Study, GESIS Data Archive, Cologne, ZA3073 Data file Version 2.0.0, https://doi.org/10.4232/1.11566.
- 2002: GLES, 2012, Long-Term Panel 2002–2005–2009 (GLES 2009), GESIS Data Archive, Cologne, ZA5320 Data file Version 2.0.0, https://doi.org/10.4232/1.11350.
- 2005: Schmitt-Beck, Rüdiger and Faas, Torsten, 2009, Federal Parliament Election 2005 Campaign Dynamics—Pre- and Post-Election Study, GESIS Data Archive, Cologne, ZA4991 Data file Version 1.0.0, https://doi.org/10.4232/1.4991.
- 2009: GLES, 2019. Pre- and Post-Election Cross Section (Cumulation) (GLES 2009), GESIS Data Archive, Cologne, ZA5302 Data file Version 6.0.2, https://doi.org/10.4232/1.13230.
- 2013: GLES, 2019, Pre- and Post-Election Cross Section (Cumulation) (GLES 2013), GESIS Data Archive, Cologne, ZA5702 Data file Version 4.0.1, https://doi.org/10.4232/1.13233.
- 2017: GLES, 2019, Pre- and Post-Election Cross Section (Cumulation) (GLES 2017), GESIS Data Archive, Cologne, ZA6802 Data file Version 3.0.1, https://doi.org/10.4232/1.13236.

A.5 Great Britain

A.5.1 Main analyses

- 1964, 1966, and 1970: Butler, David and Stokes, Donald E., Political Change in Britain, 1963–1970. [distributor], 2007, https://doi.org/10.3886/ICPSR07250.v3.

- February 1974: Alt, James, Crewe, Ivor and Sarlvik, Bo, British Election Study, February 1974; Cross-Section Survey [computer file], Colchester, Essex: UK Data Archive [distributor], 1976, https://www.britishelectionstudy.com/data-object/1974-february-bes-cross-section/.
- October 1974: Crewe, I.M., Robertson, D.R. and Sarlvik, B., British Election Study, October 1974 [computer file], Colchester, Essex: UK Data Archive [distributor], 1977, https://www.britishelectionstudy.com/data-object/1974-october-bes-cross-section/.
- 1979: Crewe, I.M., Robertson, D.R., and Sarlvik, B., British Election Study, May 1979; Cross-Section Survey [computer file], Colchester, Essex: UK Data Archive [distributor], 1981, https://www.britishelectionstudy.com/data-object/1979-bes-cross-section/.
- 1983: Heath, A., Jowell, R., and Curtice, J.K., British General Election Study, 1983; Cross-Section Survey [computer file], Colchester, Essex: UK Data Archive [distributor], 1983, https://www.britishelectionstudy.com/data-object/1983-bes-cross-section/.
- 1987: Heath, A., Jowell, R., and Curtice, J.K., British General Election Study, 1987; Cross-Section Survey [computer file], 2nd edn, Colchester, Essex: UK Data Archive [distributor], April 1993, https://www.britishelectionstudy.com/data-object/1987-bes-cross-section/.
- 1992: Heath, A. et al., British General Election Study, 1992; Cross-Section Survey [computer file], Colchester, Essex: UK Data Archive [distributor], April 1993, https://www.britishelectionstudy.com/data-object/1992-bes-cross-section/.
- 1997: Heath, A. et al., British General Election Study, 1997; Cross-Section Survey [computer file], 2nd edn, Colchester, Essex: UK Data Archive [distributor], May 1999, https://www.britishelectionstudy.com/data-object/1997-bes-cross-section/.
- 2001: Clarke, H. et al., British General Election Study, 2001; Cross-Section Survey [computer file], Colchester, Essex: UK Data Archive [distributor], March 2003, https://www.britishelectionstudy.com/data-object/2001-bes-cross-section-2/.

- 2005: Clarke, H. et al., British Election Study, 2005: Face-to-Face Survey [computer file], Colchester, Essex: UK Data Archive [distributor], November 2006, https://www.britishelectionstudy.com/data-object/2005-bes-post-election-survey/.
- 2010: Whiteley, P.F. and Sanders, D., British Election Study, 2010: Face-to-Face Survey [computer file], Colchester, Essex: UK Data Archive [distributor], August 2014, https://www.britishelectionstudy.com/data-object/2010-bes-cross-section/.
- 2015: Fieldhouse, E., Green, J., Evans, G., Schmitt, H., van der Eijk, C., Mellon, J., and Prosser, C., 2016, British Election Study, 2015: Face-to-Face Post-Election Survey [data collection], UK Data Service, SN: 7972, http://dx.doi.org/10.5255/UKDA-SN-7972-1.
- 2017: Fieldhouse, E., Green, J., Evans, G., Schmitt, H., van der Eijk, C., Mellon, J., and Prosser, C., 2018, British Election Study, 2017: Face-to-Face Post-Election Survey [data collection], http://doi.org/10.5255/UKDA-SN-8418-1.
- 2019: Fieldhouse, E., J. Green., J., Evans., G., Mellon, J., Prosser, C., de Geus, R., and Bailey, J., 2021, 2019 BES Post-Election Random Probability Survey v.1.1.1 [computer file], May 2021, http://www.britishelectionstudy.com/data-object/2019-british-election-study-post-election-random-probability-survey/.

A.5.2 Panel analyses

- 1964–1966: Butler, David and Donald E. Stokes, Political change in Britain, 1963–1970 [computer file], ICPSR07250-v3, Conducted by David Butler, Bibliographic Citation: Nuffield College, Oxford and Donald E. Stokes, University of Michigan, 1979, Ann Arbor, MI: Inter-University Consortium for Political and Social Research [producer and distributor], https://www.britishelectionstudy.com/data-object/1963-1970-political-change-in-britain/.
- 1983–1987: Heath, A., Jowell, R., and Curtice, J.K., British Election Panel Study, 1983, 1986, and 1987 [computer file], Colchester, Essex: UK Data Archive [distributor], July 1999, https://www.britishelectionstudy.com/data-object/1983-1986-and-1987-bes-panel-study-part-1/.
- 1992–1997: Heath, A., Jowell, R., and Curtice, J.K., British Election Panel Study, 1992-1997 [computer file], Colchester, Essex: UK Data Archive

[distributor], July 1998, https://www.britishelectionstudy.com/data-object/1992-1997-bes-panel-study/.
- 1997–2001: Heath, A., Jowell, R., and Curtice, J.K., British Election Panel Study, 1997–2001; Waves 1–8 [computer file], 4th edn, Colchester, Essex: UK Data Archive [distributor], July 2002, https://www.britishelectionstudy.com/data-object/1997-2001-bes-panel-study/.
- 2015–2017: Fieldhouse, E., Green, J., Evans, G., Mellon, J., and Prosser, C., 2020, British Election Study Internet Panel Waves 1–19, https://www.britishelectionstudy.com/data-object/british-election-study-combined-wave-1-19-internet-panel-open-ended-response-data/.

A.6 The Netherlands

- 1971, 1972, 1977, 1981, 1982, 1986, 1989, 1994, 1998, 2002, 2003, and 2006: Aarts Kees, Bojan Todosijevic and van der Kaap, Harry, 2010, Dutch Parliamentary Election Study Cumulative Dataset, 1971–2006, ICPSR 28221.
- 2010: Van der Kolk, Henk, Aarts, Kees and Tillie, Jean 2012, Nationaal Kiezersonderzoek, 2010—NKO, 2010, DANS, http://dx.doi.org/10.17026/dans-xvh-tghy.
- 2012: Van der Kolk, Henk, Tillie, Jean, van Erkel, Patrick, van der Velden, Mariken and Damstra, Alyt, 2012, Dutch Parliamentary Election Study 2012—DPES, 2012, DANS, https://doi.org/10.17026/dans-x5h-akds.
- 2017: Van der Meer, Tom, van der Kolk, Henk and Rekker, Roderik 2017, Dutch Parliamentary Election Study 2017—DPES/NKO, 2017, DANS, https://doi.org/10.17026/dans-xby-5dhs.

A.7 Sweden

- 1956: Westerståhl, Jörgen and Särlvik, Bo, Swedish Election Study 1956, Swedish National Data Service, SND 0020, 1982, https://snd.gu.se/en/catalogue/study/snd0020.
- 1960: Särlvik, Bo, Swedish Election Study 1960, Swedish National Data Service, SND 001, 1982, https://snd.gu.se/en/catalogue/study/snd0001.
- 1964: Särlvik, Bo, Swedish Election Study 1964, Swedish National Data Service, SND 0007, 1982, https://snd.gu.se/en/catalogue/study/snd0007.

- 1968: Särlvik, Bo, Swedish Election Study 1968, Swedish National Data Service, SND 0039, 1982, https://snd.gu.se/en/catalogue/study/snd0039.
- 1970: Särlvik, Bo, Swedish Election Study 1970, Swedish National Data Service, SND 0047, 1983, https://snd.gu.se/en/catalogue/study/snd0047.
- 1973: Petersson, Olof and Särlvik, Bo, Swedish Election Study 1973, SND 0040, 1982, https://snd.gu.se/en/catalogue/study/snd0040.
- 1976: Petersson, Olof, Swedish Election Study 1976, SND 0008, 1982, https://snd.gu.se/en/catalogue/study/snd0008.
- 1979: Holmberg, Sören, Swedish Election Study 1979, SND 0089, 1984, https://snd.gu.se/en/catalogue/study/snd0089.
- 1982: Holmberg, Sören, Swedish Election Study 1982, SND 0157, 1986, https://snd.gu.se/en/catalogue/study/snd0157.
- 1985: Holmberg, Sören; Gilljam, Mikael, Swedish Election Study 1985, SND 0217, 1988, https://snd.gu.se/en/catalogue/study/snd0217.
- 1988: Holmberg, Sören and Gilljam, Mikael, Swedish Election Study 1988, SND 0227, 1991, https://snd.gu.se/en/catalogue/study/snd0227.
- 1991: Holmberg, Sören and Gilljam, Mikael, Swedish Election Study 1991, SND 0391, 1993, https://snd.gu.se/en/catalogue/study/snd0391.
- 1994: Holmberg, Sören and Gilljam, Mikael, Swedish Election Study 1994, SND 0570, 1997, https://snd.gu.se/en/catalogue/study/snd0570.
- 1998: Holmberg, Sören, Swedish Election Study 1998, SND 0750, 2001, https://snd.gu.se/en/catalogue/study/snd0750.
- 2002: Holmberg, Sören and Oscarsson, Henrik Ekengren, Swedish Election Study 2002, SND 0812, 2004, https://snd.gu.se/en/catalogue/study/snd0812.
- 2006: Holmberg, Sören and Oscarsson, Henrik Ekengren, Swedish Election Study 2006, SND 0861, 2006, https://snd.gu.se/en/catalogue/study/snd0861.
- 2010: Holmberg, Sören and Oscarsson, Henrik Ekengren, Swedish National Election Study 2010, SND 0876, 2017, https://snd.gu.se/en/catalogue/study/snd0876.
- 2014: Oscarsson, Henrik Ekengren, Berg, Linda, Hedberg, Per, and Oleskog Tryggvason, Per, Swedish National Election Study 2014, SND 1039, 2021, https://snd.gu.se/en/catalogue/study/snd1039.
- 2018: Oscarsson, Henrik, Andersson, Dennis, Hedberg, Per, and Svensson, Richard, Swedish National Election Study 2018–CSES Edition, SND 2020-159, 2021, https://snd.gu.se/en/catalogue/study/2020-159.

A.8 The United States

- 1952–2016: ANES Time Series Cumulative Data File, https://electionstudies.org/data-center/anes-time-series-cumulative-data-file/.

Appendix B
Percentage of campaign deciders by election

Table 1.2 in Chapter 1 shows the average percentage of campaign deciders by decade for each of the eight countries. Tables B.1–B.8 in this Appendix provide more detail and list the exact percentage of respondents that is coded as campaign decider for each election for which this information is available.

Table B.1 Percentage of campaign deciders by election, Australia

Country	Election	% Campaign deciders
Australia	1990	35.74
	1993	37.65
	1996	31.41
	1998	42.21
	2001	34.63
	2004	32.40
	2007	23.23
	2010	34.08
	2013	29.76
	2016	37.44
	2019	32.10

Table B.2 Percentage of campaign deciders by election, Canada

Country	Election	% Campaign deciders
Canada	1972	51.33
	1974	36.59
	1979	43.99
	1980	33.74
	1988	52.44
	1993	60.52
	1997	48.75
	2000	47.12
	2004	51.27
	2006	43.04
	2008	46.51
	2011	43.20

Table B.3 Percentage of campaign deciders by election, Denmark

Country	Election	% Campaign deciders
Denmark	1971	14.52
	1973	32.80
	1975	25.89
	1977	26.90
	1979	23.10
	1981	28.15
	1984	22.80
	1987	20.98
	1990	20.97
	1994	27.52
	1998	28.87
	2001	29.41
	2005	37.12
	2007	40.96
	2011	44.35
	2015	50.19

Table B.4 Percentage of campaign deciders by election, Germany

Country	Election	% Campaign deciders
Germany	1965	7.65
	1969	9.64
	1972	8.97
	1976	6.94
	1980	9.42
	1983	15.66
	1987	12.51
	1990	10.67
	1994	12.93
	2002	17.97
	2005	41.57
	2009	21.54
	2013	26.38
	2017	39.55

Table B.5 Percentage of campaign deciders by election, Great Britain

Country	Election	% Campaign deciders
Great Britain	1964	11.74
	1966	11.34
	1970	8.04
	1974 February	22.67
	1974 October	22.03
	1979	28.04
	1983	21.86
	1987	20.85
	1992	24.10
	1997	26.26
	2001	23.30
	2005	33.25
	2010	34.39

Table B.6 Percentage of campaign deciders by election, The Netherlands

Country	Election	% Campaign deciders
The Netherlands	1971	22.31
	1977	20.81
	1981	27.76
	1982	21.93
	1986	21.51
	1989	28.66
	1994	42.66
	1998	39.98
	2002	45.57
	2003	37.57
	2006	53.16
	2010	59.88
	2012	59.26
	2017	60.83

Table B.7 Percentage of campaign deciders by election, Sweden

Country	Election	% Campaign deciders
Sweden	1964	17.82
	1968	23.34
	1970	96.81
	1973	27.76
	1976	28.80
	1979	29.61
	1982	17.51
	1985	20.19
	1988	21.27
	1991	28.60
	1994	27.47
	1998	36.04
	2002	34.42
	2006	35.76
	2010	44.69
	2014	32.29
	2018	32.84

Table B.8 Percentage of campaign deciders by election, United States

Country	Election	% Campaign deciders
United States	1948	12.57
	1952	11.40
	1956	9.76
	1960	12.09
	1964	12.67
	1968	21.77
	1972	13.79
	1976	23.87
	1980	25.91
	1984	13.37
	1988	17.35
	1992	24.32
	1996	18.17
	2000	22.35
	2004	15.23
	2016	18.28

Appendix C
Socio-demographic variables

C.1 Australia

C.1.1 Elections included

1966, 1969, 1977, 1987, 1993, 1996, 1998, 2001, 2004, 2007, 2010, 2013, 2016, and 2019

C.1.2 Operationalization of independent variables

Class	Self-identification of class, distinguishing lower class, working class, middle class, and upper class.
Religious denomination	Categorical variable distinguishing between different pre-coded religious denominations, including no religious denomination or atheist.
Urban–rural	From 1966 to 1987: categorical variable distinguishing between respondents living in a rural, urban, or metropolitan district. In 1993, four categories: rural, provincial, outer metropolitan. and inner metropolitan. From 1996–2019, five categories: rural/village, small country town, larger country town, large town, and major city.
Sex	Categorical variable distinguishing between women (= 1) and men (=0).
Age	Continuous variable.
Education	Treated as a continuous variable from lowest to highest level of education. Based on highest attained level of education. In 2010 and 2013, based on age at which respondent left education. In 2016 and 2019, based on obtained qualification, degree, or diploma.

C.2 Canada

C.2.1 Elections included

1965, 1968, 1972, 1974, 1979, 1980, 1984, 1988, 1993, 1997, 2000, 2004, 2006, 2008, 2011, 2015, and 2019.

C.2.2 Operationalization of independent variables

Note that a measure of the rural–urban character of respondents' place of living is not consistently included in Canadian election studies. The urban–rural cleavage is therefore not taken into account for the Canadian case.

Class	Income as a proxy measure for class, measured through varying income groups and consistently treated as a continuous variable.
Religious denomination	Categorical variable, consistently coded to distinguish between the non-religious, Catholics, Protestants, and other religions.
Sex	Categorical variable distinguishing between women (= 1) and men (=0).
Age	Continuous variable. Age group variable with eleven categories is used in 1972.
Education	Treated as a continuous variable from lowest to highest level of education. Based on highest attained level of education.
Regional differences	A dichotomous variable distinguishing between Quebec and the other provinces.

C.3 Denmark

C.3.1 Elections included

1971, 1975, 1977, 1979, 1981, 1984, 1987, 1990, 1994, 1998, 2001, 2005, 2007, 2011, and 2015.

C.3.2 Operationalization of independent variables

Note that a measure of religious denomination or church attendance is not consistently included in Danish election studies. The religious cleavage is therefore not taken into account for the Danish case.

Class	Income as a proxy measure for class, measured through varying income groups and consistently treated as a continuous variable.
Urban–rural	Categorical variable. Measure of childhood city in 1971 (large city, mid-sized royal borough, smaller royal borough, suburb, railway town, rural). Distinction between districts in 1975 and 1977 (rural districts, provincial towns, Copenhagen suburbs, and Copenhagen/Frederiksberg/Gentofte). Measure distinguishing between three categories in 1979 (rural, provincial city/town, metropolitan Copenhagen). Four categories in 1981 (rural area, provincial towns, Copenhagen suburbs, Copenhagen). Seven categories in 1984 (city over 50,000 inhabitants, city 10,000–49,999 inhabitants, city 2,000–9,999 inhabitants, rural district, downtown Copenhagen, northern suburbs of Copenhagen, southern/western suburbs of Copenhagen). Nine categories in 1987 (city over 50,0000 inhabitants, city 20,000–49,999 inhabitants, city 10,000–19,999 inhabitants, city 2,000–9,999 inhabitants, rural district, downtown Copenhagen, northern suburbs of Copenhagen, southern/western suburbs of Copenhagen, outskirts of Copenhagen). Seven categories in 1990 (provincial town over 50,000 residents, provincial town less than 50,000 residents, rural districts, downtown Copenhagen, northern suburbs of Copenhagen, southern/western suburbs of Copenhagen, midtown Copenhagen). Twelve categories in 1994 (eight categories for municipalities of different sizes, the capital, suburbs of the capital,

	other municipality in the capital, restgroup in the region around the capital). Five categories in 1998, 2001, 2005, and 2007 (rural district, city with less than 10,000 inhabitants, city with 10,000–50,000 inhabitants, city with 50,001–500,000 inhabitants, metropolitan Copenhagen). Seven categories in 2011 (farm/country house, small town between 200 and 9,999 inhabitants, city between 10,000 and 49,999 inhabitants, suburb of major city, larger city with more than 50,000 inhabitants, suburb of Copenhagen, Copenhagen). Nine categories in 2015 (seven categories by population size, Aarhus/Aalborg/Odense, Copenhagen/Copenhagen area).
Sex	Categorical variable distinguishing between women (= 1) and men (=0).
Age	Continuous variable. Age groups instead of full range in 1975, 1981, 1984, 1987, 1990, and 1994.
Education	Treated as a continuous variable from lowest to highest level of education. Based on indicator of highest attained education (number of categories varies by election).

C.4 Germany

C.4.1 Elections included

1961, 1965, 1969, 1972, 1976, 1980, 1983, 1987, 1990, 1994, 1998, 2002, 2005, 2009, 2013, and 2017.

C.4.2 Operationalization of independent variables

Class	Income as a proxy measure for class, measured through varying income groups and consistently treated as a continuous variable. Income is a fully continuous measure in 1994. No income variable is included in 1980, 1983, 1987, 1990, and 2005.

Religious denomination	Categorical variable, consistently coded to distinguish between the non-religious, Catholics, Protestants, and other religions. Because of small numbers, 'other' religions and 'none' are combined in 1961 and 1965.
Urban–rural	Nine categories capturing towns of different population size in 1961 and 1965. Twelve categories capturing towns of different population size in 1969. Eight categories in 1972. Ten categories in 1976, 1980, 1983, 1987, and 1990. Seven categories in 1994. Nine categories in 1998. Five categories in 2002. Seven categories in 2005. Eight categories in 2009 and 2013. Four categories in 2017.
Sex	Categorical variable distinguishing between women (= 1) and men (=0).
Age	Continuous variable. Age group is used in 1961 (thirteen different categories), 1965 (ten categories) and 1969 (eleven categories).
Education	Treated as a continuous variable, from lowest to highest level of education. Based on indicator of highest attained education (number of categories varies by election).
Regional differences	A dichotomous variable distinguishing between East and West is included from 1994 onwards.

C.5 Great Britain

C.5.1 Elections included

1964, 1966, 1970, 1979, 1983, 1987, 1992, 1997, 2001, 2005, 2010, 2015, 2017, and 2019.

C.5.2 Operationalization of independent variables

Note that a measure of the rural–urban character of respondents' place of living is not consistently included in British election studies. The urban–rural cleavage is therefore not taken into account for the British case.

Class	Categorical variable distinguishing between respondents who indicate no class identity, the working class, and the middle class.
Religious denomination	Categorical variable, consistently coded to distinguish between the non-religious, Catholics, Anglicans, other Protestants, and other religions. Religious denomination is not included in the 1970 and 1974 surveys.
Sex	Categorical variable distinguishing between women (= 1) and men (=0).
Age	Continuous variable.
Education	Categorical variable that distinguishes between those with and without post-secondary education.

C.6 the Netherlands

C.6.1 Elections included

1971, 1972, 1977, 1981, 1982, 1986, 1989, 1994, 1998, 2002, 2003, 2006, 2010, 2012, and 2017.

C.6.2 Operationalization of independent variables

Class	Categorical variable capturing self-identified membership of a social class, in five categories (working class, upper working class, middle class, upper middle class, upper class).
Religious denomination	Categorical variable, consistently coded to distinguish between the non-religious, Catholics, Protestants, and other religions.
Urban–rural	Five categories in elections from 1971 to 2006 (not urban, hardly urban, mildly urban, strongly urban,

	very strongly urban). Five categories in 2010, 2012, and 2017 (very low, low, medium, high, and very high urbanization).
Sex	Categorical variable distinguishing between women (= 1) and men (=0).
Age	Continuous variable. Measure of age group (treated as continuous) in 1971 and 1989.
Education	Treated as a continuous variable from lowest to highest level of education. Based on indicator of highest attained education (number of categories varies by election).

C.7 Sweden

C.7.1 Elections included

1960, 1964, 1976, 1979, 1982, 1985, 1988, 1994, 1998, 2002, 2006, 2010, 2014, and 2018.

C.7.2 Operationalization of independent variables

Note that a measure of religious denomination or church attendance is not consistently included in Swedish election studies. The religious cleavage is therefore not taken into account for the Swedish case.

Class	Income as a proxy measure for class, measured through varying income groups and consistently treated as a continuous variable.
Urban/rural	Eight categories in 1960 (rural area, small towns—low industrialization, small towns—high industrialization, big towns—low industrialization, big towns—high industrialization, Malmö, Göteborg, Stockholm). Four categories (of different

	population sizes) in 1964, 1976, and 1979. Six categories (of different population sizes) in 1982. Four categories in 1985 (pure countryside, small town, city or town, Stockholm/Göteborg). Four categories in 1988, 1994, 1998, 2002, 2006, 2010, and 2014 (countryside, town or village, large town or city, Stockholm/Göteborg/Malmö). Seven categories in 2018 (countryside, smaller urban area, larger urban area, suburb of a city, city centre, suburb of metropolitan area, metropolitan area).
Sex	Categorical variable distinguishing between women (= 1) and men (=0).
Age	Measure of age group (treated as continuous). Full age range included in 1960, 1964, 1976, and 1979.
Education	Treated as a continuous variable from lowest to highest level of education.

C.8 United States

C.8.1 Elections included

1948, 1952, 1956, 1960, 1964, 1968, 1972, 1976, 1980, 1984, 1988, 1992, 1996, 2000, 2004, 2008, 2012, and 2016.

C.8.2 Operationalization of independent variables

Note that a measure of the rural–urban character of respondents' place of living is not consistently included in the American National Election Studies (ANES). The urban–rural cleavage is therefore not taken into account for the United States.

Class	Categorical variable capturing subjective social class. Six categories: average working class, average or upper working class, upper working class, average middle class, average or upper middle class, upper middle class.

Religious denomination	Categorical variable, consistently coded to distinguish between Protestants, Catholics, Jewish, and others (including no religious denomination).
Sex	Categorical variable distinguishing between women (= 1) and men (=0).
Age	Continuous variable.
Education	Treated as a continuous variable from lowest to highest level of education. Consistently distinguishes between grade school or less, high school, some college, and college or advanced degree.
Regional differences	A dichotomous variable distinguishing states in the South versus others.
Race	Categorical variable distinguishing White, Black, and others.

Appendix D
Change in the role of socio-demographics

The main analyses that are presented in Chapter 3 consist of a graphical representation of how the McFadden pseudo-R^2 of a vote-choice model that only includes socio-demographic variables fluctuates over time. The line graphs in Figures 3.1 and 3.2 suggest that the evidence for the idea that the impact of socio-demographic variables on the vote have weakened is limited overall.

Here, I more formally test whether the patterns of change that are presented in Chapter 3 amount to a *significant* decline in the effect of socio-demographic variables on individuals' vote choices.

First, in Table D.1, I present the results of a series of ordinary least-squares (OLS) regression estimations, where the dependent variable is the McFadden pseudo-R^2 statistic of a socio-demographics-only model and the independent variable is the year of the election. As can be seen from the estimates in Table D.1, there are four countries for which the overall time trend is negative and significant (Australia, Denmark, the Netherlands, and Sweden). With the exception of the Netherlands, however, the substantive importance of the estimated time trend is very small. In addition, there are two countries where the time trend is *positive* and significant (Canada and the United States).

The final model in Table D.1 assesses the pooled over-time trend in the pseudo-R^2 statistic across the elections in the 8 countries that are analysed in this book. The coefficient on the election-year variable in this model is essentially zero, which further confirms the lack of an across-the-board decline in the role of socio-demographic characteristics for explaining vote choices in established democracies. This is also further illustrated in Figure D.1, which visualises the linear fit between time and the pseudo-R^2 statistics from the vote-choice models.

Finally, Tables D.2 and D.3 break apart the results by type of socio-demographic variable and test for the time trend of the decomposed pseudo-R^2 statistic for 'old' and 'new' cleavage variables, respectively. As can be seen from the estimates in these tables, the results for the 'old' cleavage variables are very similar to those of the overall models. For 'new' cleavage variables, the main take-away is that there is hardly any evidence of change in the extent to which these variables explain variation in vote choices across the eight established democracies.

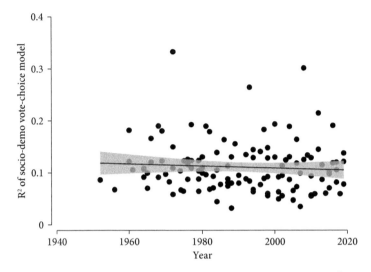

Figure D.1 Bivariate association between time and pseudo-R^2 statistic of a socio-demographic-only model

Note: Each observation represents one election study. The solid line indicates a linear fit and the shaded area the 95 per cent confidence intervals around that linear fit.

Table D.1 Association between election year and McFadden pseudo-R^2 statistics of a socio-demographic vote-choice model

	Australia	Canada	Denmark	Germany	Great Britain	The Netherlands	Sweden	United States	All
Election year	−0.001* (0.001)	0.002* (0.001)	−0.001* (0.001)	−0.000 (0.000)	−0.000 (0.000)	−0.003* (0.001)	−0.001*** (0.000)	0.002* (0.001)	−0.000 (0.000)
Country FE	✗	✗	✗	✗	✗	✗	✗	✗	✓
Intercept	2.355* (1.027)	−3.270* (1.042)	2.518* (1.085)	0.440 (0.563)	0.836 (0.623)	6.292* (2.170)	2.039*** (0.340)	−2.948* (1.265)	0.347 (0.520)
N	14	17	15	16	16	14	14	17	123
R^2	0.366	0.226	0.423	0.019	0.123	0.590	0.774	0.326	0.366

Note: Robust standard errors in parentheses. * $p < 0.05$, ** $p < 0.01$, *** $p < 0.001$.

Table D.2 Association between election year and McFadden pseudo-R^2 statistic of a socio-demographic vote-choice model (old cleavages only)

	Australia	Canada	Denmark	Germany	Great Britain	The Netherlands	Sweden	United States	All
Election year	-0.001** (0.000)	0.002* (0.001)	-0.001* (0.000)	-0.000 (0.000)	-0.000 (0.000)	-0.003* (0.001)	-0.000** (0.000)	0.002* (0.001)	-0.000 (0.000)
Country FE	✗	✗	✗	✗	✗	✗	✗	✗	✓
Intercept	2.852** (0.850)	-3.055* (1.063)	1.280* (0.547)	0.388 (0.532)	0.986 (0.565)	6.316* (2.229)	0.826** (0.253)	-3.237* (1.238)	0.154 (0.512)
N	14	17	15	16	16	14	14	17	123
R^2	0.573	0.209	0.378	0.018	0.200	0.585	0.536	0.380	0.488

Note: Robust standard errors in parentheses. *$p < 0.05$, **$p < 0.01$, ***$p < 0.001$.

Table D.3 Association between election year and McFadden pseudo-R^2 statistic of a socio-demographic vote-choice model (new cleavages only)

	Australia	Canada	Denmark	Germany	Great Britain	The Netherlands	Sweden	United States	All
Election year	0.000 (0.000)	0.000 (0.000)	−0.001 (0.000)	−0.000 (0.000)	0.000 (0.000)	0.000 (0.000)	−0.001*** (0.000)	−0.000 (0.000)	−0.000 (0.000)
Country FE	✗	✗	✗	✗	✗	✗	✗	✗	✓
Intercept	−0.497 (0.336)	−0.214 (0.213)	1.238 (0.625)	0.052 (0.258)	−0.149 (0.320)	−0.023 (0.254)	1.213*** (0.218)	0.290 (0.238)	0.194 (0.123)
N	14	17	15	16	16	14	14	17	123
R^2	0.199	0.111	0.327	0.000	0.026	0.003	0.711	0.084	0.534

Note: Robust standard errors in parentheses. * $p < 0.05$, ** $p < 0.01$, *** $p < 0.001$.

Appendix E
Partisanship in Germany
West versus East

The drop in the percentage of partisans in German election studies, as shown in Figure 4.1, coincides with reunification. Therefore, it is important to disentangle what part of the change is due to the inclusion of respondents from East Germany in the samples and what part is a 'real' decline of partisanship in the West. To that end, Figure E.1 plots the share of respondents that is a partisan in Länder in West (black circles) and East Germany (white circles) separately.

This graph illustrates that the decline in partisanship is not entirely driven by the inclusion of respondents from the East in election surveys from 1994 onwards. Even when restricting the sample to respondents in Länder in the West, there is a notable decline in levels of partisanship between the 1990 and 1994 election surveys.

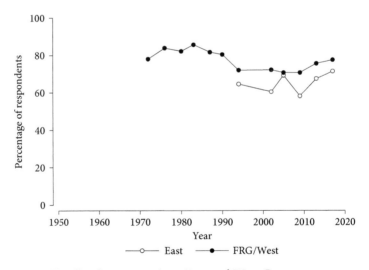

Figure E.1 Partisans over time, East and West Germany

Appendix F
Partisanship over time

In Chapter 4, I focus on visualizing levels of partisanship over time in each of the eight countries that is studied in this book. Here, I present a more formal test of the over-time trend in partisanship in each of the democracies studied.

I present the results of two sets of ordinary least-squares (OLS) regression estimates. First, in Table F.1, I list the results of nine linear models in which the dependent variable is the share of partisans in an election survey and the independent variable is the year of the election. I show the estimates by country before pooling the data and estimating a model for the 111 election-years for which there is information on partisanship. As can be seen in Table F.1, the linear time trend is negative and significant in five of the eight countries and also in the pooled estimation. The substantive size of the coefficients, however, is modest. The coefficient for the pooled data set suggests that the percentage of partisans in these eight democracies on average declines by about three percentage points every ten years.

Second, Table F.2 presents the results for similar analyses that use the share of strong partisans as a dependent variables. For this indicator, there is evidence of a negative and significant over-time decline in the share of strong partisans in three countries: Australia, Great Britain, and Sweden. The coefficient for the pooled regression as well reaches significance. Again, however, these results point to effect sizes that are substantively moderate. More precisely, the pooled estimate suggests that the percentage of strong partisans on average drops about two percentage points every ten years.

Table F.1 Association between election year and the share of partisans

	Australia	Canada	Denmark	Germany	Great Britain	The Netherlands	Sweden	United States	All
Election year	−0.001 (0.001)	0.003* (0.001)	−0.002* (0.001)	−0.003* (0.001)	−0.002*** (0.000)	−0.001 (0.002)	−0.009*** (0.000)	−0.003*** (0.000)	−0.003*** (0.000)
Country FE	✗	✗	✗	✗	✗	✗	✗	✗	✓
Intercept	2.585* (1.060)	−5.086* (1.974)	3.657* (1.265)	7.025** (2.046)	4.753*** (0.711)	2.909 (3.239)	17.757*** (0.833)	5.784*** (0.982)	5.930*** (0.696)
N	15	10	13	12	16	13	15	17	111
R^2	0.168	0.520	0.362	0.484	0.679	0.053	0.971	0.644	0.916

Note: Robust standard errors in parentheses. $^*p < 0.05$, $^{**}p < 0.01$, $^{***}p < 0.001$.

Table F.2 Association between election year and the share of strong partisans

	Australia	Canada	Denmark	Germany	Great Britain	The Netherlands	Sweden	United States	All
Election year	−0.002** (0.001)	0.005*** (0.001)	−0.001 (0.001)	−0.002 (0.001)	−0.006*** (0.001)	0.000 (0.001)	−0.005*** (0.000)	0.000 (0.001)	−0.002*** (0.000)
Country FE	✗	✗	✗	✗	✗	✗	✗	✗	✓
Intercept	4.420** (1.259)	−9.913** (1.982)	2.882 (1.456)	4.237 (2.481)	11.904*** (2.169)	0.183 (2.162)	10.418*** (0.903)	0.224 (1.231)	4.667*** (0.786)
N	15	10	13	12	16	13	15	17	111
R^2	0.412	0.778	0.225	0.191	0.658	0.000	0.907	0.000	0.877

Note: Robust standard errors in parentheses. * $p < 0.05$, ** $p < 0.01$, *** $p < 0.001$.

Appendix G
Wording of partisan strength measures

G.1 Australia

- 1966, 1969, 1977: Now, thinking of the federal parties, how strongly (name of federal party) do you feel: very strongly, fairly strongly, or not very strongly?
- 1987, 1990, 1993, 1996, 1998, 2001, 2004, 2007, 2010, 2013, 2016, 2019: Would you call yourself a very strong, fairly strong, or not very strong supporter of that party?

G.2 Canada

- 1988, 1993, 1997, 2000, 2004, 2006, 2008, 2011, 2015, 2019: How strongly (party identified in PID question) do you feel: very strongly, fairly strongly, or not very strongly?

G.3 Denmark

- 1971, 1973, 1977, 1979, 1984, 1990, 1994, 2001, 2005, 2007, 2011, 2015: Some are strongly convinced adherents of their party while others are not so convinced. Do you consider yourself a strongly convinced adherent of your party or not strongly convinced?

G.4 Germany

- 1972, 1976, 1980, 1983, 1987, 1990, 1994: Taken altogether, how strongly or weakly do you lean towards this party: very strongly, fairly strongly, moderately, fairly weakly, or very weakly?
- 2002, 2005, 2009, 2013, 2017: All in all, how strongly or weakly attached are you to this party? Very strongly, fairly strongly, moderately, fairly weakly, or very weakly?

Note that for consistency with the measures of partisan strength in the other countries, the partisan strength variable in Germany has been recoded to distinguish between non-partisans, weak partisans (= very weakly, fairly weakly, and moderately), and strong partisans (= fairly strongly and very strongly).

G.5 Great Britain

- 1964, 1966, 1970: Well how strongly (chosen party) do you feel—very strongly, fairly strongly, or not very strongly?
- February 1974, October 1974, 1979, 1983, 1987, 1992, 1997, 2001, 2005, 2010, 2015, 2017, 2019: Would you call yourself a very strong (chosen party), fairly strong, or not very strong?

G.6 The Netherlands

- 1971: Some people are very convinced adherents of their party, others are not. Do you consider yourself a very convinced adherent of the party you just named or not?
- 1972, 1977, 1981, 1982, 1986, 1989, 1994: Would you call yourself a convinced adherent to this party, or do you not consider yourself to be a convinced adherent?
- 1998, 2002, 2006, 2010, 2012, 2017: Would you call yourself a very convinced adherent to this party, a convinced adherent, or do you consider yourself not to be an adherent?

Note that before 1998 the partisan strength questions distinguished between convinced and non-convinced adherents. From 1998 onwards, the questions distinguished between strongly convinced, convinced, and not so convinced adherents. I coded all convinced and strongly convinced adherents as 'strong partisans' and all those indicating they are not so convinced as 'weak partisans'.

G.7 Sweden

- 1968, 1970, 1973, 1976, 1979, 1982, 1985, 1988, 1991, 1994, 1998, 2002, 2006, 2010, 2014: Some people are strongly convinced adherents of their party. Others are not so strongly convinced. Do you yourself belong to the strongly convinced adherents of your party?

G.8 United States

- 1952, 1956, 1960, 1964, 1968, 1972, 1976, 1980, 1984, 1988, 1992, 1996, 2000, 2004, 2008, 2016: Would you call yourself a strong (REP/DEM) or a not very strong (REP/DEM)?

Appendix H
Strength of partisanship, stacked area graphs

An alternative way of assessing change over time in the strength of partisanship is to examine what share of respondents falls in the non-partisan, weak partisan, and strong partisan categories, respectively. Figures H.1 and H.2 allow the relative importance of each of these three categories to be gauged over time by plotting the stacked distributions of the partisanship variables in each country, including the non-partisans (lightest grey), weak partisans (darkest grey), and strong partisans.

Looking at the figures, they show important variation between countries in the relative size of the weak and strong partisan groups, which might, in part, be a function of differences in question wording. Regardless of such differences, if dealignment mostly takes the form of a weakening of the strength of citizens' partisan attachments, we should see that the size of the top section in each graph (strong partisans) takes up less space over time—relative to the middle section (weak partisans). While there is some evidence for this in some of the countries (e.g. in Australia, Germany, and Great Britain), the trend seems to reverse during the most recent time period. In other countries, the relative size of the weak and strong partisan groups remains fairly stable over time (e.g. in Sweden) or the group of strong partisans gains in weight (e.g. in the United States).

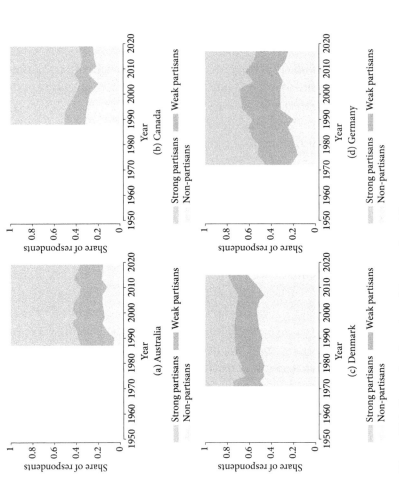

Figure H.1 Strength of partisanship over time (1)

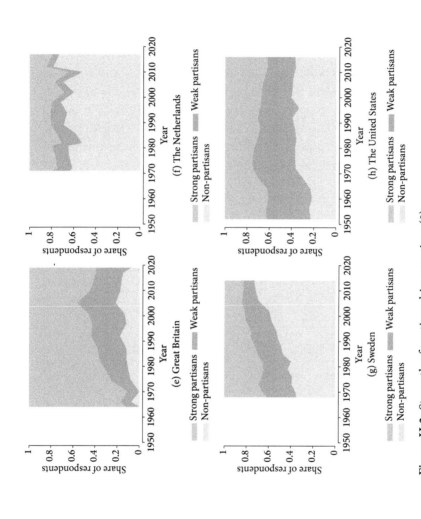

Figure H.2 Strength of partisanship over time (2)

Appendix I
Long-term and short-term factors, illustration

Table I.1 shows the results of a linear probability model to explain voting for the incumbent president (Obama) in the 2016 American National Election Study (ANES). The model includes an interaction between the strength of partisanship (independents, leaners, and partisans) and a measure of respondents' sociotropic retrospective economic evaluation. The estimates in Table I.1 are used to obtain the average marginal effects that are shown in Figure 5.2.

Table I.1 Economic evaluations and support for the incumbent, ANES 2016

	Vote for Obama in 2016
Pure independent (ref.)	
Leaner	−0.222*
	(0.088)
Partisan	−0.206**
	(0.077)
Economic evaluation	0.136***
	(0.028)
Leaner × Economic evaluation	0.085**
	(0.032)
Partisan × Economic evaluation	0.111***
	(0.029)
Intercept	−0.016
	(0.074)
N	2,795
R^2	0.258

Note: Robust standard errors in parentheses. *$p < 0.05$, **$p < 0.01$, ***$p < 0.001$.

Appendix J
Economic voting over time, alternative analytical approaches

J.1 Added pseudo-R^2 when accounting for economic evaluations

The main results in Chapter 5 assess changes in the role of economic evaluations on the vote by focusing on the estimated coefficients of economic evaluations. In line with how I evaluate changes in the impact of leader evaluations, an alternative approach is to focus on how much explanatory power adding economic evaluations adds to a model—compared to a model that only accounts for individuals' socio-demographic characteristics and incumbent partisanship.

Figures J.1 and J.2 rely on this alternative approach and show how much adding economic evaluations to a model predicting support for the incumbent, ads in terms of the decomposed pseudo-R^2 value compared to a model that only includes socio-demographic variables and an indicator of partisanship (distinguishing between non-partisans, incumbent partisans, and opposition partisans).

In line with the main results presented in Chapter 5, these graphs do not provide much evidence for the idea that economic voting has strengthened over time. The only two countries where the data suggest an upwards trend are the United States and, to a lesser extent, Canada.

J.2 Economic voting as voting for the party of the prime minister

In Chapter 5, I analyse the effects of economic evaluations on the vote by focusing on support for the incumbent. In case of a governing coalition, I code a vote for any party that is a member of the outgoing governing coalition as an incumbent. A number of studies, however, have argued that in contexts of coalition government, accountability is mostly directed towards the head of government and the party of the prime minister (Debus, Stegmaier and

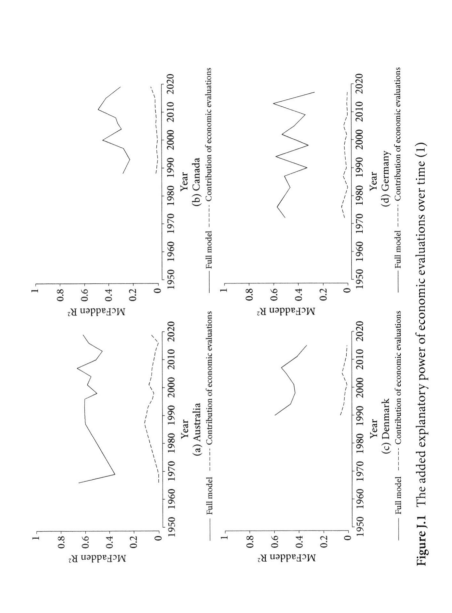

Figure J.1 The added explanatory power of economic evaluations over time (1)

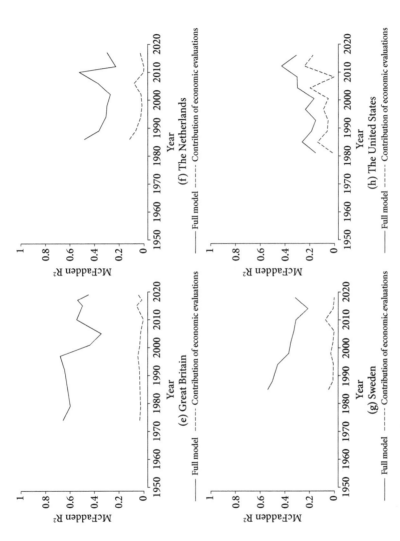

Figure J.2 The added explanatory power of economic evaluations over time (2)

Tosun, 2014; Larsen, 2016). To account for the possibility that economic voting operationalized in this way does show patterns of an increased weight of economic evaluations, I replicate the analyses with a dependent variable that takes the value of 1 if a respondent voted for the party of the prime minister and 0 otherwise.

I do not estimate these models for the United States, which has a presidential system. For Canada, it should be pointed out that given the country has never had coalition governments, the estimates are identical to those of the main results presented in Chapter 5. Figures J.3 and J.4 plot the average marginal effect of a one-unit change in economic evaluations for each of these models. As can be seen from these figures, the trends are very similar to those of the main models.

J.3 Asymmetry in economic voting

The main analyses that serve to evaluate whether there is a change in the effect of economic evaluations on the vote over time assume a linear effect of economic evaluations—which are coded to range between 0 (worse/deteriorate), over 1 (stable) to 2 (better/improve). However, given that there is work that shows that individuals react more strongly to negative than to positive information (Soroka, 2006) and because previous work has shown evidence that negative economic conditions are more strongly correlated with incumbent support than positive economic conditions (Dassonneville and Lewis-Beck, 2014), it might be important to account for such an asymmetry when studying change in the effect of individuals' evaluations of the state of the economy.

To that end, Figures J.5 and J.6 plot the average marginal effects of perceiving the economy to have gotten worse versus perceiving it to have been unchanged (black circles), and the average marginal effects of perceiving the economy to have worsened versus unchanged (white circles). These estimates are obtained from election-specific linear probability models, that explain voting for the incumbent, by means of economic evaluations, socio-demographic controls, and a measure of partisanship (whether one is a partisan of the incumbent, a partisan of the opposition, or independent). As can be seen from J.5 and J.6, there are no indications of a clear time trend for either perceptions of worsening economic conditions or for perceptions of improving economic conditions.

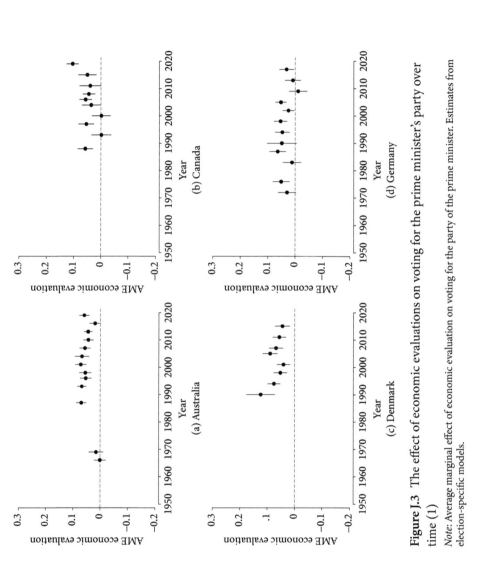

Figure J.3 The effect of economic evaluations on voting for the prime minister's party over time (1)

Note: Average marginal effect of economic evaluation on voting for the party of the prime minister. Estimates from election-specific models.

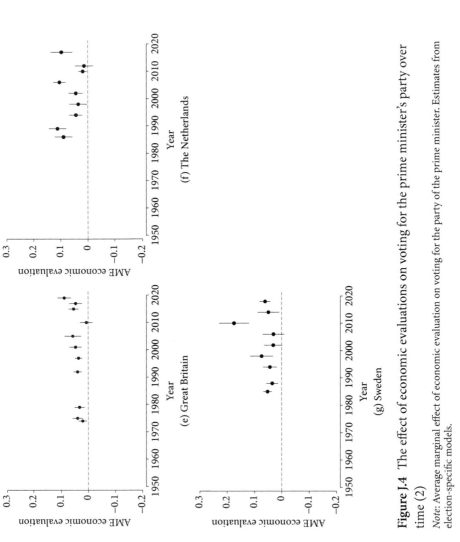

Figure J.4 The effect of economic evaluations on voting for the prime minister's party over time (2)

Note: Average marginal effect of economic evaluation on voting for the party of the prime minister. Estimates from election-specific models.

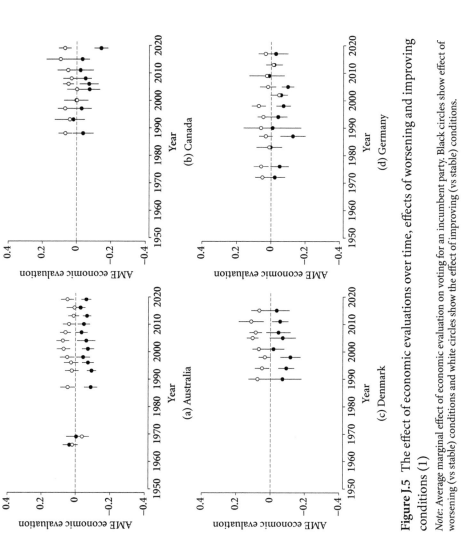

Figure J.5 The effect of economic evaluations over time, effects of worsening and improving conditions (1)

Note: Average marginal effect of economic evaluation on voting for an incumbent party. Black circles show effect of worsening (vs stable) conditions and white circles show the effect of improving (vs stable) conditions.

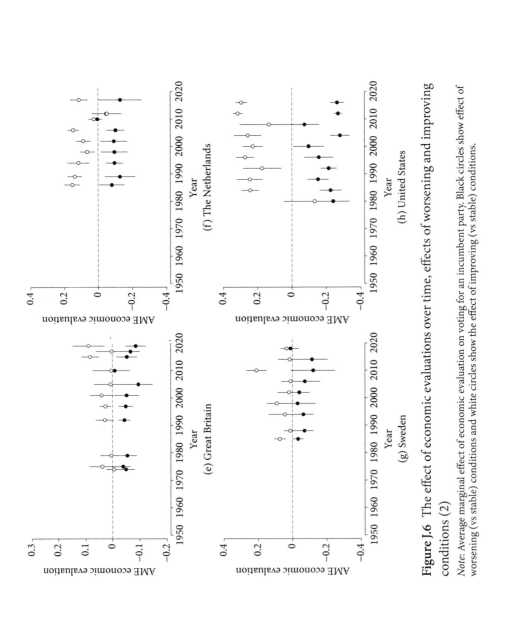

Figure J.6 The effect of economic evaluations over time, effects of worsening and improving conditions (2)

Note: Average marginal effect of economic evaluation on voting for an incumbent party. Black circles show effect of worsening (vs stable) conditions and white circles show the effect of improving (vs stable) conditions.

Appendix K
Measurement and wording of short-term variables

This appendix provides more information on the survey items that are used to operationalize respondents' evaluations of the state of the economy and their evaluations of party leaders. For economic evaluations, the measures are mostly sociotropic retrospective evaluations of the economy—though when such measures were not available, evaluations of the current state of the economy or measures that capture how respondents evaluate the government's impact on the economy were used. The reference period in the questions vary somewhat, but most items have a twelve-month reference frame.

For leader evaluations, the measures are mostly like/dislike scales or thermometer ratings of specific party leaders. When respondents were asked to rate different politicians from the same party, the most prominent leader in the election campaign was selected.

K.1 Australia

K.1.1 Economic evaluations

- 1966, 1969: We are also interested in how well off people are these days. Are you and your family better off now than you were three or four years ago, are you worse off, or have you stayed about the same?
- 1987: How do you think the general economic situation in this country has changed over the last twelve months? A lot better, a little better, about the same, a little worse, a lot worse?
- 1990, 1993: And how do you think the general economic situation in the country now compares with what it was a year ago? A lot better, a little better, about the same, a little worse, a lot worse?
- 1996, 1998, 2001, 2004, 2007, 2010, 2013, 2016, 2019: And how do you think the general economic situation in Australia now compares with

what it was twelve months ago? A lot better, a little better, about the same, a little worse, a lot worse?

K.1.2 Leader evaluations

- 1966: 'Summary attitudes' towards Holt, Whitlam, and McEwen are included. These are the holtsumm, whitsumm, and mewnsumm variables in the original data set. These summary variables combine information on a series of like and dislike mention items in the data set and are scaled to range between 0 (lowest like/dislike score) and 10 (highest like/dislike score).
- 1987: The variables q19bobh, q19johnh, q19ians, and q19janh from the original data set are included. These variables capture respondents, like/dislike feelings about Bob Hawke, John Howard, Ian Sinclair, and Janine Haines, respectively. The measures range between 0 (very unfavourable) and 10 (very favourable).
- 1993: The variables c1pk, c1jhew, c1tf, and c1jcou from the original data set are included. These variables capture feelings about Paul Keating, John Hewson, Tim Fischer, and John Coulter, respectively. The measures range between 0 (very unfavourable) and 10 (very favourable).
- 1996: The variables c1keat, c1how, c1fisch, and c1kern from the original data set are included. These variables capture feelings about Paul Keating, John Howard, Tim Fischer, and Cheryl Kernot, respectively. The measures range between 0 (strongly dislike) and 10 (strongly like).
- 1998: The variables C1BEAZ, C1HOW, C1FISCH, C1LEES, and C1HANS from the original data set are included. These variables capture feelings about Kim Beazley, John Howard, Tim Fischer, Meg Lees, and Pauline Hanson, respectively. The measures range between 0 (strongly dislike) and 10 (strongly like).
- 2001: The variables C1BEAZ, C1HOW, C1AND, C1STOTD, C1HANS, and C1BROWN from the original data set are included. These variables capture feelings about Kim Beazley, John Howard, John Anderson, Natasha Stott Despoja, Pauline Hanson, and Bob Brown, respectively. The measures range between 0 (strongly dislike) and 10 (strongly like).
- 2004: The variables c1lath, c1how, c1and, c1bart, and c1brown from the original data set are included. These variables capture feelings about Mark Latham, John Howard, John Anderson, Andrew Bartlett, and Bob Brown, respectively. The measures range between 0 (strongly dislike) and 10 (strongly like).

- 2007: The variables c1howard, c1rudd, c1vaile and c1brown from the original data set are included. These variables capture feelings about John Howard, Kevin Rudd, Mark Vaile, and Bob Brown, respectively. The measures range between 0 (strongly dislike) and 10 (strongly like).
- 2010: The variables c3julia, c3abbott, c3truss, and c3brown from the original data set are included. These variables capture feelings about Julia Gillard, Tony Abbott, Warren Truss, and Bob Brown, respectively. The measures range between 0 (strongly dislike) and 10 (strongly like).
- 2013: The variables c1rudd, c1abbott, c1truss, and c1milne from the original data set are included. These variables capture feelings about Kevin Rudd, Tony Abbott, Warren Truss, and Christine Milne, respectively. The measures range between 0 (strongly dislike) and 10 (strongly like).
- 2016: The variables C1_1, C1_2, C1_3, and C1_5 from the original data set are included. These variables capture feelings about Shorten, Turnbull, Joyce, and Di Natale, respectively. The measures range between 0 (strongly dislike) and 10 (strongly like).
- 2019: The variables C1_1, C1_2, C1_3, and C1_5 from the original data set are included. These variables capture feelings about Morrison, Shorten, McCormack, and Di Natale, respectively. The measures range between 0 (strongly dislike) and 10 (strongly like).

K.2 Canada

K.2.1 Economic evaluations

- 1988: Would you say that over the past year the economy of the country has got better, stayed the same, or got worse?
- 1993: Would you say that over the past year Canada's economy has got better, stayed the same, or got worse?
- 1997, 2000, 2004, 2006, 2008, 2011: Over the past year, has Canada's economy got better, stayed the same, or got worse?
- 2015: Over the past, has Canada's economy: got better, got worse, stayed about the same?
- 2019: Thinking about the economy, over the past year, has Canada's economy got better, worse, or stayed about the same?

K.2.2 Leader evaluations

- 1968: The variables var208, var209, var210, and var212 from the original data set are included. These variables capture the thermometer ratings of Trudeau, Stanfield, Douglas, and Patterson, respectively. The measures range between 1 (lowest rating) and 10 (highest rating).
- 1974: The variables v187, v190, and v193 from the original data set are included. These variables capture the thermometer ratings of Trudeau, Stanfield, and Lewis, respectively. The thermometer ratings range between 0 (lowest rating) and 100 (highest rating).
- 1979: The variables v1261, v1264, and v1267 from the original data set are included. These variables capture the thermometer ratings of Trudeau, Clark, and Broadbent, respectively. The thermometer ratings range between 0 (lowest rating) and 100 (highest rating).
- 1980: The variables v2080, v2083, and v2086 from the original data set are included. These variables capture the thermometer ratings of Trudeau, Clark, and Broadbent, respectively. The thermometer ratings range between 0 (lowest rating) and 100 (highest rating).
- 1984: The variables var301, var302, and var3030 from the original data set are included. These variables capture the thermometer ratings of Turner, Mulroney, and Broadbent, respectively. The thermometer ratings range between 0 (lowest rating) and 100 (highest rating).
- 1988: The variables d2a, d2b, and d2c of the original data set are included. These variables capture thermometer ratings of Mulroney, Turner, and Broadbent, respectively. The thermometer ratings range between 0 (very negative) and 100 (very positive).
- 1993: The variables CPSD2A, CPSD2B, and CPSD2C from the original data set are included. These variables capture thermometer ratings of Campbell, Chretien, and McLaughlin, respectively. The thermometer ratings range between 0 (very unfavourable) and 100 (very favourable).
- 1997: The variables cpsd1a, cpsd1b, and cpsd1d from the original data set are included. These variables capture thermometer ratings of Charest, Chretien, and Manning, respectively. The thermometer ratings range between 0 (really dislike) and 100 (really like).
- 2000: The variables cpsclark, cpschret, cpsmcdon, and cpsstock from the original data set are included. These variables capture thermometer ratings of Clark, Chretien, McDonough, and Stockwell Day, respectively. The thermometer ratings range between 0 (really dislike) and 100 (really like).

- 2004: The variables cps_g1, cps_g2, and cps_g3 from the original data set are included. These variables capture thermometer ratings of Harper, Martin, and Layton, respectively. The thermometer ratings range between 0 (really dislike) and 100 (really like).
- 2006: The variables ces06_CPS_G1, ces06_CPS_G2, and ces06_CPS_G3 from the original data set are included. These variables capture thermometer ratings of Harper, Martin, and Layton, respectively. The thermometer ratings range between 0 (really dislike) and 100 (really like).
- 2008: The variables ces08_CPS_G1, ces08_CPS_G2, ces08_CPS_G3, and ces08_CPS_G5 from the original data set are included. These variables capture thermometer ratings of Harper, Dion, Layton, and May, respectively. The thermometer ratings range between 0 (really dislike) and 100 (really like).
- 2011: The variables CPS11_23, CPS11_24, CPS11_25, and CPS11_27 from the original data set are included. These variables capture thermometer ratings of Harper, Ignatieff, Layton, and May, respectively. The thermometer ratings range between 0 (really dislike) and 100 (really like).
- 2015: The variables ldrfeel_hrpr, ldrfeel_trud, ldrfeel_mulc, and ldrfeel_may from the original data set are included. These variables capture thermometer ratings of Harper, Trudeau, Mulcair, and May, respectively. The thermometer ratings range between 0 (really dislike) and 100 (really like).
- 2019: The variables q20, q21, q22, q24, and q25 from the original data set are included. These variables capture thermometer ratings of Trudeau, Sheer, Singh, May, and Bernier, respectively. The thermometer ratings range between 0 (lowest rating) and 100 (highest rating).

K.3 Denmark

K.3.1 Economic evaluations

- 1998: Would you say the country's economy situation has become better, stayed the same, or has become worse during the last twelve months?
- 2001: How do you think the economic situation for Denmark is today compared to three to four years ago? Much better, better, no change, worse, much worse?
- 2005: How do you think the economic situation for Denmark is today compared to three to four years ago? Much better, better, no change, worse, much worse?

- 2007, 2011, 2015: How do you think Denmark's economic situation is today compared to three years ago? Much better, better, no change, worse, much worse?

K.3.2 Leader evaluations

- 1971: The variables v383, v385, v386, and v388 from the original data set are included. These variables capture thermometer ratings of Ninn-Hansen, Baunsgaard, Krag, and Hartling, respectively. The thermometer ratings range between 0 (lowest rating) and 300 (highest rating).
- 1994: The variables v130, v131, v133, v134, and v135 from the original data set are included. These variables capture evaluations of Nyrup, Jelved, Jacobsen, Nielsen, and Jensen, respectively. The measure ranges between 0 (lowest rating) and 10 (highest rating).
- 1998: The variables v48, v49, v50, v51, v53, v53, v54, v55, v56, and v57 from the original data set are included. These variables capture evaluations of Nyrup, Jelved, Moeler, M. Jacobsen, Nielsen, Kjaersgaard, Sjursen, Ellemann, K. Jacobsen, and Aaen, respectively. The measure ranges between 0 (lowest rating) and 10 (highest rating).
- 2001: The variables v41, v42, v43, v44, v45, v46, v47, and v48 from the original data set are included. These variables capture sympathy ratings of N. Rasmussen, Jelved, Bendtsen, Nielsen, Kjaersgaard, Sjursen, F. Rasmussen, and Aaen, respectively. The measure ranges between 0 (view very poorly) and 10 (view very favourably).
- 2005: The variables v79, v80, v81, v82, v83, and v84 from the original data set are included. These variables capture sympathy ratings of Lykketoft, Jelved, Bendtsen, Nielsen, Kjaersgaard, and Fogh, respectively. The measure ranges between 0 (view very poorly) and 10 (view very favourably).
- 2007: The variables v96, v97, v98, v99, v101, v102, v103, and v104 from the original data set are included. These variables capture sympathy ratings of Thorning, Vestager, Bendtsen, Søvndal, Kjaersgaard, Fogh, Khader, and Barfod, respectively. The measure ranges between 0 (view very poorly) and 10 (view very favourably).
- 2011: The variables v76, v77, v78, v79, v80, v81, v82, and v83 from the original data set are included. These variables capture sympathy ratings of Thorning-Schmidt, Vestager, Barfod, Søvndal, Samuelsen, Kjaersgaard, Løkke Rasmussen, and Schmidt-Nielsen, respectively. The measure ranges between 0 (view very poorly) and 10 (view very favourably).
- 2015: The variables V76, V77, V78, V79, V80, V81, V82, V83, and V84 from the original data set are included. These variables capture sympathy

ratings of Thorning-Schmidt, Østergaard, Pape, Olsen Dyhr, Samuelsen, Thulesen Dahl, Løkke Rasmussen, Schmidt-Nielsen, and Elbaek, respectively.

K.4 Germany

K.4.1 Economic evaluations

- 1972: How would you, quite generally, evaluate the present economic situation in the Federal Republic? Very good, good, part good/part bad, more bad, or bad?
- 1976, 1983, 1987, 1990: How would you, quite generally, evaluate the present economic situation in the Federal Republic (of Germany)? Very good, good, part good/part bad, bad, very bad?
- 1994: How would you, quite generally, evaluate the present economic situation in Germany? Very good, good, part good/part bad, bad, very bad?
- 1998: Would you say that the economic situation in Germany has improved over the past twelve months, has it remained unchanged, or has it deteriorated?
- 2002: How has the general economic situation in the old/new federal states developed in the last one to two years? The general economic situation has improved a lot, improved a bit, stayed the same, got a bit worse, got a lot worse?
- 2005, 2009, 2013, 2017: And has the general economic situation in Germany improved considerably, improved somewhat, remained the same, deteriorated somewhat, or deteriorated considerably in the last one to two years?

K.4.2 Leader evaluations

- 1961: The variables v64, v68, and v69 from the original data set are included. These variables capture attitudes towards Adenauer, Brandt, and Mende respectively. Attitudes were originally measured on a scale from −5 (rejects politician) to +5 (likes politician) but were rescaled to range between 0 and 10.

- 1976: The variables v69, v70, and v71 from the original data set are included. These variables capture attitudes towards Genscher, Kohl, and Schmidt, respectively. Attitudes were originally measured on a scale from −5 (do not think much of politician) to +5 (think a great deal of politician) but were rescaled to range between 0 and 10.
- 1980: The variables v30, v32, and v33 from the original data set are included. These variables capture attitudes towards Genscher, Schmidt, and Strauss, respectively. Attitudes were originally measured on a scale from −5 (do not think much of politician) to +5 (think a great deal of politician) but were rescaled to range between 0 and 10.
- 1983: The variables v33, v34, and v39 from the original data set are included. These variables capture attitudes towards Genscher, Vogel, and Kohl, respectively. Attitudes were originally measured on a scale from −5 (do not think much of politician) to +5 (think a great deal of politician) but were rescaled to range between 0 and 10.
- 1987: The variables v29, v32, and v34 from the original data set are included. These variables capture attitudes towards Bangemann, Kohl, and Rau. Attitudes were originally measured on a scale from −5 (do not think much of politician) to +5 (think a great deal of politician) but were rescaled to range between 0 and 10.
- 1990: The variables v33, v34, and v38 from the original data set are included. These variables capture attitudes towards Kohl, Lambsdorff, and Lafontaine. Attitudes were originally measured on a scale from −5 (do not think much of politician) to +5 (think a great deal of politician) but were rescaled to range between 0 and 10.
- 1994: The variables v19, v20, v21, v22, and v23 from the original data set are included. These variables capture attitudes towards Kohl, Scharping, Kinkel, Fischer, and Gysi, respectively. Attitudes were originally measured on a scale from −5 (do not think much of politician) to +5 (think a great deal of politician) but were rescaled to range between 0 and 10.
- 1998: The variables v46, v50, v51, v53, and v55 from the original data set are included. These variables capture attitudes towards Kohl, Schröder, Gerhardt, Trittin, and Bisky, respectively. Attitudes were originally measured on a scale from −5 (do not think much of politician) to +5 (think a great deal of politician) but were rescaled to range between 0 and 10.
- 2005: The variables Q31_A, Q31_B, Q31_C, Q31_D, and Q31_E are included. These variables capture attitudes towards Schroeder, Merkel, Fischer, Westerwelle, and Lafontaine, respectively. Attitudes were originally measured on a scale from −5 (do not think much of politician) to

+5 (think a great deal of politician) but were rescaled to range between 0 and 10.
- 2009: The variables vn166a, vn166c, vn166d, vn166e, and vn166f are included. These variables capture attitudes towards Merkel, Steinmeier, Westerwelle, Kuenast, and Lafontaine, respectively. Attitudes were originally measured on a scale from −5 (do not think much of politician) to +5 (think a great deal of politician) but were rescaled to range between 0 and 10.
- 2013: The variables vn22a, vn22b, vn22c, vn22d, and vn22e are included. These variables capture attitudes towards Merkel, Steinbrueck, Bruederle, Gysi, and Trittin, respectively. Attitudes were originally measured on a scale from −5 (do not think much of politician) to +5 (think a great deal of politician) but were rescaled to range between 0 and 10.
- 2017: The variables vn21a, vn21b, vn21c, vn21d, vn21e, and vn21f are included. These variables capture attitudes towards Merkel, Schulz, Wagenknecht, Oezdemir, Lindner, and Petry, respectively. Attitudes were originally measured on a scale from −5 (do not think much of politician) to +5 (think a great deal of politician) but were rescaled to range between 0 and 10.

K.5 Great Britain

K.5.1 Economic evaluations

- October 1974: Looking back over the last six months, would you say that the state of Britain's economy has stayed about the same, got better, or got worse?
- 1979: Looking back over the last year or so, would you say that the state of Britain's economy has stayed about the same, got better, or got worse?
- 1992: Looking back over the last year or so, would you say that Britain's economy has got stronger, got weaker, or stayed about the same?
- 1997, 2001: And how do you think the general economic situation in Britain has changed over the last twelve months? Has it got a lot better, got a little better, stayed the same, got a little worse, got a lot worse?
- 2005, 2010, 2015, 2017, 2019: How do you think the general economic situation in this country has changed over the last twelve months? Got a lot worse, got a little worse, stayed the same, got a little better, got a lot better?

K.5.2 Leader evaluations

- 1964: The variables v1077, v1093, and v1099 from the original data set are included. These variables capture attitudes towards Home, Wilson, and Grimmond, respectively. Attitudes are measured on a scale from 0 (lowest rating) to 10 (highest rating).
- 1966: The variables v1078 and v1094 from the original data set are included. These variables capture attitudes towards Heath and Wilson, respectively. Attitudes are measured on a scale from 0 (lowest rating) to 10 (highest rating).
- 1970: The variables v1079 and v1095 from the original data set are included. These variables capture attitudes towards Heath and Wilson, respectively. Attitudes are measured on a scale from 0 (lowest rating) to 10 (highest rating).
- February 1974: The variables feb147, feb148, and feb149 from the original data set are included. These variables capture attitudes towards Heath, Wilson, and Thorpe, respectively. Attitudes are measured on a scale from 0 (lowest mark) to 10 (highest mark).
- October 1974: The variables oct147, oct148, and oct149 from the original data set are included. These variables capture attitudes towards Heath, Wilson, and Thorpe, respectively. Attitudes are measured on a scale from 0 (lowest mark) to 10 (highest mark).
- 1979: The variables m000173, m000174, and m000175 from the original data set are included. These variables capture attitudes towards Thatcher, Callaghan, and Steel, respectively. Attitudes are measured on a scale from 0 (lowest mark) to 10 (highest mark).
- 1997: The variables majlike, blrlike, and ashlike from the original dataset are included. These variables capture attitudes towards Major, Blair, and Ashdown, respectively. Attitudes are measured on a scale from 0 (strongly dislike) to 10 (strongly like).
- 2001: The variables aq17a, aq17b, and aq17c from the original data set are included. These variables capture attitudes towards Blair, Hague, and Kennedy, respectively. Attitudes are measured on a scale from 0 (strongly dislike) to 10 (strongly like).
- 2005: The variables aq14a, aq14b, and aq14c from the original data set are included. These variables capture attitudes towards Blair, Howard, and Kennedy, respectively. Attitudes are measured on a scale from 0 (strongly dislike) to 10 (strongly like).
- 2010: The variables aq14_1, aq14_2, and aq14_3 from the original data set are included. These variables capture attitudes towards Brown,

Cameron, and Clegg, respectively. Attitudes are measured on a scale from 0 (strongly dislike) to 10 (strongly like).
- 2015: The variables i01_1, i01_2, i01_3, i01_4, and i01_5 from the original data set are included. These variables capture attitudes towards Miliband, Cameron, Clegg, Bennett, and Farage, respectively. Attitudes are measured on a scale from 0 (strongly dislike) to 10 (strongly like).
- 2017: The variables i01_3, i01_4, i01_5, and i01_7 from the original data set are included. These variables capture attitudes towards Corbyn, May, Farron, and Nuttall, respectively. Attitudes are measured on a scale from 0 (strongly dislike) to 10 (strongly like).
- 2019: The variables i01_1, i01_2, i01_3, and i01_6 from the original data set are included. These variables capture attitudes towards Corbyn, Johnson, Swinson, and Farage, respectively. Attitudes are measured on a scale from 0 (strongly dislike) to 10 (strongly like).

K.6 The Netherlands

K.6.1 Economic evaluations

- 1986, 1989, 1994, 1998, 2002, 2006: First, the economic situation in the Netherlands: do you think that the economic situation has been influenced favourably, unfavourably, or neither by the government policies?
- 2010: Would you say that the general economic situation of our country over the last twelve months has improved, deteriorated, or stayed the same?
- 2012: Would you say that over the past twelve months, the Dutch economy's condition has got better, stayed about the same, or got worse?
- 2017: Would you say that over the past twelve months, the state of the economy in the Netherlands has got better, stayed about the same, or has got worse?

K.6.2 Leader evaluations

- 1986: Variables V32_1, V32_2, V32_3, and V32_4 from the original data set are used. These variables capture sympathy scores for Lubbers, Den Uyl, Nijpels, and Mierlo, respectively. Attitudes are measured on a scale from 0 (very unsympathetic) to 10 (very sympathetic).
- 1989: Variables V32_1, V32_2, V32_3, and V32_4 from the original data set are used. These variables capture sympathy scores for Lubbers, Kok,

Voorhoeve, and Van Mierlo, respectively. Attitudes are measured on a scale from 0 (very unsympathetic) to 10 (very sympathetic).
- 1994: Variables V32_1, V32_2, V32_4, V32_5, and V32_8 from the original data set are used. These variables capture sympathy scores for Lubbers, Kok, Bolkestein, Brouwer, and Van Mierlo, respectively. Attitudes are measured on a scale from 0 (very unsympathetic) to 10 (very sympathetic).
- 1998: Variables V32_1, V32_2, V32_3, V32_4, V32_5, and V32_7 from the original data set are used. These variables capture sympathy scores for Kok, de Hoop Scheffer, Bolkestein, Borst, Rosenmöller, and Marijnissen, respectively. Attitudes are measured on a scale from 0 (very unsympathetic) to 10 (very sympathetic).
- 2002: Variables V32_1, V32_3, V32_4, V32_5, V32_6, V32_8, and V32_9 from the original data set are used. These variables capture sympathy scores for Kok, Balkenende, Dijkstal, de Graaf, Rosenmoller, Marijnissen, and Fortuyn, respectively. Attitudes are measured on a scale from 0 (very unsympathetic) to 10 (very sympathetic).
- 2010: Variables v351, v352, v353, v354, v355, v356, and v357 from the original data set are used. These variables capture sympathy scores for Balkenende, Cohen, Rutte, Pechtold, Halsema, Roemer, and Wilders, respectively. Attitudes are measured on a scale from 0 (very unsympathetic) to 10 (very sympathetic).
- 2012: Variables V200, V201, V203, V204, V205, V206, V207, and V209 from the original data set are used. These variables capture sympathy scores for Buma, Samson, Rutte, Pechtold, Sap, Roemer, Wilders, Slob, and Thieme, respectively. Attitudes are measured on a scale from 0 (very unsympathetic) to 10 (very sympathetic).
- 2017: Variables V213, V214, V215, V216, V217, V218, V219, V220, and V222 from the original data set are included. These variables capture sympathy scores for Rutte, Asscher, Wilders, Buma, Roemer, Pechtold, Segers, Klaver, and Thieme, respectively. Attitudes are measured on a scale from 0 (very unsympathetic) to 10 (very sympathetic).

K.7 Sweden

K.7.1 Economic evaluations

- 1985, 1988, 1994: How has, in your opinion, the Swedish economy changed in the last two or three years? Has it improved, remained about the same, or has it got worse?

- 1998, 2002, 2006, 2010, 2014: Would you say that the economic situation in Sweden has improved, remained the same, or gone worse during the last twelve months?
- 2018: How do you think that the economic situation in Sweden has changed during the past twelve months? Improved a lot, somewhat improved, neither improved nor deteriorated, somewhat deteriorated, deteriorated a lot?

K.7.2 Leader evaluations

- 1979: The variables sympl1, sympl2, sympl3, sympl4, and sympl5 from the original data set are used. These variables capture like/dislike ratings for Fäldin, Bohman, Werner, Ullsten, and Palme, respectively. Attitudes are measured on a scale from −5 (dislike strongly) to +5 (like strongly)
- 1982: Variables V102, V103, V104, V105, and V106 from the original data set are included. These variables capture like/dislike ratings for Fäldin, Adelsohn, Werner, Ullsten, and Palme, respectively. Attitudes are measured on a scale from −5 (dislike strongly) to +5 (like strongly) and were rescaled to range between 0 and 10.
- 1985: Variables V89, V90, V91, V92, V93, and V94 from the original data set are included. These variables capture like/dislike ratings for Fäldin, Adelsohn, Werner, Westerberg, Palme, and Svensson, respectively. Attitudes are measured on a scale from −5 (dislike strongly) to +5 (like strongly) and were rescaled to range between 0 and 10.
- 1988: Variables V78, V79, V80, V81, and V82 from the original data set are included. These variables capture like/dislike ratings for Johansson, Bildt, Werner, Westerberg, and Carlsson, respectively. Attitudes are measured on a scale from −5 (dislike strongly) to +5 (like strongly) and were rescaled to range between 0 and 10.
- 1994: Variables v96, v97, v98, v99, v100, v101, and v102 from the original data set are included. These variables capture like/dislike ratings for Johansson, Bildt, Schyman, Westerberg, Carlsson, Schlaug, and Svensson, respectively. Attitudes are measured on a scale from −5 (dislike strongly) to +5 (like strongly) and were rescaled to range between 0 and 10.
- 1998: Variables v101, v102, v103, v104, v105, v106, and v107 from the original data set are included. These variables capture like/dislike ratings of Daleus, Bildt, Schyman, Leijonborg, Persson, Schlaug, and Svensson, respectively. Attitudes are measured on a scale from −5 (dislike strongly) to +5 (like strongly) and were rescaled to range between 0 and 10.

- 2002: Variables V110, V111, V112, V113, V114, and V117 are included. These variables capture like/dislike ratings of Olofsson, Lundgren, Schyman, Leijonborg, Persson, and Svensson, respectively. Attitudes are measured on a scale from −5 (dislike strongly) to +5 (like strongly) and were rescaled to range between 0 and 10.
- 2006: Variables v244, v245, v246, v247, v248, v250, and v251 are included. These variables capture like/dislike ratings of Olofsson, Reinfeldt, Ohly, Leijonborg, Persson, Wetterstrand, and Hägglund, respectively. Attitudes are measured on a scale from −5 (dislike strongly) to +5 (like strongly) and were rescaled to range between 0 and 10.
- 2010: Variables VU10_V292, VU10_V293, VU10_V294, VU10_V295, VU10_V296, VU10_V298, VU10_V299, and VU10_300 from the original data set are included. These variables capture like/dislike ratings of Olofsson, Reinfeldt, Ohly, Björklund, Sahlin, Wetterstrand, Hägglund, and Åkesson, respectively. Attitudes are measured on a scale from −5 (dislike strongly) to +5 (like strongly) and were rescaled to range between 0 and 10.
- 2014: Variables f10ba, f10bb, f10bc, f10bd, f10be, f10bg, f10bh, f10bi, and f10bj from the original data set are used. These variables capture like/dislike ratings of Lööf, Reinfeldt, Sjöstedt, Björklund, Löfven, Romson, Hägglund, Åkesson, and Schyman, respectively. Attitudes are measured on a scale from −5 (dislike strongly) to +5 (like strongly) and were rescaled to range between 0 and 10.
- 2018: Variables q318a, q318b, q318c, q318d, q318e, q318f, q318h, and q318i from the original data set are used. These variables capture like/dislike ratings of Lööf, Kristersson, Sjöstedt, Björklund, Löfven, Fridolin, Busch Thor, and Åkesson, respectively. Attitudes are measured on a scale from −5 (dislike strongly) to +5 (like strongly) and were rescaled to range between 0 and 10.

K.8 United States

K.8.1 Economic evaluations

- 1980, 1988, 1992: How about the economy. Would you say that over the past year the nation's economy has got better, stayed about the same, or got worse?
- 1984: How about the economy? Would you say that over the past year the nation's economy has got better, stayed the same, or got worse?

- 1996, 2000, 2004, 2008, 2012, 2016: Now thinking about the economy in the country as a whole. Would you say that over the past year the nation's economy has got better, stayed about the same, or got worse?

K.8.2 Leader evaluations

- 1992–2004: Variables VCF0403 and VCF0407 from the original data set are included. These variables capture affect towards the Democratic and Republican Presidential Candidates, respectively. Attitudes are measured on a scale from −5 (maximum negative) to +5 (maximum positive) and were rescaled to range between 0 and 10.

Appendix L
Change in the role of economic and leader evaluations

In Chapter 5, I assess over-time changes in the effect and roles of economic evaluations and leader evaluations on the vote choice. The main results that are presented in that chapter consist of visualizations of the coefficient of individuals' economic evaluation on their likelihood to vote for the incumbent (Figures 5.3 and 5.4) and the over-time trend in the decomposed share of the pseudo-R^2 that can be explained by leader evaluations (Figures 5.5 and 5.6).

Those visualizations do not provide much evidence for the idea that the impact of short-term factors, such as economic evaluations and evaluations of leaders, has increased over time.

Here, I more formally estimate the over-time trends in the effect of economic evaluations on the vote and in the explanatory power of leadership evaluations on the vote.

First, Table L.1 shows the results of a series of regression estimation in which the dependent variable is the coefficient for economic evaluation (i.e. the estimates visualized in Figures 5.3 and 5.4). The main independent variable is the election year. The results in Table L.1 confirm the conclusions that I drew based on a visual assessment of the economic evaluation coefficients. There is not a single country where a linear time trend reaches statistical significance. A pooled estimation also returns a coefficient that is close to zero and not statistically significant.

Second, to assess more formally whether there are indications of change in the impact of leader evaluations on the vote choice, Table L.2 shows the estimates of regression estimations in which the decomposed pseudo-R^2 of leader evaluations is the dependent variable and the election year the (main) independent variable. The results suggest that there are two countries where there is evidence of a significant over-time increase in the extent to which leader evaluations contribute to explaining variation in the vote choice: Denmark and the United States. In the six other countries, the estimated time trend is not significant and often close to zero. When pooling all the data, the time trend is positive and significant, but the effect size is substantively very small.

Table L.1 Association between election year and coefficient of economic evaluations

	Australia	Canada	Denmark	Germany	Great Britain	The Netherlands	Sweden	United States	All
Election year	0.001 (0.000)	0.002 (0.001)	−0.000 (0.000)	−0.001 (0.000)	0.001 (0.000)	−0.002 (0.002)	0.001 (0.001)	0.002 (0.002)	0.001 (0.000)
Country FE	✗	✗	✗	✗	✗	✗	✗	✗	✓
Intercept	−1.932 (0.993)	−3.120 (2.431)	0.103 (0.972)	1.134 (0.907)	−1.374 (0.712)	4.719 (3.148)	−1.069 (2.965)	−3.958 (3.424)	−0.964 (0.687)
N	13	10	8	12	11	9	9	10	82
R^2	0.313	0.258	0.000	0.096	0.290	0.260	0.016	0.150	0.695

Note: Robust standard errors in parentheses. $^*p < 0.05$, $^{**}p < 0.01$, $^{***}p < 0.001$.

Table L.2 Association between election year and decomposed McFadden pseudo-R^2 statistic of leader evaluations

	Australia	Canada	Denmark	Germany	Great Britain	The Netherlands	Sweden	United States	All
Election year	0.003 (0.002)	0.001 (0.000)	0.009*** (0.001)	0.001 (0.001)	0.001 (0.001)	0.001 (0.002)	0.001 (0.001)	0.003*** (0.001)	0.002*** (0.001)
Country FE	✗	✗	✗	✗	✗	✗	✗	✗	✗
Intercept	−6.704 (4.141)	−1.470 (0.888)	−17.010*** (1.999)	−2.544 (1.294)	−2.029 (1.529)	−1.361 (4.870)	−1.905 (2.706)	−4.967** (1.192)	−3.909*** (1.029)
N	12	15	8	12	13	8	11	14	93
R^2	0.413	0.186	0.885	0.130	0.189	0.020	0.073	0.650	0.557

Note: Robust standard errors in parentheses. * $p < 0.05$, ** $p < 0.01$, *** $p < 0.001$.

Specifically, the coefficient of 0.002 suggests that the decomposed pseudo-R^2 of leader evaluations increases by 0.02 every decade.

Overall, the additional analyses that are presented here substantiate the conclusion that the evidence for an increase in the impact of short-term factors on the vote is very weak.

Appendix M
Full variation method

As indicated in Chapter 7, to operationalize group-based cross-pressures, I follow the empirical approach suggested by Brader, Tucker and Therriault (2014). The starting point is to estimate vote-choice models, including as independent variables the indicators that are a source of cross-pressure. The predicted probabilities of those vote-choice models are then saved to assess variation in predicted probabilities. In this step, one has to decide how many parties to include when assessing variation. In their paper, Brader, Tucker and Therriault (2014) obtain a cross-pressure (CP) score measure for all parties (full variance method), one that is limited to the top three parties, and another one that is limited to the top two parties. On this point, they indicate (p. 35):

> If voters simply decide between their two most preferred parties, then it is best to calculate CP scores using only the variance across the two largest predicted probabilities of party choice; inclusion of additional probabilities may simply add noise. If, however, voters consider the full range of parties, then we should include all of the predicted probabilities in the calculation of her CP score. Ultimately, this is a conceptual question: which parties truly matter to the respondent's decision making process?

For the main analyses that are presented in this book, I relied on the top-two variance approach. This means that I operationalized cross-pressure based on the variation in predicted probabilities between the two parties for which a voter has the highest probability of voting. In this appendix, I verify whether the main results hold when taking a different decision and using the variation in predicted probabilities for *all* parties included in the estimation.

I first validate whether the patterns and findings with respect to over-time change in group-based cross-pressures hold when using the full variance method. Subsequently, I verify whether there is also evidence of an association between group-based cross-pressures and late deciding and volatility, respectively when using the full variance method.

Note that given that the US estimations consistently include two parties only (Democrats and Republicans), the top-two variance method and the full variance method are identical for the United States. Therefore, the results in this appendix are limited to the other seven countries.

M.1 Cross-pressure over time

Figures M.1, M.2, M.3, and M.4 show the distribution of the group-based CP score measure (using the full variance method), by election year. Comparing distributions from bottom (the oldest election) to the top (the most recent elections), the ridgeplots indicate change over time. More specifically, and in line with the main results, there are indications that the median CP score (the vertical lines in the plots) has increased over time. Furthermore, there are indications that the share of high cross-pressured respondents in surveys has substantially increased over time. The two settings where this trend is less clear and pronounced are Australia and Great Britain. Overall, these trends and patterns of change are very much in line with the main results, which focused on variance between the top two parties only.

Furthermore, as can be seen from the estimates of seven country-specific linear probability models in Table M.1, the time trend in group-based cross-pressures is consistently positive and significant. The effect sizes that are reported in Table M.1, furthermore, are substantively very similar to those reported in Chapter 8.

M.2 Cross-pressure and campaign deciding

Turning to the association between group-based cross-pressure and campaign deciding, Tables M.2, M.3, and M.4 replicate the main results, relying on a full variance method to obtain individual-level measures of group-based cross-pressure. As can be seen from the estimates, using this approach as well, there is evidence of a strong association between group-based cross-pressures and deciding during the campaign. The association is significant in each of the seven countries, holds when accounting for a linear time trend (Table M.3), and is also apparent when focusing on the association between cross-pressure and campaign deciding *within* elections (Table M.4).

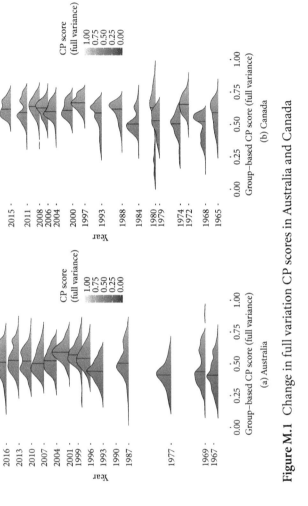

Figure M.1 Change in full variation CP scores in Australia and Canada

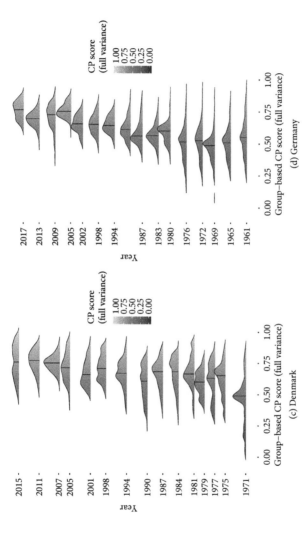

Figure M.2 Change in full variation CP scores in Denmark and Germany

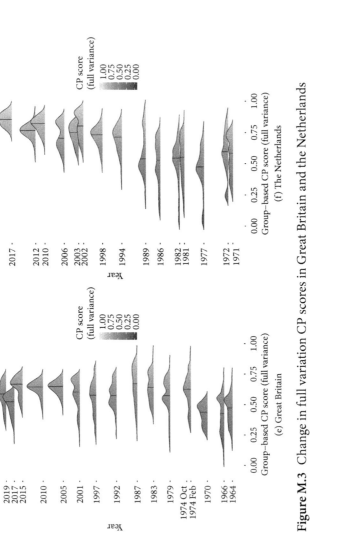

Figure M.3 Change in full variation CP scores in Great Britain and the Netherlands

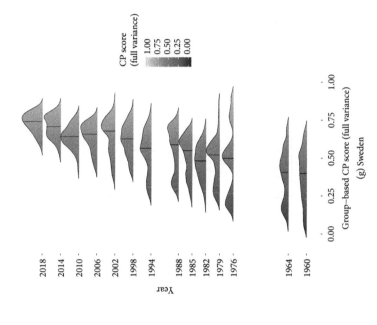

Figure M.4 Change in full variation CP scores in Sweden

Table M.1 Explaining full variation CP score, change over time

	Australia	Canada	Denmark	Germany	Great Britain	The Netherlands	Sweden
Year	0.002***	0.003***	0.005***	0.005***	0.001***	0.008***	0.006***
	(0.000)	(0.000)	(0.000)	(0.000)	(0.000)	(0.000)	(0.000)
Intercept	−3.377***	−4.697***	−8.503***	−8.810***	−1.152***	−14.820***	−11.538***
	(0.109)	(0.077)	(0.151)	(0.106)	(0.098)	(0.141)	(0.092)
N	23,434	26,934	20,214	17,886	30,936	20,466	29,168
R^2	0.063	0.152	0.194	0.379	0.011	0.402	0.359

Note: Robust standard errors in parentheses. * $p < 0.05$, ** $p < 0.01$, *** $p < 0.001$.

Table M.2 Association between group-based cross-pressure and campaign deciding

	Australia	Canada	Denmark	Germany	Great Britain	The Netherlands	Sweden
Group-based cross-pressure	0.279***	0.282***	0.681***	0.785***	0.315***	0.782***	0.426***
	(0.030)	(0.039)	(0.024)	(0.024)	(0.018)	(0.017)	(0.016)
Intercept	0.166***	0.303***	−0.152***	−0.298***	0.046***	−0.130***	0.044***
	(0.016)	(0.023)	(0.016)	(0.014)	(0.010)	(0.012)	(0.009)
N	17,504	15,772	17,658	14,230	24,716	19,426	26,382
R^2	0.005	0.003	0.041	0.070	0.011	0.080	0.025

Note: Robust standard errors in parentheses. * $p < 0.05$, ** $p < 0.01$, *** $p < 0.001$.

Table M.3 Association between group-based cross-pressure and campaign deciding, accounting for linear time trend

	Australia	Canada	Denmark	Germany	Great Britain	The Netherlands	Sweden
Group-based cross-pressure	0.294***	0.278***	0.515***	0.423***	0.257***	0.398***	0.299***
	(0.030)	(0.039)	(0.027)	(0.030)	(0.018)	(0.023)	(0.020)
Year	−0.003***	0.000	0.004***	0.004***	0.003***	0.007***	0.002***
	(0.000)	(0.000)	(0.000)	(0.000)	(0.000)	(0.000)	(0.000)
Intercept	6.709***	0.068	−7.363***	−8.671***	−6.305***	−14.803***	−4.626***
	(0.819)	(0.564)	(0.554)	(0.496)	(0.411)	(0.605)	(0.425)
N	17,504	15,772	17,658	14,230	24,716	19,426	26,382
R^2	0.008	0.003	0.050	0.087	0.021	0.105	0.029

Note: Robust standard errors in parentheses. * $p < 0.05$, ** $p < 0.01$, *** $p < 0.001$.

Table M.4 Association between group-based cross-pressure and campaign deciding, within-election effects

	Australia	Canada	Denmark	Germany	Great Britain	The Netherlands	Sweden
Group-based cross-pressure	0.340***	0.261***	0.512***	0.275***	0.244***	0.402***	0.304***
	(0.032)	(0.042)	(0.028)	(0.031)	(0.020)	(0.024)	(0.020)
Election FE	✓	✓	✓	✓	✓	✓	✓
N	17,504	15,772	17,658	14,230	24,716	19,426	26,382
R^2	0.018	0.015	0.057	0.114	0.026	0.113	0.047

Note: Robust standard errors in parentheses. * $p < 0.05$, ** $p < 0.01$, *** $p < 0.001$.

Table M.5 Association between group-based cross-pressure and volatility

	Australia	Canada	Denmark	Germany	Great Britain	The Netherlands	Sweden
Group-based cross-pressure	0.380***	0.409***	0.561***	0.526***	0.261***	0.384***	0.561***
	(0.022)	(0.030)	(0.024)	(0.026)	(0.018)	(0.018)	(0.019)
Intercept	0.008	0.051**	−0.057***	−0.083***	0.054***	0.055***	−0.060***
	(0.011)	(0.017)	(0.016)	(0.016)	(0.011)	(0.012)	(0.010)
N	20,846	20,154	17,291	14,434	24,206	16,728	10,693
R^2	0.013	0.009	0.027	0.026	0.008	0.023	0.073

Note: Robust standard errors in parentheses. * $p < 0.05$, ** $p < 0.01$, *** $p < 0.001$.

Table M.6 Association between group-based cross-pressure and volatility, accounting for linear time trend

	Australia	Canada	Denmark	Germany	Great Britain	The Netherlands	Sweden
Group-based cross-pressure	0.365***	0.307***	0.314***	0.381***	0.234***	0.280***	0.218***
	(0.023)	(0.033)	(0.027)	(0.034)	(0.018)	(0.023)	(0.023)
Year	0.001**	0.001***	0.006***	0.002***	0.002***	0.002***	0.005***
	(0.000)	(0.000)	(0.000)	(0.000)	(0.000)	(0.000)	(0.000)
Intercept	−1.241**	−2.771***	−10.908***	−3.495***	−3.355***	−3.876***	−9.869***
	(0.380)	(0.391)	(0.572)	(0.491)	(0.305)	(0.588)	(0.486)
N	20846	20154	17291	14434	24206	16728	10693
R^2	0.014	0.011	0.047	0.029	0.013	0.025	0.110

Note: Robust standard errors in parentheses. *($p < 0.05$, **$p < 0.01$, ***$p < 0.001$

Table M.7 Association between group-based cross-pressure and volatility, within-election effects

	Australia	Canada	Denmark	Germany	Great Britain	The Netherlands	Sweden
Group-based cross-pressure	0.316***	0.279***	0.340***	0.400***	0.195***	0.324***	0.216***
	(0.024)	(0.036)	(0.028)	(0.036)	(0.021)	(0.024)	(0.023)
Election FE	✓	✓	✓	✓	✓	✓	✓
N	20,846	20,154	17,291	14,434	24,206	16,728	10,693
R^2	0.020	0.032	0.105	0.041	0.016	0.061	0.113

Note: Robust standard errors in parentheses. * $p < 0.05$, ** $p < 0.01$, *** $p < 0.001$.

M.3 Cross-pressure and volatility

Finally, the findings with regard to the association between group-based cross-pressure and volatility as well hold when using a full variation method to operationalize group-based cross-pressure. Tables M.5, M.6, and M.7 show strong and significant associations between group-based cross-pressures and volatility (i.e. party switching) in each country. This also holds when accounting for a linear time trend (Table M.6) and when focusing on the association between cross-pressure and campaign deciding *within* elections (Table M.7).

Appendix N
European Election Study voter survey analyses

N.1 Information on the datasets

- 1979 European Election Study voter survey:
  Commission of the European Communities (2012): Eurobarometer 11 (Apr 1979), GESIS Data Archive, Cologne, ZA1036 Data file Version 1.0.1, doi:10.4232/1.10866.
- 2018 European Election Study voter survey:
  Schmitt, Hermann, Hobolt, Sara B., van der Brug, Wouter, and Popa, Sebastian Adrian (2020), European Parliament Election Study 2019, Voter Study, GESIS Data Archive, Cologne, ZA7581 Data file Version 1.0.0, https://doi.org/10.4232/1.13473.

N.2 Operationalization of socio-demographic variables

N.2.1 1979 voter survey

- I include a measure for gender, using v120 in the original data set. This variable is coded so female = 1 and male = 0.
- Age is included as a continuous measure (v121 in the original data set).
- For the measure of education, I make use of v118 from the original data set. The measure captures the age a respondent left education (coded as a continous variable). Respondents who were still studying were coded as missing.
- To capture the role of religion, I include v116 from the original data set, which captures the importance that individuals attach to religion in their daily life (from 1 = no importance to 4 = great importance).
- To capture the role of the rural–urban cleavage, I include v131 from the original data set as a categorical variable. This measure distinguishes between 'rural/village', 'small/middle town', and 'big town'.

- Finally, for income, I make use of v125 from the original data set, which distinguishes between country-specific income categories.
- Note that, in the absence of a measure of social class, an interaction between education and income was included in the vote-choice models.

N.2.2   2019 voter survey

- I include a measure for gender, using D3 in the original data set. This variable is coded so female = 1 and male = 0.
- To account for the role of age, I subtract respondents' year of birth (variable D4) from 2019 (i.e. the year of the election) and include this as a continuous measure in the vote-choice models.
- Education is measured by means of a categorical variable (EDU in the original data set) based on the age at which respondents left school (fifteen years and less; sixteen to nineteen; twenty and more). Respondents who were still studying are coded as missing.
- For religion, I make use of variable D9 in the original data set, which captures respondents' religious denomination. I recode this variable to distinguish between those with no religion (or atheists), Catholics, Protestants, and any other religious denomination.
- The rural–urban cleavage is captured through variable D8 in the original data set. This variable distinguishes between 'rural area or village', 'small or middle size town', and 'large town'.
- Social class is measured by means of variable D7 in the original data set. This variable indicates whether respondents identify as 'working class', 'lower middle class', 'middle class', 'upper middle class', and 'upper class'. This variable is included as a continuous measure. Respondents indicating 'other' are coded as missing.

N.3   Wording of issue measures

N.3.1   1979 voter survey

We'd like to hear your views on some important political issues. Could you tell me whether you agree or disagree with each of the following proposals? How strongly do you feel? (Answer options: Strongly agree, agree, disagree, strongly disagree, don't know.)

- Strong public control should be exercised over the activities of multinational corporations.
- Nuclear energy should be developed to meet future energy needs.
- Greater effort should be made to reduce inequality of income.
- More severe penalties should be introduced for acts of terrorism.
- Public ownership of private industry should be expanded.
- Government should play a greater role in the management of the economy.
- Western Europe should make a stronger effort to provide adequate military defence.
- Women should be free to decide for themselves in matters concerning abortion.
- Employees should be given equal representation with share holders on the governing boards of large companies.
- Economic aid to Third World countries should be increased.
- Stronger measures should be taken to protect the environment against pollution.
- Stronger measures should be taken to protect the rights of individuals to express their own political views.
- Economic aid to the less developed regions of the European Community should be increased.

N.3.2 2019 voter survey

Now I would like you to tell me your views on various issues. For each issue, we will present you with two opposite statements and we will ask your opinion about these two statements. We would like to ask you to position yourself on a scale from 0 to 10, where '0' means that you 'fully agree with the statement at the top' and '10' means that you 'fully agree with the statement at the bottom'. Then, if your views are somewhere in between, you can choose any number that describes your position best.

- What do you think of state regulation and control of the economy?
  - 0: You fully favour state intervention in the economy.
  - 10: You fully oppose state intervention in the economy.
- Redistribution of wealth.
  - 0: You fully favour redistribution from the rich to the poor in [country].

- 10: You fully oppose redistribution of wealth from the rich to the poor in [country].
- Same-sex marriage.
  - 0: You fully favour same-sex marriage.
  - 10: You fully oppose same-sex marriages.
- Civil liberties.
  - 0: You fully support privacy rights even if they hinder efforts to combat crime.
  - 10: You fully support restricting privacy rights in order to combat crime.
- Immigration.
  - 0: You fully favour a restrictive policy on immigration.
  - 10: You fully oppose a restrictive policy on immigration.
- Environment.
  - 0: Environmental protection should take priority even at the cost of economic growth.
  - 10: Economic growth should take priority even at the cost of environmental protection.

N.4 Cross-pressures, most preferred party, and differences between parties: full results

Tables N.1 and N.2 show the full estimates of the results that are visually summarised in Figures 7.4 and 7.5.

Table N.1 Cross-pressure and the most preferred party

	Denmark	Germany	The Netherlands	Sweden	Great Britain
CP score	−0.325**	−0.304**	−0.239*	0.110	0.066
	(0.099)	(0.096)	(0.102)	(0.115)	(0.140)
1989 (ref.)					
1994	−0.964***	−0.871***	−0.950***	–	−0.448***
	(0.056)	(0.063)	(0.068)	–	(0.089)
1999	−0.468***	−0.350***	−0.412***	(ref.)	−0.524***
	(0.072)	(0.079)	(0.071)	–	(0.103)
2004	−0.125*	−0.733***	−0.294***	−0.448***	−0.612***
	(0.060)	(0.119)	(0.065)	(0.109)	(0.092)
2009	−0.268***	−0.140	−0.429***	0.169	−0.396***
	(0.060)	(0.077)	(0.066)	(0.112)	(0.093)

318 SUPPLEMENTARY MATERIALS

2014	−0.250***	0.005	−0.426***	0.399***	−0.031
	(0.061)	(0.066)	(0.073)	(0.109)	(0.107)
2019	−0.338***	−0.165*	−0.990***	0.272*	−0.196*
	(0.068)	(0.078)	(0.088)	(0.117)	(0.092)
Intercept	9.717***	9.348***	9.502***	8.773***	8.851***
	(0.072)	(0.066)	(0.081)	(0.131)	(0.110)
N	5,453	5,582	5,707	3,787	4,801
R^2	0.048	0.050	0.047	0.056	0.016

Note: Robust standard errors in parentheses. $^*p < 0.05$, $^{**}p < 0.01$, $^{***}p < 0.001$.

Table N.2 Cross-pressure and differences between parties

	Denmark	Germany	The Netherlands	Sweden	Great Britain
CP score	−1.803***	−1.617***	−1.172***	−1.467***	−0.889***
	(0.201)	(0.170)	(0.176)	(0.183)	(0.200)
Max. PTV	0.675***	0.702***	0.616***	0.612***	0.736***
	(0.024)	(0.020)	(0.021)	(0.022)	(0.020)
1989 (ref.)	–	–	–		–
1994	−0.014	−0.245*	−1.280***	–	−0.919***
	(0.146)	(0.120)	(0.155)	–	(0.170)
1999	−0.415**	−0.159	−1.747***	(ref.)	−1.121***
	(0.145)	(0.132)	(0.147)	–	(0.157)
2004	−0.055	−0.336*	−1.554***	−1.749***	−0.726***
	(0.141)	(0.155)	(0.141)	(0.135)	(0.146)
2009	−0.793***	−0.758***	−2.341***	−0.535***	−1.735***
	(0.138)	(0.136)	(0.142)	(0.151)	(0.145)
2014	−0.488***	0.174	−1.603***	−0.581***	0.182
	(0.142)	(0.128)	(0.144)	(0.152)	(0.181)
2019	−0.549***	−0.614***	−1.632***	−0.531*	−1.810***
	(0.140)	(0.139)	(0.149)	(0.163)	(0.148)
Intercept	−1.711***	−1.681***	−0.727**	−1.353***	−1.310***
	(0.282)	(0.209)	(0.239)	(0.236)	(0.234)
N	5,453	5,582	5,707	3,787	4,801
R^2	0.131	0.184	0.200	0.227	0.233

Note: Robust standard errors in parentheses. $^*p < 0.05$, $^{**}p < 0.01$, $^{***}p < 0.001$.

Appendix O
Age, period, and cohort effects

The main results for the age–period–cohort analysis that is presented in Chapter 8 rely on a categorization of individuals in six different generations, based on their year of birth. Given that generations are formed through shared experiences, it could be argued that the categorizations of generations should be country-specific. To relax the assumption that the generations that are distinguished between in Table 8.2 are comparable across countries, in this appendix, I take a more data-driven approach and evaluate whether there are differences based on respondents' birth cohorts. I distinguish between five-year birth cohorts. As can be seen from Table O.1, for this approach as well the only country for which there are indications of higher levels of group-based cross-pressure in each subsequent birth cohort is Australia.

Alternatively, it could be argued that the main results and those presented in Table O.1 obfuscate the main generational distinction in electorates: that between older and younger generations. Much previous work that discusses generational change draws attention to a change following the baby-boom generations. To assess this possibility, in Table O.2, I limit the categorization in generations to a dichotomous distinction between the baby-boomers and older generations, on the one hand, and younger generations, on the other. This approach suggests that in three of the seven countries included in these analyses, younger generations are significantly more cross-pressured than older generations. The differences between generations, however, are substantively limited. Furthermore, in two of the seven countries, younger generations are significantly *less* cross-pressured than older generations. Overall, these additional analyses do not provide strong evidence for the idea that change is driven by generational replacement either.

Table O.1 Explaining CP score, age, period, and cohort effects

	Australia	Canada	Denmark	Germany	Great Britain	The Netherlands	United States
Year	0.001**	0.004***	0.005***	0.003***	−0.000*	0.004***	−0.002***
	(0.000)	(0.000)	(0.000)	(0.000)	(0.000)	(0.000)	(0.000)
18–29 (ref.)							
30–49	0.042***	0.017***	0.003	0.001	0.015**	−0.022***	−0.002
	(0.005)	(0.005)	(0.006)	(0.005)	(0.005)	(0.005)	(0.008)
50–64	0.057***	0.021*	0.001	0.011	0.039***	−0.030***	0.006
	(0.008)	(0.008)	(0.009)	(0.009)	(0.008)	(0.009)	(0.013)
65+	0.030**	0.017	−0.040**	0.018	0.005	−0.034**	0.052**
	(0.012)	(0.012)	(0.012)	(0.012)	(0.012)	(0.012)	(0.019)
1910–14 (ref.)							
1915–19	0.010	−0.008	0.015	0.020	0.013	0.008	0.009
	(0.012)	(0.011)	(0.027)	(0.012)	(0.008)	(0.017)	(0.010)
1920–24	0.017	−0.009	0.054*	0.026*	0.009	0.019	0.006
	(0.011)	(0.010)	(0.024)	(0.011)	(0.008)	(0.016)	(0.011)
1925–29	0.014	−0.012	0.071**	0.022*	0.019*	0.024	0.016
	(0.011)	(0.010)	(0.023)	(0.011)	(0.008)	(0.015)	(0.011)
1930–34	0.030**	−0.016	0.042	0.030**	0.025**	0.054***	0.005
	(0.011)	(0.010)	(0.023)	(0.011)	(0.008)	(0.015)	(0.013)
1935–39	0.032**	−0.016	0.040	0.038***	0.023*	0.066***	0.001
	(0.011)	(0.011)	(0.023)	(0.011)	(0.009)	(0.015)	(0.014)
1940–44	0.037**	−0.014	0.020	0.035**	0.026**	0.095***	0.016
	(0.012)	(0.011)	(0.023)	(0.012)	(0.010)	(0.015)	(0.014)
1945–49	0.048***	−0.017	0.012	0.041***	0.046***	0.110***	0.032*
	(0.012)	(0.012)	(0.024)	(0.012)	(0.010)	(0.016)	(0.016)

1950–54	0.054***	−0.015	0.006	0.050***	0.066***	0.118***	0.041*
	(0.013)	(0.012)	(0.024)	(0.013)	(0.011)	(0.017)	(0.017)
1955–59	0.069***	−0.007	0.008	0.063***	0.072***	0.123***	0.037
	(0.014)	(0.014)	(0.025)	(0.014)	(0.012)	(0.017)	(0.019)
1960–64	0.080***	−0.005	0.011	0.072***	0.083***	0.141***	0.047*
	(0.015)	(0.015)	(0.025)	(0.015)	(0.013)	(0.018)	(0.021)
1965–69	0.093***	−0.010	0.016	0.073***	0.094***	0.136***	0.017
	(0.016)	(0.015)	(0.026)	(0.015)	(0.014)	(0.019)	(0.024)
1970–74	0.106***	−0.020	0.015	0.061***	0.110***	0.142***	0.005
	(0.017)	(0.017)	(0.026)	(0.016)	(0.015)	(0.020)	(0.025)
1975–79	0.127***	−0.015	0.042	0.070***	0.111***	0.139***	0.012
	(0.018)	(0.018)	(0.027)	(0.018)	(0.017)	(0.020)	(0.027)
1980–84	0.143***	−0.018	0.046	0.081***	0.114***	0.125***	0.010
	(0.018)	(0.019)	(0.027)	(0.018)	(0.018)	(0.021)	(0.028)
1985–89	0.158***	−0.021	0.049	0.074***	0.115***	0.108***	−0.039
	(0.020)	(0.020)	(0.029)	(0.019)	(0.019)	(0.022)	(0.032)
1990–94	0.180***	0.008	0.044	0.045	0.069**	0.092***	−0.014
	(0.021)	(0.022)	(0.029)	(0.025)	(0.023)	(0.024)	(0.034)
1995–99	0.184***	−0.014	−0.050	0.048*	0.013	0.116***	0.045
	(0.024)	(0.023)	(0.035)	(0.023)	(0.026)	(0.025)	(0.044)
Intercept	−0.759	−6.872***	−9.816***	−5.613***	1.599***	−7.412***	4.124***
	(0.458)	(0.454)	(0.571)	(0.475)	(0.456)	(0.483)	(0.723)
N	22,571	24,819	13,104	14,604	28,774	18,444	19,997
R^2	0.060	0.107	0.148	0.127	0.026	0.219	0.016

Note: Robust standard errors in parentheses. * $p < 0.05$, ** $p < 0.01$, *** $p < 0.001$.

Table O.2 Explaining CP score, old and young generations

	Australia	Canada	Denmark	Germany	Great Britain	The Netherlands	United States
Year	0.002***	0.004***	0.005***	0.004***	0.001***	0.006***	−0.001***
	(0.000)	(0.000)	(0.000)	(0.000)	(0.000)	(0.000)	(0.000)
18–29 (ref.)							
30–49	0.013**	0.016***	−0.000	−0.010*	−0.001	−0.041***	−0.005
	(0.004)	(0.004)	(0.004)	(0.004)	(0.004)	(0.004)	(0.006)
50–64	0.004	0.020***	0.006	−0.019***	−0.002	−0.095***	−0.010
	(0.005)	(0.005)	(0.006)	(0.005)	(0.004)	(0.005)	(0.007)
65+	−0.049***	0.015**	−0.012*	−0.028***	−0.061***	−0.141***	0.019*
	(0.006)	(0.005)	(0.006)	(0.005)	(0.005)	(0.006)	(0.008)
Post-baby boomer generations	0.029***	−0.003	0.019***	−0.001	0.017***	−0.028***	−0.043***
	(0.004)	(0.004)	(0.004)	(0.004)	(0.004)	(0.004)	(0.007)
Intercept	−3.686***	−6.875***	−8.647***	−7.422***	−0.999***	−11.833***	2.646***
	(0.205)	(0.197)	(0.361)	(0.237)	(0.197)	(0.255)	(0.266)
N	22,576	24,837	13,104	14,604	28,803	18,444	19,997
R^2	0.056	0.106	0.137	0.124	0.019	0.205	0.014

Note: Robust standard errors in parentheses. $^*p < 0.05$, $^{**}p < 0.01$, $^{***}p < 0.001$.

Appendix P
Party system fragmentation over time

In addition to growing more volatile, election outcomes in established democracies have gradually grown more fragmented. The 1990s were marked by a surge of radical right-wing parties throughout Europe Mudde (2013), while green parties managed to stabilize their electoral support Dolezal (2010). More recently, scholars have noted the rise of 'challenger parties' Hobolt (2016) and populists have gained across established democracies (Kriesi, 2014; Mudde, 2016). Irrespective of how exactly certain ideological families gain or lose popularity, what all of this contributes to is a rather fundamental change towards more party system fragmentation. Each new party family that has emerged since the 1950s has contributed to growing levels of fragmentation across democracies. And each newly emerging party is only a part of the bigger story: that of a remarkable surge in the number of parties.

To get a sense of the extent to which party systems in established democracies have become fragmented, we can look at data on the effective number of parties Laakso and Taagepera (1979). To that end, Figure P.1 plots the average effective number of electoral parties, by decade, in twenty established democracies. The plot shows evidence of a striking over-time surge in the effective number of parties that gain votes in these twenty established democracies. At the start of the time series, the average party system was one in which around 3.5 effective parties competed. In elections in the same set of countries between 2010 and 2019, in contrast, about 5.5 effective parties gain votes.

Figure P.1 also clarifies that the trend takes the form of a continuing but step-wise increase. Party systems became more fragmented in the 1970s, a new surge followed in the 1990s, and the 2010s have been marked by a third and sharp increase in party system fragmentation. Each and every new party family that has entered the electoral arena—green parties in the 1970s and 1980s, radical right-wing parties in the 1990s, and populist parties more recently—seems to have structurally and stably contributed to more party system fragmentation.

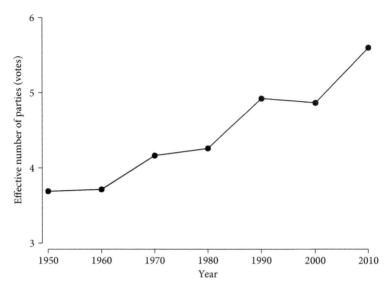

Figure P.1 Effective number of electoral parties by decade

Note: Average effective number of electoral parties by decade, in Australia, Austria, Belgium, Canada, Denmark, Finland, France, Germany, Iceland, Ireland, Israel, Italy, Japan, Luxembourg, Netherlands, New Zealand, Norway, Sweden, Switzerland, and the UK. Data on the effective number of parties in each election are retrieved from Döring and Manow (2021).

Figure P.1 only offers an insightful but crude summary of the trend in party system fragmentation across established democracies. We know, however, that there is substantial between-country variation in the extent to which party system are fragmented (Farrell, 2001). In addition, the trend towards more party system fragmentation as well might vary substantially between countries.

When taking into account such differences, and looking at country-specific patterns of change in the effective number of parties, the evidence of change is even more striking. Table P.1 lists the average effective number of parties in elections in the 1950s, the 1970s, the 1990s, and the 2010s in each of the twenty established democracies for which Döring and Manow (2021) offer data.

Looking at the country-specific patterns in Table P.1, Belgium appears to be an exceptional case. The strong surge in the effective number of parties between the 1950s and the 1970s, however, can be explained by the splits of all main parties along language lines in this time period (Deschouwer, 2009). In the more recent time period, the fragmentation of the Belgian party system has continued further but at a pace much more similar to what holds for other countries. The most noteworthy observation from Table P.1, however, is that—without a single exception—the effective number of parties in elections in the 2010s is systematically higher than it was in either the 1950s or the 1970s.

Table P.1 Effective number of parties by decade and country

Country	1950s	1970s	1990s	2010s
Australia	2.65	2.81	3.22	4.18
Austria	2.57	2.28	3.61	4.48
Belgium	2.88	6.42	9.85	10.19
Canada	2.69	3.15	4.01	3.52
Denmark	3.91	5.49	4.78	6.02
Finland	5.06	5.95	5.88	6.84
France	5.99	5.93	6.99	6.06
Germany	3.89	2.88	3.76	5.50
Iceland	3.71	3.92	4.02	6.35
Ireland	3.26	2.78	3.99	5.24
Israel	5.57	4.44	7.08	7.21
Italy	4.02	3.83	4.19	5.04
Japan	3.52	3.73	4.29	5.20
Luxembourg	3.14	4.43	4.73	5.60
The Netherlands	4.58	5.96	5.43	7.16
New Zealand	2.26	2.62	3.64	3.11
Norway	3.48	4.38	4.90	5.28
Sweden	3.32	3.55	4.26	5.33
Switzerland	5.04	5.82	6.71	6.22
United Kingdom	2.25	2.90	3.13	3.44

Note: Data on the effective number of parties in each election are retrieved from Döring and Manow (2021).

Figure P.1 shows evidence of a strong increase in party system fragmentation in established democracies. Based on the more detailed view that Table P.1 offers, we can conclude that this increase in the effective number of parties is a widespread phenomenon. Over the past half-century, all established democracies have seen the number of parties that gain electoral support increase. In every single one of the twenty established democracies included in Table P.1, election outcomes are more fragmented now than ever.

Appendix Q
Group-based cross-pressure and strength of partisan attachments

The main analyses that examine the association between group-based cross-pressure and partisanship in Chapter 9 rely on a dichotomous operationalization of partisanship (partisans versus non-partisans) that does not take into account the strength of party attachments. Here, I verify whether the conclusions from those analyses hold when using a measure of partisan strength instead. The analyses that are presented in Tables Q.1 and Q.2 are based on ordinary least-square (OLS) estimations in which the dependent variable takes the value of 0 when a respondent is a non-partisan, 1 when they are a weak partisan, and 2 when they are a strong partisan.

Table Q.1 Cross-pressure and partisan strength (1)

	Australia	Australia	Canada	Canada	Denmark	Denmark	Germany	Germany
Year	−0.002***	−0.002***	−0.004***	−0.004***	−0.006***	−0.003***	−0.003***	−0.002***
	(0.000)	(0.000)	(0.000)	(0.000)	(0.000)	(0.001)	(0.000)	(0.000)
Group-based cross-pressure	–	−0.183***	–	−0.137***	–	−0.365***	–	−0.175***
	–	(0.025)	–	(0.026)	–	(0.038)	–	(0.038)
Intercept	5.579***	4.964***	10.444***	9.603***	12.010***	7.702***	7.182***	6.089***
	(0.548)	(0.552)	(0.572)	(0.591)	(0.989)	(1.084)	(0.646)	(0.687)
N	22,408	22,408	22,853	22,853	16,579	16,579	16,648	16,648
R^2	0.002	0.005	0.010	0.011	0.008	0.014	0.004	0.005

Note: Robust standard errors in parentheses. * $p < 0.05$, ** $p < 0.01$, *** $p < 0.001$.

Table Q.2 Cross-pressure and partisan strength (2)

	Great-Britain	Great Britain	The Netherlands	The Netherlands	Sweden	Sweden	United States	United States
Year	−0.004***	−0.004***	−0.003***	−0.001**	−0.001	0.002***	0.001*	0.000
	(0.000)	(0.000)	(0.000)	(0.001)	(0.000)	(0.000)	(0.000)	(0.000)
Group-based cross-pressure	–	−0.192***	–	−0.325***	–	−0.336***	–	−0.322***
		(0.018)		(0.035)		(0.026)		(0.020)
Intercept	10.023***	9.874***	7.197***	3.742***	2.226**	−2.454**	−0.120	0.805
	(0.402)	(0.402)	(0.909)	(0.989)	(0.857)	(0.930)	(0.508)	(0.510)
N	27,735	27,735	17,115	17,115	24,146	24,146	22,507	22,507
R^2	0.013	0.017	0.003	0.008	0.000	0.007	0.000	0.011

Note: Robust standard errors in parentheses. * $p < 0.05$, ** $p < 0.01$, *** $p < 0.001$.

Appendix R
Broader indicator of cross-pressure

The main analyses that are presented in Chapter 10 show that group-based cross-pressures are significantly associated with a higher likelihood of campaign deciding and of volatility. I theorize, however, that the effect of cross-pressures is not limited to socio-demographic variables and argue that group-based cross-pressures trickle down in the funnel of causality to lead to a voting decision that is less constrained overall. Not only group-based cross-pressures but also cross-pressures based on other determinants of the vote choice should hence be associated with electoral instability.

To show the role of a more general indicator of cross-pressure, which is not limited to cross-pressure based on socio-demographic characteristics, in this appendix, I present a replication that relies on a broader indicator of cross-pressure. More specifically, I obtain a measure of cross-pressure that combines information on socio-demographic characteristics and the indicators used for the measure of short-term cross-pressures used in Chapter 9. More specifically, this broad indicator of cross-pressure is based on an estimation of vote-choice models that include, in addition to socio-demographic variables, indicators of respondents' evaluation of the state of the economy and their leader ratings.

Tables R.1, R.2, and R.3 show the results for the analyses that focus on campaign deciding. The estimates in these tables show that the broad measure of cross-pressure is positively and strongly associated with campaign deciding, even when accounting for a time trend in campaign deciding and also when focusing on within-election effects. It is also noteworthy, but not surprising, that the estimated effects of this cross-pressure indicator are larger than those of the group-based cross-pressure measure that is focused on in Chapter 10.

Tables R.4, R.5, and R.6 show the associations between the broad measure of cross-pressure and volatility in each of the eight countries. In line with the main results, the measure of cross-pressure is found to be positively associated with volatility. This also holds when accounting for a time trend and when assessing this association within elections. Like the association between cross-pressure and campaign deciding, the effects for volatility as well are more sizeable when the broad indicator of cross-pressure is used than when the focus is on group-based cross-pressure.

Table R.1 Association between overall cross-pressure and campaign deciding

	Australia	Canada	Denmark	Germany	Great Britain	The Netherlands	Sweden	United States
Broad cross-pressure	0.398***	0.428***	0.284***	0.333***	0.360***	0.390***	0.328***	0.418***
	(0.012)	(0.017)	(0.017)	(0.015)	(0.013)	(0.017)	(0.013)	(0.019)
Intercept	0.171***	0.280***	0.199***	0.063***	0.102***	0.196***	0.112***	0.083***
	(0.005)	(0.010)	(0.009)	(0.007)	(0.006)	(0.010)	(0.007)	(0.005)
N	15,906	7,244	8,727	8,969	10,756	7,791	11,028	6,709
R^2	0.069	0.072	0.030	0.052	0.066	0.057	0.051	0.094

Note: Robust standard errors in parentheses. $^*p < 0.05$, $^{**}p < 0.01$, $^{***}p < 0.001$.

Table R.2 Association between overall cross-pressure and campaign deciding, accounting for linear time trend

	Australia	Canada	Denmark	Germany	Great Britain	The Netherlands	Sweden	United States
Broad cross-pressure	0.413***	0.425***	0.285***	0.279***	0.353***	0.323***	0.312***	0.418***
	(0.012)	(0.017)	(0.016)	(0.014)	(0.013)	(0.017)	(0.013)	(0.019)
Year	−0.005***	−0.004***	0.011***	0.007***	0.001**	0.009***	0.004***	0.000
	(0.000)	(0.001)	(0.001)	(0.000)	(0.000)	(0.001)	(0.000)	(0.001)
Intercept	9.970***	9.256***	−21.181***	−14.630***	−1.885**	−18.544***	−7.572***	−0.477
	(0.842)	(1.635)	(1.603)	(0.597)	(0.604)	(1.018)	(0.666)	(1.189)
N	15,906	7,244	8,727	8,969	10,756	7,791	11,028	6,709
R^2	0.077	0.076	0.049	0.106	0.066	0.096	0.062	0.094

Note: Robust standard errors in parentheses. *$p < 0.05$, **$p < 0.01$, ***$p < 0.001$.

Table R.3 Association between overall cross-pressure and campaign deciding, within-election effects

	Australia	Canada	Denmark	Germany	Great Britain	The Netherlands	Sweden	United States
Broad cross-pressure	0.414***	0.431***	0.287***	0.232***	0.352***	0.321***	0.305***	0.414***
	(0.012)	(0.017)	(0.017)	(0.015)	(0.013)	(0.018)	(0.013)	(0.019)
Election FE	✓	✓	✓	✓	✓	✓	✓	✓
Intercept	0.283***	0.300***	0.107***	−0.033***	0.086***	0.042**	0.046***	0.129***
	(0.011)	(0.017)	(0.018)	(0.009)	(0.010)	(0.014)	(0.009)	(0.015)
N	15,906	7,244	8,727	8,969	10,756	7,791	11,028	6,709
R^2	0.085	0.082	0.051	0.130	0.072	0.101	0.070	0.100

Note: Robust standard errors in parentheses. *$p < 0.05$, **$p < 0.01$, ***$p < 0.001$.

Table R.4 Association between overall cross-pressure and volatility

	Australia	Canada	Denmark	Germany	Great Britain	The Netherlands	Sweden	United States
Broad cross-pressure	0.281***	0.303***	0.173***	0.298***	0.308***	0.295***	0.339***	0.241***
	(0.011)	(0.016)	(0.018)	(0.017)	(0.013)	(0.017)	(0.029)	(0.023)
Intercept	0.110***	0.172***	0.305***	0.130***	0.095***	0.144***	0.251***	0.137***
	(0.004)	(0.008)	(0.010)	(0.009)	(0.005)	(0.010)	(0.017)	(0.007)
N	16,343	8,029	8,265	7,986	10,388	7,082	2,951	4,676
R^2	0.044	0.042	0.011	0.037	0.053	0.037	0.042	0.029

Note: Robust standard errors in parentheses. *p < 0.05, **p < 0.01, ***p < 0.001.

Table R.5 Association between overall cross-pressure and volatility, accounting for linear time trend

	Australia	Canada	Denmark	Germany	Great Britain	The Netherlands	Sweden	United States
Broad cross-pressure	0.282***	0.303***	0.174***	0.279***	0.305***	0.261***	0.345***	0.242***
	(0.011)	(0.016)	(0.018)	(0.017)	(0.013)	(0.017)	(0.029)	(0.023)
Year	−0.000	0.000	0.013***	0.002***	0.002***	0.005***	0.007***	0.000
	(0.000)	(0.001)	(0.001)	(0.000)	(0.000)	(0.001)	(0.002)	(0.001)
Intercept	0.648	−0.464	−25.396***	−4.784***	−3.279***	−9.413***	−13.195***	−0.066
	(0.631)	(1.052)	(1.687)	(0.733)	(0.449)	(1.021)	(3.570)	(1.546)
N	16,343	8,029	8,265	7,986	10,388	7,082	2,951	4,676
R^2	0.044	0.043	0.036	0.042	0.058	0.049	0.047	0.029

Note: Robust standard errors in parentheses. * $p < 0.05$, ** $p < 0.01$, *** $p < 0.001$.

Table R.6 Association between overall cross-pressure and volatility, within-election effects

	Australia	Canada	Denmark	Germany	Great Britain	The Netherlands	Sweden	United States
Broad cross-pressure	0.282*** (0.011)	0.300*** (0.016)	0.141*** (0.017)	0.260*** (0.018)	0.307*** (0.013)	0.242*** (0.018)	0.345*** (0.029)	0.246*** (0.023)
Election FE	✓	✓	✓	✓	✓	✓	✓	✓
Intercept	0.079*** (0.011)	0.167*** (0.017)	0.151*** (0.018)	0.099*** (0.015)	0.093*** (0.010)	0.106*** (0.015)	0.185*** (0.024)	0.144*** (0.017)
N	16,343	8,029	8,265	7,986	10,388	7,082	2,951	4,676
R^2	0.049	0.048	0.111	0.050	0.060	0.056	0.047	0.036

Note: Robust standard errors in parentheses. $^{*}p < 0.05$, $^{**}p < 0.01$, $^{***}p < 0.001$.

Appendix S
Measures of sophistication and frustration

S.1 Australia

S.1.1 Political trust

- 1977 (TRUSGV79): 'In general, do you feel that the people in government are too often interested in looking after themselves, or do you feel that they can be trusted to do the right thing nearly all the time?' Coded so that respondents saying people in government do the right thing are coded 1 and others are coded 0.
- 1987 (q53): 'How much of the time do you think you can trust the government in Canberra to do what is right?' Answer options are 'just about always', 'most of the time', 'some of the time', and 'not at all'. Coded to range between 0 and 1, where 0 corresponds to 'not at all' and 1 corresponds to 'just about always'.
- 1993 (h3), 1998 (C5), 2001 (C8), 2004 (c4), 2007 (c8), 2010 (c9), 2013 (c5), 2016 (C6), 2019 (C6): 'In general, do you feel that the people in government are too often interested in looking after themselves, or do you feel that they can be trusted to do the right thing nearly all the time?' Answer options are 'usually look after themselves', 'sometimes look after themselves', 'sometimes can be trusted to do the right thing' and 'usually can be trusted to do the right thing'. Coded to range between 0 and 1, where 0 corresponds to 'usually look after themselves' and 1 corresponds to 'usually can be trusted'.

S.1.2 Political interest

- 1969 (intspol9): respondent's interest in politics, with answer options 'good deal', 'some', 'not much', and 'none'. Coded to range between 0 and 1, where 0 corresponds to 'none' and 1 to 'good deal'.
- 1977 (INTPOL79): 'How much interest do you generally have in what's going on in politics–a good deal, some, not much or none?' Coded to range between 0 and 1, where 0 corresponds to 'none' and 1 to 'good deal'.

- 1987 (q14): 'How much interest do you usually have in what's going on in politics?' Answer options are 'a good deal', 'some', 'not much', and 'none'. Coded to range between 0 and 1, where 0 corresponds to 'none' and 1 to 'good deal'.
- 1993 (a3), 1996 (a1), 1998 (A1), 2001 (A1), 2004 (a1), 2007 (a1), 2010 (a1), 2013 (a1), 2016 (A1), 2019 (A1): 'Generally speaking, how much interest do you usually have in what's going on in politics?' Answer options are 'a good deal', 'some', 'not much', and 'none'. Coded to range between 0 and 1, where 0 corresponds to 'none' and 1 to 'good deal'.

S.1.3 Satisfaction with democracy

- 1996 (a12): 'On the whole, are you satisfied, fairly satisfied, not very satisfied or not at all satisfied with the way democracy works in Australia?' Coded to range between 0 and 1, where 0 is 'not at all satisfied' and 1 is 'satisfied'.
- 1998 (B9), 2001 (C7), 2004 (c7), 2007 (c7), 2010 (c7), 2013 (c4), 2016 (C5), 2019 (C5): 'On the whole, are you very satisfied, fairly satisfied, not very satisfied or not at all satisfied with the way democracy works in Australia?' Coded to range between 0 and 1, where 0 is 'not at all satisfied' and 1 is 'very satisfied'.

S.2 Germany

S.2.1 Political interest

- 1965 (v58): 'Do you feel that you are personally well informed about current events in politics or not so well?' Answer options are 'not at all interested in politics', 'know only very little about politics', 'barely know about important things in politics', 'am somewhat informed about politics', and 'am fairly accurately informed about politics'. Coded to range between 0 and 1, where 0 is 'not at all interested' and 1 is 'fairly accurately informed'.
- 1969 (v12): 'How interested are you in politics: very strongly, strongly, somewhat, a little or not at all?'. Coded to range between 0 and 1, where 0 is 'not at all' and 1 is 'very strongly'.
- 1972 (v15): 'Quite generally, are you interested in politics?' Answer options are 'yes', 'not particularly', and 'not at all'. Coded to range between 0 and 1, where 0 is 'not at all' and 1 is 'yes'.

- 1976 (v11 and v12) 1983 (v8), 1987 (v6 and v7), 1990 (v7 and v8): 'Quite generally, are you interested in politics?' Answer options are 'yes', 'not particularly', and 'not at all'. If, the respondent answers yes, the follow-up question is 'How strongly are you interested in politics: very strongly, strongly or not so strongly?' Coded to range between 0 and 1, where 0 is 'not at all' and 1 is 'yes, very strongly'.
- 1994 (v8): 'How strongly are you interested in politics?' Answer options are 'very strongly', 'strongly', 'somewhat', 'a little', and 'not at all'. Coded to range between 0 and 1, where 0 is 'not at all' and 1 is 'very strongly'.
- 2002 (c50), 2005 (Q1): 'In general terms: How interested in politics are you?' Answer options are 'extremely interested', 'very interested', 'moderately interested', 'slightly interested', and 'not interested at all'. Coded to range between 0 and 1, where 0 is 'not interested at all' and 1 is 'extremely interested'.
- 2009 (vn217), 2013 (vn3), 2017 (vn3): 'Quite generally, how interested are you in politics: very interested, somewhat interested, in between, not very interested, or not at all interested?' Coded to range between 0 and 1, where 0 is 'not at all interested' and 1 is 'very interested'.

S.2.2 Satisfaction with democracy

- 1972 (v35), 1976 (v63): 'What would you generally say about democracy in the Federal Republic of Germany, that is, about our political parties and our entire political system? Are you very satisfied, somewhat satisfied, or not satisfied with it?' Coded to range between 0 and 1, where 0 is 'not satisfied' and 1 is 'very satisfied'.
- 1983 (77), 1987 (v78): 'What would you generally say about democracy in the Federal Republic of Germany, that is about our political parties and our entire political system? Are you very satisfied, somewhat satisfied, somewhat dissatisfied, or very dissatisfied with it?' Coded to range between 0 and 1, where 0 is 'very dissatisfied' and 1 is 'very satisfied'.
- 1990 (v19): 'What would you generally say about democracy in the FRG, that is, about our entire political system? Are you very satisfied, somewhat satisfied, somewhat dissatisfied or very dissatisfied with it?' Coded to range between 0 and 1, where 0 is 'very dissatisfied' and 1 is 'very satisfied'.
- 1994 (v94): 'Now about democracy in Germany: How satisfied or dissatisfied are you—in general—with democracy as it is in Germany?' Answer options are 'very satisfied', 'somewhat satisfied', 'fairly satisfied', 'fairly

dissatisfied', 'somewhat dissatisfied', and 'very dissatisfied'. Coded to range between 0 and 1, where 0 is 'very dissatisfied' and 1 is 'very satisfied'.
- 2002 (c40), 2009 (vn291), 2013 (vn6), 2017 (vn6): 'On the whole, how satisfied or dissatisfied are you with democracy in Germany? Are you very satisfied, fairly satisfied, neither satisfied nor dissatisfied, fairly dissatisfied, very dissatisfied?' Coded to range between 0 and 1, where 0 is 'very dissatisfied' and 1 is 'very satisfied'.
- 2005 (Q33): 'How satisfied or dissatisfied are you, overall, with democracy as it is in Germany? Are you very satisfied, somewhat satisfied, partly satisfied partly dissatisfied, fairly dissatisfied, or very dissatisfied?' Coded to range between 0 and 1, where 0 is 'very dissatisfied' and 1 is 'very satisfied'.

S.3 The Netherlands

S.3.1 Political interest

- 1971, 1972, 1977, 1981, 1982, 1986, 1989, 1994, 1998, 2002, 2006 (V1_4), 2010 (v024), 2012 (v014), 2017 (V024): 'Are you very interested in political subjects, fairly interested or not interested?' Coded to range between 0 and 1, where 0 is 'not interested' and 1 is 'very interested'.

S.3.2 Satisfaction with democracy

- 1998, 2006 (V35_1), 2010 (v720), 2012 (V232), 2017 (V232): 'On the whole, are you very satisfied, fairly satisfied, not very satisfied, or not at all satisfied with the way democracy works in the Netherlands?' Coded to range between 0 and 1, where 0 is 'not at all satisfied' and 1 is 'very satisfied'.

S.4 United States

S.4.1 Political interest

- 1952, 1956, 1960, 1964, 1968, 1972, 1980, 1988, 1992, 1996 (VCF0310): 'Some people don't pay much attention to political campaigns. How about you? Would you say that you have been/were very much interested, somewhat interested, or not much interested in following the political campaigns (so far) this year?' Coded to range between 0 and 1, where 0 is 'not much interested' and 1 is 'very much interested'.

- 2000, 2004, 2008, 2016 (VCF0310): 'Some people don't pay much attention to political campaigns. How about you? Would you say that you have been/were very much interested, somewhat interested, or not much interested in the political campaigns (so far) this year?' Coded to range between 0 and 1, where 0 is 'not much interested' and 1 is 'very much interested'.

S.4.2 Political trust

- 1964 (VCF0604): 'I'd like to talk about some of the different ideas about the government in Washington. These ideas don't refer to Democrats or Republicans in particular, but just to government in general. We want to see how you feel about these ideas. How much of the time do you think you can trust the government in Washington to do what is right–just about always, most of the time, or only some of the time ?' Coded to range between 0 and 1, where 0 is 'only some of the time' and 1 is 'just about always'.
- 1968, 1972, 1976, 1980, 1988, 1992 (VCF0604): 'People have different ideas about the government in Washington. These ideas don't refer to Democrats or Republicans in particular but just to government in general. We want to see how you feel about these ideas. How much of the time do you think you can trust the government in Washington to do what is right–just about always, most of the time, or only some of the time ?' Coded to range between 0 and 1, where 0 is 'only some of the time' and 1 is 'just about always'.
- 1996 (VCF0604): 'People have different ideas about the government in Washington. These ideas don't refer to Democrats or Republicans in particular, but just to government in general. We want to see how you feel about these ideas. For example: How much of the time do you think you can trust the government in Washington to do what is right–just about always, most of the time, or almost never?' Coded to range between 0 and 1, where 0 is 'almost never' and 1 is 'just about always'.
- 2000, 2004, 2008 (VCF0604): 'People have different ideas about the government in Washington. These ideas don't refer to Democrats or Republicans in particular, but just to government in general. We want to see how you feel about these ideas. For example: How much of the time do you think you can trust the government in Washington to do what is right–just about always, most of the time, or only some of the time ?' Coded to range between 0 and 1, where 0 is 'only some of the time' and 1 is 'just about always'.

Bibliography Supplementary Materials

Brader, Ted, Joshua A. Tucker, and Andrew Therriault. 2014. 'Cross pressure scores: An individual-level measure of cumulative partisan pressures arising from social group memberships'. *Political Behavior* 36(1): 23–51.

Dassonneville, Ruth and Michael S. Lewis-Beck. 2014. 'Macroeconomics, economic crisis and electoral outcomes: A national European pool'. *Acta Politica* 49(4): 372–394.

Debus, Marc, Mary Stegmaier, and Jale Tosun. 2014. 'Economic voting under coalition governments: Evidence from Germany'. *Political Science Research and Methods* 2(1): 49.

Deschouwer, Kris. 2009. *The Politics of Belgium: Governing a Divided Society*. Basingstoke: Palgrave Macmillan.

Dolezal, Martin. 2010. 'Exploring the stabilization of a political force: The social and attitudinal basis of Green parties in the age of globalization'. *West European Politics* 33(3): 534–552.

Döring, Holger and Philip Manow. 2021. 'Parliaments and governments database (ParlGov): Information on Parties, Elections and Cabinets in Modern Democracies.' http://www.parlgov.org/.

Farrell, David M. 2001. *Electoral Systems: A Comparative Introduction*. Basingstoke: Palgrave Macmillan.

Hobolt, Sara B. and James Tilley. 2016. 'Fleeing the centre: The rise of challenger parties in the aftermath of the Euro crisis'. *West European Politics* 39(5): 971–991.

Kriesi, Hanspeter. 2014. 'The populist challenge'. *West European Politics* 37(2): 361–378.

Laakso, Markku and Rein Taagepera. 1979. 'The "Effective" Number of Parties: A Measure with Application to West Europe'. *Comparative Political Studies* 12(1): 3–27.

Larsen, Martin Vinæs. 2016. 'Economic conditions affect support for prime minister parties in Scandinavia'. *Scandinavian Political Studies* 39(3): 226–241.

Mudde, Cas. 2013. 'Three decades of populist radical right parties in Western Europe: So what?' *European Journal of Political Research* 52(1): 1–19.

Mudde, Cas. 2016. 'Europe's populist surge: A long time in the making'. *Foreign Affairs* 95(6): 25–30.

Soroka, Stuart N. 2006. 'Good news and bad news: Asymmetric responses to economic information'. *Journal of Politics* 68(2): 372–385.

Index

ancillary organizations, 112–17
  church, 32, 33, 38, 40–1, 112, 117
  labour union, 104, 112–13
  trade union, 38, 40, 41, 112–14
Australia
  Australian Election Studies, 14
  party, 57
    Labor, 57
    Liberal, 57
    National, 57
average marginal effect, 83

Belgium
  Dehaene, Jean-Luc, 1, 2, 3, 14, 177
  party system, 307–8
birth cohort, 150

Canada
  party, 57
    Bloc Québécois, 47, 57, 87
    Conservative, 57
    Liberal, 57
    Green, 57
    NDP, 57
    Reform, 47
ceiling effects, 137
Christian-Democratic parties, 25, 35, 40
class stratification, 34
cognitive mobilization, 178, 194–6
Columbia school, 103, 120, 121
Comparative Study of Electoral Systems (CSES), 55
confidence interval, 4
consistency bias, 6, 69
constraint, 2, 14, 16, 100–8, 112, 118, 119, 139, 161–2, 167, 168, 177–8, 186, 198, 202, 203, 204, 205
cross-cutting influences, 100, 101, 103, 104, 111, 112, 114, 123, 127, 161, 186, 198, 206, 208, 210, 213

cross-pressure
  issue-based, 170–5
  group-based, 2, 13, 14, 16–17, 30, 100–22, 123, 125, 127, 129–31, 137, 141–2, 146–7, 156, 158, 160, 161–76, 177–98, 202–13
cross-pressure (CP) score
  group-based, 123–40, 141–58, 163, 166, 168, 169, 173, 174, 177, 179, 189, 190, 193, 196, 205
  short-term, 168, 169, 174
cross-sectional data, 5, 15, 17, 148, 198, 200, 203, 209, 210

dealignment, 24, 26, 27, 51, 52, 61, 73, 178, 186, 201, 211
Denmark
  party, 57
    Communist, 57
    Conservative, 57
    Liberal, 57
    Social Democrat, 57
    Social Liberal, 57
    Socialist People's, 87
democratic attitudes, 195
dissatisfaction with politics, 178, 195

economic condition, 12, 14, 23, 25, 28, 29, 30, 75, 77, 80–2, 86–91
economic evaluation, 76, 80–91, 168, 173, 201
effect size, 169, 174
effective number of parties, 156
election campaign, 9–10, 11, 21, 23, 29, 49, 113, 120, 121, 122, 179–183, 186, 194, 195, 200, 203
  debates, 181
  events, 181
election outcome, 3, 5, 10, 11, 113, 212
electoral change, 11, 14, 212

electoral choice, 2, 13, 17, 25, 26, 31, 32, 33, 51, 54, 76, 78, 79, 85, 104, 108, 119, 133, 147, 155, 159, 161, 199, 209, 211
electoral politics, 2, 34
electoral rule, 15, 54, 55, 204, 205
  majoritarian, 145, 204, 205
  proportional, 54, 145, 160, 198, 203
elite cue, 29
encapsulation, 111–17, 119, 207, 208
established democracies, 3, 4, 5, 6, 10, 17, 21, 25, 26, 30, 31, 33, 37, 39, 41, 50, 65, 74, 75, 76, 78, 91, 94, 95, 108, 141, 159, 175, 177, 184, 196, 198, 200, 201, 202, 204, 209, 212
European Election Study (EES), 15, 135, 137, 140, 158, 159, 173, 174
European unification, 78
explanatory power, 33, 40–9, 91, 94, 99, 159, 201

fixed effects, 137, 169, 170, 181, 186, 190
floor effects, 137
France
  Macron, Emmanuel, 40
  2017 presidential elections, 40
funnel of causality, 12, 17, 21–2, 24–7, 75, 79, 100, 105, 107, 108, 119, 130, 160, 161, 162, 168, 169, 175, 178, 202, 203
  long-term determinants, 11–12, 22, 27–30, 75, 79, 99, 102, 105, 107, 117, 118, 147, 201, 208, 213
  party identification, 12, 22, 24, 25, 27, 28, 51–74, 75, 79, 86, 101–2, 105, 118, 121, 161–3, 167, 186, 198, 211
    evaluation-based, 53
    identity-based party, 53
  socio-demographic characteristics, 2, 11, 12, 16, 17, 21, 23–6, 32–3, 49–50, 51, 85, 86, 99–102, 104, 106, 108, 111, 117, 119, 122, 123, 131, 134, 137, 140, 147, 158, 160, 161, 163, 167, 170, 173, 175–6, 177, 178, 181, 186, 189, 198, 201, 202, 203, 204, 207, 209, 211–2, 213
    age, 26, 32, 37, 39–41, 42, 43, 44, 48, 50, 78, 108, 110, 124, 126, 133, 137, 148–154
    education, 13, 26, 32, 37, 39–41, 42, 43, 44, 47, 50, 102, 108, 110, 111, 124, 133, 137, 149, 173, 174, 194, 195, 206, 208, 209
    gender, 13, 26, 33, 37–9, 41, 42, 43, 44, 47, 48, 50, 108, 110, 111, 124, 133, 137, 173, 206, 208, 210
    place of living, 32, 33, 36–7, 38, 41, 42, 47, 50, 132, 133, 137, 174
      centre-periphery cleavage, 33, 36
      rural-urban cleavage, 26, 36, 43, 101
    race, 41, 42, 43, 44, 47, 48, 124, 206, 207
      Black, 126, 206
      White, 126, 210
      Latino, 126
    religion, 12, 23, 25, 26, 28, 33, 35–6, 37, 38, 40, 41, 42, 43, 47, 50, 104, 112, 113, 114–16, 117, 124, 132, 148, 149, 206, 207
      denomination, 32, 33, 35, 36, 43, 114, 126, 133, 137, 173, 207
        Catholic, 35, 104, 109, 120, 126
        Protestant, 35, 104, 120, 126
      religiosity, 32, 36, 43, 113
        church attendance, 35, 114–16, 207
    social class, 12, 28, 32, 33–4, 43, 47, 102, 137, 148, 149, 174, 207, 209
      white-collar, 104
      blue-collar/working class, 33, 34, 40, 41
      upper service class, 33
  short-term factors, 12–14, 16, 17, 22–3, 25, 27–30, 31, 74, 75–95, 99, 100, 103, 105, 160, 170, 196, 201
    issue position, 14, 25, 29, 65, 105, 107, 162, 173, 174

funnel of causality (*Continued*)
    abortion, 173
    civil liberties, 173
    defence, 173
    economy, 173
    environment, 173
    foreign policy, 173
    immigration, 39, 78, 173
    inequality, 173
    law and order, 173
    redistribution, 78, 173
    leader effects, 13, 78, 85, 91, 173, 203
    like/dislike ratings, 85, 135
    thermometer scale, 86
    political evaluations, 74, 80, 81
    economic voting, 76, 82, 87, 90, 99
frustrated floating voter, 195

gender gap, 13, 37–9
Germany
  Christian Democratic Union (CDU), 109, 110
  German Election Study, 131
  unification, 43, 47, 61
government of coalition, 87, 91
Great Britain
  Brexit referendum, 39
  British Election Panels, 71
  British Election Studies, 177
  British Election Study Internet Panel, 193
  party, 57
    Conservative, 57
    Labour, 57
    Liberal Democrat, 57
    Plaid Cymru, 57
    Scottish National Party, 87
  Political Change in Britain, 71
green party, 40, 111
group decider, 132–3
group membership, 101, 103–4, 109–10, 111, 112, 120, 122, 123, 139, 142, 155, 162, 167, 175, 176, 178, 179, 181, 202, 207–8, 210, 213

habituation, 154

identity, 14, 34, 53, 55, 61, 65, 95, 107, 108, 110, 111–12, 113, 118, 119, 120, 162, 207, 208, 210, 211

incumbent party, 81, 82, 87, 90, 91
Industrial Revolution, 33, 36
International Social Survey Program (ISSP), 116
issue ownership, 78
issue voting, 76, 78, 105
  proximity, 78
  valence, 78

late deciding, 10, 122, 134, 177–83, 184, 199, 205, 213
left-wing party, 33, 34, 35, 38, 40, 111, 113
legislative election, 137
linear probability model, 65, 67, 82, 162, 166, 179, 184, 189, 190
logistic regression, 42, 87, 91, 124, 125, 168, 174
longitudinal analysis, 5, 6, 13, 15, 17, 36, 37, 51, 55, 69, 78, 124, 141, 159, 168, 170, 174, 177, 184, 201

mediation, 35, 186, 189, 193
Michigan school, 51, 54, 65, 162
motivated reasoning, 106, 107–8
multinomial logit model, 124

opposition party, 85
ordinary least-squares (OLS) model, 137, 150, 169
Organisation for Economic Co-operation and Development (OECD), 39, 114

panel data, 15, 17, 66, 71, 72, 177, 190, 193, 198, 200, 203
participation, 120, 131
partisan anchor, 65–73, 167, 176
partisan strength, 24, 27, 52, 55, 56, 62, 83, 121, 162, 163
partisanship
  incumbent, 81, 85
  non-partisan, 66, 67, 71, 72, 73, 74, 85, 189, 194, 201
  opposition, 80, 81, 85
party closeness, 55
party elites, 107
party loyalty, 9, 103, 116, 117, 156, 212
party preferences, 32, 37, 38, 39, 65, 99, 103, 109, 121, 122, 149, 155, 167, 207, 208, 210

party switching, 6, 24, 67, 69, 142, 146–7, 177, 184–95, 198, 203, 213
party system, 5, 11, 15, 23, 32, 36, 37, 54, 109, 205
  fragmentation, 155, 156, 160
Pedersen's index of net volatility, 3
personalization, 13, 94
polarization, 39, 52, 54, 69, 81, 205, 206
political cleavage, 26, 33, 38, 40, 104, 109, 113, 120, 208
political efficacy, 195
political interest, 111, 194–6
political knowledge, 194
political preferences, 53, 105, 130, 170, 175, 176, 207
political sophistication, 194–5
political trust, 195–6
predispositions, 14, 30, 101, 102, 106, 107, 108, 118
propensity to vote (PTV), 15, 34, 136, 137, 138, 148, 158, 202
pseudo-R^2, 42, 44, 47, 48, 49, 50, 85, 91
psychological attachment, 24, 26, 51, 52, 53, 162

radical right-wing party, 25, 36, 38, 40, 42, 49
representative democracy, 2
representative sample, 15
retrospective evaluations, 77, 81, 84, 86
right-wing party, 34, 109, 112
running tally, 53

satisfaction with democracy, 195, 196
selective exposure, 106, 107
social anchor, 11, 16, 102, 112, 113, 117, 159, 181, 198
social change, 2
social cleavage, 11, 23–4, 33, 41, 48, 101, 103, 119, 124, 160
social democratic parties, 34
social interactions, 121
social modernization, 24
social network, 112, 121, 130
socialization, 53
split-ticket voting, 105
survey data, 5, 13, 17, 41, 47, 51, 65, 67, 77, 78, 85, 114, 120, 122, 123, 127, 141, 200, 210

Sweden
  party, 57
    Centerpartist, 57
    Folkpartist, 57
    Kristdemokrat, 57
    Miljö-partist, 57
    Moderat, 57
    Socialdemokrat, 57
    Vänsterpartist, 57

time effects
  period effects, 78, 141, 147–55
  generation effects, 147–55
    Baby-boomers (1946–1964), 150, 154
    Generation X (1965–1980), 39, 150
    Generation Y (1981–1996), 39, 150
    Generation Z (1997–), 150
    Greatest generation (1910–1924), 150, 154
    Silent generation (1925–1945), 150
  life-cycle effects, 147–9, 154
time series, 10, 14, 49, 58, 61, 67, 73, 116, 145, 207, 211
trade union density, 113–16

United States
  American National Election Study, 56, 81, 126
  congressional election, 56
  McCain, John, 126
  Obama, Barack, 126
  party, 57
    Democratic party, 42, 126, 206
    Republican party, 42, 126
  presidential election, 56, 111, 126
unmoved mover, 54, 74
urbanization, 43, 124, 137, 148, 173

Vietnam war, 61
vote share, 5, 87, 200
voter ambivalence, 135–6, 137, 141, 158, 160
voter alienation, 134–6, 140
voting-decision process, 16, 17, 100, 102, 103, 107, 108, 111, 118

World Values Survey (WVS), 114